Caravan
& Camping
France 2008

Produced by AA Publishing
Contents, pictures, and text compiled from information
supplied by ANWB bv, The Hague, The Netherlands
Campsites © ANWB bv, The Hague, The Netherlands
This 5th edition published 2008
© Automobile Association Developments Limited 2008
Maps prepared by the Mapping Services Department of the
Automobile Association
Maps © Automobile Association Developments Limited 2008
The product includes mapping data licensed from IGN (France)
© Institut Géographique National (France)

The contents of this book are believed correct at the time of printing.
Nevertheless, the Publisher cannot be held responsible for any errors or
omissions, or for changes in the details given in this guide, or for the conse-
quences of any reliance on the information provided.

Page layout by Jamie Wiltshire
Printed by Graficas Estella, S.A., Navarra, Spain
To contact us: lifestyleguides@theAA.com

Picture credit: Front cover : AA World Travel Library/R Moore

The Automobile Association would like to thank the following photographers,
companies and picture libraries for their assistance in the preparation of this
book.

Abbreviations for the picture credits are as follows: (t) top; (b) bottom; (l) left;
(r) right; (AA) AA World Travel Library.

1 AA/J A Tims; 2l AA/B Smith; 3tr AA/A A Kouprianoff; 3bl AA/R Strange; 3br
AA/A Baker; 4tl AA/M Jourdan; 4b AA/P Kenward; 5tr AA/A Kouprianoff; 6tl
AA/M Jourdan; 6b AA/J Miller; 7tr AA/A Kouprianoff; 8tl AA/M Jourdan; 8c AA/J
Wyand; 9tr AA/A Kouprianoff; 10tl AA/M Jourdan; 11tr AA/A Kouprianoff; 11b
AA/R Strange; 12tl AA/M Jourdan; 13tr AA/A Kouprianoff; 13b AA/C Sawyer;
14tl AA/M Jourdan; 14tr AA/R Strange; 15tr AA/A Kouprianoff; 15b AA/R
Strange; 16tl AA/M Jourdan; 17tr AA/A Kouprianoff; 17br AA/C Sawyer; 18tl
AA/M Jourdan; 19tr AA/A Kouprianoff; 19b AA/S L Day; 20tl AA/M Jourdan;
21tr AA/A Kouprianoff; 21b AA/R Day; 22tl AA/M Jourdan; 23tr AA/A
Kouprianoff; 24tl AA/M Jourdan; 25tr AA/A Kouprianoff; 26tl AA/M Jourdan;
27tr AA/A Kouprianoff; 37 AA/C Sawyer; 56b AA/P Kenward; 73b AA/P
Kenward; 79 AA/P Kenward; 93b AA/R Moss; 112b AA/P Kenward; 126b AA/T
Oliver; 154b AA/P Kenward; 195b AA/N Setchfield; 196b AA/N Setchfield; 203b
AA/M Short.

A CIP record for this book is available from the British Library
pPublished by AA Trading which is a trading name of Automobile
Association Developments Limited, whose registered office is
Fanum House, Basing View, Basingstoke, Hampshire, RG21 4EA
Registered number 1878835

ISBN-13: 978-0-7495-5573-3

A03289

Contents

Using the guide

Where in France?

This guide aims to provide you with a choice of around 400 great caravan and camping parks throughout France. To ensure that you have the most accurate and up-to-date information, these sites have all been inspected by the Dutch camping organisation ANWB, which has rated them according to the quality and provision of their facilities.

In this guide France has been divided into 19 regions which are colour-coded on the map on page 28. The map also shows the départements into which French regions are divided. Each département has a standard number, as shown on the map and in the key (see page 28-29), which for postal purposes in France replaces its name. These numbers also form part of the registration number of

French cars, thus indicating the département in which the car was registered.

To find the general area of France that you want to visit you can use the map on page 30 and the key on page 28 to identify the French region (e.g. Picardy). The regional name appears at the top of each page of the guide in its easily-identifiable colour. Regions are in alphabetical order throughout the guide and then the département name (e.g. Aisne in Picardy) is listed alphabetically within each region.

The locations of the sites that appear in this guide are marked on the maps on pages 31-36 and are also listed alphabetically in the index at the back.

Sample Entry

① **La Côte d'Argent**

② **Rating** 7.9
③ **Tariff range** €€€€
④ **Town** Hourtin
⑤ **Department** Gironde
⑥ **Postal Code** 33990
⑦ **Map** 4 C4
    Tel 05-56091025
    Fax 05-56092496
    e-mail info@camping-cote-dargent.com
    Open 13 May – 17 Sep
⑧ Site on D101 E, just before Hourtin-Plage.
⑨ **Size (hectares)** 20
    Touring pitches 550
    Sanitary facilities rating 8.4
⑩
⑪ modern swimming pool • riding centre • day-care for children • Atlantic Ocean • wine châteaux • Hourtin (8 km)
⑫ **Electric hook-ups/amps** 550/6

⑬

Since arriving here the owner has made improvements throughout the site in order to meet modern campers' demands. Camping on La Côte d'Argent offers pure luxury, yet the rates are still average compared with campsites elsewhere in the region.
    The heated swimming pool has five water slides and a **⑭** jacuzzi, and you can ride a horse in the equestrian centre or go off pony trekking. Everything is professionally run here, and the entertainment team is also qualified: they offer a wide choice of activities for young children in the miniclub as well as games and competitions for older ones. The campsite is situated in a pine forest with broad lanes, spacious pitches and clean sanitary facilities. The sandy beaches of the Atlantic Ocean are only 300m away, and restaurants and snack bars are within walking distance. But you can also have a meal in the snack bar or the restaurant (with a terrace) on the site. Hourtin-Plage, a seaside resort, offers beaches and entertainment.

① Name of site

② Rating
All the sites in this guide have been assessed by ANWB according to a strict set of criteria. ANWB grades from 7 to 8.8. For further details see page 6

③ Tariff range
€=under €10, €€=€10-€20, €€€=€20-€30, €€€€=over €30. For further details see page 7

④ Town
This is the nearest town or village to the site. (Some sites are rurally located)

⑤ Name of Département
One of 92 départements in France. See pages 28-29 for map and key

⑥ Postcode
The first two digits of this postal code represent the number of the département

⑦ Map Reference
The map page number is given first followed by the grid square in which the location can be found. The maps are on pages 31-36

⑧ Directions
Brief directions to the site are given

⑨ Site size and number of pitches
Area given in hectares (1 hectare=2.47 acres)

⑩ Sanitary facilities rating
This rating is taken into consideration to give the site its overall rating

⑪ Additional information
Shows the characteristics of the site and the surrounding area, nearby places of interest, local activities, largest nearby town and (distance)

⑫ Electric hook-ups/amps
Number of hook-ups on site and amperage

⑬ Site symbols
Full explanation on page 7

⑭ Description
A description of the site based on the inspector's findings

Inspection requirements

All of the campsites featured in this guide have been inspected by the respected Dutch camping organisation, ANWB. Their inspectors have been to every site at least once within the past three years, and assessed its facilities, its maintenance, and its ability to cope with visitor numbers. The inspectors use a mathematical formula to achieve two scores for each site: one is an overall rating that represents the total park, and the other relates only to the sanitary facilities, and their state of cleanliness and maintenance during the site visit. The ratio of toilets, wash basins and showers to the number of campers is also taken into account. In the overall rating, the inspectors look at swimming pools, restaurants and shops and any other facility provided by the site, as well as taking the measurements of an average pitch.

Provided that the overall rating is 7.5, and the sanitary rating is 7, an ANWB classification is given.

Symbols & abbreviations

⊘	Quiet Area	🚲	Cycles for hire
❀	Pretty Area		BBQ not allowed
≋	Beside river/lake		Dogs not allowed
	On the coast		Campervans not allowed
	Beach sand		
	Beach pebbles	[CCI]	Discount with Camping Card International (see page 18 for further information)
	Beach grass		
	Beach rock		
	Beach concrete	EUROTOP	The Eurotop label is awarded by the ANWB to recognize the very best campsites in Europe
♣♣♣	Situated in woodland		
	Minimal or no shelter		
	Sufficient shelter		

	(Partly) Nudist
◀))	Potential noise of train/traffic
	Grassland
	Sandy soil
	Woodland soil
	Rocky soil
⊕	Food available
¶◎¶	Restaurant
⊜	Snack bar
◎	Disco
⊓	Playground
⊈	Tennis court
	Swimming pool
	Paddling pool
	Canoes for hire

Tariff range

The tariff range is per tent or caravan per night, based on 2 adults and 2 children, 1 car and tourist tax. Please note that hot water and electricity may not be included.

€	under €10
€€	€10 – €20
€€€	€20 – €30
€€€€	over €30

Abbreviations

km	– kilometres
m/mtrs	– metres
N	– North
S	– South
E	– East
W	– West
NW	– North-west

Hints on booking your stay

Despite the carefree nature of a camping or caravanning holiday, it is best to book well in advance for peak holiday seasons, or for your first and last stop close to a ferry crossing point. Despite there being over 10,000 campsites throughout France, during July and August they are heavily booked, especially on the Mediterranean coast and other popular holiday destinations.

Advance Planning

Preparing for your journey means having your car and caravan or motorvan properly checked and serviced. For information on what to do before setting off, see pages 10-11. As well as booking your actual holiday destination in advance, it is a good idea to know where you will be staying en route both in this country and in France. On pages 20-21 we provide a list of strategically-located UK sites throughout the country that are close to the main roads leading to the ferry ports on the south coast. We also list sites that are handy for the ports themselves, enabling you to make a stop either before or after a ferry crossing. On pages 24-27 we show a selection of aires for motorvans on autoroutes, and sites close to autoroutes where you can stop overnight with a caravan or tent. Ferry information is given on page 22.

Most sites will require a booking fee in advance, especially for the high season. Some will only accept bookings for a minimum period. You should also be aware that, occasionally, some campsites may regard your deposit as a booking fee which is non-deductible from the final account. You are advised to check when booking if this is the case.

Cancellations

Some parks may not return a booking fee if you have to cancel your holiday. If you do have to cancel, notify the proprietor at once or you may be liable for partial or full payment unless the pitch can be re-let. You would be wise to take out cancellation insurance to cover this eventuality.

Payment

Check which payment methods are acceptable when booking. Many campsites will accept payment in cash, and most will accept travellers cheques or credit cards, though these methods may incur additional charges.

Sample Letter

Monsieur

Je me propose de séjourner à votre terrain de camping pour ..... jours, depuis le ..... jusqu'a ....

Nous sommes .... personnes en tout, y compris ...... adultes et .... enfants (âgés de ....) et nous aurons besoin d'un emplacement pour .... tente(s), et/ou un parking pour notre voiture/caravan /remorque/camping-car.

Veuillez me donner dans votre réponse une idée de vos prix, m'indiquant en même temps le montant qu'il faut payer en avance, ce qui vous sera envoyé sans délai.

Sample Letter translated

Dear Sir

I would like to stay at your camping site for ..... days, from ..... (date and month) to .... (date and month)

We are a group of ...... people including ...... adults and .... children (aged ....) and would like to book a pitch for .... tent(s), and/or a parking space for our car/caravan/trailer/motorvan.

Please quote full charges when replying and advise on the deposit required, which I will forward without delay.

Public Holidays in France 2008

1 Jan	New Year's Day
23 Mar	Good Friday
25 Mar	Easter Sunday (Pâques)
26 Mar	Easter Monday
1 May	Labour Day (Fête du premier mai)/ Ascension Day (l'Ascension)
8 May	WWII Victory Day (Fête de la Victoire; Fête du huitième mai)
1 May	Whit Sunday (la Pentecôte)
12 May	Whit Monday
14 Jul	Bastille Day
15 Aug	Assumption of Blessed Virgin Mary

1 Nov	All Saints Day (La Toussaint)
11 Nov	Armistice Day (Jour d'armistice)
25 Dec	Christmas Day
26 Dec	2nd Day of Christmas (Alsace-Lorraine only)

Please note that if a holiday falls on a Tuesday or Thursday many French people take the respective Monday or Friday as leave as well. This does not apply to government or to banks but may cause problems with certain businesses on occasions.

Preparing for your journey

Please read this section before you set off on your journey to France, especially if you are new to driving abroad. There are certain preparations you should make, and some regulations you should know about. Also read the following section on Essential Motoring Information (Pages 12-17).

Preparing Your Caravan

Having your caravan regularly serviced can save you from encountering serious problems on your journey. The following tips could also prove useful, especially for the first trip out of winter storage.

- Give the caravan a good airing
- Where a water pump is fitted, check the flow, sterilize the system, and flush with clean water to remove staleness
- Check for leaks and replace doubtful washers
- Examine window rubbers, rear light clusters and roof lights for leaks, applying sealing compound as necessary
- Test cupboard, locker and window catches
- Clean rain gutters, down spouts and window channel drainpipes
- Check braking mechanism for correct adjustment
- Check rear lights, stop lights, number-plate lights, rear fog guard lamps, flashers and indicators
- Check for tread and wear to tyres, including cracks and cuts that may have developed over the winter

Preparing Your Tent

- Choose a fine day to test your tent before travelling
- Inspect potential stress points, i.e. where guy lines attach, where tent walls meet the groundsheet, where frame poles touch fabric
- Look out for mildew if the tent has been stored damp
- Check the tent's proofing, and re-spray if necessary
- Repair holes or tears with a suitable patch kit

Loading Your Caravan and Good Road Handling

Before loading luggage and equipment into the caravan, check on the weight restrictions that apply to it and the towing vehicle. The laden weight of the caravan should ideally be no more than 85 per cent of the kerbside weight of the towing vehicle. Check the manufacturer's handbook for both.

- Keep as much weight as possible near the trailer axle
- Store heavy equipment on caravan floor
- Never store heavy items at the rear of the caravan as a counterbalance - this causes instability and can be very dangerous
- Keep the roof lockers free of heavy luggage if possible
- Ensure lockers, drawers and cupboards are securely closed
- After loading the caravan should be level or slightly nose down when coupled to the car

A Few Final Checks

- Corner steadies are fully wound up. Brace is handy for arrival at site
- Windows, vents and doors are firmly shut
- Any fires or flames are extinguished. Gas cylinder tap is fully turned off
- The coupling is firmly in position and the breakaway cable is attached
- The over-run brake is working correctly
- Both car mirrors give good visibility
- All the car and caravan lights are working
- The safety catch on the hitch is on
- The jockey wheel is raised and secured, the handbrake is released, and the fire extinguishers are operational and close at hand

Tips on Towing

- Know your car well before attempting to tow
- Stop before you get tired
- Plan to use roads suitable for towing
- Have the appropriate mirrors and use them
- If traffic builds up behind you, pull up safely and let it pass
- Keep a safe stopping distance between you and the vehicle in front
- Switch on your headlights when visibility becomes poor
- Make good use of the gears on hills
- Allow plenty of time when overtaking or pulling across a main road
- Never stop on narrow roads, bends, crests of hills, or anywhere that could be dangerous
- In case of breakdown or accident, use hazard flashers and warning triangle(s)

Taking out insurance

- A certificate for motor insurance must be carried at all times in France.
- The AA can quote by phone or online for many types of insurance including
  Car Insurance 0800 316 2456
  Caravan Insurance 0870 010 1893
  Travel Insurance 0800 085 7240
  www.theAA.com/insurance

Check List of Essentials

Passports ❏
Tickets ❏
Driving licence (if you hold a photocard take counterpart document too) ❏
Holiday insurance ❏
Motor insurance ❏
Green Card ❏
Vehicle registration certificate (V5C) ❏
Breakdown cover ❏
EHIC (European Health Insurance Card) ❏
Euros/travellers cheques ❏
Credit card(s) ❏
Maps/road atlases/guidebooks ❏
Campsite guidebook ❏
GB stickers ❏
Headlamp beam convertors ❏
Red warning triangle ❏
Fire extinguisher ❏
Spare car/caravan light bulbs & fuses ❏
First aid kit/insect repellant ❏
Torch ❏
Polarity tester ❏

Essential information for motoring in France

Accidents

If you are involved in an accident you must stop. A warning triangle must be placed on the road at a suitable distance to warn following traffic of the obstruction. Hazard lights may be used, but not as a substitute for the triangle. Get medical assistance for anyone injured in the accident. Be sure to notify your insurance company within 24 hours of the accident. If a third party is injured, contact your insurers for advice or, if you have a Green Card, notify the company on the back of it. Try to take photographs of the scene, including registration plates of other vehicles involved.

Breakdown

If your car breaks down try to move it to the side of the road. Place a warning triangle at an appropriate distance on the road behind any obstruction. Hazard lights may be used in addition to the triangle, but may not work if the fault is electrical. Although high visibilty jackets are not compulsory it is recommended that you carry one for everyone in the vehicle. Breakdown insurance is vital, as towing in France can be expensive. For information on the AA's European Breakdown Cover see the inside front cover or visit the AA's website **www.theAA.com**

Caravans, Trailer Tents and Luggage Trailers

Take a list of contents, especially if any valuable or unusual equipment is being carried, as this may be required at Customs. A towed vehicle should be readily identifiable by a plate in an accessible position. Number plates can include the Euro symbol and GB national identifier.

This will dispence with the need for a seperate GB sticker.

Children in Cars

Children under the age of 10 are not permitted to travel on the front seats of vehicles, unless there are no rear seats or the rear seats are already occupied with children under 10 or there are no seatbelts. In these circumstances a child must not be placed in the front seats with their back to the road if the vehicle is fitted with a passenger airbag, unless it is deactivated. They must travel in an approved child seat or restraint adapted to their size. A baby up to 13kg must be carried in a rear facing baby seat. A child between 9 and 18kg must be seated in a child seat and a child from 15kg up to 10 years can use a booster seat with a seat belt or a harness. It is the driver's responsibility to ensure all passengers under 18 are appropriately restrained.

Cycle Carriers

If you intend taking your bicycles on a rear-mounted cycle rack, make sure that they do not obstruct rear lights and/or number plate, or you would risk an on-the-spot fine. The AA recommends roof-mounted racks.

Disabled Drivers

All EU member states now operate a Blue Badge Scheme. Badge holders can enjoy the same parking concessions available to disabled drivers in the host country. To obtain a booklet outlining details of these reciprocal arrangements, call the AA on 0800 262050 or visit the Department for Transport website (**www.dft.gov.uk**). As in the UK these arrangements apply only to badge holders themselves. Wrongful display of the badge may incur local penalties.

Drinking and Driving

There is only one safe rule - if you drink, don't drive. Laws are strict and the penalties severe. Maximum permissible alcohol levels are very low (0.05%), and random breath tests are frequent. Saliva tests are now used to detect the influence of drugs.

Driving Licence and International Driving Permit

You should carry your national driving licence with you even when you hold an International Driving Permit (IDP), which is not necessary when driving in EU countries like France. The IDP, for which a statutory

charge is made, is issued by the AA to an applicant over 18 who holds a valid full British driving licence. (Application form available on-line on the AA website **www.theAA.com**). The minimum age for driving a temporarily imported vehicle in France is 18.

Fuel

Petrol stations in France no longer sell leaded petrol, which has been replaced with a substitute unleaded petrol (Super ARS) that can be used in vehicles that normally use leaded fuel. Unleaded (sans plomb) may be found as 98 or 95 octane, 'super plus' or 'premium'. Diesel (Gazole) and LPG are available. There are many automatic petrol pumps operated by credit/debit cards. However cards issued outside France are not always accepted. Check with your card issuer.

Horn

In built-up areas, the general rule is that you should not use one unless safety demands it. In many large towns and resorts, and in areas indicated by the international sign (a horn inside a red circle, crossed through), use of the horn is totally banned.

Lights

Yellow tinted headlights are no longer necessary in France. Headlights should be adjusted so that the dipped beam does not dazzle oncoming drivers. This can easily be done by using headlamp beam converters; this is compulsorary in France. Remember to have the lamps set to the correct height to compensate for the load being carried or towed.

Continued

The French Government highly recommends that 4+ vehicles and vehicles towing a caravan or trailer use dipped headlights day and night. (Already compulsory for motorcycles). Driving on side lights alone is prohibited. Dipped headlights* should be used in fog, snowfall, heavy rain and in tunnels. Police may wait at the end of the tunnel to check. Headlight flashing is only used to signal approach or as an overtaking signal at night. At other times it is taken as a sign of irritation, and may lead to misunderstandings.

You should also carry a spare bulb kit. This will not avoid a fine if you are travelling with faulty lights, but being able to replace a bulb on the spot may save you the cost and inconvenience of a garage call-out. AA Headlamp Beam Converters and AA Bulb Kits can be purchased at the AA Dover shop, or the AA Folkestone shop at the Eurotunnel Passenger Terminal.

*also recommended outside built up area at all times

Luggage or Roof Racks

Only use equipment suitable for your vehicle. Distribute the load evenly, taking care not to exceed the vehicle manufacturer's roof rack load limit. A roof rack laden with luggage increases fuel consumption, so remember when calculating mileage per gallon. It also reduces stability, especially when cornering.

Mirrors

When driving or towing on the right, it is essential to have clear all-round vision. Ideally, external rear-view mirrors should be fitted to both sides of your vehicle, but at minimum on the left to allow for driving on the right. When towing a caravan or trailer tent it is essential to fix mirror accessories for better rear vision. These include clip-on extension arms to extend wing mirrors, and long arm wing or door mirrors.

The longer the mirror arm, the more rigid its mounting has to be.

A mirror mounted on the door pillar gives a wide field of vision because it is close to the driver, but it is at a greater angle to the forward line of sight. Convex mirrors give an even wider field of vision, but practice is needed in judging distance due to the diminished image.

Motor Insurance

When driving in France you must carry your certificate of motor insurance with you at all times. Third-party is the minimum legal requirement, although you are recommended to arrange for the same level of cover as you have at home. Therefore, before taking a motor vehicle, caravan or trailer abroad, contact your insurance company and arrange cover. Some will produce a Green Card for you, and others will automatically cover your trip abroad at no extra cost.

Parking

Parking restrictions are indicated by signs or yellow lines on the kerb. Stopping and parking is prohibited if the yellow line is continuous; parking is allowed if it is broken. In Paris parking is forbidden in many city centre streets, and wheelclamps are in use. It is absolutely forbidden to stop or park on a red route.

Police Fines

In France, on-the-spot fines can be imposed by the police under certain circumstances. If you haven't got the cash, they will escort you to a cash point or bank to access the money. In some cases an immediate deposit is levied, followed by a fine which may be the same as, or greater or lesser than, this sum. They are normally paid in cash, either to the police or at a local post office against a ticket issued by the police. The amount can exceed the equivalent of £1,000 for the most serious offences. The reason for the fines is to penalize, and to keep minor motoring offences out of the courts.

Disputing the fine usually leads to a court appearance, delays and expense. If the fine is not paid, legal proceedings will usually follow. Once paid, a fine cannot be recovered, but a receipt should always be obtained as proof of payment.

Anyone caught exceeding the speed limit by more than 40kph will lose their licence on the spot, so without another driver to take over you will be forced to end your journey immediately. Police may stop drivers seen using a hand-held mobile phone and issue an on-the-spot fine (approx max £150).

Priority including roundabouts

In built-up areas you must give way to traffic coming from the right – priorité à droite. However, at roundabouts (sometimes with signs bearing the words Vous n'avez pas la priorité or Cédez le passage), traffic on the roundabout always has priority.

Outside built-up areas, all main roads of any importance have right of way. This is indicated by a red-bordered triangle showing a black cross on a white background with the words Passage Protégé underneath; or a red-bordered triangle showing a pointed black upright with horizontal bar on a white background; or a yellow square within a white square with points vertical.

Registration Documents

You must take the vehicle's registration certificate (V5C) with you. It should be in your name and kept with you. If you plan to use a borrowed vehicle you will need a letter of authority from the registered keeper as well as the V5C form. If you plan to use a hired or leased vehicle, you will need a Vehicle on Hire Certificate. This will normally be provided by the hiring/leasing operator.

Continued

Essential information for
motoring in France *continued*

Roads

France has more than 8,000 kilometres of motorway (autoroute). With the exception of a few sections into or around large cities, tolls are payable. Emergency telephones which connect the caller to the police are located approximately every two kilometres. There is also a very comprehensive network of other roads, and surfaces are generally good. Exceptions are usually signed Chaussée déformée. The camber is often severe and the edges rough.

During July and August, and especially at weekends, traffic on main roads is likely to be very heavy. Special signs are erected to indicate alternative routes with the least traffic congestion. Wherever they appear, it is usually advantageous to follow them, although you may not save time. The alternative routes are quiet, but they are not as wide as the main roads. They are not suitable for caravans.

A free road map showing the marked alternative routes, plus information centres and petrol stations open 24 hours, is available from service stations displaying the Bison Futé poster.

Road Signs

Road signs conform to international standards and should be familiar. Watch out for road markings - do not cross a solid white or yellow line marked on the road centre.

Seat Belts

Compulsory for front/rear seat belts to be worn if fitted. See also 'Children in cars' (page 12).

Spares

The spares you should carry depend on the vehicle and how long you are likely to be away. Useful items include a set of windscreen wiper blades (one for the rear window in a hatchback). See also Lights. Remember that when ordering spare parts for dispatch abroad, you must be able to identify them clearly by the manufacturer's part numbers if known. Always quote your engine and vehicle identification (VIN).

Speed Limits

Built-up areas 50kph (31mph)
Outside built-up areas on normal roads 90kph (55mph)
Dual carriageways separated by a central reservation 110kph (68mph)
Motorways 130kph (80mph)

The minimum speed in the outside lane on a level stretch of motorway during good daytime visibility is 80kph (49mph), and drivers travelling below this speed are liable to be fined. The maximum speed on the Paris périphérique (ring road) is 80kph (49mph), and on other stretches of urban motorway, 110kph (68mph).

In fog when visibility is reduced to 50 metres (55yds), the speed limit on all roads is 50kph (31mph). In wet weather speed limits outside built-up areas are reduced to 80kph (49mph), 100kph (62mph) and 110kph (68mph) on motorways. These limits apply to cars, and cars towing a trailer or caravan if the latter's weight does not exceed that of the car and the total weight is less than 3.5 tonnes. However, if the weight of the trailer exceeds that of the car by less than 30%, the speed limit is 65kph (40mph), or if more then 30% the speed limit is 45kph (28mph). These combinations must also display a disc at the rear of the trailer/caravan showing the maximum speed. They must not be driven in the outside lane of a 3-lane motorway.

Motorists who have held a full driver's licence for less than two years must not exceed 80kph (49mph) outside built-up areas, 100kph (62mph) on dual carriageways separated by a central reservation, and 110kph (68mph) on motorways. Holders of EU driving licences exceeding the speed limit by more than 40km/h will have their licences confiscated on the spot by the police.

Tolls (péage)

Tolls are payable on most motorways in France. Over long distances the charges can be quite considerable. Compare the cost against time and convenience (e.g. overnight stops), particularly as some of the all-purpose roads can also be very fast. Always have some

currency ready to pay the tolls, although you may prefer to pay by credit card. A list of tolls and charges can be found on page 23 and on the AA website.

Traffic Lights

Traffic lights are often suspended over the road, and they change from red to green without going to amber. The density of the light may be so poor that lights could be missed - especially those overhead. There is usually only one set on the right-hand side of the road some distance before the road junction, and if you stop too close to the corner the lights will not be visible. Look out for 'filter' lights enabling you to filter right with care. If you wish to go straight ahead, do not enter a lane leading to 'filter' lights or you may obstruct traffic trying to turn right.

Tyres

Inspect your tyres carefully. If you notice uneven wear, scuffed treads or damaged walls, get expert advice on whether or not the tyres are suitable for further use. The AA strongly advises against using tyres with 2mm or less of tread, ideally changing any tyres worn down to 3mm before setting off on a long journey. Tyres wear down quickly once they reach this point, and wet grip is markedly reduced.
Check the car handbook for recommended tyre pressures. Different pressures will be recommended for a fully-loaded car travelling at motorway speeds. Remember that pressures can only be checked accurately when the tyres are cold, and don't forget the spare wheel.

Vehicle Licence

When you take a vehicle into France from the UK its vehicle licence (tax disc) should be valid on your return. If it will expire when you are abroad, you can apply for a new one up to 42 days in advance of the expiry date. Apply in writing either to a Post Office that deals with postal applications (if a vehicle registration document is enclosed), or to a DVLA local office.

Warning Triangle/ Hazard Warning

The use of a warning triangle or hazard-warning lights is compulsory in the event of accident or breakdown. This is important as the hazard-warning lights may be damaged or inoperative. This should be placed on the road 30 metres (33yds) behind the vehicle and clearly visible from 100 metres (109yds).
If your vehicle is equipped with hazard warning lights, it is also compulsory to use them if you are forced to drive temporarily at a greatly reduced speed. However, when slow-moving traffic is established in an uninterrupted lane or lanes, this only applies to the last vehicle in the lane.

Useful Websites

www.theAA.com
(route planning, motoring advice, traffic information, insurance and much more)
www.autoroutes.fr
(information on motorways in France - road works, tolls etc)
www.franceguide.com
(information on motoring in France)
www.sytadin.tm.fr
(traffic reports around Paris)
www.fco.gov.uk
(Foreign & Commonwealth Office website)

Useful information

British Consulate

18 bis, rue d'Anjou,
75008 Paris
Tel 01 44 51 31 00
Fax 01 44 51 31 27
Office hours (GMT):
Mon-Fri 8.30-11.30, 13.30-15.30
There are also Consulates in Bordeaux, Lille, Lyon
and Marseille. You will find British Consulates with
Honorary Consuls in Amiens, Boulogne-sur-Mer,
Calais, Cherbourg, Clemont-Ferrand, Dunkerque,
Le Havre, Lorient, Montpellier, Nantes, Nice,
St-Malo-Dinard, Saumur, Toulouse and Tours.

Camping Card International

A Camping Card International (CCI) is recognized at
most campsites in France; in some cases it is essential
and you will not be allowed to camp without one. At
certain campsites a reduction to the advertised charge
may be allowed on presentation of the camping card.
It is valid for 12 months, and provides third-party
insurance cover for up to 11 people camping away
from home.

On arrival at the campsite, report to the campsite
manager who will tell you where you may pitch your
tent or caravan. You may be asked to pay in advance,
or to hand over your card for the duration of your
stay. Some campsite managers may insist on keeping
all passports as well.

AA personal members may purchase a CCI from the
Caravan Club. If you require further information please
contact the Caravan Club on 01342 327410 (Mon-Fri
09.15-15.15), and be prepared to quote your AA
membership number. For further information on CCIs
visit www.campingcardinternational.com.

Customs Regulations within the EU

People travelling within the EU are free to take not
only personal belongings but a motor vehicle, boat,
caravan or trailer across the internal frontiers without
being subject to Customs formalities. When you return
to the UK, use the blue exit reserved for EU travellers.

You do not have to pay any tax or duty in the UK on
goods you have bought in other EU countries for your
own use. Note that you may be breaking the law if you
sell alcohol or tobacco you have bought. If you are
caught you face imprisonment, and/or confiscation
of the goods and the vehicle in which they were
transported.

To help protect people in the UK, Customs carry out
checks on some EU travellers to look for prohibited or
restricted goods, including drugs, indecent or obscene
material, firearms, ammunition, unlicensed animals
and endangered species. This means they may ask you
about your baggage. The law sets out guidelines for
the amount of alcohol and tobacco you may bring
into the UK. If you bring in more, you must satisfy the
Customs Officer that the goods are for your own use.

The guidelines are 3200 cigarettes, 400 cigarellos,
200 cigars, 3kg smoking tobacco, 10 litres spirits, 20
litres fortified wine, 90 litres wine, 110 litres beer.
Anyone under 18 is not allowed to bring in alcohol or
tobacco.

Emergency Numbers

Fire	18
Police	17
Ambulance (SAMU)	15
Operator	13
Directory Enquiries	12
European Emergency Number (use for any emergency services from a mobile phone)	112

Insurance

Car Insurance 0800 316 2456
Caravan Insurance 0870 010 1893
Travel Insurance 0800 085 7240
www.theAA.com/insurance

Medical Treatment and Health Insurance

If you regularly take certain medicines, do make sure
that you have a sufficient supply before travelling. If
for health reasons you carry drugs or appliances (such
as a hypodermic syringe), a letter from your doctor

explaining the condition and treatment required may save you from encountering difficulties on entering France. Before travelling make sure you are covered by insurance for emergency medical and dental treatment as a minimum. Before taking out extra insurance check whether or not your homeowner or medical insurance covers travel abroad. British holidaymakers in France can now enjoy the same health care as French citizens. To prove your entitlement to this you should carry an European Health Insurance Card (EHIC), obtainable by calling 0845 606 2030. To apply by post pick up a pre-paid addressed envelope from the Post Office or online at www.ehic.org.uk. (More information is also available on www.dh.gov.uk/travellers). The EHIC doesn't replace travel insurance, but is in addition to it.

Pet Travel Scheme

For further information contact the Pets Helpline on 0870 2411710, or visit the DEFRA website at **www.defra.gov.uk/animalh/quarantine** The Pet Travel scheme, which applies to dogs (including assistance dogs), cats, ferrets, and certain other pets, enables pets resident in the UK to enter, without quarantine restrictions, certain (listed) countries throughout the world and then return to Britain. Thanks to the relaxation of quarantine controls in this country, they can go straight home on arrival.

In order to bring your pet into, or back into, the UK from one of the listed countries (inc. France) the scheme requires that your pet must be fitted with a microchip, be vaccinated against rabies, pass a blood test and be issued with a pet passport (or hold a valid pet certificate dated before 1/10/2004). Before entering the UK, your animal will also need to receive both tapeworm and tick treatments. Remember it is necessary for your pet to have passed a satisfactory blood test at least 6 calendar months before travel commences. Your pet cannot travel under this scheme unless this time has elapsed.

The following breeds of dog are not allowed to be imported into France: Mastiff (also known as 'Boerbulls'), Staffordshire Terrier without a pedigree, American Staffordshire Terrier without a pedigree (also known as 'Pitbulls'), Tosa without a pedigree.

Useful stopover sites

Holidaymakers heading for France from the Channel ports come from all over the UK, with many families travelling long distances before even reaching their ferry or the Eurotunnel. For them it may be essential to make an overnight stop either near the ferry port itself or en route through the country.

  The following list is a selection of UK sites which have all been inspected by the Automobile Association, and awarded a high quality percentage in addition to a pennant rating. Sites can be found near all of the Channel ports, and are in strategic positions on motorways and major routes connecting the ferries with other parts of the country. Further sites can be found in the AA Caravan and Camping Britain & Ireland Guide (available on **www.theAA.com/bookshop**).

FOLKESTONE

Camping & Caravanning Club Site, Folkestone, **Kent.** Tel 01303 255093

Little Satmar Holliday Park, Folkestone, Kent. Tel 01303 251188

DOVER

Hawthorn Farm Caravan Park, Martin Mill, Kent. Tel 01304 852658 & 852914

PORTSMOUTH

Chichester Camping & Caravanning Club Site, Southbourne, W Sussex. Tel 01243 373202

POOLE

South Lytchett Manor Caravan Park, Lytchett Minster, Dorset. Tel 01202 622577

Beacon Hill Touring Park, Poole, Dorset. Tel 01202 631631

Wilksworth Farm Caravan Park, Wimborne Minster, Dorset. Tel 01202 885467

PLYMOUTH

Riverside Caravan Park, Plymouth, Devon. Tel 01752 344122

Langstone Manor Camping & Caravan Park, Tavistock, Devon. Tel 01822 613371

Higher Longford Caravan & Camping Park, Tavistock, Devon. Tel 01822 613360

WEYMOUTH

East Fleet Farm Touring Park, Weymouth, Dorset. Tel 01305 785768

NEWHAVEN

Bay View Park, Pevensey Bay, East Sussex. Tel 01323 768688

M6, JUNCT 38

Westmorland Caravan Park, Tebay, Cumbria. Tel 01539 711322

M5 JUNCT 13

Tudor Caravan & Camping, Slimbridge, Gloucestershire. Tel 01453 890483

M5 JUNCT 25

Ashe Farm Camping & Caravan Site, Taunton, Somerset. Tel 01823 442567

M5 JUNCT 31

Kennford International Caravan Park, Kennford, Devon. Tel 01392 833046

M1 JUNCT 28

Teversal Camping & Caravanning Club Site, Teversal, Nottinghamshire. Tel 01623 551838

A1(M) JUNCT 48

Boroughbridge Camping & Caravanning Club Site, Boroughbridge, N Yorks. Tel 01423 322683

A1/A66

Scotch Corner Caravan Park, Scotch Corner, North Yorkshire. Tel 01748 822530

M1 JUNCT 24

Shardlow Marina Caravan Park, Shardlow, Derbyshire. Tel 01332 792832

M42 JUNCT 9

Kingsbury Water Park Camping & Caravanning Club Site, Kingsbury, Warwickshire. Tel 01827 874101

M40 JUNCT 11

Barnstones Caravan & Camping Site, Banbury, Oxon. Tel 01295 750289

M25 JUNCT 25

Theobalds Park Camping & Caravanning Club Site, Waltham Cross, Herts. Tel 01992 620604

M25 JUNCT 11

Chertsey Camping & Caravanning Club Site, Chertsey, Surrey. Tel 01932 562405

M25 JUNCT 2A/3

Gate House Wood Touring Park, Wrotham Heath, Kent. Tel 01732 843062

M20 JUNCT 10

Broad Hembury Caravan & Camping Park, Ashford, Kent. Tel 01233 620859

M4 JUNCT 45

Riverside Caravan Park, Swansea. Tel 01792 775587

Crossing the Channel

There are many different ways to travel to France with a caravan, motorvan or trailer tent, depending on where you live or wish to travel from, and whether your preference is for sailing or going by Eurotunnel. The busy ferry ports on England's south coast offer great versatility, allowing you to head for various French ports on the north and north-west coasts, as well as northern Spain for easy access to south-west France and Belgium for the north of France. You may also choose whether to travel by day or overnight, and by normal ferry or by a fast service. Irish travellers can sail directly from two ports to two destinations in France.

BRITTANY FERRIES
Tel: 08709 076 103
www.brittanyferries.com
Plymouth to Roscoff
Plymouth to Santander
Portsmouth to Caen
Poole to Cherbourg
Portsmouth to Cherbourg
Portsmouth to St Malo

CONDOR FERRIES
Tel: 0870 243 5140
www.condorferries.co.uk
Poole to St Malo
(via Channel Islands, 22nd May-30 Sep)
Portsmouth to Cherbourg
(Sundays, 15 Jul-9 Sep)
Weymouth to St Malo
(via Channel Islands, 22 May-30 Sep)

EUROTUNNEL
Tel: 08705 35 35 35
www.eurotunnel.com
Folkstone to Calais (Channel Tunnel)

IRISH FERRIES
Tel: 08705 17 17 17
www.irishferries.com
Rosslare to Cherbourg
Rosslare to Roscoff

L D LINES
Tel: 0844 576 8836
www.ldline.co.uk
Portsmouth to Le Havre
Newhaven to Le Haure (1 May-30 Sep)

NORFOLK LINE
Tel: 0870 870 10 20
www.norfolkline.com
Dover to Dunkerque

P&O FERRIES
Tel: 08705 980 333
www.poferries.com
Dover to Calais
Portsmouth to Bilbao
Hull to Zeebrugge
Hull to Rotterdam

SEAFRANCE
Tel: 0871 663 2546
www.seafrance.com
Dover to Calais

SPEED FERRIES
Tel: 0871 222 7456
www.speedferries.com
Dover to Boulogne

TRANSMANCHE FERRIES
Tel: 0800 917 12 01
www.transmancheferries.com
Newhaven to Dieppe
Newhaven to Le Haure
Portsmouth to Le Haure

Tolls

Road name	Toll description	Car	Car & Caravan
A1	Lille - Paris	€13.10	€19.20
A2/A1	Valenciennes - Paris	€12.00	€17.60
A2/A26	Valenciennes - Reims	€10.60	€15.90
A4	Paris - Reims	€9.00	€13.50
A4	Paris - Metz	€21.00	€31.50
A4	Metz - Strasbourg	€10.90	€16.70
A4	Paris - Strasbourg	€31.90	€48.20
A5/A31/A6	Paris - Lyon (via Troyes)	€28.20	€36.90
A6	Paris - Beaune	€17.90	€23.40
A6	Paris - Macon	€23.40	€30.60
A6	Paris - Lyon	€28.20	€36.90
A7/A8	Lyon - Aix-en-Provence	€20.60	€31.80
A7/A9	Lyon - Montpellier	€20.90	€32.50
A8	Aix-en-Provence - Cannes	€12.00	€18.20
A8	Cannes - Nice	€3.80	€5.70
A8	Nice - Menton (Italian frontier)	€1.90	€2.90
A9	Orange - Montpellier	€6.50	€10.00
A9	Montpellier - Le Perthus (Spanish frontier)	€16.50	€17.90
A9/A54	Montpellier - Arles	€4.60	€7.10
A10	Paris - Tours	€19.60	€31.30
A10	Tours - Bordeaux	€27.80	€43.30
A10	Tours - Poitiers	€8.70	€14.50
A10	Poitiers - Saintes	€9.30	€14.30
A10/A71	Paris - Clermont-Ferrand	€31.50	€46.80
A10/A837	Bordeaux - Rochefort	€11.30	€17.30
A11	Paris - Angers	€23.10	€35.30
A11	Angers - Nantes	€7.50	€11.40
A11/A81	Paris - Rennes	€25.20	€39.10
A13	Le Havre-St Saens	€6.30	€9.50
A13	Caen - Paris	€18.80	€31.60
A13	Le Havre - Paris	€16.10	€27.40
A13	Rouen - Paris	€11.50	€20.80
A14	Orgeval-Paris (La defense)	€8.80	€13.00
A16	Calais - Paris	€18.50	€28.20
A26	Calais - Reims	€18.70	€27.00
A26	Reims - Troyes	€9.20	€13.40
A26/A1	Calais - Paris	€18.50	€28.20
A26/A5	Reims - Lyon	€33.80	€45.60
A26/A5/ A39/A40	Reims - Chamonix	€47.00	€66.80
A29	Le Havre - St Saens (A28)	€6.50	€9.80
A29/A26	Amiens - Reims	€10.90	€16.40
A31	Toul - Langres	€7.40	€9.70
A31	Langres - Dijon	€3.20	€4.20
A31	Dijon - Beaune	€2.20	€2.60
A36	Beaune - Besancon	€6.20	€8.10
A36	Besancon - Belfort	€6.30	€8.30
A36	Belfort - Mulhouse	€2.40	€3.00
A39	Dijon - Dole	€2.50	€3.30
A39	Dole - Bourg-en-Bresse	€7.40	€9.70
A40	Macon - Geneve	€13.50	€20.00
A40	Geneve - Chamonix	€5.00	€8.80
A41	Grenoble -Chambery	€5.10	€7.40
A41	Chambery - Geneve	€4.80	€7.50
A41/A40	Chambery - Chamonix	€11.00	€17.40
A42/A40	Lyon - Geneve	€13.30	€19.70
A43	Lyon - Chambery	€9.40	€15.10
A43/A48	Lyon - Grenoble	€8.90	€14.30
A43/A430	Chambery - Albertville	€4.60	€7.10
A49	Valence - Grenoble	€7.60	€12.00
A52/A50	Aix-en-Provence - Toulon	€6.50	€9.80
A51	Aix-en-Provence - La Saulce	€9.90	€16.10
A54/A7	Montpellier - Aix-en-Provence	€8.30	€12.70
A57	Toulon - Le Cannet de Maures	€2.00	€3.00
A61/A9	Toulouse - Montpellier	€17.40	€26.40
A61/A9	Toulouse - Le Perthus	€16.20	€25.10
A62	Bordeaux - Toulouse	€15.40	€24.00
A63	Bordeaux - Hendaye (Spanish frontier)	€6.40	€9.90
A64	Bayonne - Toulouse	€16.20	€24.80
A72	Clermont-Ferrand - St Etienne	€9.30	€14.40
A83/A10	Nantes - Bordeaux	€24.30	€37.10
A85	Angers - Bourgueil	€5.40	€7.60
A87	Angers - Cholet	€4.40	€4.90
A89	Bordeaux - Mussidan	€5.40	€8.40
A89	Tulle- St Julien	€8.40	€13.10

Tunnels and bridges

		Car	Car & Caravan
Pont de Normandie		€5.00	€5.80
Pont de Tancarville		€2.30	€2.90
Tunnel du Puymorens		€5.40	€10.90
Tunnel Maurice Lemaire (due to re-open in 2008)			
Tunnel du Frejus		€31.20	€41.30
Tunnel du Mont Blanc		€31.90	€42.10
Tunnel Prado Carenage (cars only)		€2.40	
le Viaduc de Millau (summer) on A75		€6.50	€9.70
le Viaduc de Millau (rest of the year) on A75		€4.90	€7.30

Aires on autoroutes with facilities for motorvans

Compared with the UK, France is a very large country with driving times to match. Travelling from the ferry ports of Brittany and Normandy to central or southern regions takes a long time, and frequent stopping is both recommended and desirable. While some drivers with plenty of time may like to plan their journeys using smaller roads, and seeing quiet parts of the countryside, others will wish to cover the distance to their holiday destination as quickly as possible using the excellent system of autoroutes. The following list provides information on Aires on autoroutes which all offer the means of emptying waste water and chemical toilets, and filling up with drinking water. The list on pages 26-27 gives some stopover campsites close to autoroutes.

A4 – SW of Verdun
55 - Meuse
Aire Verdun-St Nicholas
accessed from Strasbourg towards Paris

A4 – Near Strasbourg
67 - Bas-Rhin
Aire de Monswiller
accessed from Paris towards Strasbourg

A5 – W of Troyes
89 - Yonne
Villeneuve-L'Archeveque
accessed from Paris towards Langres

A5b – N of Melun
77 - Seine-et-Maritime
Aire Station Shell

A6 – S of Mâcon
69 - Rhône
Aire de Taponas et de Drace accessed: Drace - from Paris towards Lyon; Taponas - from Lyons towards Paris

A6 – S of Villefranche-sur-Saône
69 - Rhône
Aire les Cheres
accessed from Lyon towards Paris

A6 – N of Mâcon
71 - Saône-et-Loire
Mâcon la Salle
accessed from Lyon towards Paris

A6 – N of Mâcon
71 - Saône-et-Loire
Mâcon Saint Albain
accessed from Paris towards Lyon

A6 – S of Paris
77 - Seine-et-Maritime
Acheres
accessed from Lyon towards Paris

A6 – Near Precy-de-Vrin
89 - Yonne
Precy-de-Vrin
accessed from Lyon towards Paris

A7 – N of Marseille
13 - Bouches-du-Rhône
Lancon-Provence
accessed from Lyon towards Marseille

A7 – N of Valence
26 - Drôme
Aire Latitude 45
accessed from Valence towards Lyon

A7 – SE of St Etienne
26 - Drôme
Aire de Saint-Rambert-d'Albon
accessed by BP station

A7 – SE of Montelimer
26 - Drôme
Aire de Montelimer
accessed both directions

A7 – N of Orange
84 - Vaucluse
Aire d'Orange-le-Gres
accessed from Lyon towards Marseille

8 – E of Aix-de-Provence
13 - Bouches-du-Rhône
Aire de l'Arc

A8 – N of Toulon
83 - Var
Aire de Brignoles-Cambarette
accessed both directions

A8 – N of Orange
84 - Vaucluse
Aire de Mornas-Village
accessed from Lyon towards Marseille

A9 – Near Narbonne
11 - Aude
Aire Narbonne-Vinassan
accessed both directions

A9 – S of Narbonne
11- Aude
Aire de Lapalme
accessed both directions

A9 – NE of Nimes
30 - Gard
Aire de Nimes-Marguerittes
accessed from Orange towards Spain

A9 – SW of Nimes
34 - Herault
Aire Aubrussum-Nord
accessed from Orange towards Spain

A9 – SE of Montpellier
34 - Herault
Béziers Montblanc Sud
accessed from Spain towards Orange

A9 – SE of Montpellier
34 - Herault
Béziers Montblanc Nord
accessed Orange towards Spain

A9 – S of Perpignan
66 - Pyrénées-Orientales
Village Catalan Est
accessed from Spain towards Orange

A9 – S of Perpignan

66 - Pyrénées-Orientales
Village Catalan Ouest
accessed from Orange towards Spain

A10 – N of Saintes

17 - Charente-Maritime
Aire de Fenioux
accessed from Bordeaux towards Paris

A10 – S of Saintes

17 - Charente-Maritime
Aire de Saint-Leger
accessed from Paris towards Bordeaux

A10 – N of Orleans

28 - Eure-et-Loire
Aire du Heron Cendre
accessed from Paris towards Orleans

A10 – N of Bordeaux

33 - Gironde
Saugon
accessed both directions

A10 – SE of Niort

79 - Deux-Sévres
Poitou-Charentes nord
accessed from Poitiers towards
Bordeaux

A10 – NE of Niort

79 - Deux-Sévres
Rouille Pamproux Sud
accessed from Bordeaux towards Paris

A16 – N of Abbeville

80 - Somme
Station Shell (Sailly-Flibeaucourt)
accessed both directions

A19 – SE of Sens

89 - Yonne
Villeroy
accessed both directions

A20 – N of Cahors

46 - Lot
Aire Jardin des Causses du Lot
accessed both directions

A26 – N of Troyes

51 - Marne
Aire de Sommesous
accessed both directions

A29 – NE of Le Havre

76 - Seine-Maritime
Aire de Bolleville
accessed both directions

A33 – NE of Lunéville

54 - Meurthe-et-Marne
Aire de Virtimont
accessed between
Lunéville-Centre & Lunéville Château
exits. Follow heavy lorry signs

A36 – NE of Dole

21 - Cote-d'Or
Pont Chene d'Argent
accessed from Dijon towards Bourg-
en-Bresse

A36 – W of Besançon

25 - Doubs
Aire de Besançon-Marchaux
accessed from Beaune towards
Mulhouse

A36 – W of Besançon

25 - Doubs
Aire de Besançon-Champoux
accessed from Mulhouse towards
Besançon

A39 – N of Bourg-en-Bresse

71 - Saône-et-Loire
Poulet de Bresse
accessed from both directions by
road bridge

A43 – E of Lyon

38 - Isère
Aire de Isle-d'Abeau
accessed from Lyon towards
Chambery

A43 – SE of Chambery

73 - Savoie
Aire de l'Arclusaz
accessed from Albertville towards
Chambery before Montmelian exit.
Behind Fina station

A43 – SW of Albertville

73 - Savoie
Aire de Val-Gelon
accessed from Chambery towards
Albertville

A46 – S of Lyon

69 - Rhône
Aire Total de Communay
accessed from Lyon towards
St Etienne

A49 – NE of Valence

26 - Drôme
Aire de la Baume d'Hostun
accessed both directions

A57 – W of Toulon

83 - Var
Aire de Repos de la Bigue

A61 – Near Carcassonne

11 - Aude
Aire Les Corbieres
accessed both directions

A61 – SE of Toulouse

31 - Haute-Garonne
Aire de Port-Lauragais
accessed from Toulouse towards
Carcassonne

A62 – S of Montauban

31 - Haute-Garonne
Frontonnais Nord
accessed from Toulouse towards
Bordeaux

A62 – SE of Bordeaux

33 - Gironde
Saint-Michel-de-Rieufret
accessed both directions

A62 – W of Agen

47 - Lot-et-Garonne
Agen Porte d'Aquitaine nord
accessed from Agen towards
Marmande

A64 – E of Bayonne

40 - Landes
Hastingues
accessed both directions

A64 – SW of d'Orthez

64 - Pyrénées-Atlantiques
Aire de Lacq-Audejos Sud
accessed from Bayon towards
Toulouse

A64 – Near Tarbes

64 - Pyrénées-Atlantiques
Les Pyrénées
accessed from directions by road
bridge

A75 – SE of Millau

34 - Herault
Le Caylar

A75 – N of St-Chely-d'Apcher

48 - Lozère
Aire de Lozère
accessed from St Flour towards Millau

A84 – NE of Avranches

50 - Manche
La Vallee de la Vire Gouvets
accessed from Caen towards
Avranches

A89 – Near Perigeaux

24 - Dordigne
Aire du Manoir
accessed both directions

A89 – E of Clermont-Ferrand

42 - Loire
Haut Forez Sud
accessed from Clermont-Ferrand
towards St Etienne

Campsites handy for autoroutes and other main roads

OFF A1 BOIRY-NOTRE-DAME

(Pas de Calais)

Camping La Paille Haute.
Rue Verte,
62156 Boiry-Notre-Dame.
Tel 03-21481540
Fax 03-21220724
Open Apr to Oct

OFF A1 ORVILLERS-SOREL

(Oise)

Camping de Sorel.
60490 Orvillers-Sorel.
Tel 03-44850274
Open 1 Feb to 15 Dec

OFF A10 CHARTRES

(Eure-et-Loir)

Les Bordes de l'Eure.
9, rue de Launay,
28000 Chartres.
Tel 02-37287943
Open 30 Apr to 4 Sep

OFF A11 DURTAL

(Maine-et-Loire)

Camping L'international.
9 rue de Camping,
43430 Durtal.
Tel 02-41763180
Open 6 Apr to 30 Sep

OFF A10/A7 OLIVET

(Loiret)

Municipal d'Olivet.
rue de Pont-Bouchet,
45160 Olivet.
Tel 02-38635394
Fax 02-38635896
Open 1 Apr to 15 Oct

OFF A61 CARCASSONNE

(Aude)

Campeole de la Cite.
rte de St-Hilaire,
11000 Carcassonne.
Tel 04-68251177
Open 15 May to 10 Oct

OFF A71 BOURGES

(Cher)

Municipal de Bourges.
26 boulevard de l'Industrie,
18000 Bourges.
Tel 02-48201685
Fax 02-48503239
Open 15 Mar to 15 Nov

OFF A71 CHÂTELGUYON

(Pay-de-Dôme)

Clos de las Balanenède.
route de la Piscine,
63140 Châtelguyon.
Tel 04-73860247
Open 15 Apr to 2 Oct

OFF A75 MASSIAC

(Cantal)

Municipal de L'Allagnon.
av de Courcelles,
15500 Massiac.
Tel 04-71230393
Fax 04-71230393
Open May to Sep

OFF A9 BOULOU

(Pyrénées-Orientales)

Camping Mas Llinas.
66165 La Boulou.
Tel 04-68832546
Open Feb to Nov

OFF A71 SAZERET

(Allier)

La Petite Valette.
03390 Sazeret.
Tel 04-70076457
Fax 04-70072548
Open 1 Apr to 31 Oct

OFF A6 AUXERRE

(Yonne)

Municiple.
8 route de Vaux,
89000 Auxerre.
Tel 03-86521115
Fax 03-86511754
Open 1 Apr to 30 Sep

OFF A6 DARDILLY

(Rhône)

International de Lyon.
Porte de Lyon,
69570 Dardilly.
Tel 04-78356455
Fax 04-72170426
Open all year

OFF A7 TAIN-L'HERMITAGE

(Drôme)

Municipal les Lucs.
24 av Pres-Roosevelt,
26600 Tain-l'Hermitage.
Tel 04-75083282
Fax 04-75083206
Open 15 Mar to Oct

OFF A7 REMOULINS

(Gard)

La Sousta.
Avenue du Pont-du-Gard,
30210 Remoulins.
Tel 04-66371280
Fax 04-66372369
Open 1 Mar to 31 Oct

OFF N10 SALLES
(Gironde)

Val de l'Eyre.
route de Lugos,
33770 Salles.
Tel 05-556884703
Fax 05-556884727
Open all year

OFF A11 SAINTES
(Charente-Maritimes)

Au Fil de l'Eau.
6, rue de Courbiac,
17100 Saintes.
Tel 05-46930800
Fax 05-46936188
Open May to Sep

OFF A11 NEUVILLE-SUR-SARTHE
(Sarthe)

Le Vieux Moulin.
route de Vieux Moulin,
72190 Neuville-sur-Sarthe.
Tel 02-43253182
Fax 02-43253811
Open 1 May to 30 Sep

OFF A13 LOUVIERS
(Eure)

Bel Air.
Hameau de St-Lubin,
rte de la haye Malherbe,
27400 Louviers.
Tel/Fax 02-32401077
Open 1 Mar to 30 Oct

OFF A26 SERAUCOURT-LE-GRAND
(Aisne)

Le Vivier aux Carpes.
10, rue Ch-Voyeux,
02790 Seraucourt-le-Grand.
Tel 03-23605010
Fax 03-23605169
Open Mar to Oct

OFF A4 VERDUN
(Meuse)

Camping Des Breuils.
Allée des Breuils,
55100 Verdun.
Tel 03-29861531
Fax 03-29867576
Open Apr to Sep

OFF A6/A31 BEAUNE
(Côte-d'Or)

Municipal Les Cent Vignes.
10, rue August-Dubois,
21200 Beaune.
Tel 03-80220391
Open 15 Mar to 31 Oct

OFF A6 LAIVES
(Saône-et-Loire)

Camping la Heronniere.
Les Bois de Laives,
71240 Laives.
Tel/Fax 03-85449885
Open 15 May to 15 Sep

OFF A6 GREZ-SUR-LOING
(Seine-et-Marne)

Camping les Près.
chemin des Près,
77880 Grez-sur-Loing.
Tel/Fax 01-64457275
Open 20 Mar to 11 Nov

OFF A7 VALENCE
(Drôme)

Camping L'Epervière.
Chemin de L'Epervière,
26000 Valence.
Tel 04-75423200
Fax 04-75562067
Open 20 Jan to 15 Dec

OFF A7 BOLLÈNE
(Vaucluse)

Camping La Simioune.
Quarter Guffiage,
84500 Bollène.
Tel 04-90304462
Fax 04-90304477
Open all year

OFF A8 ST MAXIMIN-LA-STE-BAUME
(Var)

Camping Provençal.
rte de Mazaugues,
83470 St Maximin-la-Ste-Baume.
Tel 04-94781697
Open Apr to Sep

OFF A64 MARTRES-TOLOSANE
(Haute-Garonne)

Camping le Moulin.
31220 Martres-Tolosane.
Tel 05-61988640
Fax 05-61986690
Open 15 Mar to 15 Oct

OFF A64 URT
(Pyrénées-Atlantiques)

d'Etche Zahar.
Allée de Mesples,
64240 Urt.
Tel 05-59562736
Open mid Mar to mid Nov

OFF A20 SOUILLAC
(Lot)

Domaine de la Paille Basse.
46200 Souillac.
Tel 05-65378548
Fax 05-65370958
Open 15 May to 15 Sep

OFF A20 VELLES
(Indre)

Les Grand Pins.
Les Maisons Neuves,
36330 Velles.
Tel 02-54366193
Open 1 Apr to 15 Oct

OFF N137 NOZAY
(Loire-Atlantique)

Municipal 'Henri Dubourg'.
rte de Rennes,
44170 Nozay.
Tel 02-40879433
Fax 02-40793564
Open 15 May to 15 Sep

Region names and département numbers with colour-coding

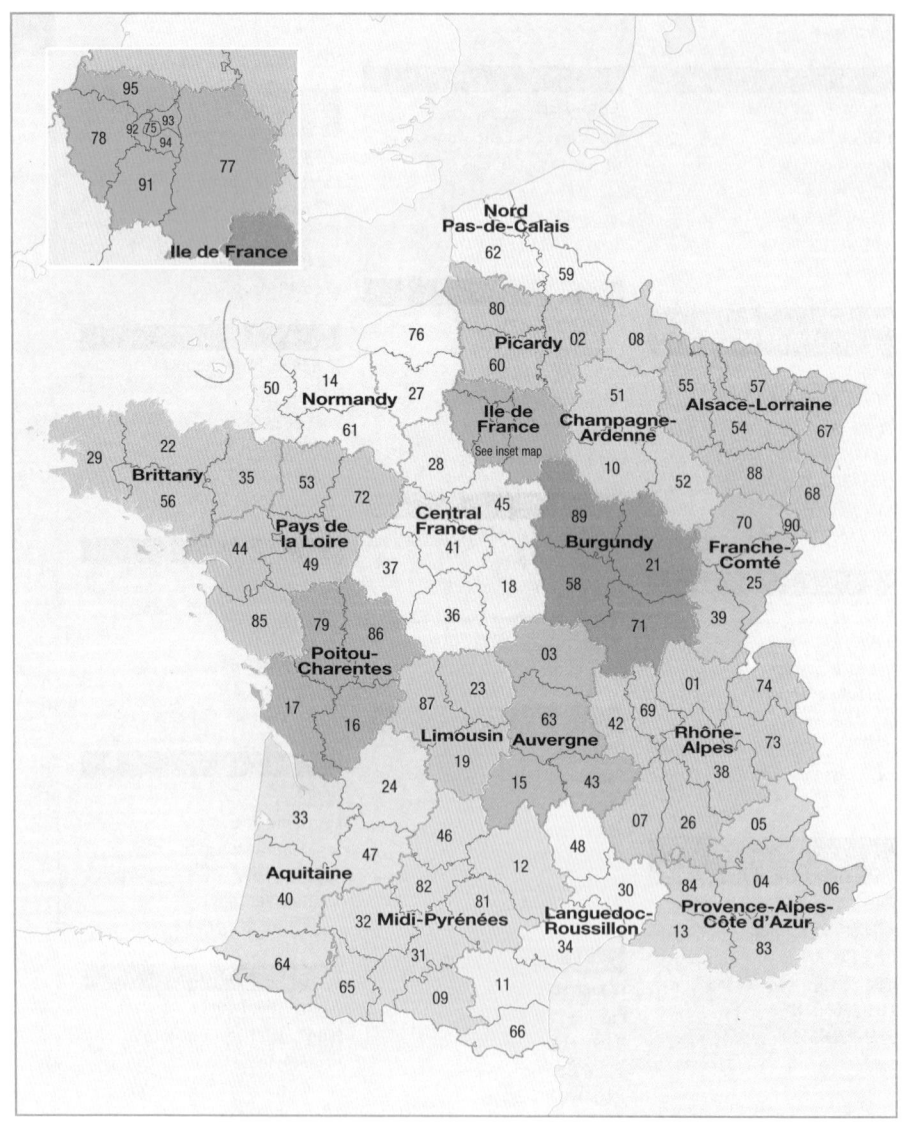

95
78 92 75 93
        94
91   77
Ile de France

Nord
Pas-de-Calais
62
59
80
76
Picardy 02 08
60
50 14 27 51 55 57
Normandy Alsace-Lorraine
61 Ile de Champagne- 54 67
France Ardenne
See inset map 10
22 28 52 88
29 35 53 45 89 68
Brittany 72 Central 70 90
56 France Burgundy Franche-
Pays de 41 Comté
44 la Loire 37 18 21 25
49 58
85 79 86 36 71 39
Poitou- 03
Charentes 23 01 74
17 87 63 42 69
16 Limousin Auvergne 19 Rhône- 73
24 15 43 Alpes
33 38
46 07 26 05
47 48
Aquitaine 82 12 30 84 04 06
40 81 Languedoc- Provence-Alpes-
32 Midi-Pyrénées Roussillon 13 Côte d'Azur
64 34 83
31
65 09 11
66

28

List of regions

ALSACE-LORRAINE
54	Meurthe-et-Moselle
55	Meuse
57	Moselle
67	Bas-Rhin
68	Haut-Rhin
88	Vosges

AQUITAINE
24	Dordogne
33	Gironde
40	Landes
47	Lot-et-Garonne
64	Pyrénées-Atlantiques

AUVERGNE
3	Allier
15	Cantal
43	Haute-Loire
63	Puy-de-Dôme

BRITTANY
22	Côtes-d'Armor
29	Finistère
35	Ille-et-Vilaine
56	Morbihan

BURGUNDY
21	Côte-d'Or
58	Nièvre
71	Saône-et-Loire
89	Yonne

CENTRAL FRANCE
18	Cher
28	Eure-et-Loir
36	Indre
37	Indre-et-Loire
41	Loir-et-Cher
45	Loiret

CHAMPAGNE-ARDENNE
8	Ardennes
10	Aube
51	Marne
52	Haute-Marne

FRANCHE-COMTÉ
25	Doubs
39	Jura
70	Haute-Saône
90	Territoire de Belfort

ILE-DE-FRANCE
75	Ville de Paris
77	Seine-et-Marne
78	Yvelines
91	Essonne
92	Hauts-de-Seine
93	Seine-St-Denis
94	Val-de-Marne
95	Val-d'Oise

LANGUEDOC-ROUSSILLON
11	Aude
30	Gard
34	Hérault
48	Lozère
66	Pyrénées-Orientales

LIMOUSIN
19	Corrèze
23	Creuse
87	Haute-Vienne

MIDI-PYRÉNÉES
9	Ariège
12	Aveyron
31	Haute-Garonne
32	Gers
46	Lot
65	Hautes-Pyrénées
81	Tarn
82	Tarn-et-Garonne

NORD-PAS-DE-CALAIS
59	Nord
62	Pas-de-Calais

NORMANDY
14	Calvados
27	Eure
50	Manche
61	Orne
76	Seine-Maritime

PAYS-DE-LA-LOIRE
44	Loire-Atlantique
49	Maine-et-Loire
53	Mayenne
72	Sarthe
85	Vendée

PICARDY
2	Aisne
60	Oise
80	Somme

POITOU-CHARENTES
16	Charente
17	Charente-Maritime
79	Deux-Sèvres
86	Vienne

PROVENCE-ALPES-CÔTE D'AZUR
4	Alpes-de-Haute-Provence
5	Hautes-Alpes
6	Alpes-Maritimes
13	Bouches-du-Rhône
83	Var
84	Vaucluse

RHÔNE-ALPES
1	Ain
7	Ardèche
26	Drôme
38	Isère
42	Loire
69	Rhône
73	Savoie
74	Haute-Savoie

KEY TO ATLAS

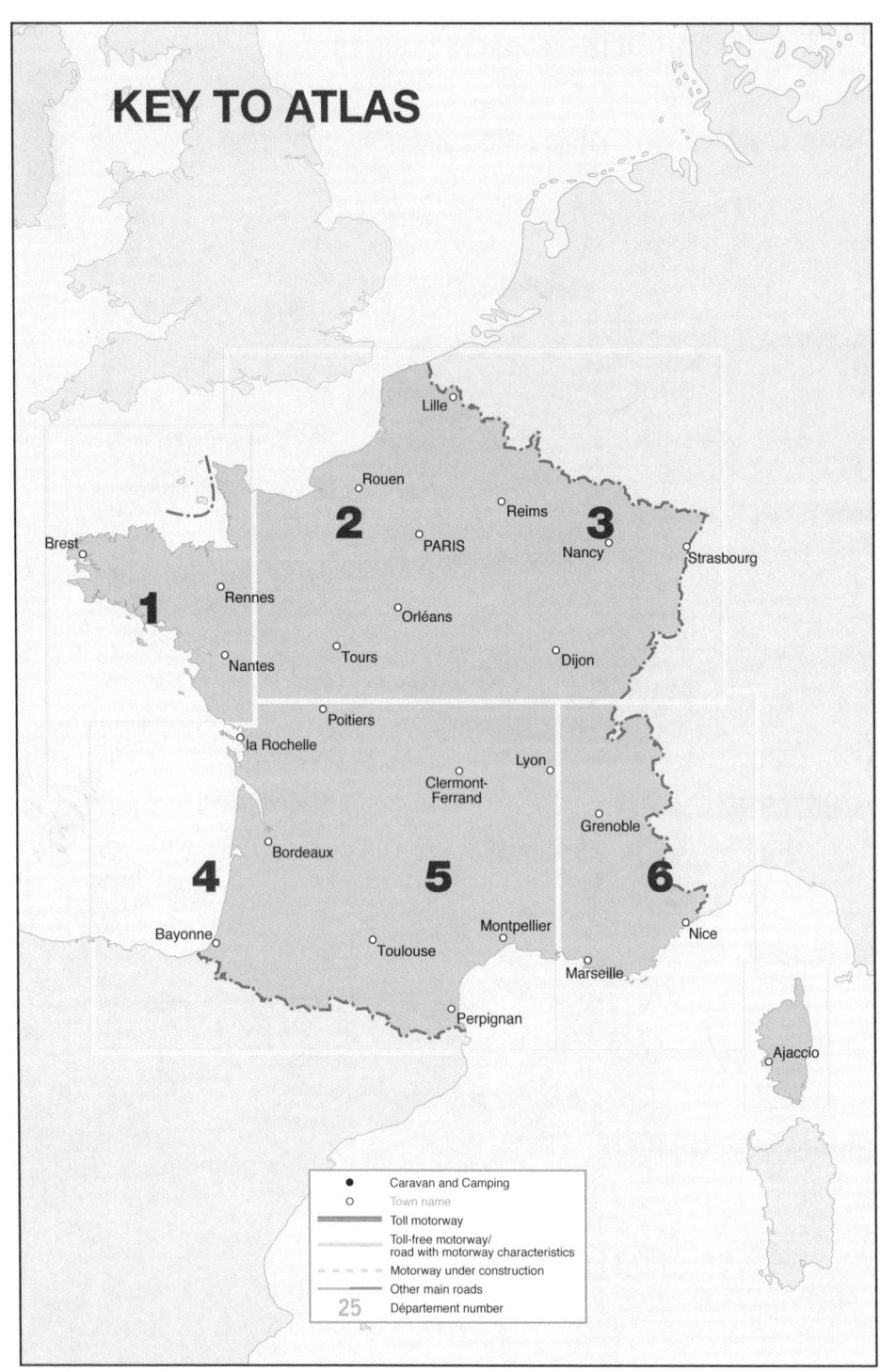

Lille

Rouen

Reims

2

Brest

PARIS

Nancy

3

Strasbourg

Rennes

Orléans

Nantes

Tours

Dijon

1

Poitiers

la Rochelle

Lyon

Clermont-
Ferrand

Grenoble

Bordeaux

4

5

6

Bayonne

Montpellier

Nice

Toulouse

Marseille

Perpignan

Ajaccio

●	Caravan and Camping
○	Town name
▬▬	Toll motorway
	Toll-free motorway/ road with motorway characteristics
- - -	Motorway under construction
───	Other main roads
25	Département number

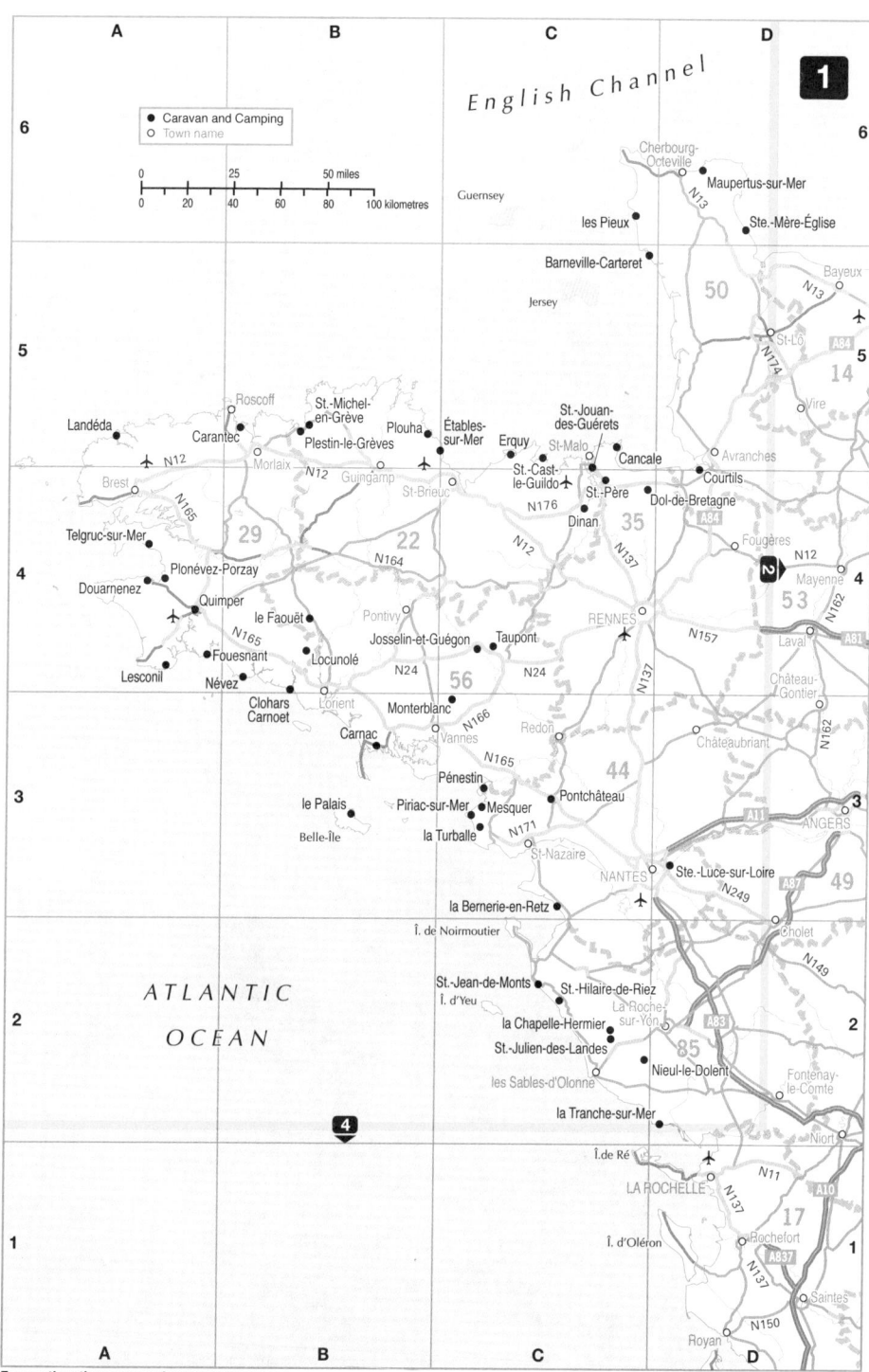

A **B** **C** **D**

1

English Channel

6 6

● Caravan and Camping
○ Town name

0   25   50 miles
0 20 40 60 80 100 kilometres

Guernsey

Cherbourg-Octeville

Maupertus-sur-Mer
N13

les Pieux

Ste.-Mère-Église

Barneville-Carteret

Jersey

Bayeux
N13

50

St-Lô
A84

5 5

N174

14

Roscoff

St.-Michel-en-Grève

Landéda

Carantec

Plouha

Plestin-le-Grèves

Étables-sur-Mer

Erquy

St.-Jouan-des-Guérets

Vire

Morlaix

N12

N12

Guingamp

St-Malo

Cancale

Avranches

St-Brieuc

St-Cast-le-Guildo

Courtils

Brest

N165

N176

St.-Père

Dol-de-Bretagne

A84

Telgruc-sur-Mer

29

Dinan

35

Fougères

N12

22

N164

N12

N137

Douarnenez

Plonévez-Porzay

Mayenne

4 4

Quimper

le Faouët

Pontivy

RENNES

N157

53

N162

N165

Josselin-et-Guégon

Taupont

Laval

A81

Fouesnant

Locunolé

N24

N24

N137

Château-Gontier

Lesconil

Névez

56

N162

Clohars-Carnoet

Lorient

Monterblanc

N166

Redon

Châteaubriant

Carnac

Vannes

N165

44

3 3

Pénestin

le Palais

Piriac-sur-Mer

Mesquer

Pontchâteau

A11

ANGERS

Belle-Île

la Turballe

N171

St-Nazaire

NANTES

Ste.-Luce-sur-Loire

N249

49

la Bernerie-en-Retz

Cholet

Î. de Noirmoutier

N149

St.-Jean-de-Monts

St.-Hilaire-de-Riez

2 2

Î. d'Yeu

la Chapelle-Hermier

La Roche-sur-Yon

A83

ATLANTIC

St.-Julien-des-Landes

85

OCEAN

les Sables-d'Olonne

Nieul-le-Dolent

Fontenay-le-Comte

la Tranche-sur-Mer

Niort

4

Î.de Ré

N11

LA ROCHELLE

N137

A10

17

1 1

Î. d'Oléron

Rochefort

A837

N137

Saintes

N150

Royan

A **B** **C** **D**

For continuation pages refer to numbered arrows

31

English Channel

| | A | B | C | D |

2

GB

● Caravan and Camping
○ Town name

| 0 | 25 | 50 miles |
| 0 20 40 60 80 | 100 kilometres |

○ Dover
Folkestone ○ Calais
Dunkerque ○
BRUGGE ○

6 ○ Portsmouth
Guînes ● Éperlecques ●
Boulogne-sur-Mer ○ Saint-Omer ○
LILLE ○
N42
Montreuil ○ 62 Béthune ○
Lens ○ Douai ○
Villers-sur-Authie ● Arras ○ Camb
Abbeville ○

5 ○ Dieppe
Bertangles ● 80
Veules-les-Roses ● Petit-Appeville ● AMIENS St-Quen
76 N27 60 N29 St-Quen

○ Cherbourg-
Octeville
Le Havre ○ Beauvais ○ 60 N31 Soissons ○
N13 N151 ROUEN ○ N31 Compiègne ○
N13 Bayeux ○ Houlgate ● Creil ○ N2
4 50 Martragny ● CAEN Moyaux ● 95 Pontoise ○ Meaux ○
N174 St-Lô ○ Pont- Bernay ○ Villevaudé ●
14 l'Evêque Évreux ○ N154
Vire ○ 27 PARIS
Argentan ○ N12 Évry ○ 77
Avranches ○ 61 St-Rémy- Dreux ○ 78 91 N36
3 Ambrières- sur-Avre ● N154 Chartres ○ N4 Provins ○
Fougères ○ les-Vallées ● Alençon ○ N12 91 Melun ○
N12 Nogent- N154 A10 Fontainebleau ○
Mayenne ○ le-Rotrou ○ N20 N6
N157 53 72 N10 28 N152 Pithiviers ○
Laval ○ Châteaudun ○ ORLÉANS N60 Montargis ○
Château- LE MANS ● Cloyes-sur-le-Loir N60 45
Gontier ○ Vendôme ○ A10 18
2 ○ Châteaubriant Luché-Pringé ● Suèvres ● Gien ○ 89
○ Muides-sur-Loire ●
ANGERS Blois ○ 41 Pierrefitte- Cosne-Cours-
Ballan-Miré ● TOURS Limeray ● sur-Sauldre ● sur-Loire
49 Saumur ● Chenonceaux ● Romorantin-Lanthenay ○ 18
N249 Concourson- Varennes- 37 Loches ○ Vierzon ○ N1
sur-Layon ● sur-Loire ● BOURGES
1 Cholet ○ Thouars ○ Vatan ● Nevers ○
N149 Châtellerault ○ Velles ● N76 N7
Airvault ● St-Cyr ● Châteauroux ○
85 A83 79 POITIERS le Blanc ○ la Châtre ○ Moulins

A84 ◄ 1
4 ▼
5 ▼

A | B | C | D

For continuation pages refer to numbered arrows

GENT (GAND)

E ANTWERPEN/ANVERS

F

NL

G

KÖLN

H

3

6

BRUXELLES/BRUSSEL

Aachen

Bonn

Siegen

B

LIÈGE / LUIK

Koblenz

Frankfurt A.M.

Valenciennes

Charleroi

D

MAINZ

5

Maubeuge

59

N2

Hirson

L

Mannheim

Vervins

les Mazures

LUXEMBOURG

02

Laon

Charleville-Mézières

Rethel

08

le Chesne

Longuyon

Thionville

SAARBRÜCKEN

4

Vouziers

KARLSRUHE

Reims

Verdun

Forbach

Sarreguemines

Ste-Menehould

METZ

Niederbronn-les-Bains

Épernay

Châlons-en-Champagne

N35

55

St-Mihiel

Morhange

57

Oberbronn

Haguenau

51

N4

N44

Vitry-le-François

St-Dizier

Bar-le-Duc

Toul

Sarrebourg

Saverne

STRASBOURG

ézanne

N4

NANCY

Villey-le-Sec

Villers-lès-Nancy

54

67

Obernai

St.-Pierre

52

N67

Neufchâteau

N57

St-Dié-des-Vosges

N59

Sélestat

Kaysersberg

Troyes

N60

Bar-sur-Aube

Vittel

Épinal

88

Xonrupt-Longemer

Colmar

FREIBURG I.B.

10

Chaumont

le Tholy

68

Ste-Croix-en-Plaine

N77

St-Florentin

Montigny-le-Roi

Bannes

Saulxures-sur-Moselotte

la Bresse

Kruth

uxerre

N6

Châtillon-sur-Seine

Langres

N19

N57

Fresse

N66

N83

A35

Mulhouse

2

Montbard

21

70

Gray

Vesoul

Montbéliard

90

Belfort

BASEL

Clamecy

Avallon

DIJON

Rougemont

A36

25

Montsauche-les-Settons

Vandenesse-en-Auxois

BESANÇON

LUZERN

Château-Chinon

N81

Autun

Beaune

N73

Dole

N73

N83

N57

D461

BERN

CH

1

58

N80

Santenay

Chalon-sur-Saône

Parcey

Montbarrey

Ounans

N5

Pontarlier

Le Creusot

N70

Lons-le-Saunier

Marigny

Doucier

6

LAUSANNE

Louhans

N78

E

F

G

H

33

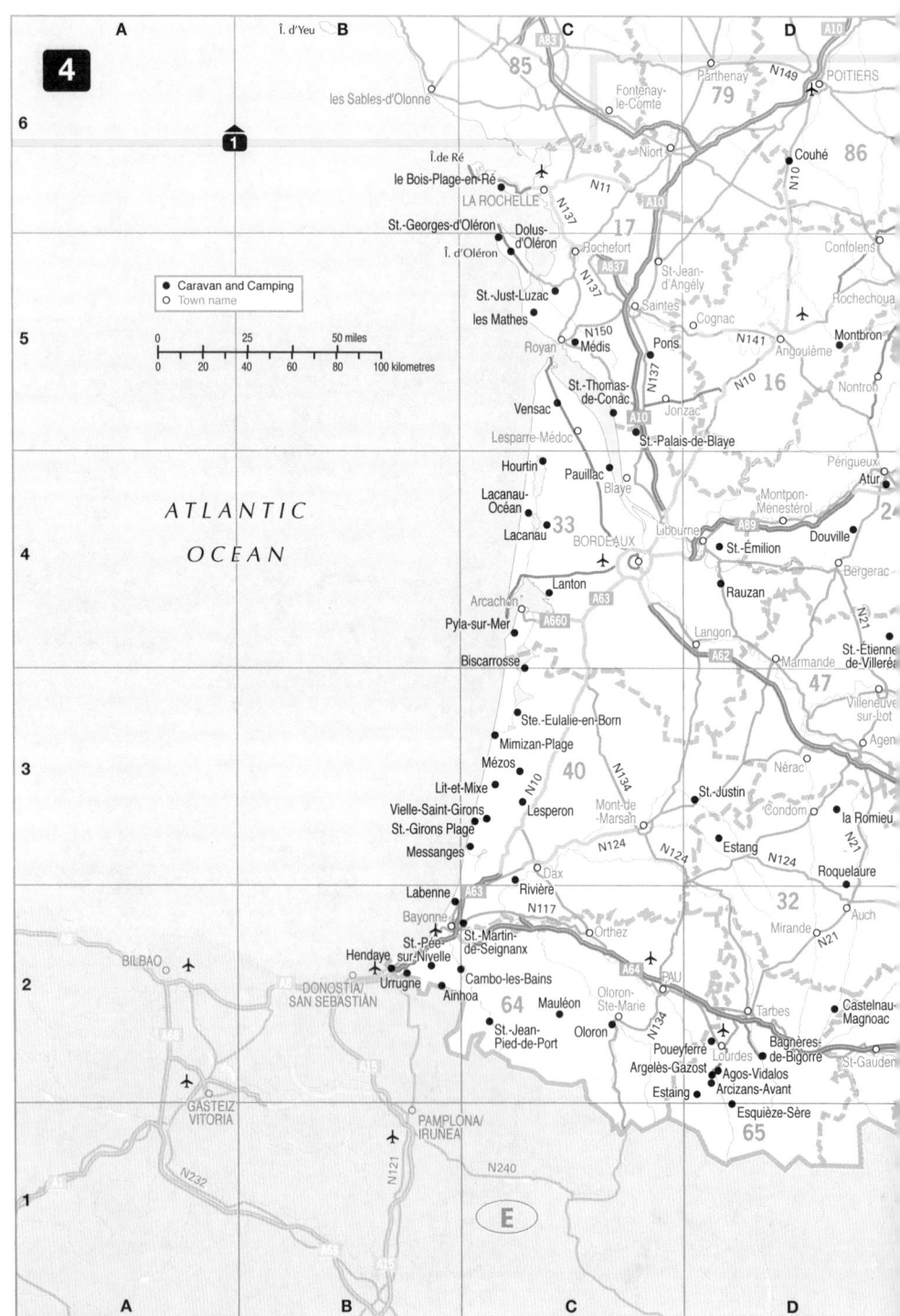

4

A   Î. d'Yeu   B   C   D

A83
85
Parthenay
N149
POITIERS
A10
les Sables-d'Olonne
Fontenay-
le-Comte
79

6

Niort
Couhé
86
Î.de Ré
le Bois-Plage-en-Ré
N11
LA ROCHELLE
N137
N10
St.-Georges-d'Oléron
Dolus-
d'Oléron
17
A10
Rochefort
Confolens
Î. d'Oléron
St-Jean-
d'Angély
Rochechoua
St.-Just-Luzac
A837
les Mathes
Saintes
N141
Montbron
N150
Royan
Médis
Pons
Cognac
Angoulême
16

5

St.-Thomas-
de-Conac
N137
N10
Nontron
Vensac
Jonzac
Lesparre-Médoc
A10
St.-Palais-de-Blaye
Périgueux
Atur
Hourtin
Pauillac
Blaye
2
Lacanau-
Océan
Montpon-
Ménestérol
Lacanau
33
BORDEAUX
Libourne
A89
Douville
St.-Émilion
Bergerac

4

● Caravan and Camping
○ Town name

0   25   50 miles
0   20   40   60   80   100 kilometres

ATLANTIC

OCEAN

Lanton
Rauzan
Arcachon
A63
Pyla-sur-Mer
A660
Langon
N21
St.-Étienne
de-Villeré
Biscarrosse
A62
Marmande
47
Villeneuve
sur-Lot
Ste.-Eulalie-en-Born
Agen
Mimizan-Plage
Nérac

3

Mézos
40
N134
St.-Justin
Condom
la Romieu
Lit-et-Mixe
N10
Vielle-Saint-Girons
Lesperon
Mont-de-
Marsan
Estang
N124
Roquelaure
St.-Girons Plage
N124
N21
Messanges
N124
Dax
Auch
Labenne
A63
Rivière
Mirande
32
Bayonne
N117
Orthez
N21
St.-Martin-
de-Seignanx
St.-Pée-
sur-Nivelle
A64
PAU
BILBAO
Hendaye
Cambo-les-Bains
64
Mauléon
Oloron-
Ste-Marie
Tarbes
Castelnau-
Magnoac
DONOSTIA/
SAN SEBASTIAN
Urrugne
Ainhoa
Oloron
N134
Bagnères-
de-Bigorre
St-Gauden

2

St.-Jean-
Pied-de-Port
Poueyferré
Lourdes
Argelès-Gazost
Agos-Vidalos
Arcizans-Avant
Estaing
GASTEIZ
VITORIA
Esquièze-Sère
65

1

PAMPLONA/
IRUNEA
N232
N121
N240
E

A   B   C   D

For continuation pages refer to numbered arrows

E
2

F

G

H
5

le Blanc
36
A20

Châteauroux

la Châtre
N79

N147

N145
la Souterraine
Guéret
N145
23

Boussac-
Bourg

Montluçon

Sazeret
N79
03

Moulins
N79

N7

Le Creusot

N78
Long-le-
Saunier
3
A6
Gigny-sur-Saône
71
Louhans
39

Palinges

Charolles
N79
Dompierre-les-Ormes

N6
Mâcon
A39
Bourg-en-
Bresse
A40

Bellac

N141

N147

LIMOGES

Aubusson

Vichy

Gannat

Chauffailles
69

Roanne

Villefranche-
sur-Saône

N7

Ambérieu-
en-Bugey
A42

Aixe-sur-Vienne
87
A20

Treignac

CLERMONT-
FERRAND

Nébouzat

Chambon-
sur-Lac
Orcet
63
Issoire
Murol

Thiers

A72

Ambert

les Pradeaux

Montbrison

Feurs

ST-ÉTIENNE

LYON
A47

St-Clair-du-Rhône

la Tour-
du-Pin
A43
5
Vienne
A48

Aubervives-
sur-Varèze
A49

N21

Tourtoirac

St-Antoine-
d'Auberoche
1
Montignac
8 2 5 4
9 3 6
5
10 11 7 Vitrac
12 13
Daglan 14
elvès
Monpazier
Sauveterre-la-Lémance
Montcabrier Cahors
Duravel

A89

Tulle
19

Brive-la-
Gaillarde

Souillac Bretenoux
Padirac
Payrac
Thégra

Carlucet

Argentat

Calviac

St.-Cirq-Lapopie

Palisse Lanobre

Mauriac

Vic-sur-Cère
A75

Aurillac

N122

St.-Amans-des-Cots

Figeac
46

Cassaniouze

Rodez

St.-Flour
15

Brioude

N102

Le Puy-
en-Velay

N88

Vorey-sur-Arzon

Eclassan

le Chambon-
sur-Lignon

Goudet
07

les Ollières-
sur-Eyrieux

Privas

Ucel

Largentière
Joyeuse

N88

Romans-
sur-Isère
A7
A49

Valence
St.-Laurent-du-Pape
4

Die
26

Baix
9
Montélimar

Villeneuve-de-Berg

82

Moissac

Montauban

Mirandol-Bourgnounac

Cordes-
sur-Ciel
Albi
N88

Villefranche-
de-Rouergue
A20

Séverac-l'Église
N88

Pont-de-Salars

St.-Geniez-d'Olt

12

Canet-de-
Salars

Teillet
81

Beaumont-
de-Lomagne
A62

N124

TOULOUSE
N126

N112

Brousses-
et-Villaret

Muret
A64
N20
A61

A68

Nages

Castres

Villardonnel

Villemoustaussou

Rivière-
sur-Tarn

Meyrueis

Millau

Nant

Florac

N106

Vagnas

St.-Alban-Auriolles
15
16
Balazuc

St.-Remèze
St.-Martin-d'Ardèche

Barjac

Goudargues

St.-Victor-de-Malcalp

Cendras
Allègre-
les-Fumades

Villeneuve-lès-Avignon

Remoulins

Orange
84
3

Carpentras

Apt

St.-Jean-
du-Gard

Anduze

Ales

AVIGNON

le Vigan

Lodève

Boisseron

NÎMES
A9

St-Rémy-
de-Provence

Salon-de-
Provence

Arles

13
Istres
A8
A51
2
MARSEILLE

Villefranche-
de-Panat

34

Clermont-
l'Hérault

MONTPELLIER

Lattes

Frontignan

Sète

31

A66

Carcassonne

Narbonne

Montclar

Limoux
11

Béziers
Sérignan

Agde
Valras-
Plage
Vias-Plage
Sérignan-Plage

Marseillan-Plage

A9

09
Surba
Mercus-Garrabet
Tarascon-sur-Ariège
Aston
N20

St-Girons

Foix

Prades

PERPIGNAN
66

le Barcarès
Ste.-Marie-la-Mer
Canet-en-Roussillon
St.-Cyprien-Plage
Argelès-sur-Mer

AND
ANDORRA
LA VELLA

Estavar
Err

Maureillas-las-Illas

N116

MEDITERRANEAN SEA

1. Plazac
2. St.-Léon-sur-Vézère
3. Marcillac-Saint-Quentin
4. St.-Crépin-et-Carlucet
5. Vézac
6. Ste.-Nathalène
7. Sarlat-la-Canéda
8. le Bugue

9. Alles-sur-Dordogne
10. Coux-et-Bigaroque
11. Beynac-et-Cazenac
12. Castelnaud-la-Chapelle
13. Groléjac
14. le Vigan
15. Sampzon
16. Vallon-Pont-d'Arc

1

E

F

G

H

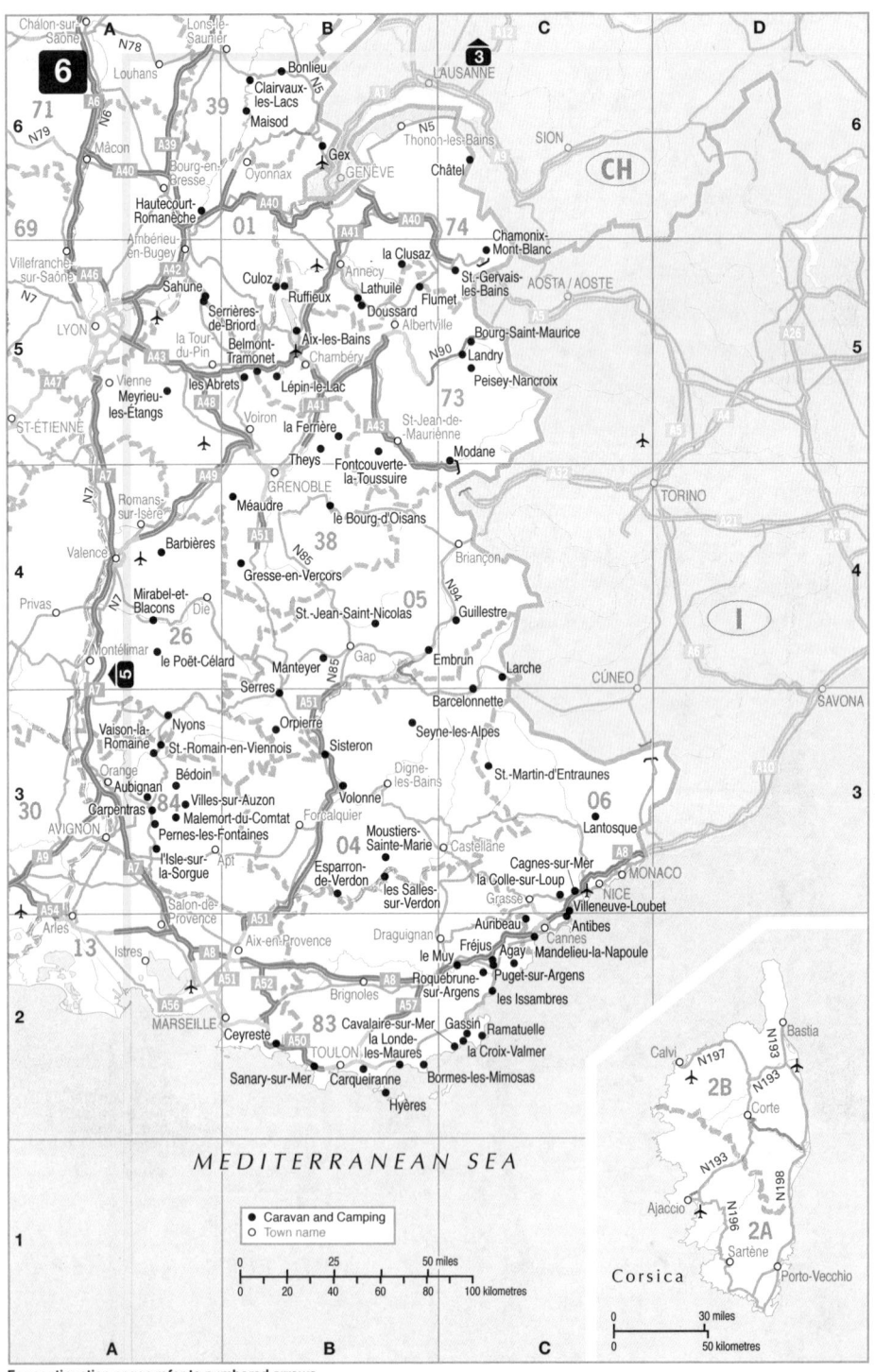

MEDITERRANEAN SEA

● Caravan and Camping
○ Town name

| 0 | | 25 | | 50 miles |
| 0 | 20 | 40 | 60 | 80 | 100 kilometres |

CH

Corsica

| 0 | | 30 miles |
| 0 | | 50 kilometres |

For continuation pages refer to numbered arrows

Heidenkopf

Rating	7.8
Tariff range	€€
Town	Niederbronn-les-Bains
Department	Bas-Rhin
Postal code	67110
Map	3 H4
Tel	03-88090846
Fax	03-88090846
e-mail	heidenkopf@tiscali.fr
Open	01 Mar – 31 Oct

N62, junct Niederbronn-Nord. From rdbt follow signs to site, 3 km N of Niederbronn.

Size (hectares) 2

Touring pitches 50 **Static pitches** 30

Sanitary facilities rating 7.7

quiet • rural character • suitable for the elderly camper • thermal baths • walking tours • Niederbronn (1 km)

Electric hook-ups/amps 50/6-16

A visit to the thermal baths at Niederbronn-les-Bains is one of the main reasons for staying at Camping Heidenkopf. The town had its heyday in the 19th century, but even now some 4,000 guests annually seek a cure for rheumatism and other ailments. The campsite is generally quiet but not really suitable for children. The fortifications at Schoenenbourg (part of the Maginot Line) that withstood heavy attacks from the German army in 1940 are very interesting.

Sports enthusiasts will enjoy a family excursion on foot or mountain bike to the Winterberg hills. Provided that you are well equipped, you can make the same trip in winter, as Heidenkopf is an all-seasons campsite. The municipal swimming and sports complex is only 600m away. The high trees around the park attract thousands of birds, and offer shade and shelter at the same time. The washing and toilet facilities have seen better days but are perfectly adequate. Once you have conquered the steep hill and narrow road to the entrance and found a piece of flat surface for your tent or caravan, you won't care about such trivialities.

Le Vallon de l'Ehn

Rating	7.9
Tariff range	€€
Town	Obernai
Department	Bas-Rhin
Postal code	67210
Map	3 H3
Tel	03-88953848
Fax	03-88483147
e-mail	camping@obernai.fr
Open	01 Jan – 31 Dec

From Strasbourg follow A35 & A352 to Molsheim. From junct 11 take D500 to Bischoffsheim & Obernai. At rdbt follow 'Route de Contournement' leading to Rue de Berlin.

Size (hectares) 3

Touring pitches 149

Sanitary facilities rating 7.9

friendly reception • rural views • brand new washing facilities • Sainte-Odile Castle • Alsatian Wine Route • Obernai (0.5 km)

Electric hook-ups/amps 119/16

The village of Obernai is set in this fascinating region where two cultures meet. Sometimes the scenery looks very German, but around the next bend it is typically French again. You are guaranteed a friendly reception at Le Vallon de l'Ehn thanks to managers Madame Senecal and Madame Guinchard. The campsite is located between vast vineyards which are very busy in harvest time.

A renovation has resulted in perfect sanitary facilities which are a delight to use. A plantation of young trees is growing well, and will soon provide plenty of shade. From the spacious pitches there is a magnificent view of the Vosges mountains. Young children should enjoy playing in the modest garden, on the mini golf course or in the recreation area. Older ones can play table tennis, badminton or volleyball, and next to the campsite is an Olympic-sized municipal swimming pool. It takes about 15 minutes to walk to the shops and restaurants in Altstadt Obernai (free parking), or you can go to Mont-Sainte-Odile where the castle is worth a visit. From the banks of the Rhine there is a fine view over the Alsatian plain, itself an excellent cycling area.

Municipal L' Oasis

Rating 8.3
Tariff range €€
Town Oberbronn
Department Bas-Rhin
Postal code 67110
Map 3 H4
Tel 03-88097196
Fax 03-88099787
e-mail oasis-oberbronn@laregie.fr
Open 12 Mar – 11 Nov
D28 to Zinswiller. Turn left after 1 km, as signed.
Site S of Oberbronn.
Size (hectares) 9
Touring pitches 150   **Static pitches** 35
Sanitary facilities rating 8.2
quiet • views • sports and games • plenty of footpaths •
Alsatian villages • Niederbronn (6 km)
Electric hook-ups/amps 150/10

Walking and relaxing are the main attractions of the municipal campsite at Eichelgarten, just a 15-minute walk from Oberbronn. Wake up to the joyful sound of birdsong, pack your rucksack with food for a tasty lunch and walk away. At reception there are details of local footpaths of varying lengths beginning at the site. Wherever you choose to go, there are plenty of beautiful spots where you can open the thermos flask and soak up the views; Wasenburg Castle, about one hour away, is one of these.

In the evening you can enjoy the view from the wide open space near the woods around the site. They don't offer much shade, but there is always a gentle wind blowing around the hills at the foot of the Vosges range. The washing facilities at Eichelgarten are somewhat outdated but nevertheless adequate. Children will enjoy the shallow swimming pool, the playground and the lawn next to it. Older kids will gather around the table tennis table, the volleyball pitch or the video games; playing tennis is free for all. Niederbronn-les-Bains (6 km) offers an extensive range of swimming and sports facilities.

Beau Séjour

Rating 7.6
Tariff range €€
Town St. Pierre
Department Bas-Rhin
Postal code 67140
Map 3 H3
Tel 03-88085224
Fax 03-88085224
e-mail commune.saintpierre@wanadoo.fr
Open 15 May – 01 Oct
N422 (Strasbourg-Sélestat) and onto Gertwiller & St-Pierre.
Size (hectares) 0.8
Touring pitches 47
Sanitary facilities rating 7.8
cosy and well tended • spacious stands • large playgrounds •
medieval villages • walking and cycling • Mittelbergheim (5 km)
Electric hook-ups/amps 47/6

This cosy campsite bordering the vast vineyards in the magnificent Pays de Barr et du Bernstein is one of the best kept secrets of the annual exodus to and from Southern France. Camping Beau Séjour is such a great place to stay that those who plan to use it for relaxation after a tiring journey often end up staying for much longer. The spacious pitches offer plenty of privacy, and the lack of trees guarantees a fine view when the sun goes down.

The washing and toilet facilities are well cared for by friendly caretakers. Children will easily find their way to the extensive playgrounds in the village square facing the campsite, which are also near the tennis courts and the community centre. Swimming in the lake near Benfeld (12 km) is a refreshing experience. Although there are plenty of dining outlets in Mittelbergheim and Barr, you should also try the two local restaurants. Don't forget to take a walk or a ride to the medieval villages and castles in the surrounding area.

Alsace-Lorraine

ClairVacances

Rating	8.4
Tariff range	€€€€
Town	Ste-Croix-en-Plaine
Department	Haut-Rhin
Postal code	68127
Map	3 H2/3
Tel	03-89492728
Fax	03-89493137
e-mail	clairvacances@wanadoo.fr
Open	01 Apr – 21 Oct

A35, junct 27 (Ste-Croix-en-Plaine), D1 towards Herrlisheim. 2 km before Herrlisheim site on left, (6-km S of Colmar)
Size (hectares) 3.5
Touring pitches 135
Sanitary facilities rating 8.9
neatly laid out • very clean washing rooms • fine swimming pool • take-away • Colmar, the wine capital • half-timbered houses • Equisheim (8 km)
Electric hook-ups/amps 120/8-13

Pierre and Monique Hauser have created a site that is not too big yet still able to offer good facilities and a swimming pool, where guests can enjoy a few days of rest. Far away from the traffic noise, on an open space in the woods near the village of Herrlisheim, Clair Vacances offers a sheltered oasis which holiday visitors can share with the birds. Privacy is guaranteed on the tidy, level pitches, and when the trees, shrubs and hedges mature over the next few years it will get even better. Washing and toilet facilities are truly luxurious (heated on cold days).

With the kids enjoying the fine swimming pool you can relax in your reclining chair under a parasol; there is an extra paddling pool for the youngest visitors. Cycling is easy around here: the vineyards are flat and you can easily ride from village to village, passing half-timbered houses adorned with roses and geraniums. Colmar is undoubtedly the food and wine capital of the Alsace region, so do not use Clair Vacances as merely a transit site.

Le Schlossberg

Rating	7.5
Tariff range	€€
Town	Kruth
Department	Haut-Rhin
Postal code	68820
Map	3 G2
Tel	03-89822676
Fax	03-89822017
e-mail	contact@schlossberg.fr
Open	22 Mar – 01 Oct

Beyond Remiremont follow N66 to Fellering. Sharp left and follow D13 to Kruth. Site N of Kruth.
Size (hectares) 5.2
Touring pitches 160   **Static pitches** 40
Sanitary facilities rating 7.9
nature all around • very well kept • quiet • reservoir • natural park Les Ballons • Thann or La Bresse (18 km)
Electric hook-ups/amps 140/2-6

From the high Vosges mountains you can watch paragliders jump off the 'ballons' (round mountain tops). Le Schlossberg itself is one of these high spots in the natural park named 'Les Ballons'. The site offers plenty of space, quiet pitches, spotless washing rooms and well kept grounds. A fast-running rivulet winds its way delightfully through the site. Although there are trees and shrubs all around, you can always find a sunny place, which is most welcome at a cool altitude of 500m. The large open-air café and the bar offer plenty of refreshments, and in the high season there is some entertainment.

During the rest of the year campers have to make do with table tennis, volleyball and boules, while for the younger children there is a large playground. A short 300m walk will take you to a large reservoir where you can go swimming or sunbathing, and there are some nice spots for a family picnic. Hikers who prefer even higher altitudes can use the 450-km network of footpaths, some of which lead to 'ballons' of 1300m or more.

Municipal

Rating 7.7
Tariff range €€
Town Kaysersberg
Department Haut-Rhin
Postal code 68240
Map 3 H3
Tel 03-89471447
Fax 03-89471447
e-mail camping@ville-kaysersberg.fr
Open 21 Mar – 30 Sep
N415 Colmar-St-Dié. Right after Kaysersberg/Alspach sign. Follow signs to site (NW of Kaysersberg)
Size (hectares) 1.5
Touring pitches 115
Sanitary facilities rating 8.1
well tended • next to a nice village • starting point for walks • walking • wine tasting • Colmar (10 km)
Electric hook-ups/amps 110/8-13

Only the gurgling of the Weiss River disturbs the silence at the municipal campsite of Kaysersberg, which is set very close to the village. When the weather is fine, the open air cafés in the picturesque streets of Kaysersberg look inviting. A walk on a windy autumn evening will lead you, in the footsteps of Dr Albert Schweitzer, to a quiet restaurant for a good Alsatian dish. In spring and summer the high trees and lower vegetation bring an extra beauty to the site, as do the sun-washed vineyards.

The site owes its reputation, among other things, to the excellent washing facilities. Entertainment is limited, but there is table tennis and a tennis court, and the baker pays a visit every morning. About 500m away there is a tropical swimming paradise with slide and jacuzzi. The footpath to the village centre runs along the river, passing a number of children's playing facilities. Or you can take a longer walk over the southern ridge to Riquewihr and back through the not-so-steep vineyards. More villages steeped in character are within easy reach by car.

Campéole de Nancy/Brabois

Rating 7.5
Tariff range €€€
Town Villers-lès-Nancy
Department Meurthe-et-Moselle
Postal code 54600
Map 3 G3
Tel 03-83271828
Fax 03-83400643
e-mail campeoles.brabois@wanadoo.fr
Open 01 Apr – 15 Oct
A33, junct 2b (Nancy-Brabois). Turn left at 2nd lights, follow signs. Site S of town.
Size (hectares) 6
Touring pitches 186
Sanitary facilities rating 7.3
well tended transit site • quiet • good food • palaces in Nancy • botanical garden (Montet) • Nancy (3 km)
Electric hook-ups/amps 159/5-15

British-born Michael Massy has rented this former municipal campsite from the town council of Nancy for a few years now, and he has provided a decent site where transit campers feel at home. The spacious pitches look well tended, and the toilet facilities are clean and easy to use; one of the toilet buildings has been adapted for less mobile guests which has been a popular move. Recreational facilities consist of a playground, a hard surface volleyball field, table tennis tables and an area for playing boules. You can borrow a book from the library or even exchange your own finished book for another one.

Most visitors use this site on their way through the region, although those who love culture may stay longer. The beautiful town of Nancy, only 3 km away, is easily accessible by bus (bus stop 15 mins walking distance away). The Musée de l'Ecole de Nancy and the botanical garden in Montet are not far away. Don't forget to ask Michael to show you the way to the restaurant. Two chefs prepare excellent regional dishes, and the 'quiche lorraine' and the salmon are very good indeed.

Alsace-Lorraine

Villey le Sec

Rating 8.1
Tariff range €€
Town Villey-le-Sec
Department Meurthe-et-Moselle
Postal code 54840
Map 3 F3
Tel 03-83636428
Fax 03-83636428
e-mail info@campingvilleylesec.com
Open 01 Apr – 30 Sep
A31, junct 15, then D400/D909 to Maron. Turn right in Dommartin. After Villey-le-Sec turn right again, follow signs to 'Base de Loisirs'. Site downhill, 1 km S.
Size (hectares) 2.5
Touring pitches 82   **Static pitches** 45
Sanitary facilities rating 8.1
quiet • beautiful view • friendly owners • fortified town Villey-le-Sec • walking and cycling • Toul (8 km)
Electric hook-ups/amps 80/6-10

Villey-le-Sec is set in a beautiful valley on the banks of the Moselle River. It is not just a comfortable and practical stop on your way to the south, but also a perfect starting point for excursions. The village itself, built on a hill, is interesting from a historic and architectural point of view. It was surrounded by walls after the Franco-German War of 1870, and became part of a defensive line. The campsite is attractive because of the fine view over the green hills that offer great opportunities for walking and cycling. There is a good choice of sunny open pitches.

Anglers can try their luck in the inviting rivers, but success is only guaranteed in the trout basins near Pierre-la-Treiche. Those who bring their own canoes can try a paddling tour on the Moselle River. For a swim, head for the town of Toul (8 km), where you will find both an indoor and an open air pool. The site shop sells regional products, among which is a genuine AOC-wine from the Côtes de Toul. At the bar you can have a drink with the owners, Monsieur and Madame Evrard.

Les Breuils

Rating 7.4
Tariff range €€€
Town Verdun
Department Meuse
Postal code 55100
Map 3 F4
Tel 03-29861531
Fax 03-29867576
e-mail contact@camping-lesbreuils.com
Open 01 Apr – 30 Sep
A4, junct Verdun-Ouest. Then take N35 & N3 to Chalôns-en-Champagne. Site SW of Verdun.
Size (hectares) 5.5
Touring pitches 144   **Static pitches** 20
Sanitary facilities rating 7.6
strategic position • beautiful towns • good swimming pool • biking in the Meuse Valley • Verdun (0.5 km) • Douaumont
Electric hook-ups/amps 144/6

CCI

Many campers are familiar with Les Breuils, now run by Miss Madrigal while her brother tends the bar. Their parents ran the campsite for nearly 30 years before retiring, and the many repeat bookings show the soft spot that campers have for this place. The site is located near the gates of Verdun, a town with many terrible memories of the First World War. To balance the sadness of these associations there is the beautiful 'campagne', the countryside around the Meuse Valley that offers wonderful opportunities for bicycle trips.

If you arrive early or late in the season you may find a prime spot near the pond, where hours can be spent angling or just relaxing. All pitches are good, however, and the grass is well cut. The toilet facilities are perfectly reasonable, but don't forget to bring your own toilet paper. The main attraction is the swimming pool with slides and paddling pool, and from a strategic position on the indoor terrace parents can also keep an eye on the playground. Try the 'plat du jour' in the small and far from expensive restaurant in the evening, and finish off with a night cap in the bar.

La Mutche

Rating 7.8
Tariff range €€
Town Morhange
Department Moselle
Postal code 57340
Map 3 G4
Tel 03-87862158
Fax 03-87862488
e-mail mutche@wanadoo.fr
Open 01 Apr – 31 Oct

Metz-D999 Baronville-N74 passing Morhange. Turn left at sign showing car with caravan, follow D78. Site N of Morhange. Follow signs 'Site touristique de la Mutche'.

Size (hectares) 5
Touring pitches 90   **Static pitches** 20
Sanitary facilities rating 7.6

lakeside • (water)sport facilities • spacious • sailing school • bicycle tours • take-away • Morhange (3 km)

Electric hook-ups/amps 90/16

Arriving out of season you may find that La Mutche is nearly empty, unless the local villagers are using the huge leisure centre on a sunny weekend. The camping and caravan pitches occupy a large lawn at the lakeside with enough room for sports and games, but there is also sufficient privacy. The lake is a big attraction both for watersports fans and a group of wood owls who have taken up residence. Close to the campsite there is a boat house where you can rent all sorts of equipment, ranging from canoes and surfboards to catamarans. You can also take lessons. Most anglers bring their own equipment and can look forward to a good catch.

Just outside the grounds there is a fine swimming pool with a sunbathing area, with free admission when you show your guest card. There is also a lake with a sandy beach, part of which is reserved for swimmers. La Mutche offers daily entertainment for children in July and August. There is a small shop in reception selling some basic items, and the local baker brings fresh bread every morning, but not before 10am!

Domaine du Haut des Bluches

Rating 7.5
Tariff range €€
Town la Bresse
Department Vosges
Postal code 88250
Map 3 G2
Tel 03-29256480
Fax 03-29257803
e-mail hautdesbluches@labresse.fr
Open 01 Jan – 04 Nov, 19 Dec – 31 Dec

From Gérardmer follow D486 via la Bresse to Col de la Schlucht (D34). Right after 3 km, site on left.

Size (hectares) 4
Touring pitches 124   **Static pitches** 30
Sanitary facilities rating 7.8

fine views of woods and mountains • reasonable fees • very clean and well tended • lakes near La Bresse • winter sports • La Bresse (4 km)

Electric hook-ups/amps 124/4-13

Big boulders arranged harmoniously mark the entrance to this municipal campsite. A great variety of plants and flowerpots, along with the humble river aptly named La Moselotte and the sound of gurgling water, contribute to the rustic atmosphere. Everywhere, in the valley or from the terraces, there are fine views over the wooded slopes. The charges are quite reasonable, and the facilities are clean and very good. The simple restaurant offers a changing menu of the day, and even a take-away service. There is also a small café, and the modest recreational area allows youngsters to play a game of table tennis, table football or pool.

A good swimming pool and a discotheque can both be found in La Bresse, and small restaurants here serve delicious regional dishes. You can also visit Gérardmer for some shopping or take a stroll along the lake. For a picnic go to Lac de Longemer, where you will find boating and swimming facilities. Walking is a popular activity in the vicinity of the campsite, and experienced bikers will be fascinated by the sight of the Honneck (1362m).

Alsace-Lorraine

Noirrupt

Rating	7.4
Tariff range	€€€
Town	le Tholy
Department	Vosges
Postal code	88530
Map	3 G3
Tel	03-29618127
Fax	03-29618305
e-mail	info@jpvacances.com
Open	15 Apr – 15 Oct

D11 (Epinal-Gérardmer).Route to Noirrupt signed; site on right of D11, just NW of le Tholy.

Size (hectares) 3
Touring pitches 77
Sanitary facilities rating 8.1

beautiful stands • well planted • good washing facilities • cascades of Tendon • several lakes • Gérardmer (10 km)

Electric hook-ups/amps 77/2-10

A wonderful variety of flowers, trees and hedges awaits you at the entrance to this site, where the hardest thing you will have to do is select a pitch. You can leave your car and walk uphill to find your preferred spot. Every pitch on this terraced site has its own charm, surrounded by plants, shrubs, trees, flowers and rocks in a harmonious setting, with wonderful views over the woods and fields of the low mountain range. There is plenty of shade if you prefer, and once you've made your selection you can return to your car. The washing and toilet facilities here are excellent, and it is evident that every single detail is lovingly cleaned and cared for.

There is a fine tennis court, and a swimming pool (next to which are some tent-shaped chalets for rent). Once a week table tennis and boule competitions are held, and there is a guided walking tour every Saturday; a ride by tilt-car is a favourite with the children. Enjoy the views along the Route des Crêtes, the villages on the Route du Vin or the waterfalls near Tendon on a day trip.

Lac de la Moselotte

Rating	7.2
Tariff range	€€€
Town	Saulxures-sur-Moselotte
Department	Vosges
Postal code	88290
Map	3 G2
Tel	03-29245656
Fax	03-29245831
e-mail	lac-moselotte@ville-saulxures-mtte.fr
Open	All year

From Remiremont on N57, D417 & D243 to Saulxures-sur-Moselle. Follow signs 'Lac de la Moselotte'. Site W of village.

Size (hectares) 3
Touring pitches 75
Sanitary facilities rating 7.1

primarily a transit site • by a lake • recreational area nearby • walking and cycling • winter sports • La Bresse (15 km)

Electric hook-ups/amps 75/10

Municipal campsites in France are often located near a recreational area frequented by the French as well. In the case of Lac de la Moselotte, its proximity to the lake with its charming views is what distinguishes the site. A pleasant walk through the fence near reception leads to the swimming, boating and beach activities beloved of French holiday makers. Anglers can rent a boat, climbers use the climbing wall, and skate boarders show their skills on the track. There is also a games room, toy corner, playground, simple snack counter and an open air café overlooking the lake. The washing and toilet facilities are clean and well maintained.

Pitches are surrounded by hedges for privacy, but otherwise there is little room to park your car. The surrounding area offers lots of opportunities for walking and hiking, and you can take a trip round the mountains to Gérardmer for shopping or a picnic at the Lac de Longemer and then back via La Bresse. Lac de la Moselotte is an excellent site for an extended stay, but it is also a good transit site.

Camping de Vittel

Rating	8.3
Tariff range	€€€
Town	Vittel
Department	Vosges
Postal code	88800
Map	3 F3
Tel	03-29080271
Fax	03-86379583
e-mail	aquadis1@wanadoo.fr
Open	01 Apr – 31 Oct

A31, junct 9 (Contrexéville-Vittel), D164 & D429 to Vittel. Then take D68 to They-sous-Montfort. Site on right after 600mtrs, NE of Vittel.
Size (hectares) 3.5
Touring pitches 130
Sanitary facilities rating 8.1
nice transit site • on the outskirts of town • simple and tidy • Vittel mineral water • thermal baths • Vittel (2 km)
Electric hook-ups/amps 130/10

Only a short distance away from the centre of Vittel lies this municipal campsite, close to a residential area on the outskirts. Many visitors to France use it as a favoured transit site for one night, sometimes taking the opportunity to visit the town and the factory where the famous mineral water is bottled. Add a visit to the thermal baths and you will need an extra night. In the summer time this is a busy site, frequented by campers on their way to Southern France.

The small but spacious pitches are either grass or gravel, or a combination of both, and surrounded by well-tended hedges. The washing facilities are simple, clean and old fashioned, including the 13 'pissoirs' in the main building. On a transit campsite you would not expect to find a good choice of sport and playing facilities, and a small playground is actually all there is. Every morning begins in style with the arrival of the baker sounding her horn and selling baguettes, flûtes, croissants and pain au chocolat. There is no need to hurry, as madame always completes two rounds of the entire site.

La Vologne

Rating	7.2
Tariff range	€€
Town	Xonrupt-Longemer
Department	Vosges
Postal code	88400
Map	3 G3
Tel	03-29608723
Fax	03-29608723
e-mail	camping@lavologne.com
Open	15 Apr – 15 Sep

From Gérardmer follow D417; beyond Xonrupt turn left at 'Caravaneige/Retournemer' sign (D67). Site E of Xonrupt between Longemer & Retournemer lakes.
Size (hectares) 2.5
Touring pitches 100
Sanitary facilities rating 7
on the bank of the Vologne • overlooking woods and mountains • simple and clean • Lac de Longemer • waterfalls of Tendon • Gérardmer (10 km)
Electric hook-ups/amps 100/2-10

The Vologne River runs straight through the campsite, and you can admire wonderful views of the wooded slopes. The planting of trees here on La Vologne is still in its early days, and the open aspect ensures a much wider view than will be possible in a few years. The washing and toilet rooms are very clean and well tended, and there are family cabins and facilities for less able guests. The use of the washing machines is included in the fee. There is no entertainment here, but you can go sailing, swimming, windsurfing and canoeing on Lac de Longemer (5 mins walking distance).

Gérardmer is an enjoyable place for a stroll, being beautifully situated at the border of the lake with the same name. For an interesting day out you could go to the waterfalls at Tendon or enjoy the scenery along the Route des Crêtes. Mountain bikers and motor cyclists should try to climb the Col de la Schlucht, as this is a cyclists paradise and there are plenty of routes to explore. For the hiker, footpaths lead off the site in all directions. All this makes La Vologne an attractive home base for campers who enjoy an active holiday.

Le Port de Limeuil

Rating	8.2
Tariff range	€€€€
Town	Alles-sur-Dordogne
Department	Dordogne
Postal code	24480
Map	5 E4
Tel	05-53632976
Fax	05-53630419
e-mail	didierbonvallet@aol.com
Open	01 May – 30 Sep

From Le Buisson, take D51 NW towards Le Bugue. Approx 3 km turn left to Limeuil, left again after few km, cross bridge towards Alles-sur-Dordogne. Site immediately on right.

Size (hectares) 5.5
Touring pitches 90
Sanitary facilities rating 8.4

marvellous location • 400 metres of riverside beach • weekly circus • Dordogne valley • prehistoric finds • Le Bugue (6 km)

Electric hook-ups/amps 90/5-10

At the confluence of two of France's most beautiful rivers, the Dordogne and the Vézère, two ancient bridges span the water. From this campsite's gravel beach you look out onto this almost magical place. On the other side lies Limeuil, nominated as one of the most beautiful villages in France. There are only 90 pitches on the whole site, so even in the high season there is plenty of space.

Between the pitches and the river lies a rolling field where the lightweight tents belonging to canoeists are pitched. The site has canoes for hire, and the owner can take you to your start point and pick you up later. Some families prefer pitches further from the river next to broad fields, because they don't have to keep such a close eye on the children there. On the other hand, the 400-metre beach by the Dordogne is child-friendly, as there is plenty of shallow water. A weekly circus with animals is organised for children, but there are not many organised activities. If they like canoeing, raft building and sitting around a campfire with other children, they will love it here.

Le Grand Dague

Rating	8.5
Tariff range	€€€€
Town	Atur
Department	Dordogne
Postal Code	24750
Map	4 D4
Tel	05-53042101
Fax	05-53042201
e-mail	info@lagranddague.fr
Open	25 Apr – 28 Sep

From Périgueux centre towards Brive: From Périgueux (built-up area) take D2 S to Atur. Site approx 4 km E of Atur.

Size (hectares) 7
Touring pitches 65
Sanitary facilities rating 8.7

very clean, green and spacious • nice swimming pool (including baby pool) • Dutch owners • medieval villages • prehistoric finds • Périgueux (10 km)

Electric hook-ups/amps 65/6-12

The first things you notice about Le Grand Dague are the beautiful flowers, maintained not by a full-time gardener, but by the campsite's owner, Marly Reimersma. The sanitary facilities are exceptionally clean, and the owner's sense of order is also reflected in the high hedgerows that surround the pitches on three sides. Catalpa trees, which have huge leaves, grow through the hedgerows, creating some much-needed shade. The large fields in front of the pitches add a nice touch, and compensate for the sheltered atmosphere around the caravan. The fields tend to be used as playing areas by children.

The campsite also has other facilities for children, including a sculptured fountain in the baby pool and an enclosed waterslide (twister) near the swimming pool. There's also a small field with several animals. The café cum bar is located in a converted barn, and as it is pretty well sound-proof, you can enjoy yourself here until the early hours of the morning. Orderliness and a convivial atmosphere don't always go hand in hand, but at Le Grand Dague they do.

RCN Le Moulin de la Pique

Rating	8.3
Tariff range	€€€€
Town	Belvès
Department	Dordogne
Postal code	24170
Map	5 E4
Tel	05-53290115
Fax	05-53282909
e-mail	info@rcn-lemoulindelapique.fr
Open	12 Apr – 11 Oct

S on D710 (passing Belvès). 2 km and site on left.

Size (hectares) 12
Touring pitches 138
Sanitary facilities rating 8.7

family atmosphere • located amid natural beauty • picturesque buildings • River Dordogne • Gardens • Belvès (2 km)

Electric hook-ups/amps 138/6-10

In the heart of the beautiful Dordogne nature reserve lies Le Moulin de la Pique. Set on a splendid country estate with picturesque 18th-century buildings, exotic gardens and idyllic water features, this centre offers spacious pitches, comfortable static caravans and a number of holiday chalets in the typical Périgord style. In the main building, you will find the reception, restaurant, bar with terrace and a small shop that sells snacks and takeaway meals. Water enthusiasts will relish the four swimming baths, and especially the slide which can take four abreast. There is also a toddler pool for the youngest guests.

At the heart of the site is a recreational pond where you can try your hand at fishing, or paddle a rubber boat. From May to September, the recreation team organises activities throughout the day for young and old. These vary from theme days to barbecue evenings, and there are games in the woods, canoe trips, survival trips and games afternoons. A tennis court, a variety of climbing equipment, a football field, a volleyball court, ping-pong tables, a boules pitch and an exotically arranged mini-golf course should satisfy sports lovers.

Les Hauts de Ratebout

Rating	8
Tariff range	€€€€
Town	Belvès
Department	Dordogne
Postal code	24170
Map	5 E4
Tel	05-53290210
Fax	05-53290828
e-mail	camping@hauts-ratebout.fr
Open	12 May – 09 Sep

S on D710 (passing Belvès). Approx 2 km turn onto D54 towards St-Foy-de-Belvès. Left again after 2 km; site in 2 km.

Size (hectares) 12
Touring pitches 140
Sanitary facilities rating 8.7

swimming complex • excellent sanitary facilities • wonderful atmosphere • caves • medieval villages • Sarlat-la-Canéda (35 km)

Electric hook-ups/amps 140/6

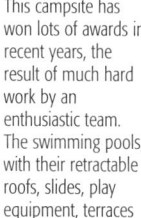 

This campsite has won lots of awards in recent years, the result of much hard work by an enthusiastic team. The swimming pools, with their retractable roofs, slides, play equipment, terraces and reclining chairs, are the main attraction.

The complex has been built around three former farms on the Ratebout Mountain, and the buildings themselves are of historic interest; a special feature is the 400-year-old storage cave, and there are many caves to visit in the surrounding area, such as at Proumeyssac and Padirac. If you want to see the famous Lascaux cave paintings in the high season, you will need to book in advance.

The site's spacious pitches are laid out on a terraced hillside, separated in some places by flowering shrubs or hedges. The view all around, over meadows and woods, is magnificent; the site has a park-like appearance, with its acacias, nut trees, plum and apple trees, and tubs full of geraniums and other flowering plants. The atmospheric restaurant serves regional specialities, and cabarets, discothèques and bingo evenings are organised two or three times a week for guests of all ages.

Aquitaine

Le Capeyrou

Rating 8.2
Tariff range €€€
Town Beynac-et-Cazenac
Department Dordogne
Postal code 24220
Map 5 E4
Tel 05-53295495
Fax 05-53283627
e-mail lecapeyrou@wanadoo.fr
Open 20 Mar – 30 Sep
Site E of Beynac on D703 (Bergerac-Sarlat). Site entrance directly opposite filling station.
Size (hectares) 5
Touring pitches 100
Sanitary facilities rating 7.9
fantastic location • quiet, spacious and clean • walking distance from the village • the Dordogne valley • prehistoric remains • Beynac (1 km)
Electric hook-ups/amps 100/6-10

Most people choose this campsite for its location: from the swimming pool and the pitches you can enjoy views of the limestone cliffs and the château of Beynac towering above. The banks of the Dordogne are right by the campsite and also offer spectacular views. This is one of the most picturesque parts of the Dordogne, with its dramatic countryside, wild river and peaceful campsite. Being able to walk to the shops and restaurants in only five minutes is a bonus.

Le Capeyrou is surrounded by sights, and along this section of the river you can always see at least two châteaux from wherever you are standing. The campsite offers clean, modern sanitary facilities and tidy, well-maintained grounds. Each pitch has enough shade. The generous pitches have hedges over half their length. Three hundred metres downstream is a child-friendly beach where canoes are available for hire, and there is also a swimming pool. There is no organised entertainment, so it is quiet during the day. Next door to the site is a small shop selling local produce including foie gras, with a restaurant upstairs.

Maisonneuve

Rating 7.7
Tariff range €€€
Town Castelnaud-la-Chapelle
Department Dordogne
Postal code 24250
Map 5 E4
Tel 05-53551063
Fax 05-53551063
e-mail camping.maisonneuve@wanadoo.fr
Open 01 Apr – 31 Oct
From Castelnaud take D57 over bridge towards Domme. Approx 3 km turn left at Pont-de-Causse, turn left again in approx 500mtrs. Site in 500mtrs.
Size (hectares) 10.5
Touring pitches 40
Sanitary facilities rating 8.1
fantastic river • spacious and fine views • popular with rock climbers • historical villages • cave paintings • Castelnaud (1 km)
Electric hook-ups/amps 40/10

A crystal clear river and open aspects towards the château at Castelnaud make this campsite special. Only 800m further downstream, the River Céou joins the Dordogne. The river is great for swimming, and the campsite has installed a diving board above a deep section of the river behind a natural dam. There are also stone steps going down into the water in a semi-circle, making it the favourite spot of older children. Smaller children have their own shallow paddling area.

Maisonneuve is a former farm that has managed to retain the open atmosphere of the wide Céou valley ground by leaving most of the site free of pitches. Tents and caravans surround an enormous field and look out onto the château rather than other campers. There is a summerhouse in the field, overgrown with climbing plants, and this contains a shower. There is a lack of shade here, and it can only be found near the entrance where there are trees and hedges between the pitches, or near the banks of the Céou. A swimming pool on the other side of the campsite is much frequented by everyone.

Les Valades

Rating	8.5
Tariff range	€€€€
Town	Coux-et-Bigaroque
Department	Dordogne
Postal code	24220
Map	5 E4
Tel	05-53291427
Fax	05-53281928
e-mail	camping.valades@wanadoo.fr
Open	01 Apr – 30 Oct

From Coux-et-Bigaroque take D703 towards Le Bugue. After approx 4.5 km turn left to Les Valades. Site on right in 1 km.

Size (hectares) 12
Touring pitches 50
Sanitary facilities rating 8.6

lake with sandy beach • shop and restaurant • space, peace and scenery • prehistoric finds • Dordogne valley with its castles • Le Bugue (10 km)

Electric hook-ups/amps 50/10

This site runs from the top of a hill right down to the valley bottom, and is largely made up of a rolling field on which no tents are allowed. This guarantees that everyone has a view over the neighbouring fields, woods and hills, dotted with cattle and the occasional farmhouse. At the foot of the hill lies a clear lake with lots of fish; with its sandy beach, it is a favourite place for children, because they can swim, float on airbeds and paddle canoes (on hire at the site).

The big surprise about this campsite is the location of the swimming pool. It is nowhere near the tents, but instead is next to the lake, just behind the little beach, and surrounded by grass on which you can sunbathe at your ease. As a result, the pitches uphill are quiet even in the daytime. The owner, who gave up a busy, successful career in Paris to start this campsite far from the rat race, knows exactly what campers want. He also provides well-maintained sanitary facilities, water, electricity, a restaurant that serves some local specialities, and a shop that sells local handicraft. The place is so quiet that the owner even guarantees your money back if you are disturbed!

Le Moulin de Paulhiac

Rating	8.6
Tariff range	€€€€
Town	Daglan
Department	Dordogne
Postal code	24250
Map	5 E4
Tel	05-53282088
Fax	05-53293345
e-mail	francis.armagnac@wanadoo.fr
Open	17 May – 13 Sep

From Daglan, follow the D57 towards St-Cybranet. The campsite is 4 km down this road on the right, to the NW of Daglan.

Size (hectares) 5
Touring pitches 100
Sanitary facilities rating 8.3

large swimming pool complex • for all ages • spacious pitches • numerous castles • by the River Céou • Daglan (3 km)

Electric hook-ups/amps 100/6

This is one of those campsites where the owner seems to be continually on the go, but he always finds time for a chat and a laugh. That is why campers are so keen to come back here, and many who came as children now bring their own. It is an ideal location for youngsters, with its swimming complex complete with four pools and three slides. Serious swimmers can plunge into their own pool without disturbing those who are out for a quiet paddle. Another magnet is the little River Céou, where children build dams, float on air mattresses and fish while their parents lie close by on the grassy turf, next to a large play area.

The restaurant is the third magnet, and prices are so low and the quality so good that you have to book in advance. Many activities are organised at the campsite, like the children's club, show evenings and competitions in every sport that the site can offer. There are also activities such as mountain biking and canoeing. In the evening, children from twelve to sixteen gather around a supervised campfire on a field outside the campsite, and this age group is always the first to ask if they can come back next year.

Aquitaine

Lestaubière

Rating	8.6
Tariff range	€€€€
Town	Douville
Department	Dordogne
Postal Code	24140
Map	4 D4
Tel	05-53829815
Fax	05-53829017
e-mail	lestaubiere@cs.com
Open	26 Apr – 01 Oct

From Périgueux, take N21 towards Bergerac. Site 29 km on left just before Pont-Saint-Mamet.

Size (hectares) 24
Touring pitches 104
Sanitary facilities rating 8.8

parkland grounds • great view • spacious camping areas • villages from Roman times • châteaux • Bergerac (18 km)

Electric hook-ups/amps 104/4-10

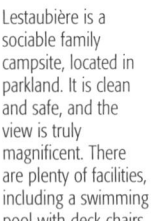 

Lestaubière is a sociable family campsite, located in parkland. It is clean and safe, and the view is truly magnificent. There are plenty of facilities, including a swimming pool with deck chairs, a sunbathing area, a lake with a diving pontoon, a baby pool (near the playground), several table-tennis tables, and pétanque facilities. You can also play football and (beach) volleyball, and there's a tennis court in the nearby village, and no fewer than six golf courses in the surrounding area.

The site is located on the edge of a forest on the Château Lestaubière estate, so is fairly open with no hedgerows or fences; though pitches are large. Apart from a shop, where you can buy the bare essentials, there are no restaurants, snack bars or other eating outlets. You are, however, more than welcome to barbeque near your caravan or tent. If you want to serve a truly memorable meal, why not buy some delicious foie gras in Douville, followed by confit or rillettes the day after! All you need to complete your banquet is a bottle of Bergerac. And there's no need to travel to Bergerac to get one (18 km).

Les Granges

Rating	8.5
Tariff range	€€€
Town	Groléjac
Department	Dordogne
Postal code	24250
Map	5 E4
Tel	05-53281115
Fax	05-53285713
e-mail	contact@lesgranges-fr.com
Open	26 Apr – 14 Sep

Site signed from D704 (Sarlat-Gourdon). Turn off at Groléjac, under viaduct, left towards site.

Size (hectares) 6.5
Touring pitches 64
Sanitary facilities rating 8.5

three swimming pools • many activities during the day • good sanitary facilities • close to the river Dordogne • picture-postcard Sarlat • Groléjac (1 km)

Electric hook-ups/amps 64/6

Les Granges boasts three large swimming pools with slides, modern and clean sanitary facilities, a restaurant, a bar and lots of organised activities. The campsite is situated in the heart of the Dordogne close to all the sights, and just 700m from the river and a canoe hire centre. Other campsites in the Dordogne are slightly better located, offering fine views or direct access to the river. Les Granges looks out towards its own static caravans, which not everyone will appreciate. They are separate from the touring caravans, but the rented tents do not have their own special area.

In the summer none of this matters, but people coming in the late season are usually looking for space as well as quiet. Many pitches are taken up by large tents, and high hedges between the pitches don't quite make up for this. So Les Granges is essentially a campsite for the high season when the many daytime facilities and activities will keep the children happy while their parents visit the sights just a short distance from the site. It is quiet in the evenings, which is perhaps not what the older children will be looking for.

Saint Avit Loisirs

Rating	8.8
Tariff range	€€€€
Town	le Bugue
Department	Dordogne
Postal Code	24260
Map	5 E4
Tel	05-53026400
Fax	05-53026439
e-mail	contact@saint-avit-loisirs.com
Open	01 Apr – 30 Sep

N from le Bugue take D710 towards Périgueux. Approx 3.5 km left onto C201 towards Saint-Avit. Site 5 km.

Size (hectares) 7

Touring pitches 60   **Static pitches** 50

Sanitary facilities rating 8.9

luxurious facilities • large swimming pool complex • located in oak forest • Dordogne Valley with châteaux • prehistoric paintings • Le Bugue (8 km)

Electric hook-ups/amps 60/6-10

A luxury campsite with all the amenities you could wish for, and new octagonal buildings with central heating and plenty of lights housing the sanitary facilities. These feature individual cubicles with washing areas and separate showers. The swimming pool complex, which comprises two separate pools - one with a waterslide, two baby pools and an indoor swimming pool - has been enlarged, and now includes two 'crazy rivers' - wider-than-usual waterslides that may only be used by children wearing a water ring.

The campsite also has a professional-sized basketball field with baskets at either end, and a well-designed mini golf course. The shop offers more than a normal campsite shop, the restaurant serves gastronomic dishes (there's also a self-service restaurant), and the organised entertainment is about as well-organised as it gets. As the ground is quite narrow, many pitches are located on the edge of the forest, enjoying either morning or evening sun, and a great view across the playing fields that form part of the complex.

Les Tailladis

Rating	8.2
Tariff range	€€€
Town	Marcillac-Saint-Quentin
Department	Dordogne
Postal code	24200
Map	5 E4
Tel	05-53591095
Fax	05-53294756
e-mail	tailladis@aol.com
Open	All year

From Sarlat, take D704 N towards Montignac. Turn left towards Marcillac-St-Quentin after approx 7 km. From Marcillac 1.5 km to site on left.

Size (hectares) 8

Touring pitches 78

Sanitary facilities rating 8.4

relaxed atmosphere • horse riding on the campsite • lake for fishing and paddling • old villages and castles • cave paintings • Sarlat (12 km)

Electric hook-ups/amps 78/6

The owner of this campsite once used to do his rounds on a white horse. Every afternoon, he would swim a few lengths in what is now the fishing lake, with his straw hat on his head, a Gauloise in his mouth and the same three ducks following behind him. Even then the campsite was a big hit with the children. His son, who now runs Les Tailladis, is a little less eccentric, but he still shares the same love of life and cares just as much about his guests. Understandably, there is a good relationship between the guests and the owner.

This campsite is hidden away in a small but beautiful corner in the centre of the splendid sights of the Dordogne. You are more than welcome to enjoy a drink on the large terrace between the pool and the restaurant, and when you get up in the morning to fetch the croissants just tell them your pitch number, and pay at the end of the week. The same applies when ordering local specialities in the evening, or a snack in the afternoon. Although the owner Philip is the epitome of the French joie de vivre, he is actually from Holland.

Aquitaine

Moulin de David

Rating 8.9
Tariff range €€
Town Monpazier
Department Dordogne
Postal code 24540
Map 5 E4
Tel 05-53226525
Fax 05-53239976
e-mail contact@village-center.com
Open 31 May – 07 Sep
Take N89 to Périgueux-Brive. At Niversac take D710 towards Le Bugue. In Belvès turn right to Monpazier. Site SE of Monpazier, by D2.
Size (hectares) 14
Touring pitches 80
Sanitary facilities rating 8.5
quiet and friendly • child-friendly • good campsite shop • Château de Biron • Vézère valley • Villeréal (12 km)
Electric hook-ups/amps 80/6-10

Campsite owner Jean-Claude Ballay has turned a very overgrown piece of land into a natural paradise where attention is lavished on guests. Traces of the millers and farmers who once used the little brook by the river have not been completely eradicated. The simple restaurant uphill from the stream has a covered terrace that is housed in splendid old restored farm buildings. The pitches vary in size from big to very big, and thanks to the luxuriant plant growth, the main site has adequate privacy. A section that was laid out more recently still has immature greenery.

The sanitary facilities are divided among three buildings and range from good to luxurious, all equally well maintained. Fitness coaching is given at the swimming pool, and there is also a natural pool (cleaned every week) with slides; both are surrounded by grass. There is also play equipment and a trampoline, with games facilities and organised activities aimed towards children of up to about 14. Adults tend to concentrate on the fascinating attractions in the surrounding area, such as the châteaux and caves.

La Fage

Rating 8.4
Tariff range €€€
Town Montignac
Department Dordogne
Postal code 24290
Map 5 E4
Tel 05-53507650
Fax 05-53507919
e-mail camping.lafage@wanadoo.fr
Open 01 May – 30 Sep
From Montignac S on D704e past 'Lascaux II', and turn off towards La Chapelle-Aubareil. Through woods for approx 7 km. Turn left towards site 500mtrs after La Chapelle-Abareil.
Size (hectares) 2.5
Touring pitches 58
Sanitary facilities rating 8.6
rest and relaxation • safe for children • beautiful trees • Lascaux II • castles and gardens • Sarlat (18 km)
Electric hook-ups/amps 58/6-10

La Fage is a quiet, well-cared for site with acacia trees, oaks, chestnut trees and many flowering plants and bushes. It is surrounded by forest, and the village is only a short distance away. The pitches are generous and are separated by natural features, and though the sanitary facilities are somewhat dated, they are generally fine and kept clean. Sun worshippers will be drawn to the swimming pool set in a sunny meadow, and the terrace café is very inviting. This campsite is ideal for children up to about ten years old, as it is a quiet, safe play haven.

With no bingo or karaoke evenings, you can always try your hand at boules, football or volleyball. Older guests will only be looking for the basics at La Fage while they concentrate on discovering the attractions of the surrounding area. Most notably, there is Lascaux II with its recreated cave that can hardly be distinguished from the original. But the caves of Les Eyzies are also worth a visit, as are the beautiful gardens of Manoir d'Eyrignac and the fantastic wall carpets at Château de Losse.

Aquitaine

Le Lac

Rating	8.4
Tariff range	€€€
Town	Plazac
Department	Dordogne
Postal code	24580
Map	5 E4
Tel	05-53507586
Fax	05-53505836
e-mail	contact@campinglelac-dordogne.com
Open	01 May – 15 Sep

Take D706 (Montignac-Les-Eyzies): approx 7 km after Thonac turn right onto D45 towards Plazac. Site approx 7 km on right (just before village of Plazac).

Size (hectares) 2.5
Touring pitches 70
Sanitary facilities rating 8.3

quiet family campsite • lake (well-suited to children) • spacious camping areas with hedgerows • cave paintings • Dordogne valley with châteaux • Plazac (1 km)

Electric hook-ups/amps 70/10

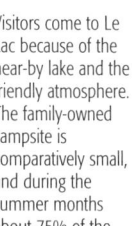 

Visitors come to Le Lac because of the near-by lake and the friendly atmosphere. The family-owned campsite is comparatively small, and during the summer months about 75% of the guests are families with small children. You can see the sandy beach from the terrace beside the snack bar, which is a great place to enjoy a snack, pizza or local dish in the shade of the weeping willows. Fresh water is constantly fed into the crystal-clear lake from wells on the bottom. Apart from going for a swim, you can hire pedalos, or bob about in your own rubber dinghy. An attendant supervises the lake in the afternoons in high season, while the swimming pool has a permanent attendant.

Both swimming facilities are located away from the site, which means it's fairly quiet during the day. There is some organised entertainment: the morning sessions are intended for toddlers and the afternoon sports sessions are for older children. A soirée dansante is held once a week. The pitches are spacious, and separated by hedgerows (flowery bushes on the rear field). The campsite offers clean and exceptionally modern sanitary facilities.

La Pélonie

Rating	8.5
Tariff range	€€€
Town	St-Antoine-d'Auberoche
Department	Dordogne
Postal Code	24330
Map	5 E4
Tel	05-53075578
Fax	05-53037427
e-mail	lapelonie@aol.com
Open	01 Apr – 30 Oct

On N89 (Périgueux-Brive), approx 5 km after St-Pierre-de-Chignac: towards St-Antoine/Limeyrat immediately after corner. Site 500mtrs after small tunnel (SW of St-Antoine).

Size (hectares) 2.9
Touring pitches 60
Sanitary facilities rating 8.9

quiet family campsite • restaurant annex café-bar • swimming pool (with baby pool) • prehistoric paintings • Périgueux en Sarlat • Thenon (9 km)

Electric hook-ups/amps 60/6

La Pélonie is a quiet campsite frequented by families with small children during the high season, and guests aged between 30 and 80 (without children) in the low season. Both groups appreciate the cleanliness of the sanitary facilities, and the restaurant/café-bar serves meals and drinks on the terrace in the sun. With the exception of the pizzas and snacks, all dishes are regional (or at least French). The swimming pool has a toddler's section and though there are no deck chairs, you'll find outdoor tables, chairs and sunshades. As people tend to walk around the pool area barefoot, you are not allowed to eat or drink near it.

The pitches are spacious, and you can choose how much sunshine you want; there are also several off-the-beaten-track spots in the forest which some people prefer to occupy. People visit La Pélonie for its natural surrounding, and the local walking, cycling tours and sights. Saint-Antoine lies between the old city of Périgueux and the Vézère Valley, with its record number of prehistoric cave paintings (at Lascaux, for example).

Aquitaine

Les Péneyrals

Rating 8.5
Tariff range €€€€
Town St-Crépin-et-Carlucet
Department Dordogne
Postal code 24590
Map 5 E4
Tel 05-53288571
Fax 05-53288099
e-mail camping.peneyrals@wanadoo.fr
Open 10 May – 13 Sep
From Salignac, take D60 towards Sarlat. After about 4 km, take D56 from St-Crépin to Proissans. Site approx 1 km. Site S of St-Crépin.
Size (hectares) 12
Touring pitches 85
Sanitary facilities rating 8.6
large swimming pool complex • quiet and secluded • many activities available for the kids • prehistoric remains • Dordogne valley and castles • Salignac-Eyvigues (5 km)
Electric hook-ups/amps 85/5-10

This campsite manages to keep the older kids happy at the same time as entertaining families with small children. They do this by preserving large areas away from the pitches and other facilities. For example, there is a fishing lake from which you cannot see the tents, which creates a calm spot and allows you to stay away from the bustle surrounding the swimming pool complex. Five slides ensure that everyone has fun, and two of the pools are heated. There are all sorts of organised activities on the agenda, from cycle rides and competitions (including bicycle decorating) to a football tournament, where teams from four campsites compete on a full-sized pitch.

The evenings have their fair share of entertainment too: a singer, an evening of clowns, a conjuror, a casino where you play with toy money, a pop band and a weekly disco. These are just details, as the real charm of this campsite lies in the natural countryside that surrounds it. No two pitches are the same, and the tall hedges guarantee privacy.

Le Paradis

Rating 9
Tariff range €€€€
Town St-Léon-sur-Vézère
Department Dordogne
Postal code 24290
Map 5 E4
Tel 05-53507264
Fax 05-53507590
e-mail le-paradis@perigord.com
Open 22 Mar – 25 Oct
Take D706 towards Montignac-Les Eyzies, then take D706 from St-Léon to Les Eyzies. After 3.5 km, site on left.
Size (hectares) 6
Touring pitches 147
Sanitary facilities rating 9.1
luxury • subtropical flora • activities • Dordogne valley • prehistoric remains • Montignac (12 km)
Electric hook-ups/amps 147/10

Le Paradis lives up to its name by being an oasis of flowers, bushes, plants and trees, with banana and palm trees surrounding the swimming pool subtropics. The standard of facilities and the design of the site are far removed from the traditional image of camping. But if you appreciate luxurious sanitary facilities and other added extras, then you will certainly have a good time. There are plenty of attractions for the more sporting campers, too: canoe trips along the Vézère are a must for beginners and for more advanced canoeists.

The valley and the surrounding hills provide you with a completely different perspective, whether you choose to walk or cycle (mountain bikes can be hired on the campsite). There are two large swimming pools, play areas for all sorts of ball games, and in the summer organised entertainment is laid on in the form of rafting, archery, pot-holing and rock climbing. Regular party evenings are held with music and theatre shows for young and old. The restaurant serves excellent specialities from the region, such as duck and all sorts of mushrooms.

         EUROTOP

Aquitaine

Domaine des Mathévies

Tariff range €€€
Town Ste-Nathalène
Department Dordogne
Postal code 24200
Map 5 E4
Tel 05-53592086
Fax 05-53592086
e-mail marcel.tiemens@wanadoo.fr
Open 29 Apr – 16 Sep
Site 2 km N of Ste-Nathalène and signed. Site 7 km from Sarlat.
Size (hectares) 1.5
Touring pitches 24
space, peace and scenery • child-friendly • stylish terrace • medieval villages • Dordogne valley • Sarlat-la-Canéda (7 km)
Electric hook-ups/amps 18/6

Campers at this child-friendly site can look forward to peace and quiet in rural surroundings, along with a high standard of quality. The swimming pool is big enough for all the campers and the guests from the six chalets. Pitches are spacious, and have water and electricity supplies close by. There is also a restaurant, where meals (simple but good, and very affordable) are prepared daily. Although it is cosy inside, everyone eats on the terrace under the old linden trees with a view of the hills. It is a popular spot, and as darkness falls, the lanterns and candles are lit making the site very pretty indeed.

It is run by a Dutch couple who adore France and also children. They have provided plenty of room for youngsters on this safe, well laid-out site, which includes a play area and a paddling pool. Parents can make use of the free tennis, volleyball and badminton courts. You can book an hour or two of horse riding at a local stable, and Vitrac, six kilometres away, has a golf course. There are marvellous opportunities for walking and cycling.

Les Grottes de Roffy

Rating 8.5
Tariff range €€€€
Town Ste-Nathalène
Department Dordogne
Postal code 24200
Map 5 E4
Tel 05-53591561
Fax 05-53310911
e-mail roffy@perigord.com
Open 26 Apr – 21 Sep
From Sarlat take D47 NE towards Ste-Nathalène. Turn right at Croix-d'Alon, then after approx 4 km turn right just before Ste-Nathalène, then uphill to site.
Size (hectares) 5.5
Touring pitches 78
Sanitary facilities rating 8.9
friendly atmosphere • carefully designed • excellent restaurant • prehistoric remains • Dordogne valley and castles • Sarlat-la-Canéda (7 km)
Electric hook-ups/amps 78/6

This is a campsite where people feel as if they are personal guests of the Deneuve family. The owner, Jérome, is also head chef in the excellent restaurant, and now and again he will fire up the old village oven for a pizza evening. The oven dates from the time when the campsite buildings were home to farming families. Jérome's wife runs the épicerie, which is more than just a campsite shop because it sells everything from fresh meat, to fruit, vegetables, salads and delicious cakes and pies made by Jérome himself. The reception is looked after by his sister.

When one of the regulars turns up, the whole family appears to welcome them with open arms, and birthdays are often celebrated in style. The attention they lavish on their guests goes hand in hand with their attention for detail. You can keep an eye on the playground from the terrace and from the swimming pool, and an underwater window in the pool means that you can be entertained by what is happening below the surface, making a great holiday photo. Children have even got their own skating track.

Aquitaine

Les Périères

Rating	8.5
Tariff range	€€€€
Town	Sarlat-la-Canéda
Department	Dordogne
Postal code	24203
Map	5 E4
Tel	05-53590584
Fax	05-53285751
e-mail	les-perieres@wanadoo.fr
Open	01 Apr – 30 Sep

From Sarlat centre take D47 towards Ste-Nathalène-Proissans. Site on right in approx 1 km.

Size (hectares) 11

Touring pitches 100

Sanitary facilities rating 8.6

quiet, green campsite • heated swimming pool and sauna • walking distance from the town • prehistoric remains • Dordogne valley and castles • Sarlat-la-Canéda (1 km)

Electric hook-ups/amps 100/6

The old town of Sarlat is one of the main attractions of the Dordogne, with its colourful Saturday market that attracts tourists and inhabitants from the whole département. Les Périères is about 15 to 20 minutes walk from the centre of town and is set in beautiful green countryside. The trees are mature and tall, and the semicircular terraced slope looks out onto the green hills, while the fitness course heads off towards the woods. The site is quiet even in summer.

The open-air pools remain open all year because the sun can be very strong in the Dordogne. The pitches are large and have their own water and electric hook-up, while caravan pitches also have a waste point. There is no restaurant, but the gastronomic delights of Sarlat are only a short distance away. However, there is a café and bar offering simple bar snacks as well as organised entertainment three times a week. During the day, an activities leader is on hand to keep the children busy, though about half of the guests are adults visiting Sarlat. All the sights of the Dordogne are within reach.

Le Moulin du Roch

Rating	8.7
Tariff range	€€€€
Town	Sarlat-la-Canéda
Department	Dordogne
Postal code	24200
Map	5 E4
Tel	05-53592027
Fax	05-53592095
e-mail	moulin.du.roch@wanadoo.fr
Open	30 Apr – 12 Sep

From Sarlat, take D6 then D47, approx 10 km NE towards Les Eyzies. Site on left.

Size (hectares) 8
Touring pitches 100
Sanitary facilities rating 8.6

good family campsite • large swimming pool complex • good service and hygiene • prehistoric remains • Dordogne valley and castles • Sarlat-la-Canéda (6 km)

Electric hook-ups/amps 100/6-10

The huge swimming pool complex at this campsite provides a lot of water for playing and paddling in, as well as plenty of space for sunbathing and sitting on the café terrace. There are no enormous slides, as the family who run the campsite want to keep it as a quiet place for families with small children. With high scores for the site itself as well as the sanitary facilities, you would be forgiven for thinking that it couldn't get much better. The site offers generous pitches that are fairly easy to get caravans onto, and there is also plenty of shade.

The buildings are in the Périgord style, and once formed part of the water mill which operated from this spot. The site is on an incline at one end, and while the lower end looks like a park, the higher area is wooded and has paths that will take you straight into the countryside. The large variety of plants lends the place an attractive garden feel, as does the fishing lake with ducks, surrounded by grass and with a bench on the banks. One small drawback is the road that runs alongside one row of pitches. The owners have found a creative solution for the noise by adding a four-metre high bamboo hedge and a stream.

Les Terrasses du Périgord

Rating	8.9
Tariff range	€€€
Town	Sarlat-la-Canéda
Department	Dordogne
Postal code	24200
Map	5 E4
Tel	05-53590225
Fax	05-53591648
e-mail	terrasses-du-perigord@wanadoo.fr
Open	01 May – 22 Sep

In Sarlat take D704, at 1st rdbt follow Proissans signs. Turn left twice at D47 & D56, again follow Proissans signs. Turn left after approx 300mtrs.

Size (hectares) 6
Touring pitches 74
Sanitary facilities rating 9.2

lovely views • clean, quiet and safe • wine cellar in the campsite shop • castles and caves • prehistoric paintings • Sarlat-la-Canéda (3 km)

Electric hook-ups/amps 74/6-16

You will not find a more open aspect around Sarlat than the one from this campsite, and wherever you look you see the rolling hills of Périgord. Les Terrasses is literally perched on a hilltop; the higher section is flat, its pitches are easier to reach by caravan, and they offer more shade though less of a view. The terraces on the hillside are sunnier but smaller, and better suited to tents, and the views here are excellent.

The owner, Jacques, was born 100m from the hilltop, and camped here for twenty years before he turned this farmland into a campsite. He has created the type of place where he would like to stay, and he is always on hand to provide tips on castles, caves and Sarlat, of course, which is only 2.5 km away. He can provide regional specialities to order, though otherwise the site only has a snack bar which is located in a former barn. Jacques also has a small wine cellar. His collection includes many Bergerac wines, which are just as good as Bordeaux but less expensive. Children have their own games room, a mountain bike course and a cable slide.

Aquitaine

Aqua Viva

Rating	8.3
Tariff range	€€€€
Town	Sarlat-la-Canéda
Department	Dordogne
Postal code	24200
Map	5 E4
Tel	05-53314600
Fax	05-53293637
e-mail	aqua-viva@perigord.com
Open	15 Apr – 23 Sep

From Sarlat, take D704 towards Cahors/Souillac. After 3.5 km follow D704a to Souillac. Site on right in 3 km.

Size (hectares) 11
Touring pitches 151
Sanitary facilities rating 8.6
excellent mini golf course • beautiful nature • lively yard • caves • castles and gardens • Sarlat (6 km)
Electric hook-ups/amps 151/3-10

Thirty years ago, Aqua Viva was bought by a Dutch couple and transformed from a natural campsite on a former farm to a modern site with lots of facilities. It is now in French hands again, but the trees, flowers, space, shade, sun and water remain the same. The site is split in two by a public road, and the first section, where most of the facilities are, is flat; the upper section is wooded, more attractive and further away from where the children like to hang out in the evenings. Lots of greenery provides plenty of shade and privacy, and the pitches are spacious enough.

The sanitary facilities are good too, and there are special facilities for babies, small children and the less able. The two swimming pools are nicely secluded or, if you prefer, you could cool off in the lake that is fed with water from a stream. The small beach here makes it easy to launch your paddleboat for some fun on the water. The playground has its own trampoline, and there is also a mini golf course. All the main sights of the Dordogne are within 30 km.

Les Tourterelles

Rating	7.8
Tariff range	€€€
Town	Tourtoirac
Department	Dordogne
Postal Code	24390
Map	5 E4/5
Tel	05-53511117
Fax	05-53505344
e-mail	les-tourterelles@tiscali.fr
Open	19 Apr – 30 Sep

N from Tourtoirac centre take turn off from D5. Pass bridge over the Auvézère, left onto D73. Site approx 1.5 km.

Size (hectares) 12
Touring pitches 110   **Static pitches** 5
Sanitary facilities rating 7.6
real Dutch atmosphere • riding school on the grounds • jazz evenings • the old city of Périgueux • prehistoric finds • Hautefort (10 km)
Electric hook-ups/amps 110/6

Les Tourterelles lies in the north of the Dordogne region, away from the busy routes, but close enough to embark on a day trip to one of the tourist sights. Your offspring will feel right at home here, especially if they love horses as there's a riding school in the grounds. A long queue of volunteers waits to help Angelique (the owner's daughter) with mucking out. This is good news for parents, who can enjoy a peaceful holiday, though some complain that they only see their children at dinner time.

Les Tourterelles is a truly Dutch campsite, and the restaurant caters for the Dutch palate; plenty of apple sauce and imported mayonnaise are available from the snack bar! In addition to the usual sports competitions, the owner organises jazz evenings. To add a little 'couleur locale', French locals are allowed to use the swimming pool and riding school. The campsite consists of several grass pitches, which are scattered around the forest. No matter where you are, you always have the feeling that the campsite is smaller than it actually is.

Aquitaine

Les Deux Vallées

Rating	8.1
Tariff range	€€€
Town	Vézac
Department	Dordogne
Postal code	24220
Map	5 E4
Tel	05-53295355
Fax	05-53310981
e-mail	les2v@perigord.com
Open	All year

From Sarlat take D57 SW towards Vézac/Beynac. After place-name sign turn right. Turn left immediately after rail crossing. 500mtrs follow lane to site.

Size (hectares) 3.2
Touring pitches 88
Sanitary facilities rating 8.4

Dutch-owned • well-maintained and cosy • many activities available • prehistoric remains • Dordogne valley and castles • Beynac (1 km)

Electric hook-ups/amps 88/6-10

Mieke and Roel and their two daughters Kathalijn and Maartje took over the running of Les Deux Vallées in 2000, and will do everything to make sure you enjoy your stay on their cosy campsite. Tall climbing plants and flowers that bloom until late in September add to its attractiveness, and the site shop is housed in a log cabin. The pitches are surrounded by hedges and trees, and the island in the fishing lake has its own tree house. Children love it here, as do the over-sixties, and it is especially popular with the British.

The free-range chickens supply the site with freshly laid eggs that are always in high demand. Daytime is very busy during the summer, with the kids club keeping small children occupied with all sorts of water activities. The Irish pub is popular in the evenings, and the terrace is always full even when there is no talent competition, casino evening (toy money), barbecue or concert (three times a week). The footpath through the fields will take you to the picturesque village of Beynac where there are plenty of shops and restaurants. The site is open throughout the low season.

Soleil Plage

Rating	8.4
Tariff range	€€€€
Town	Vitrac
Department	Dordogne
Postal code	24200
Map	5 E4
Tel	05-53283333
Fax	05-53283024
e-mail	info@soleilplage.fr
Open	11 Apr – 28 Sep

Take N20 to Souillac, then D703 towards 'Vallée de la Dordogne'. Turn left at Domaine-de-Rochebois golf course. Site in approx 2 km.

Size (hectares) 8
Touring pitches 106
Sanitary facilities rating 8.4

adjacent river with sandy beach • good restaurant • large swimming pool complex • the Dordogne valley • prehistoric paintings • Sarlat-la-Canéda (9 km)

Electric hook-ups/amps 106/10

Few campsites have all the ingredients offered by Soleil Plage: an excellent swimming pool complex (slides for action, two quiet pools, a kiddies' pool and water jet massage), a good restaurant (specialities from the Périgord, the gastronomic capital of France), and a location in the heart of the Dordogne right next to the river. If you take a canoe trip down the Dordogne from here, you can admire the limestone cliff faces that overhang the river and the caves.

The water is shallow enough for paddling in some places, while elsewhere it is deep enough to dive from a tree trunk. Afterwards you can dry off on one of the beaches. Canoes can be hired at the site, and you can choose whether you want to be dropped off upstream in the morning or get picked up downstream at the end of the afternoon. If you do both, you will have seen the most beautiful section of the Dordogne in only two days as well as plenty of châteaux. Soleil Plage offers generous pitches, plenty of shade, modern sanitary facilities, tropical vegetation and extras such as a fitness room. A full 18-hole golf course is only 2 km away.

Aquitaine

Les Ourmes

Rating 7.7
Tariff range €€€
Town Hourtin
Department Gironde
Postal Code 33990
Map 4 C4
Tel 05-56091276
Fax 05-56092390
e-mail lesourmes@free.fr
Open 01 May – 30 Sep
Site 1.5 km W of Hourtin on D4 to Hourtin-Port.
Size (hectares) 6
Touring pitches 204   **Static pitches** 40
Sanitary facilities rating 7.6
luxurious and well tended • in a forest • swimming and paddling pool • Lac d'Hourtin-Carcans • Atlantic Ocean • Hourtin (2 km)
Electric hook-ups/amps 204/6-10

When camping on Les Ourmes you will notice that the northwestern peninsula of the Gironde region offers more than just sandy Atlantic beaches. This campite lies a stone's throw away from the largest lake of France, Lac d'Hourtin-Carcans, a nature reserve and a paradise for anglers and windsurfers. The site is in the heart of a pine forest.

At the central reception area there are plenty of facilities: a restaurant, a snack bar, a small shop for basic necessities and a completely new toilet building that is clean and well kept. The renovated swimming pool has a separate paddling pool, making the campsite popular with families with children. It is not just Lac d'Hourtin that offers so many opportunities for watersports enthusiasts – the vast sandy beaches on the Atlantic coast are only 10 km away. Hourtin-Plage, a seaside resort with restaurants, snack bars, open-air cafés and plenty of parking is a good destination for a day trip. There are many places to enjoy a cycling holiday in this area.

La Côte d'Argent

Rating 7.9
Tariff range €€€€
Town Hourtin
Department Gironde
Postal Code 33990
Map 4 C4
Tel 05-56091025
Fax 05-56092496
e-mail info@camping-cote-dargent.com
Open 13 May – 17 Sep
Site on D101 E, just before Hourtin-Plage.
Size (hectares) 20
Touring pitches 550
Sanitary facilities rating 8.4
modern swimming pool • riding centre • day-care for children • Atlantic Ocean • wine châteaux • Hourtin (8 km)
Electric hook-ups/amps 550/6

Since arriving here the owner has made improvements throughout the site in order to meet modern campers' demands. Camping on La Côte d'Argent offers pure luxury, yet the rates are still average compared with campsites elsewhere in the region.

The heated swimming pool has five water slides and a jacuzzi, and you can ride a horse in the equestrian centre or go off pony trekking. Everything is professionally run here, and the entertainment team is also qualified: they offer a wide choice of activities for young children in the miniclub as well as games and competitions for older ones. The campsite is situated in a pine forest with broad lanes, spacious pitches and clean sanitary facilities. The sandy beaches of the Atlantic Ocean are only 300m away, and restaurants and snack bars are within walking distance. But you can also have a meal in the snack bar or the restaurant (with a terrace) on the site. Hourtin-Plage, a seaside resort, offers beaches and entertainment.

Yelloh! Village Les Grands Pins

Rating 8.4
Tariff range €€€€
Town Lacanau-Océan
Department Gironde
Postal Code 33680
Map 4 C4
Tel 05-56032077
Fax 05-57700389
e-mail reception@lesgrandspins.com
Open 26 Apr – 20 Sep
From Lacanau follow D6 to Lacanau-Océan; on rdbt just before village take road to 'plages-nord' and follow signs.
Size (hectares) 12
Touring pitches 430   **Static pitches** 30
Sanitary facilities rating 8.6
guarded and safe • close to sea and beaches • clean sanitary facilities • vineyards • cycling in the dunes and woodlands • Lacanau-Océan (1 km)
Electric hook-ups/amps 430/10

Camping Les Grands Pins is a quiet family campsite set amongst the sand dunes. The security guard may look severe, but the reception you receive will be most friendly. As a result of the security presence there is no theft, one of the things that guests appreciate. The site is located in a natural dune area and has spacious pitches. The highest terraces offer a fine view over the region, and nearly everywhere there are pine trees and hedges, so shade and privacy are guaranteed. The sanitary facilities are modern and clean.

There is much to do on and around the site: the large swimming pool has a paddling pool, there is a large playground and a club for children between the ages of 4 and 10. You can play tennis, beach volleyball and pétanque, or join in the fitness training. Through the seaside exit (guarded!) you can walk straight onto the beach. Just 10 minutes away is a small, rather fashionable seaside resort with all sorts of entertainment. Cycling tours can be taken through the dune area, or you could take the car for a day trip to Bordeaux, the vineyards of the Médoc region or Arcachon. Most people staying here, however, are quite content to remain around the site.

Talaris Vacances

Rating 7
Tariff range €€€€
Town Lacanau
Department Gironde
Postal Code 33680
Map 4 C4
Tel 05-56030415
Fax 05-56262156
e-mail talarisvacances@free.fr
Open 05 Apr – 20 Sep
Site 4 km NW of Lacanau on road to Lacanau-Océan (D6).
Size (hectares) 8
Touring pitches 172
Sanitary facilities rating 7.5
beautiful swimming pool • lots of entertainment • suitable for children • cycling tours • vineyards of Médoc • Lacanau-Océan (6 km)
Electric hook-ups/amps 172/6

Swimmers will love the facilities on and around Talaris Vacances: there is a large swimming pool with terrace on the site itself, a fine beach with sun-bathing area on the freshwater lake near Moutchic (1 km), and the sandy sea beach by the high sand dunes of Lacanau-Océan (6 km).
This is a place that attracts both young families and older people. Here you can relax after a year of hard work while the children are having fun. It is never completely quiet: during the day you hear the sounds of youngsters playing, and in the evening there is the traffic and the weekend disco.

The restaurant and the snack bar both have a good selection of meals at reasonable prices, not to mention the 'brochetterie' (20 different spits with a large variety of exotic sauces). Talaris also offers a good entertainment programme for all ages. There are lots of games around the pool, but also competitions and evening performances (clown, magician, music). You can always hop on a bike for a tour of the neighbourhood or stroll along the seaside boulevard of Lacanau-Océan. If you fancy a good wine, the famous wines of the region (Bordeaux, Médoc) are sold in one of the village markets.

Aquitaine

Le Roumingue

Rating	8.3
Tariff range	€€€€
Town	Lanton
Department	Gironde
Postal code	33138
Map	4 C4
Tel	05-56829748
Fax	05-56829609
e-mail	info@roumingue.com
Open	1 Jan - 31 Dec

Situated in NW Lanton. From Lanton follow D3 towards Andernos. Campsite on left side of road 800mtrs after town hall (Mairie).

Size (hectares) 10
Touring pitches 200
Sanitary facilities rating 10
Border lake • close to sea • child friendly • beautiful scenery • boat trips
Electric hook-ups/amps 200/4/6

This very well furnished campsite lies on level ground near the Bassin d'Arcachon, which can be reached via a path across the dike. The pitches under the trees are often bordered by shrubbery. Two small lakes are located at the edge near the beach - one for swimming and one for fishing. Swimming lessons are given if required and there is a miniature golf course.

In the immediate surroundings there are extensive facilities for horseriding (in Andernos), golf (in Lanton), hang-gliding, waterskiing, biking and deep-sea fishing. The coastal path running along the grounds offers the opportunity to spot unusual species of birds in this 'mini-Camarque' landscape. The entertainment team organizes such activities as boat trips. Wine lovers will delight at wine-tasting events or a visit to one of the many famous Bordeaux châteaux. The campsite comes alive in the evening with dancing to live music, karaoke and all sorts of board games.

Municipal Les Gabarreys

Rating	8.1
Tariff range	€€€
Town	Pauillac
Department	Gironde
Postal Code	33250
Map	4 C4
Tel	05-56591003
Fax	05-56733068
e-mail	camping.les.gabarreys@wanadoo.fr
Open	21 Mar – 06 Oct

from N over N10 or A10 cross the Garonne to Le Verdon; then via St-Laurent to Pauillac and site.

Size (hectares) 1.6
Touring pitches 53
Sanitary facilities rating 7.8
perfect image • privacy • spacious pitches • wine châteaux • beautiful cycling routes • Pauillac (1 km)
Electric hook-ups/amps 45/5-10

In a region with so many top quality wines there has to be a top quality campsite, and that is precisely what Municipal Les Gabarreys is. This quiet site is located south of Pauillac, just

100m from the estuary of the Gironde. There are many trees and the spacious pitches are separated by hedges, so there is sufficient privacy. Everything looks very well tended: the hedges are neatly trimmed, the grass is regularly mown, and there is no litter whatsoever. The sanitary facilities are good and clean.

There are very few facilities for children: no swimming pool or entertainment. There is a small garden and a recreation room with a library and television. Pauillac is a small town with some restaurants; many wine producing châteaux offer Bordeaux wine tasting (and buying, of course), with prices ranging from reasonable to very expensive. A visit to Château Mouton-Rothschild (5 km) and neighbouring Château Clos d'Estournet is a great experience. The sandy beaches of the Atlantic Ocean are 50 km away, in Hourtin-Plage. This resort has good parking facilities and various restaurants.

Aquitaine

Village Panorama du Pyla

Rating 7.3
Tariff range €€€€
Town Pyla-sur-Mer
Department Gironde
Postal Code 33115
Map 4 C4
Tel 05-56221044
Fax 05-56221012
e-mail mail@camping-panorama.com
Open 18 Apr – 29 Sep
Site 7.5 km S of Pyla-sur-Mer on right towards Biscarrosse (D218).
Size (hectares) 15
Touring pitches 350
Sanitary facilities rating 7.1
pretty view • auditorium with concerts • own beach • Dune de Pilat • Atlantic Ocean • Pyla-sur-Mer (8 km)
Electric hook-ups/amps 350/3-10

The Dune de Pilat is the highest point of the largest dune area in Europe. This site lies at the foot of this dune and has direct access via an easy climb to its own beach on the Atlantic coast. The view here is wonderful: on one side you overlook the ocean, while on the other side you can see how far the sand dunes stretch. But the campsite itself also has a lot to offer. There is a very good restaurant with a sheltered terrace, serving excellent meals at reasonable prices. The spacious pitches are scattered over uneven ground, and the natural environment is dominated by a pine forest, part of the dune area. The site is well kept and tidy and so are the sanitary facilities.

Sports enthusiasts can play tennis and mini golf, go sailing or surfing, and relax afterwards in the sauna. The swimming pool is a pleasant place to stay around, with its paddling pool and mini-bar. For both young children and the nearly-grown-ups there is an extensive entertainment programme. In the open-air auditorium concerts of light classical music are held regularly. A wide selection of products is sold in the daily market in Pyla-sur-Mer. Activities take place near the entrance, well away from the pitches.

Le Vieux Château

Rating 7.4
Tariff range €€€€
Town Rauzan
Department Gironde
Postal Code 33420
Map 4 D4
Tel 05-57841538
Fax 05-57841834
e-mail hoekstra.camping@wanadoo.fr
Open 01 Apr – 01 Oct
From Libourne (D670)SE to Vignonet & St.-Jean-de-Blaignac-Rauzan. Follow signs to site, NW of Rauzan.
Size (hectares) 2.5
Touring pitches 50
Sanitary facilities rating 7.2
weekly competitions • quiet • small selection of pleasant activities • Rauzan caves • vineyards and wine routes • Saint-Emilion (13 km)
Electric hook-ups/amps 48/6-16

A quiet atmosphere in a fine natural setting is the hallmark of Le Vieux Château, a modest campsite hidden in the hills between Bordeaux and Bergerac (made famous by Cyrano and his long nose). Part of the site is located in a forest, and the rest occupies a piece of land at the bottom of a hill, dominated by the old château from which the owners took the name. The latter part is open and sunny. You can cool off in the swimming pool, a welcome feature in this hot part of southern France. There is a snack bar and a small recreation room, and an entertainment programme keeps the youngest children busy. Once a week there are competitions for volleyball teams and a pétanque tournament, and from time to time wine tasting is organised.

But this is an easy-going site, with tranquillity winning out over excitement. There is plenty to do and see in the surrounding area: visit some of the old châteaux or the caves in Rauzan, and see the medieval town of Saint-Emilion with its characteristic buildings and many restaurants. Vast vineyards produce the local wines, and Bordeaux and the Dordogne region are not far away.

Aquitaine

Domaine de la Barbanne

Rating	7.8
Tariff range	€€€€
Town	St-Émilion
Department	Gironde
Postal Code	33330
Map	4 D4
Tel	05-57247580
Fax	05-57246968
e-mail	barbanne@wanadoo.fr
Open	01 Apr – 24 Sep

From Libourne follow D670, SE ; left after 5 km to St-Émilion. (Town centre closed; follow road signs). Site 3 km N of town on D122.

Size (hectares) 10
Touring pitches 160
Sanitary facilities rating 7.6
lake • free bus to Saint-Émilion • sports and games • cycling in a wine region • visit to wine châteaux • Saint-Émilion (3 km)
Electric hook-ups/amps 160/10

Somewhere halfway between Bordeaux and the popular holiday region of the Dordogne lies Saint-Émilion, a small town that is known for the Bordeaux wine of the same name. Domaine de La Barbanne lies north of the town, between the vineyards. Under the inspiring leadership of its owner this campsite has developed into a modern enterprise with many facilities. During the high season especially, it aims at families with children under the age of 12; in spring and autumn, however, most guests are elderly people.

The swimming pool has a thrilling water slide, and there is a small lake that can be used for swimming, canoeing and angling, as well as a tennis court and a mini golf course. The Club d'Enfants brings entertainment five days a week for children between 4 and 12. The toilets are clean and well tended, and pitches are grouped between trees and hedges that offer some shade.

Saint-Émilion is a picturesque medieval town, built on a hill. The streets are steep and narrow and there are enough restaurants and wine cellars to indulge yourself. A free shuttle bus connects the campsite with the town. The surrounding area is suitable for cycling tours.

Chez Gendron

Rating	8
Tariff range	€€€
Town	St-Palais-de-Blaye
Department	Gironde
Postal Code	33820
Map	4 C5
Tel	05-57329647
Fax	05-57329647
e-mail	info@chezgendron.com
Open	All year

A10, junct 37, through Mirambeau, then towards St-Ciers-sur-Gironde. Right after 8 km and follow signs. Site 8 km SW of Mirambeau.

Size (hectares) 3.5
Touring pitches 48   **Static pitches** 1
Sanitary facilities rating 8.8
splendid location • family camp site • small-scale appearance • rural environment • ideal for biking holidays • Blaye (20 km)
Electric hook-ups/amps 48/6-10

Chez Gendron is a small campsite in the Gironde region, 50 km N of Bordeaux. It stretches attractively along the edge of a forest, and trees and hedges are plentiful. On the other side there is a vineyard.

It has the reputation of being a traditional campsite, mainly frequented by families with small children, and the entertainment is targetted at this group. The Dutch owners see their campers as one big family. An important role is played by the bar where campers can meet every evening to discuss the latest news. Children are kept busy with cutting, drawing, painting and other games. But there is more than that, like a small swimming pool for a refreshing dip. If you prefer absolute peace, relax on the terrace in the shade and order a bite to eat.

The sanitary facilities are clean but somewhat dated. The terraced pitches, some of which are shaded, offer campers a level surface. The surrounding area is a web of narrow country roads winding through the hills, and easily mastered by cyclists with some experience.

Les Acacias

Rating	7.9
Tariff range	€€€
Town	Vensac
Department	Gironde
Postal Code	33590
Map	4 C5
Tel	05-56095881
Fax	05-56095067
e-mail	contact@les-acacias-du-medoc.fr
Open	01 Jun – 16 Sep

From N follow N215 to D1E4 Vensac junct. Site on left (500mtrs), 2 km N of Vensac.

Size (hectares) 4.5
Touring pitches 136
Sanitary facilities rating 8

ideal for families • fine swimming pool • entertainment programme • forests and beaches • wine châteaux • Saint-Vivien-de-Médoc (2 km)

Electric hook-ups/amps 136/6-10

The western peninsula of the Gironde region is a mixture of woodlands, sandy Atlantic beaches, vast vineyards and the beautiful wine-producing châteaux of Médoc. Les Acacias lies at the heart of this area near a forest, but there are not many trees around the sun-drenched pitches.

The owners have done their best to turn Les Acacias into a true family holiday site. There is a swimming pool (with paddling pool), and a daily entertainment programme with lots of games for young children. Teenagers can spend the evening dancing or playing a game of boules. The restaurant has a limited number of dishes, and the sanitary facilities are well kept and tidy. There are vast forests in this area, and narrow roads that are ideal for cyclists and walkers. Not far from here are the vineyards of Médoc where you can see some wine producing châteaux. It has not yet been affected by mass tourism like the Atlantic beaches and the seaside resort of Soulac.

Les Écureuils

Rating	8.4
Tariff range	€€€€
Town	Biscarrosse
Department	Landes
Postal Code	40600
Map	4 C3/4
Tel	05-58098000
Fax	05-58098121
e-mail	camping.les.ecureuils@wanadoo.fr
Open	01 May – 30 Sep

From Sanguinet follow D652; turn right after 10 km (before Biscarrosse), take D305 to Navarrosse. Right after 1.5 km and again after 500mtrs.

Size (hectares) 6
Touring pitches 90
Sanitary facilities rating 8.5

well tended grounds • friendly reception • shade and privacy • sun, sea, beach • good cycling routes • Biscarrosse (3 km)

Electric hook-ups/amps 90/10

When you approach the very well-tended grounds of Les Écureuils, it looks as if you are entering an exclusive golf course. Everything here is well kept; wonderful gardens have been laid out around the swimming pools, the mini golf course and the playground with a bouncy castle.

Next to the modern reception building there is a snack bar and a terrace. The pitches are not really spacious, but the pine trees provide shade and the beautiful hedges guarantee privacy. You can play tennis, table tennis and boules. There is a separate room with video games, and an entertainment team organises all sorts of games for children of all ages.

A beautiful lake just a short distance from the campsite has a fine beach that is suitable for children. Biscarrosse-Plage is a seaside resort within walking distance, with unspoilt beaches and a centre full of pretty shops. Another shopping area can be found in Arcachon, but you will need a car to get there. A special attraction is the seaplane museum in Biscarrosse.

Aquitaine

Domaine de la Rive

Rating	7.4
Tariff range	€€€€
Town	Biscarrosse
Department	Landes
Postal Code	40600
Map	4 C3/4
Tel	05-58781233
Fax	05-58781292
e-mail	info@camping-de-la-rive.fr
Open	05 Apr – 07 Sep

Follow D652 to Biscarrosse. Turn right 5 km beyond Sanguinet and 8 km before Biscarrosse. Site entrance in 2.5 km.

Size (hectares) 15
Touring pitches 300
Sanitary facilities rating 7.4

many facilities • beautiful swimming pool • entertainment for children • Dune de Pyla (117 m) • lake with beaches • Biscarrosse (8 km)

Electric hook-ups/amps 200/6

Domaine de la Rive, with its harbour and beach, lies on the bank of one of the cleanest and most beautiful lakes in France. The clear water is shallow until about 100m from the shore, so it is safe for little children. The pitches are spacious but hardly separated from each other, which does result in a lack of privacy. The modern sanitary facilities are in good condition.

In summer a team of nine entertainers keeps the young guests busy with games and competitions. Teenagers will prefer a game of boules, table tennis, volleyball, archery, aquarobics, water polo or even water-skiing. Younger children gather on the playground with a bouncy castle. Windsurfing, sailing, pedalos and canoeing are available on the lake, and there is also a luxurious supervised swimming pool that resembles a tropical paradise. In the evening a disco party will keep you fit.

Because of the many good facilities (supermarket, restaurant, pizzeria, bar) you don't have to leave the campsite for shopping or dining. A good place to go is Biscarrosse-Plage with its seaside beach and high rolling waves. You can also take a look in the seaplane museum.

Yelloh! Village Sylvamar

Rating	7.9
Tariff range	€€€€
Town	Labenne
Department	Landes
Postal Code	40530
Map	4 B2
Tel	05-59457516
Fax	05-59454639
e-mail	camping@sylvamar.fr
Open	26 Apr – 17 Sep

Site in Labenne-Océan on D126. From Labenne entrance on right, just before bridge.

Size (hectares) 21
Touring pitches 200
Sanitary facilities rating 8.1

swimming paradise • children's paradise • entertainment • beach under surveillance • 100 km of cycling routes • Bayonne (20 km)

Electric hook-ups/amps 200/10-16

This large family-oriented campsite lies in a vast pine forest, 900m from a fine supervised beach. But you don't need to go to the seaside when you have a swimmer's paradise at your disposal on site. Here you can even take swimming lessons. The tidy campsite is beautifully laid out and offers spacious pitches. The sanitary facilities are good, and so are the restaurant and the sports grounds.

All day long there is plenty to do: games and cartoons for young children, perhaps, or sports competitions for the older kids, and pétanque, fitness training, aqua-gymnastics and step-aerobics for the adults. Every evening there is something special going on, like disco dances, cabarets, or demonstrations of Basque folklore. The cartoon show, performed by children, takes place on Fridays, and shouldn't be missed. Another highlight is the Miss Sylvamar competition. The whole area is a perfect location for a cycling holiday in the beautiful natural setting. A day trip to Spain, the Pyrénées or the Basque country on both sides of the border is well worth finding the time for.

Parc de Couchoy

Rating	7.2
Tariff range	€€€
Town	Lesperon
Department	Landes
Postal Code	40260
Map	4 C3
Tel	05-58896015
Fax	05-58896015
e-mail	colinmrose@aol.com
Open	01 Apr – 30 Sep

From N10 (Bordeaux-Spain) junct 13 (Lesperon). Turn left and follow C4 to village centre (1 km). Turn left again and take D331 to Linxe and site (3 km W of Lesperon).

Size (hectares) 1.3
Touring pitches 58
Sanitary facilities rating 7.5
peace and quiet • plenty of room • casual atmosphere • Cap-de-l'Homy (beach) • walking and cycling tours • Dax (30 km)
Electric hook-ups/amps 58/6

Once Gasgogne, a part of Les Landes, was English territory, but nothing remains of those turbulent times. Colin Rose, the British owner of Camping Parc de Couchoy, brought back a piece of Britain when he took over this campsite with his French wife. It lies in the middle of nowhere, an oasis of tranquillity with large pitches, a fine swimming pool, a bar and good sanitary facilities. There is not much entertainment for children, apart from a paddling pool and a very modest playground. You can go cycling or walking in the neighbourhood, where there are plenty of pretty, authentic villages with a decent café or a local dish that you must try.

Many campers use this site as a starting point for day trips to Médoc, Bordeaux, Dax, Sabres or the Pyrénées. A visit to a beach, either on the seaside or near a lake, is another option. The location, only 5 km from the N10 and halfway between Bordeaux and the Spanish border, makes it easy as you never have to spend more than an hour driving. This is an ideal site on your way to or from Spain or Portugal.

Les Vignes

Rating	8
Tariff range	€€€€
Town	Lit-et-Mixe
Department	Landes
Postal Code	40170
Map	4 C3
Tel	05-58428560
Fax	05-58427436
e-mail	contact@les-vignes.com
Open	12 May – 16 Sep

Site 2 km SW of Lit-et-Mixe on D88. From Lit-et-Mixe follow D652 to Léon, right after 1 km (D88). Site 500 mtrs on right.

Size (hectares) 15
Touring pitches 150
Sanitary facilities rating 8.1
beautiful swimming pool • lots of entertainment • primarily sports facilities • Cap-de-l'Homy • cycling tracks • Lit-et-Mixe (6 km)
Electric hook-ups/amps 150/10-16

Les Vignes lies just outside Lit-et-Mixe on the road to the beautiful beach of Cap-de-l'Homy. Its most striking aspects are the broad asphalt roads and the many chalets, behind which are 150 spacious pitches. It is a luxurious campsite, and no pets are allowed.

You will certainly be attracted by the sight of the swimming pool with the waterfalls, terraces and many exotic plants. The other facilities are of the same quality: mini golf, boules, tennis, volleyball, basketball and a putting green where you can learn to play golf. Even the entertainment programme is partly based on sports like badminton, rafting, step-aerobics, croquet and rugby.

The French entertainment team keeps the younger children busy with games and competitions, and in the evening with a clown, an impersonator or a magician. The older children meet every evening in the party tent for a music show, bingo, lotto, or dancing. A big supermarket and good eating-houses complete the facilities. A day on the beach is equally recommended.

Aquitaine

Le Vieux Port

Rating	7.8
Tariff range	€€€€
Town	Messanges
Department	Landes
Postal Code	40660
Map	4 C3
Tel	05-172039160
Fax	05-58480169
e-mail	contact@levieuxport.com
Open	01 Apr – 30 Sep

From Messanges follow D652 to rdbt in Messanges-Sud. Turn right and take Route de la Plage leading to site, 3 km SW of Messanges.

Size (hectares) 30
Touring pitches 350   **Static pitches** 635
Sanitary facilities rating 8.3
family atmosphere • lots of entertainment • riding centre • sea, beach, forest • riding, cycling • Vieux-Boucau-les-Bains (1 km)
Electric hook-ups/amps 330/6-8

Le Vieux Port is a lively super-size campsite where discriminating travellers will find anything they desire. The large pitches are surrounded by trees and hedges that guarantee enough privacy for an undisturbed stay. The sanitary facilities are well kept and clean. Every half hour a mini-train crosses the grounds to take you to the splendid supervised beach for half a euro or so. But there are also six (!) swimming pools with enormous water slides, and a riding centre with horses and ponies to take you on a trek through the pine forests. These woodlands can also be explored on bicycle, and if you haven't brought your own you can rent one of any sort and size.

An entertainment programme for all ages creates a lot of fun, and in the evening there are performances including songs, dances and folklore. You can enjoy a good meal in the restaurant, the pizzeria or the snack bar. As all these activities take place just outside Le Vieux Port, the campsite itself is relatively quiet. In 2001 Le Vieux Port was elected best campsite by French and German tourist organisations.

La Côte

Rating	8
Tariff range	€€€
Town	Messanges
Department	Landes
Postal Code	40660
Map	4 C3
Tel	05-58489494
Fax	05-58489444
e-mail	info@campinglacote.com
Open	01 Apr – 30 Sep

From Messanges follow D82 to Vieux-Boucau. Turn right 100mtrs before rdbt in Messanges-Sud. Site at end of no-through road, 1.5 km SW of Messanges.

Size (hectares) 3
Touring pitches 103
Sanitary facilities rating 8.1
hospitality • clean sanitary facilities • take-away • quiet and cosy • sea, beach, forest • thermal baths in Dax • Vieux-Boucau (1 km)
Electric hook-ups/amps 103/6-10

Hospitality in its true sense has made Camping La Côte, owned by Marilys and Bernard Moresmau, a great success. A decade ago they started their enterprise, and now it's a fully-fledged campsite with spacious pitches. They have managed to preserve the character of the 'camping-à-la-ferme', quite an achievement with so much competition in the neighbourhood. Fees are low and beach and forests are within walking distance. You can relax in the shade, and the sanitary facilities are excellent. There are some facilities for recreation, too: a playground and volleyball, table tennis, pétanque and table football.

Small children have their own playground with climbing nets and a sandbox. Close to the site is a big supermarket, but you can order bread at the reception desk. Almost every night there is someone at the entrance selling paellas or pizzas - worth trying! The lovely village of Vieux-Boucau, with its promenades, shops and restaurants around a lake that is connected to the sea, is only 1 km away. Further away lie Lac de Soustons, the thermal baths of Dax, Biarritz, Bayonne and the Ecomusée de Marquèze near Sabres.

Le Village Tropical Sen Yan

Rating 7.5
Tariff range €€€€
Town Mézos
Department Landes
Postal Code 40170
Map 4 C3
Tel 05-58426005
Fax 05-58426456
e-mail reception@sen-yan.com
Open 31 May – 14 Sep

From D63 into Mézos, turn left at rdbt (Avenue de la Gare). Site on left (1 km).

Size (hectares) 8
Touring pitches 160
Sanitary facilities rating 7.6

tropical swimming pool • fine mini golf course • entertainment for the youngsters • sea and beach • walking and cycling tours • Mimizan-Plage (20 km)

Electric hook-ups/amps 160/6

This site is quite oriental looking with its palm and banana trees and unusual architecture. However, the partly Chinese sounding name just means Saint Jean in the regional dialect. Pitches here are large, and the sanitary facilities are kept clean. The main attraction is the magnificent pool complex that looks like a tropical swimming paradise. The mini golf course is another exotic spot with its flowers and ponds where large fish add an Asian touch.

Together with the sports facilities, this is why the place attracts great numbers of older campers in spring and autumn. In summer you will mainly find families with children who can take part in the extensive programmes. In the early morning there is the miniclub for the youngest visitors with craftwork and games. Older children have games, sports competitions, aqua-gymnastics or aerobic dancing. Every evening there is cabaret, dancing, a show or a disco party. Nobody is bothered by noise, as the pitches are on the opposite side of the site. Most guests also come here to enjoy the beaches of Contis-Plage and Cap-de-l'Homy.

Club Marina Landes

Rating 7.1
Tariff range €€€€
Town Mimizan-Plage
Department Landes
Postal Code 40202
Map 4 C3
Tel 05-58091266
Fax 05-58091640
e-mail contact@clubmarina.com
Open 25 Apr – 15 Sep

From Mimizan SW to Mimizan-Plage, then left to Plage-Sud. Cross bridge, through residential area (2 km). Site on left.

Size (hectares) 9.5
Touring pitches 445
Sanitary facilities rating 6.9

good entertainment • casual atmosphere • guarded area • sea and beach • bird reserve • Mimizan-Plage (1 km)

Electric hook-ups/amps 355/10

Club Marina Landes may be a large campsite with lots of facilities, but its casual atmosphere remains. Eighty percent of the pitches are occupied by touring campers (half of them with tents). The layout is quite compact, and privacy and shade come from the planting of high hedges and old pine trees. The sanitary facilities are good and clean. Most visitors are families with children, who are sure to enjoy themselves. The fine beach, 500m away, is accessible by a footpath leading through the sand dunes.

On the campsite you will find two large heated swimming pools with a section for children. There is a supermarket, some small shops, a pizza baker and a large hall with slot machines, video games and billiard tables. The restaurant serves good meals at reasonable prices. The miniclub keeps children busy with arts and crafts, games and preparations for the Friday evening show, performed and organised by themselves. For the older children there are sports competitions, but also a picnic in the forest, disco and karaoke. A trip by canoe or a stroll on the flower promenade is a delightful alternative to all those activities on the site. Safety and service are the top priorities, which is another reason to stay here.

Aquitaine

Lou Bascou

Rating	8.5
Tariff range	€€
Town	Rivière
Department	Landes
Postal Code	40180
Map	4 C3
Tel	05-58975729
e-mail	loubascou@wanadoo.fr
Open	01 Mar – 31 Oct

On N124 (Dax-Bayonne) turn left and take D13 to Rivière (D13). Pass church and left after 200mtrs to site.

Size (hectares) 1
Touring pitches 19
Sanitary facilities rating 8.9

helpful owners • breeding area for storks • comfortable transit camp site • thermal baths in Dax • beautiful sandy beaches • St.-Paul-lès-Dax and Dax (10 km)

Electric hook-ups/amps 19/6-10

The owners left Paris in 1993 to develop this campsite. Since then the trees have grown, and hedges and plants have been added, but in summer it is still a place for sun worshippers due to the lack of shade and shelter. For those on their way to Spain or Portugal for the winter this is a good stopover. Lou Bascou is open all year and located close to the main routes. The ground is flat, with a spacious sunbathing terrace and a smaller one in the shade of trees. Both are good places to have a glass of wine.

The surrounding area is very popular with nature lovers. In the delta of the River Adour you can watch wild horses grazing, and on poles supporting the overhead wires of the railway line many storks from Algeria build their nests between January and August; they seem to be unbothered by the passing trains. In summer there is an entertainment programme for children with volleyball and table tennis competitions. Once a week a barbecue party is held, followed by dancing.

Les Bruyères

Rating	7.2
Tariff range	€€€
Town	Ste-Eulalie-en-Born
Department	Landes
Postal Code	40200
Map	4 C3
Tel	05-58097336
Fax	05-58097558
e-mail	bonjour@camping-les-bruyeres.com
Open	01 May – 30 Sep

From Ste-Eulalie-en-Born follow D652 N and turn left after 2 km.

Size (hectares) 3.8
Touring pitches 100
Sanitary facilities rating 7.5

casual atmosphere • cheap • Lac de Biscarrosse • cycling and walking tours • Mimizan-Plage (20 kms)

Electric hook-ups/amps 100/10

At first sight Les Bruyères looks like an average French campsite, but appearances are often deceptive. The reception is the domain of Nicole Claude and Cocaine, her black cat. Everything here is impeccable, especially the sanitary facilities where everyone wipes their feet before entering. The spacious pitches are not separated from each other, though, so there is hardly any privacy.

There's plenty to keep you busy: football, tennis, pétanque or just swimming in the pool (with paddling pool). Around the campsite you can go cycling, walking, horse riding, windsurfing or sailing on the nearby lake. During the high season there is entertainment for the whole family, with daytime games and competitions, dancing and bingo in the evening. No disco dancing of course, since people come here to rest. A day at the fine beach of Mimizan-Plage with its boulevard and shops is highly recommended.

Eurosol

Rating	7.8
Tariff range	€€€€
Town	St. Girons-Plage
Department	Landes
Postal code	40560
Map	4 C3
Tel	05-58479014
Fax	05-58477674
e-mail	contact@camping-eurosol.com
Open	10 May - 13 Sep

5 km W of Vielle-St. Girons on D42. Site on left just before St. Girons-Plage.

Touring pitches 402

Sanitary facilities rating 7.5

Peace and quiet • family campsite • three swimming pools • cycling tours

Electric hook-ups/amps 330/10

For more than 40 years, campsite-club Eurosol has been an oasis of rest and relaxation just 700mtrs from the Atlantic Ocean, and from what they claim to be, the 'biggest and most beautiful white sandy beach in France'. In 15 hectares of pine forest in a magnificent hilly terrain there are shady, marked pitches ranging from 100 to 140 m², with or without electricity and water, in addition to a variety of rental accommodation (mobile homes and chalets) for 2 to 6 persons. The pitches are often on an incline.

The swimming pool complex is inviting but the campsite also offers many more options for sports enthusiasts. There is a supermarket on site plus a miniclub where lots of fun activities for children are organised (NB they are run in Dutch). A third swimming pool, opened last year, is heated and covered in May, June and September so that you can swim and relax in warm water even in the low season.

Le Pin

Rating	7
Tariff range	€€€
Town	St-Justin
Department	Landes
Postal Code	40240
Map	4 C3
Tel	05-58448891
Fax	05-58448891
e-mail	camping.lepin@wanadoo.fr
Open	01 Apr – 15 Oct

From Roquefort follow D626 to St-Justin. Site NW of St-Justin.

Size (hectares) 3

Touring pitches 70

Sanitary facilities rating 7.2

lots of fun for children • fine setting, high trees • clean, good atmosphere • take-away • thermal baths • Ecomusée, bastides • Mont-de-Marsan (25 km)

Electric hook-ups/amps 64/6

Dutch couple, Hendrik and Marja Gadeyne, gave up their jobs in the restaurant trade some years ago, packed their bags and left for France with their children. They sought a new life in the countryside and the sun, with lots of room to move. And what they found was 'Le Pin', a place with stately oak trees surrounded by pine forests. They were immediately attracted by the old farmhouse, built in Les Landes style. They also built a swimming pool, bordered by rows of flower beds and banana trees. Elsewhere a pond was created and stocked with fish, where young guests can swim and play.

From this idyllic spot, day trips can be made to Saint-Justin and La Bastide-d'Armagnac. The museum of Notre-Dame-des-Cyclistes displays the yellow Tour de France jersey worn by the great Eddy Merckx. Barbotan-les-Thermes has hot springs with thermal baths and a splendid garden. Shopping can be done in Mont-de-Marsan, which has two indoor shopping centres – very convenient in the unlikely event of bad weather. Back at 'Le Pin' you can have a good meal in Marja's restaurant or a simple glass of Belgian beer on the terrace.

Aquitaine

Lou P'tit Poun

Rating 7.8
Tariff range €€€€
Town St. Martin-de-Seignanx
Department Landes
Postal Code 40390
Map 4 C2
Tel 05-59565579
Fax 05-59565371
e-mail contact@louptitpoun.com
Open 31 May – 13 Sep
A63 Bordeaux-Bayonne, then N117 to Pau. Approx 4.5 km and site on right (signed).
Size (hectares) 7
Touring pitches 142
Sanitary facilities rating 8
playgrounds for children • spacious and tidy pitches • just behind the beaches • golf course, nature • beautiful sandy beaches • St-Martin-de-Seignaux (0.5 km)
Electric hook-ups/amps 132/6-10

Some campsites in southern France have names in a regional language. Lou P'tit Poun, for instance, means 'The little bridge' in Gascon, one of the dialects of the old Occitan language. The pitches here are large and easily accessible.

Most campers are French, though in summer the number of Dutch, Spanish and British guests grows gradually. The owner has opened a playground for the smallest children, close to the pitches. The swimming pool is beautifully situated and has a large tiled terrace for sunseekers, close to the snack bar.

The site's location is perfect, just behind the fine sandy beaches of the Atlantic coast. Golfers have 20 links to try. Not far away you can visit a model railway museum and a monkey zoo; Capbreton has a sea museum. A visit to Bayonne, Biarritz or the Pyrénées is a good idea for a day trip. In the valley of the River Adour, a large area with a rich flora and fauna has been declared a nature reserve. Observation platforms are open to the public. The whole region is flat and can easily be explored on a bicycle.

Le Col Vert

Rating 7.7
Tariff range €€€€
Town Vielle-Saint-Girons
Department Landes
Postal Code 40560
Map 4 C3
Tel (+33) (0)890 710001
e-mail contact@colvert.com
Open 05 Apr – 21 Sep
N10 (Bordeaux-Biarritz), Castets junct, D142 to Léon. In Léon take road to Vielle-St-Girons (D652) to water tower.
Size (hectares) 24
Touring pitches 360
Sanitary facilities rating 7.9
lakeside location • many facilities • entertainment programme • Lac de Léon (windsurfing) • walking and cycling tours • Léon (5 km)
Electric hook-ups/amps 360/3-10

Thirty years ago Hélène Pavie started a modest family campsite, Le Col Vert, in the heart of a nature reserve in the largest pine forest in Europe. Nowadays it is a big holiday business, but it still

has a cosy atmosphere. There are many shopping, eating and sports facilities, and a health complex with heated supervised indoor swimming pool, sauna, Turkish bath, jacuzzi and fitness centre. Thanks to the unique location on the bank of Lac de Léon and the popularity of windsurfing, this became a top location. There are not many places where you can push your surfboard from your tent straight into the water.

The pitches are spacious with privacy guaranteed, and the sanitary facilities are clean. Exotic flowers and plants, complete with name-plates, are all around, and at the reception desk an artist has created a number of sculptures from trees that were uprooted in a storm. Le Col Vert has an entertainment programme for everybody that lasts all day. There is a beach section for little children by the lake and a large playground on the site. A daily market is held in the village of Léon.

Les Ormes

Rating	8.3
Tariff range	€€€
Town	St-Étienne-de-Villeréal
Department	Lot-et-Garonne
Postal code	47210
Map	4 D4
Tel	05-53366026
Fax	05-53366990
e-mail	info@campinglesormes.com
Open	26 Apr – 13 Sep

From Villéreal follow D255 towards Dévillac. Approx 1 km, turn right towards St-Etienne-de-Villeréal (C201). Turn right 500mtrs beyond church.

Size (hectares) 20

Touring pitches 90

Sanitary facilities rating 8.4

Plenty of room • easy-going • sports and games • Penne-d'Agenais • Château de Bonaguil • Monflanquin (8 km)

Electric hook-ups/amps 90/4-6

This quiet campsite, in typical French surroundings, has a beautiful view of woods and country estates. The friendly département, where time seems to pass more slowly than elsewhere, has a scattering of châteaux and villages with cosy cafés and bustling markets.

The campsite is spacious, with lots of room for children to play in safety. The picture is completed by a small lake, where you can fish or paddle a rubber boat, and an attractive swimming pool. The bar-restaurant, housed in a typical old farmhouse, serves excellent meals and also hosts musical evenings. There are all kinds of activities for children, from arts and crafts evenings to sports competitions. You can use the various sports and games facilities (which include a tennis court) at any time you like. You can also make treks on horseback directly from the campsite.

The shop supplies a basic range of groceries, and the baker brings fresh bread to the site every morning. A special feature is the bungalow park, which has pyramid-shaped chalets that can be turned towards the sun or away from it as you prefer.

Aquitaine

Moulin du Périé

Rating	7.5
Tariff range	€€€€
Town	Sauveterre-la-Lémance
Department	Lot-et-Garonne
Postal Code	47500
Map	5 E4
Tel	05-53406726
Fax	05-53406246
e-mail	moulinduperie@wanadoo.fr
Open	07 May – 20 Sep

Follow D710 from Siorac to Sauveterre, 15 km before Fumel. Cross rail line at traffic lights and follow signs to site (3 km).

Size (hectares) 5
Touring pitches 85
Sanitary facilities rating 7.7
suitable for children • woodlands • secluded location • medieval villages • caves • Monpazier (25 km)
Electric hook-ups/amps 85/6-10

A friendly campsite with a typical French atmosphere, found between wooded hills, and highly suitable for children. Even the nonchalance shown by the owners is very French. At the end of the 18th century a water mill was built on the bank of the River Sendroux, and it remains such a quiet location that visitors hardly leave the site. This is not because of a lack of interesting sights: on the contrary there are fortified medieval towns, caves with prehistoric finds and wine châteaux all waiting to be discovered.

This is also a region that meets the gourmet's demands. Sauveterre-la-Lémance has many small restaurants, great chefs and delicious regional wines. On Moulin du Périé you will find a natural swimming pool fed by a spring, with a sandy beach where children are always busy with their buckets, spades and toy boats. With a little bit of luck you might find a good pitch with a view over the water. Spend the day in the swimming pool (paddling pool included), on the trampoline, on the playground or on the sports fields. You can enjoy a glass of Bergerac or pastis on the terrace and watch the sun go down. Then head for the old granary that houses a simple bistro and a recreation room.

Xokoan

Rating	8.3
Tariff range	€€
Town	Ainhoa
Department	Pyrénées-Atlantiques
Postal Code	64250
Map	4 B2
Tel	05-59299026
Fax	05-59297382
e-mail	ezaldua@free.fr
Open	All year

Site at Dancharia border crossing point, 3 km S of Ainhoa on D20 (Bayonne-Cambo-les-Bains-Pamplona).

Size (hectares) 1
Touring pitches 23
Sanitary facilities rating 8.5
border river (Spanish border) • well kept • splendid nature • walking in the Pyrenees • prehistoric caves • Dancharia (5 km)
Electric hook-ups/amps 23/10

The Spanish border, marked by the River Nivelle (Lapitzxiry in Basque), almost touches the campsite. The village used to be a smugglers' hideaway, and even now customs officers come here for a quick search. Most campers are French with a few foreigners who come here to walk in the mountains. In the Spanish village of Dantxarinea petrol, cigarettes and spirits are cheaper, which attracts quite a few day trippers, though there is a better choice in the supermarkets across the border. A pleasant excursion is a visit to the prehistoric caves on both sides of the frontier post.

The capital city of the Spanish Navarra, Pamplona, is just 60 km further to the south. The small restaurant on the site, with its red tablecloths and Spanish decorations, offers a good à la carte menu, with trout one of the specialities. The Basque country is a region of strong men, and they love the many tug-of-war competitions, wood chopping and pelota (with bare hands!), which draw huge crowds of spectators.

Harazpy

Rating 8
Tariff range €€
Town Ainhoa
Department Pyrénées-Atlantiques
Postal Code 64250
Map 4 B2
Tel 05-59298938
Fax 05-59297382
e-mail ezaldua@free.fr
Open 15 Jun – 30 Sep
From Bayonne to Cambo-les-Bains, then towards D918/D20. Turn right in Ainhoa, just before church. Cross parking lot, follow signs to site (150mtrs).
Size (hectares) 1.5
Touring pitches 25
Sanitary facilities rating 8
quiet, close to the Pyrénées • located in a beautiful Basque village • five marked walking routes • 14th-century Basque church • cemetery with Basque tombstones • Ainhoa (1 km)
Electric hook-ups/amps 24/10

Ainhoa is one of the finest villages in the Basque country, situated in a green landscape on the route to Pamplona. It was and still is an important meeting point on the pilgrims' road to Santiago de Compostela, which is why there are so many hotels and restaurants here. On a side road behind one of these hotels you will find this campsite that aims at travellers who want to explore the Bas-Pyrénées on foot.

Harazpy is a modern site without much shade at the moment, though the trees are growing fast. There is a magnificent view over the rolling hills and the 14th-century church of Notre-Dame-de-l'Aubépine (Our Lady of the Hawthorn). On the market square, pelota, the thrilling national sport of the Basques, is played every Monday against the fronton (wall).

Take note of the beautiful half-timbered houses and the renovated old washing place. To many hikers this campsite is the starting point for the five signed walking routes that range from one to five hours. Even parents carrying babies and small children find them quite easy. This area truly is a paradise for walkers.

Bixta Eder

Rating 7.4
Tariff range €€€
Town Cambo-les-Bains
Department Pyrénées-Atlantiques
Postal Code 64250
Map 4 B/C2
Tel 05-59299423
Fax 05-59292370
e-mail camping.bixtaeder@wanadoo.fr
Open 15 Apr – 15 Oct
From Cambo-les-Bains follow D918 to St-Jean-de-Luz. Site on right (1.5 km).
Size (hectares) 1
Touring pitches 89
Sanitary facilities rating 8.3
recreation in a villa • beautiful camp site • modern sanitary facilities • Isturitz caves (3 km) • museum with French gardens • Cambo-les-Bains (1 km)
Electric hook-ups/amps 89/6-10

On the first Saturday morning of July, the holiday season in Europe begins. Campers gather at the town campsite in Cambo-les-Bains on this very busy day where many of them, mainly French, come to compete in the 'course des Crêtes', an endurance run through the hills of Espelette. At the finish line they are welcomed with a great show of Basque music, and in the evening there is a communal meal, followed by a ball. Don't expect the evening to be quiet, and in fact nobody cares.

Bixta Eder has an old villa that is now used for recreational purposes: card tables, television, library, table tennis. The municipal swimming pool is just 400m from the site. Cambo-les-Bains is a beautiful town with thermal baths, the Arnaga Museum with its French gardens and the house that belonged to Edmond Rostand, the author of 'Cyrano de Bergerac'. They are both worth a visit. There are also traditional markets and lovely open air cafés. Near St-Martin-d'Aberoue you can visit the Isturitz caves. Golf, hang-gliding and white-water canoeing are some of the sports you can practise in the vicinity (prices reduced for campsite guests).

Aquitaine

Ametza

Rating 7.2
Tariff range €€€
Town Hendaye
Department Pyrénées-Atlantiques
Postal Code 64700
Map 4 B2
Tel 05-59200705
Fax 05-59203216
e-mail ametza@neuf.fr
Open 15 May – 30 Sep
Exit A63 at junct 3 onto D913 to T-junct. Left onto D912 (coast road) 100mtrs to Hendaye. Left onto D358, cross rail bridge.
Size (hectares) 5.5
Touring pitches 200
Sanitary facilities rating 7.6
friendly family campsite • good and clean sanitary facilities • 90% French campers • beautiful sandy beach • small villages along Spanish coast • Saint Jean-de-Luz (12 km)
Electric hook-ups/amps 62/6

Ametza is a quiet terraced campsite with excellent facilities and not far from the ocean. The grounds lie high on a hill, just outside of Hendaye. Between the deciduous trees and the hedges, there are magnificent ocean views, the Pyrénées and the village of Hendaye. The pitches are fairly large and have sufficient shade and privacy. The sanitary facilities are modern; there is a wash cubicle, toilet and shower available for every four pitches, so that you never have to wait in a queue. There is a good restaurant/bar, a swimming pool and a tennis court on the grounds. Since there is no disco or noisy entertainment, peace and quiet pervade. Children can amuse themselves in the children's swimming pool and the large playground. On rainy days, there is a programme of entertainment (in French).

Not far from the campsite is a 3-km long, very wide sandy beach with a boulevard, and a bit further away, you can go windsurfing and sailing in the Baie de Chingoudy. There are many lovely trips you can take in the surrounding area, on foot, by bike, motorbike or on horseback. The campsite is perfectly located for spending a day in Spain, perhaps by car or train to San Sebastian; or you can drive along the stunning coastal road (Route de la Corniche) to the French Basque village of Saint Jean-de-Luz with its many shops and restaurants.

Uhaitza Le Saison

Rating 8.2
Tariff range €€€
Town Mauléon
Department Pyrénées-Atlantiques
Postal Code 64130
Map 4 C2
Tel 05-59281879
Fax 05-59280623
e-mail camping.uhaitza@wanadoo.fr
Open 01 Mar – 30 Nov
From Mauléon follow D918 to Tardets. After 1.8 km site on right.
Size (hectares) 1.1
Touring pitches 40
Sanitary facilities rating 8.3
very quiet • friendly, helpful owners • riverside location • walking in the mountains • châteaux, old fort • Mauléon (1.5 km)
Electric hook-ups/amps 40/4-10

The occasionally wild river Le Saison, that runs between high banks a short distance away from the campsite, drowns the traffic noise that comes from the road. The extremely clear water is the habitat of trout and otters. After torrential rains the fast-flowing water does not look very inviting, but normally children can build dams or play with the pebbles. On this welcoming site there is always a spare rental caravan for passing cyclists who do not want to put up their tent in the dark.

The owner is even willing to prepare a meal after 10pm for hungry late arrivals. The sanitary facilities are in good condition and kept very clean. A bicycle ride to the small town of Mauléon is worth the effort: here you can find the Hôpital de Saint-Blaise with a church that clearly shows Moorish influence from nearby Spain. On August 15th the town celebrates the Fête des Espadrilles, while just a few kilometres away lies Ordiarp, the historic 'village of the deer'. There is plenty to be discovered in this fascinating region.

Gîtes du Stade

Rating 7.2
Tariff range €€€
Town Oloron
Department Pyrénées-Atlantiques
Postal Code 64400
Map 4 C2
Tel 05-59391126
Fax 05-59391126
e-mail camping-du-stade@wanadoo.fr
Open 15 Apr – 30 Sep
Follow N134 via Pau (towards Zaragoza) to Oloron. Site S of Oloron in St-Pée. Follow site signs.
Size (hectares) 4.5
Touring pitches 168
Sanitary facilities rating 6.8
good transit camp site • tennis courts • organised canoe trips • water park in Estialescq (75 km) • hang-gliding, glider flying • Oloron-Sainte-Marie (2 km)
Electric hook-ups/amps 128/6-10

Oloron is a medieval town in the Béarn region, the eastern part of the lower Pyrénées. The campsite in the nearby hamlet of St-Pée lies close to the sports stadium and the swimming pool. It is a tidy campsite with spacious pitches, suitable for transit travellers on their way to or from Spain or Portugal. Cyclists can leave their trailers in a special shelter.

Families with children find enough room to play, and for a change there is a municipal pool with a large water slide, free to guests during peak season. There are also tennis courts and a golf practise range. For more fun you can go to the water paradise (75 km away) with its wave-pool. In Oloron there are regular concerts, and various events like jazz, reggae or folklore festivals. On the slopes in the mountain range you can drive a quadbike, and a bit further on lessons in hang-gliding are given. Less spectacular but still very popular are cycling tours. Turn right at the campsite and you will reach St-Pée's cemetery with a 'chemin du poète' named after the poet Tristan Derème. Culture, relaxation or physical activity is all possible here in Oloron.

Europ'Camping

Rating 7.6
Tariff range €€€
Town St-Jean-Pied-de-Port
Department Pyrénées-Atlantiques
Postal Code 64220
Map 4 C2
Tel 05-59371278
Fax 05-59372982
Web www.europ-camping.com
Open 15 Apr – 30 Sep
Site NW of St-Jean-Pied-de-Port on D918 towards Bayonne.
Size (hectares) 2
Touring pitches 78
Sanitary facilities rating 7.4
quiet • well equipped • fine view of the mountains • rafting • art and furniture shops • St-Jean-Pied-de-Port (2 km)
Electric hook-ups/amps 78/6-10

The route from Mauléon through the lower ranges of the Pyrénées, over the Col Osquich and down to St-Jean-Pied-de-Port, is a beautiful one with fantastic views. Clouds cover the upper half of the mountains, and there is hardly any traffic apart from a lonely walker or cyclist. Europ' Camping lies on the side of a historic small town. The first impression is of an uncrowded place set between surrounding slopes with vineyards, grazing sheep, and a tiny village with a white church. The campsite has a good layout, with spacious, level pitches that are either in the sun or in the shade – make your own choice. The sanitary building is large and well equipped.

St-Jean-Pied-de Port is the capital of the French part of Navarre, and owes its name to the historic mountain pass (port) of Roncevaux. It lies only 7 km from the Spanish border, and roads from all directions meet here. The market place is the starting point for a walk through the old town centre where picturesque houses with wooden balconies border the River Nivelle. Don't miss the typical half-timbered house along the steep road to the citadel. Even higher lies the Port du Roi where you can admire a wonderful view of the Pyrénées.

Aquitaine

Goyetchea

Rating 7.2
Tariff range €€€
Town St-Pée-sur-Nivelle
Department Pyrénées-Atlantiques
Postal Code 64310
Map 4 B2
Tel 05-59541959
e-mail info@camping-goyetchea.com
Open 31 May – 19 Sep
From St-Pée-sur-Nivelle follow D918 W to Ascain/St-Jean de Luz. 2 km turn right, then 800mtrs to site on right.
Size (hectares) 3
Touring pitches 124
Sanitary facilities rating 7.3
beautiful rolling landscape • quiet family camp site • organised tours • pelote matches • folk dancing • St-Pée-sur-Nivelle (1 km)
Electric hook-ups/amps 108/6

Campsites at the foot of the Pyrénées tend to be small and simple, quite different from those found nearer the coast. This one just outside St-Pée-sur-Nivelle blends into the surrounding countryside, and offers simple pleasures: the wonderful views of the mountains in the distance and the rolling fields to be lingered over, and the nearby sheep who walk behind their leader, and follow the sound of the bell that tinkles around his neck.

Staff on the campsite organise guided walking tours through the area, and one of the destinations is a wooden house in the mountains, where you can have an 'omelette au jambon' while being treated as a guest of the family. Communal meals are also served at the site from time to time. During the high season people in the village play a game of 'à grand chistera', a local version of the Basque national sport 'pelote', that originated here in St-Pée. On Thursdays there is a guided tour through the village, often combined with a musical performance. Not far from the campsite you will find a lake that is suitable for watersports.

Du Col d'Ibardin

Rating 7.1
Tariff range €€€€
Town Urrugne
Department Pyrénées-Atlantiques
Postal code 64122
Map 4 B2
Tel 05-59543121
Fax 05-59546228
e-mail info@col-ibardin.com
Open 21 Mar – 30 Sep
A63 (Bordeaux-Spain) junct 2; S on N10 and turn left after 2 km at rdbt (D4). After 3 km take Ascain road. Site in 300mtrs on right.
Size (hectares) 8
Touring pitches 143
Sanitary facilities rating 7
small-scale, cosy • tidy and well kept • take-away • La Rhune (901 m) • sea, beach, rocks • Ascain (4 km)
Electric hook-ups/amps 143/6-10

Most visitors to Camping Col d'Ibardin come here to enjoy the overwhelming natural beauty of the Pyrénées, to undertake long walking tours, or to cross the valleys on mountain bikes. Some are also attracted by the sea and the beach at Hendaye or Saint-Jean-de-Luz, not far from here. Yet others prefer to make day trips through the interior of the Basque country for its architecture and gastronomy. Wherever you spend the day, it is always good to return in the evening to this beautiful, well-kept site with its clean sanitary facilities, large swimming pool (with paddling pool), tennis court, and a multipurpose sports arena.

The spacious pitches guarantee privacy, while the small river that runs through the site and the mountain views all add to the atmosphere. There is no restaurant, but you can order a set menu to eat on the terrace or in the recreation area. The large playground keeps small children busy. The main attraction in this area is the 30-minute train ride to the mountain top La Rhune, where you look down from an altitude of 901m on magnificent views. Cross the Spanish border to Donostia-San Sebastián with its tapas bars or the Guggenheim Museum in Bilbao (120 km).

Auvergne

La Petite Valette

Rating 8.1
Tariff range €€€
Town Sazeret
Department Allier
Postal Code 03390
Map 5 F6
Tel 04-70076457
Fax 04-70072548
e-mail la.petite.valette@wanadoo.fr
Open 01 Apr – 30 Oct
Take exit 11 off A71 (Montmarault) towards Vichy on 1st rdbt. Take Deux Chaises turn at 2nd rdbt. Turn left after 3 km, follow site signs.
Size (hectares) 4
Touring pitches 55
Sanitary facilities rating 8.2
well-suited to children • slightly disorganised, but great fun • excellent kitchen • Fôret de Tronçais • Le Pal theme park • Montluçon (35 km)
Electric hook-ups/amps 55/6

Klaus Müller and Johan Lemstra have converted a 150-year-old farm into a miniature paradise. There's an enormous recreation area, a youth club and plenty of organised activities, including special ghost excursions, a junior disco and camp fires. Great hospitality, the advantages of a small-scale campsite and superb sanitary facilities all appeal to adults. The large pitches, all with electric hook-ups, are fenced off, and surrounded by plenty of trees and bushes. There's also a fishing lake, which doubles as a natural pool.

The kitchen is first class, serving meals at bistro tables on a convivial terrace. Sazeret is located in the old duchy of Bourbonnais, not far from Saint-Pourçain-sur-Sioul (centre of the local wine-growing region). The River Sioule meanders through the landscape, and has created a gorge that is worth a visit. Le Pal, an amusement park cum zoo to the east of Moulins, is a great day out for the entire family.

Le Coursavy

Rating 8.2
Tariff range €€€
Town Cassaniouze
Department Cantal
Postal code 15340
Map 5 F4
Tel 04-71499770
Fax 04-71499770
e-mail camping.coursavy@wanadoo.fr
Open 20 Apr – 20 Sep
21 km beyond Aurillac take D920. Then right onto D21, then D601. Site 10 km beyond Cassaniouze, NE of Grand-Vabre.
Size (hectares) 1.5
Touring pitches 41
Sanitary facilities rating 8.5
relaxed atmosphere • next to the river • picnic tables • walking and cycling • slow going River Lot • Conques (8 km)
Electric Hook-ups/amp 41/5

Camping Le Coursavy is located in a completely relaxed setting: a wide open space with a playground, swimming pool, sunbathing area and sports grounds stretching along the River Lot. The floating raft in the broad, slow-running river is a popular place to sit and sunbathe. On the other bank you can see a dense forest on steep slopes, while further away, in a small field, is a bench where you can relax or watch people fishing.

The same easy-going atmosphere can be found on the campsite itself, thanks to the way the Dutch owners interact with their guests. There is no reception desk, and newcomers announce their arrival by telephone at the entrance. There are only 50 pitches, all spacious and nestling in the shade of a variety of trees. The sanitary facilities are spotless. From the site you can go on long or short walking and cycling tours through an area that has hardly been touched by modern times, through deep gorges with panoramic views. With a little bit of luck you might even spot an eagle or an ermine. Back 'home', tired but satisfied, you can relax at your own picnic table.

Camping la Siauve

Rating	8.1
Tariff range	€€
Town	Lanobre
Department	Cantal
Postal Code	15270
Map	5 F5
Tel	04-71403185
Fax	05-46551000
e-mail	info@campingterreoceane.com
Open	17 Jun – 16 Sep

Take N89 (Bort-les-Orgues-Clermont-Ferrand). Turn left 3 km before Lanobre, follow site signs. Site S of Lanobre.

Size (hectares) 8
Touring pitches 214
Sanitary facilities rating 8.4
surrounded by nature • spacious camping areas • hospitable reception • many sights • nature at its best • Bort-les-Orgues (5 km)
Electric hook-ups/amps 180/6-10

Camping La Siauve is located on the shores of a large reservoir, behind the nearby Bort dam. The site is welcoming, and offers large pitches spread across several levels, with plenty of privacy and tranquillity. The sanitary facilities are well-maintained and clean. It has a reasonably large playground (with sandpit) as well as pétanque facilities and a volleyball court (just outside the campsite). However, most activities take place on, in or near the lake. A small track takes you through a dense forest to a small beach, a section of which has been reserved for swimmers.

The lake is a true mecca for watersports enthusiasts, and you can go sailing, windsurfing, canoeing or waterskiing. The Bort dam is one of the largest in France, and the free tour is both entertaining and informative. There's also a boat which leaves from the dam and takes you past the Château Val, which dates back to the 15th century and boasts no fewer than six towers, making it the best-defended château in the region. If you climb to the top floor, you'll be rewarded with a splendid view across the lake and the neighbouring countryside.

Le Val St. Jean

Rating	8.4
Tariff range	€€€
Town	Mauriac
Department	Cantal
Postal Code	15200
Map	5 F4
Tel	04-71673113
Fax	04-73347094
e-mail	contact@revea-vacances.com
Open	26 Apr – 29 Sep

From Mauriac take D681 towards Pleaux. Take D682 to 'Plan d'eau' and site (D682 is SW of Mauriac).

Size (hectares) 3
Touring pitches 100
Sanitary facilities rating 8.6
spacious • located in recreation park • peaceful • volcanoes • Bort-les-Orgues flood-control dam • Mauriac (0.5 km)
Electric hook-ups/amps 100/10

Le Val St-Jean is modern and spacious, and forms part of a large recreation park situated alongside a lake created by two local rivers. Individual pitches are generous, and offer plenty of privacy by way of hedgerows and fences. The sanitary facilities are good and the lake has plenty to offer watersports enthusiasts, including pedalos and canoes. The campsite organises children's entertainment programmes from Monday to Friday (mornings only). The programme is supervised by a French lady, and anyone aged between six and fifteen is welcome to attend.

Le Val St-Jean is also a paradise for tennis and golf enthusiasts, with its adjacent nine-hole course and golf lessons. The nearby town of Mauriac is situated 722m above sea level and is renowned for its medieval and picturesque streets, squares and museums. Puy Mary, a volcano to the south of Mauriac (in the direction of Aurillac), is worth a visit, as is the flood-control dam at Bort-les-Orgues.

Auvergne

International La Roche Murat

Rating 7.6
Tariff range €€
Town St-Flour
Department Cantal
Postal Code 15100
Map 5 F4
Tel 04-71604363
Fax 04-71600210
e-mail courrier@camping-saint-flour.com
Open 01 Apr – 01 Nov
Take exit 28 off A75 (St-Flour-Centre). Take 2nd exit on rdbt, follow site signs. Site 2 km E of St-Flour.
Size (hectares) 3
Touring pitches 110
Sanitary facilities rating 7
large transient campsite • never really quiet (A75) • inexpensive • Gustave Eiffel viaduct • hot springs (Chaudes-Aigues) • Saint-Flour (2 km)
Electric hook-ups/amps 120/10

Camping International la Roche Murat is located at the foot of a hill, just outside the village of Saint-Flour (near the A75), a good stopover on the way south. The spacious pitches are surrounded on three sides by thick hedgerows, and the sanitary facilities are simple but clean. At the top of the hill you'll find several picnic tables scattered around the forest, which offer a fantastic view. There is a playground for smaller children (with a slide, sandpit and climbing rack), but larger children will soon notice the absence of a swimming pool. The nearest pool (outdoor and indoor) is in Saint-Flour, some 2 km down the road. Luckily it has a lot more to offer than just a swimming pool, with several nice shops, museums and monuments, including Saint-Pierre cathedral. As their names suggest, the Gorge de Truyère and the Gorge de Blès are two spectacular gorges carved deep into the Auvergne's volcanic landscape, making great places to walk and a true paradise for bird-lovers.

La Pommeraie

Rating 7.6
Tariff range €€€€
Town Vic-sur-Cère
Department Cantal
Postal Code 15800
Map 5 F4
Tel 04-71475418
Fax 04-71496330
e-mail pommeraie@wanadoo.fr
Open 29 Apr – 15 Sep
Take N122 (Aurillac - Clermont-Ferrand). 19 km to centre of Vic-sur-Cère. Then take D54 towards Raulhac. Cross river, follow site signs (up steep road for 2 km).
Size (hectares) 3.5
Touring pitches 40 **Static pitches** 10
Sanitary facilities rating 7.3
varied evening programme • plenty of entertainment for children • typically French atmosphere • volcanoes • Pesteils château • Vic-sur-Cère (0,5 km)
Electric hook-ups/amps 40/6

The only thing that will get you and your caravan to La Pommeraie is the owner's Landrover, which slowly winds its way up the steep mountainside, rounding the most impossible hairpins on the way. But the effort is worth it, for the view is truly fantastic. The campsite is located in a former apple orchard with reasonably spacious pitches, and clean, well-maintained sanitary facilities.

All activities take place in or around the reception area and bar, which sells excellent home-made pizzas – best consumed with a glass of local wine. The terrace and swimming pool (with shallow section) are located beyond the bar area. There's always something to do in the evenings, from fun cabaret shows to music, karaoke, dinner/dance events, a discotheque and bingo. For children there's a small playground, a baby pool and Club Enfant. If you enjoy walking, you'll love a guided hike through the wild countryside and across the volcanic mountain tops.

Auvergne

Au Bord de l'Eau

Rating 7.7
Tariff range €€€
Town Goudet
Department Haute-Loire
Postal code 43150
Map 5 G4
Tel 04-71571682
Fax 04-71571288
e-mail auborddeleaugoudet@wanadoo.fr
Open 01 Mar – 15 Oct

From Costaros E on D49 to Goudet. Site just before bridge S of village. Narrow, steep road to entrance.

Size (hectares) 4
Touring pitches 83
Sanitary facilities rating 7.5

wild nature • very well kept • many facilities • take-away • hot springs • Le Puy (20 km)

Electric Hook-ups/amp 83/4-6

In a quiet valley, amidst the breathtaking beauty of the Haute-Loire mountains, lies Au Bord de l'Eau. In the background you can see the ruins of Château Beaufort and a basalt rock formation that deserves its name 'Le Rhinocéros'. Hardly anybody lives here, though occasionally you will come across a tiny medieval hamlet like Goudet. But the campsite offers all the comfort a traveller needs: spacious pitches with thick man-sized hedges, clean sanitary facilities, a swimming pool, a good shop and a pretty terrace with views of the Loire Valley.

Toddlers especially will like the small garden, the playground and the paddling pool. This is a splendid area for hiking and biking, but there is much more to see and do. You can visit the local festivities, ranging from musical performances to garlic festivals. Le Puy-en-Velay is proud of its religious buildings and museums – don't miss the interesting lace museum. Back on site, people enjoying a pint at the bar in the restaurant will probably have wonderful tales to tell of long mountain excursions, perhaps to Chavaniac-Lafayette château.

Les Hirondelles

Rating 8
Tariff range €€€
Town le Chambon-sur-Lignon
Department Haute-Loire
Postal code 43400
Map 5 G4
Tel 04-71597384
Fax 04-71658880
e-mail les.hirondelles.bader@wanadoo.fr
Open 01 Jul – 31 Aug

From Le Chambon centre take D151, SW, over bridge and follow to Le Puy/Mazet approx 800mtrs. Left to La Suchère (D7); turn right after 1 km.

Size (hectares) 1
Touring pitches 45
Sanitary facilities rating 8.2

quiet, nature • wonderful view • friendly atmosphere • walking and horse riding • many sights • Le Chambon (0,5 km)

Electric Hook-ups/amp 45/2-6

Les Hirondelles is a campsite set in high woodlands, with a friendly atmosphere; the majority of the guests are elderly people who come to enjoy the countryside and the silence. The site lies on the top of a hill, covered with pine forests, broad-leaved trees and tall hedges. Because of this there is enough shade everywhere and privacy is guaranteed. The pitches on this remarkably quiet campsite are spacious and offer fine views over the surrounding area.

The site was laid out 32 years ago by the Swiss architect Bader, who also built the chalet. He named the site Les Hirondelles – the Swallows – because he thought it suited a place where campers fly in and out with the seasons. It is obvious that the owners are nature lovers too; the pitches are not marked by numbers, but bear the names of birds. The sanitary facilities are excellent and clean, but the only amenities here are a table tennis table and a pétanque pitch. You can swim in the River Chambon, and close by is some very good walking country. Day trips can be made to the zoo in Tence, to Le Puy, and the Resistance museum in Lignon.

Auvergne

Les Moulettes

Rating 8.7
Tariff range €€€
Town Vorey-sur-Arzon
Department Haute-Loire
Postal code 43800
Map 5 G4
Tel 04-71037048
e-mail campinglesmoulettes@libertysurf.fr
Open 01 May – 15 Sep
On D103, 20 km N of Le Puy, in centre of Vorey; route signed.
Size (hectares) 1.3
Touring pitches 38
Sanitary facilities rating 8.3
family camp site • casual atmosphere • pétanque competitions
• walking • Le Puy-en-Velay • Vorey (0.5 km)
Electric Hook-ups/amp 38/10

There is always somebody playing pétanque in the morning sun at the entrance of Les Moulettes. Holidaymakers and locals alike enjoy meeting at ball games – in the evening they play volleyball.

The shady pitches are spacious and offer a lot of privacy, and the sanitary facilities are clean. There is no shop, but it takes only a few minutes to get to the village shops in rural Vorey. Cross the bridge over the Arzon river and you will reach the beautiful municipal pool with water slides, and free admission for campers.

The site owners organise entertainment for children, but left alone, youngsters will also have great fun in the sandbox and on the playground. In the Haute-Loire district you can take wonderful walks along the rocks and the mountain slopes, heading for famous châteaux and nature reserves. Busy Puy-en-Velay, starting point for the pilgrimage to Santiago de Compostela, is only half an hour away. Verveine-du-Velay is the place to learn more about traditional distilleries.

Le Pré Bas

Rating 8
Tariff range €€€€
Town Chambon-sur-Lac
Department Puy-de-Dôme
Postal Code 63790
Map 5 F5
Tel 04-73886304
Fax 04-73886593
e-mail prebas@lac-chambon.com
Open 01 May – 30 Sep
Take D996 (Murol-Le Mont Dore). Site on left through Lac de Chambon.
Size (hectares) 4
Touring pitches 80
Sanitary facilities rating 8.2
lakeside family campsite • plenty of facilities • numerous activities • volcanic mountains • Roman castles/museums • Murol (3 km)
Electric hook-ups/amps 80/6

Le Pré Bas is located on the shores of Lake Chambon, with a recreation room equipped with a pool table, and a table-tennis table nearer the road. If the lake is too cold for you, there's always the heated swimming pool. The bouncy castle on the playing field attracts swarms of children, who can't wait for their turn to bounce around, and the man running the snack bar tries his utmost to keep up with the stream of orders for pizzas.

Despite the hustle and bustle, the atmosphere is rural – there's enough space and you're unlikely to get under anyone's feet. The pitches are surrounded on three sides by hedgerows, so you'll have more than enough privacy. The sanitary facilities (plentiful) are kept spotless. If you enjoy hiking across volcanic mountains, the surrounding countryside offers lots of alternatives. The Vallée de Chaudefour nature reserve is also located close by. For an enjoyable daytrip, head for Chambon and Murol, two picturesque villages where you'll find excellent Cantal cheese and great local wines.

Serrette

Rating	8.3
Tariff range	€€€
Town	Chambon-sur-Lac
Department	Puy-de-Dôme
Postal Code	63790
Map	5 F5
Tel	04-73886767
Fax	04-73888173
e-mail	camping.de.serrette@wanadoo.fr
Open	15 May – 15 Sep

Take D996 (Murol-Le Mont Dore). After Chambon-sur-Lac, turn left and on to site.

Size (hectares) 3
Touring pitches 65
Sanitary facilities rating 8.5

magnificent view • homely atmosphere • tranquillity and nature • Lac-de-Chambon • wonderful hikes • Murol (6 km)

Electric hook-ups/amps 64/3-6

Camping Serrette lies on top of a hill, with ample space for caravans and tents, and hedgerows providing adequate shelter and privacy. Some pitches also offer a magnificent view across the entire valley including Lac-Chambon. In the distance, you'll just be able to make out Château Murol. The château organises special tours by guides dressed in period costumes. You can play table tennis, table football or the pinball machine. The sanitary facilities are clean and well-maintained.

The region owes much of its popularity to the walks of varying distances to the volcanoes, lakes, waterfalls and other local sights. The Serrette campsite is run by the exceptionally-friendly and helpful Mazin family. They'd be happy to provide you with a choice of hiking routes. If you're looking for a little entertainment, head for Lac-Chambon in the valley below. You'll not only find plenty of pavement cafés (along the D996), but also a sailing school and places to rent a pedalo or surfboard.

Château La Grange Fort

Rating	7.8
Tariff range	€€€€
Town	les Pradeaux
Department	Puy-de-Dôme
Postal Code	63500
Map	5 G5
Tel	04-73710243
Fax	04-73710769
e-mail	chateau@lagrangefort.eu
Open	07 Apr – 15 Oct

Take exit 13 from A75 towards Parentignat on D996. In Parentignat, turn right onto D999. After 200mtrs, take road towards Les Pradeaux-Nonette. Turn right after 1.5 km.

Size (hectares) 22
Touring pitches 105
Sanitary facilities rating 7.6

15th-century château • attractive restaurant • ample opportunity to play in or near the water • guided hikes • nature reserve • Issoire (5 km)

Electric hook-ups/amps 105/6

Château La Grange Fort is dominated by a 15th-century château which has a few Tuscan influences, courtesy of its previous Italian owner. One of the campsite's swimming pools is located underneath the old arches of one of the outbuildings and, given its surroundings, it feels very much like a Roman bathhouse.

You can dine in style in the château, and the stables have been converted to a bar and recreation area. Although you can camp out underneath the old walls of the château, the pitches are quite small. You may prefer one of the beautiful, larger spots, most of which offer sufficient shelter. The sanitary facilities are in good condition and cleaned regularly. For grown-ups there's pétanque, canoeing and mountaineering.

There's plenty to discover in the surrounding area too. From the campsite, you can walk straight into the surrounding hills, either with or without a guide. You can also rent a mountain bike.

Auvergne

L'Europe

Rating 7.5
Tariff range €€€€
Town Murol
Department Puy-de-Dôme
Postal Code 63790
Map 5 F5
Tel 04-73397666
Fax 04-73397661
e-mail europe.camping@wanadoo.fr
Open 31 May – 31 Aug
Site 1 km S of Murol on D618 to Jassat.
Size (hectares) 5
Touring pitches 59
Sanitary facilities rating 7.6
plenty of facilities • borders on nature reserve • close to Murol • in the vicinity of volcanic mountains • medieval château (Murol) • Besse-en-Chandesse (10 km)
Electric hook-ups/amps 59/5-10

The gently sloping grounds of this large, bustling campsite are well-maintained, with trees in the central camping area to keep your pitch cool, and mobile homes parked around the periphery. L'Europe has plenty to offer: there are two large heated swimming pools, one of which has a waterslide for children and a baby pool. Club Enfant organises a special programme for children every morning and afternoon.

To the side of the swimming pool there's a well-kept tennis court, and an area for playing pétanque. Although the pitches are somewhat small, their grass surface is excellent. There are no hedgerows or fences, so privacy is limited. The campsite provides washing, drying and ironing facilities, and there's also a baby washroom and amenities for less able guests. This is an excellent base from which to explore the surrounding area. If you enjoy walking, a guided hike through the nearby nature reserve including the volcanic mountains comes highly recommended.

La Ribeyre

Rating 8.3
Tariff range €€€€
Town Murol
Department Puy-de-Dôme
Postal Code 63790
Map 5 F5
Tel 04-73886429
Fax 04-73886841
e-mail laribeyre@free.fr
Open 01 May – 15 Sep
From Murol take D618 towards Jassat. Site approx 1 km on left (S of Murol).
Size (hectares) 10
Touring pitches 285
Sanitary facilities rating 8.2
tranquillity and nature • small beach with sun terrace • quality sanitary facilities • Lac de Chambon • nature hikes • Saint-Nectaire (5 km)
Electric hook-ups/amps 230/6-10

One noteworthy feature of La Ribeyre is the large oak tree near the lake, whose thick branches make it ideal for climbing. The tree and the nearby cave keep children busy for hours. On the lake, they can work off some of their energy by taking part in boat races. The Pommiers, who run La Ribeyre, have paid a lot of attention to the layout of the grounds. Even though the pitches appear to be scattered across the site at random, they offer a lot of privacy, tranquillity and space and the plentiful sanitary facilities are kept very clean.

There's a heated swimming pool near the reception area which also caters for toddlers. The pool is surrounded by a sunbathing area and a terrace with a snack bar, where you can order simple dishes. It also sells fresh bread in the mornings. The site located in a large valley is enclosed by the beautiful volcanic landscape, and there are many guided hikes on offer. Should you prefer to cycle, you can also rent a mountain bike.

Les Dômes

Rating	8.1
Tariff range	€€€
Town	Nébouzat
Department	Puy-de-Dôme
Postal Code	63210
Map	5 F5
Tel	04-73871406
Fax	04-73871881
e-mail	camping.les-domes@wanadoo.fr
Open	06 May – 15 Sep

Take N89 (Clermont-Ferrand-La Bourboule). Approx 10 km take D216 southward. Site on left in 500mtrs. Site 2 km W of Nébouzat.

Size (hectares) 1
Touring pitches 52   **Static pitches** 13
Sanitary facilities rating 8.1
homely campsite • surrounded by nature • sociable reception area • Puy de Dôme • plenty of sights • Clermond-Ferrand (15 km)
Electric hook-ups/amps 52/10-16

Les Dômes is a quiet campsite with a homely atmosphere, surrounded by a volcanic wilderness. Puy de Dôme, the most famous volcano in France, is located a mere 10 km away, down an old Roman road. You'll find plenty of information with suggestions for bicycle trips and walks in the reception area. There are not many organised activities for children at Les Dômes: in addition to the customary pétanque facilities, pool table and table-football, there's an indoor swimming pool where, if the weather is nice, the transparent roof is opened.

If swimming in the middle of nature sounds appealing, head for Lac Servière, which is located in the middle of a forest (7 km away). The pitches are enclosed by hedgerows and offer sufficient privacy, and sanitary facilities are well-maintained and clean. If you get the opportunity, visit Le Viaduc de Fades, the highest railway bridge in Europe. The town of Clermond-Ferrand is located 15 km to the northeast.

Le Clos Auroy

Rating	8.1
Tariff range	€€€
Town	Orcet
Department	Puy-de-Dôme
Postal Code	63670
Map	5 F5
Tel	04-73842697
Fax	04-73842697
e-mail	camping.orcet@wanadoo.fr
Open	All year

Take exit 5 off D75 (Orcet), take D213 & D52 towards Orcet. Turn left just before Orcet (follow site sign). Site on right just after river (200mtrs SE of Orcet).

Size (hectares) 2.5
Touring pitches 72   **Static pitches** 2
Sanitary facilities rating 8
sociable • easy to reach • clean • historic train journey • Vulcania Parc • Clermont-Ferrand (10 km)
Electric hook-ups/amps 72/5-10

A well-organised and tidy campsite located near Clermont-Ferrand, in the middle of the splendid Auvergne region. If you enjoy walking, mountain biking, kayaking or exploring places by car, Le Clos Auroy is for you. The site is situated in the Livradois-Forez park, with its steep slopes and abundance of sheep. The area's waterfalls, caves and medieval châteaux give purpose and direction to any expedition.

The volcanic landscape to the west is home to several 'puys', of which Puy de Dôme is undoubtedly the most famous. The pitches are spacious and surrounded on three sides by high hedgerows. As a result, you'll have more than enough privacy. They are arranged across different terraces and surrounded by colourful flowers. The sanitary facilities are excellent and well-maintained. Although you may prefer to visit a few sights, your children will undoubtedly want to spend their time dancing, competing in six-event competitions, dressing up, or playing table tennis and other games.

Brittany

International de la Hallerais

Rating	8.5
Tariff range	€€€
Town	Dinan
Department	Côtes-d'Armor
Postal code	22100
Map	1 C4
Tel	02-96391593
Fax	02-96399464
e-mail	camping.la.hallerais@wanadoo.fr
Open	10 Mar – 02 Nov

From Dinan towards Dinard. Turn right just before junct with 2-lane road, straight ahead over rail crossing. Right again at 'stop' sign; site on left (250mtrs).

Size (hectares) 8
Touring pitches 95
Sanitary facilities rating 8.6

luxurious sanitary facilities • beautiful landscape • free fishing in the pond • Mont-Saint-Michel • fortified town of Saint-Malo • port of Dinan (2 km)

Electric Hook-ups/amp 95/7

This spacious campsite lies just outside the port of Dinan, a convenient stopping place for travellers. There is plenty of room for tents and caravans, with high hedges and lots of trees to bring shade and privacy. The old farm house now contains two recreation rooms, and there is live music twice a week during the summer season.

The restaurant is unusually luxurious, with a menu offering a great variety of regional dishes. The sanitary facilities are the pièce de résistance of the campsite, with their new tiles and spacious shower cubicles. Walkers and cyclists will find a lot of marked and unmarked routes in the region, some of which lead through picturesque villages or to beautiful châteaux.

The site has its own swimming pool with deck chairs, as well as a number of sports facilities (among which are a mini golf course and a tennis court) which offer plenty of choice. A playground will delight the smallest children, but there is no further entertainment for them. The nearest beach is 30 km away, so it is the natural beauty and the many interesting sights that draw people here.

Le Vieux Moulin

Rating	7.5
Tariff range	€€€€
Town	Erquy
Department	Côtes-d'Armor
Postal code	22430
Map	1 C5
Tel	02-96723423
Fax	02-96723663
e-mail	camp.vieux.moulin@wanadoo.fr
Open	26 Apr – 06 Sep

On rdbt SE of Erquy, at junct of D786 & D34, turn to Les Hôpitaux. Route to site is signed (NE of Erquy).

Size (hectares) 6.6
Touring pitches 86   **Static pitches** 3
Sanitary facilities rating 7.7

lots of fun and sports • luxurious swimming pool • original merry-go-round • close to 7 beaches • flower island of Bréhat • Erquy (1 km)

Electric Hook-ups/amp 78/6

Le Vieux Moulin was founded 45 years ago by the father of the present owner, and many people have been coming here for their holidays for years. High pine trees and hedges separate the pitches from each other, and flowering plants add colour. The pleasant bar next to the luxurious swimming pool is a meeting point for guests, and in the evening lots of activities take place.

Once a week there is a disco party for the children, bands play live music and the pool tables are well used. The pride of the owners is an original fairground merry-go-round which is very popular with children. Sports fans can use the fitness room, the tennis court (half court), the table tennis tables or the pétanque pitch. Those who think that even this large swimming pool is too small for them can go to one of the seven beaches at Erquy; the nearest of these is about 1,200m from the site.

Popular sights in the region are the island of Bréhat (famous for its flowers and large sea bird colonies, accessible from Arcouest), Cap Fréhel and Fort de la Latte. Shopping can be enjoyed in Erquy or the beautiful towns of Dinan, Dinard or Saint-Malo.

L'Abri Côtier

Rating 8.2
Tariff range €€€
Town Étables-sur-Mer
Department Côtes-d'Armor
Postal code 22680
Map 1 B/C5
Tel 02-96706157
Fax 02-96706523
e-mail camping.abricotier@wanadoo.fr
Open 01 May – 08 Sep
The site lies NW of Étables-sur-Mer; follow the road signs.
Size (hectares) 2.5
Touring pitches 130
Sanitary facilities rating 8.3
peace and quiet • take-away • ports of Binic and Plouha • close to beach • coastal walks
Electric Hook-ups/amp 130/6-10

In the former vegetable garden of Château Kersaint can be found this quiet family campsite just 500m from the beach. It also boasts its own swimming pool complete with paddling pool and jacuzzi. This is a perfect place for anyone seeking relaxation, or wishing to explore the region. It is a no-nonsense site with pitches separated by hedges. The trees are a breeding place for the wood owl and the European canary, and the song of the hedge sparrow and the finch fills the air. The trees and other greenery don't offer much privacy, but there is sufficient shade.

As L'Abri Côtier is situated outside the village and far from the main routes, it is a quiet campsite. Small children will have great fun in the pool and the playground, and on the beach of Étables-sur-Mer there is a kids' club during the high season (entrance fee). Day trip destinations might be the 'falaises' of Plouha, the ports of Binic and Paimpol, and the island of Bréhat. You can walk or ride along the Côte de Granit Rose, as this part of the coastline is known. The site has a comfortable little bar, and a snack bar that sells a limited number of take-away meals.

Le Saint Efflam

Rating 8.2
Tariff range €€
Town Plestin-les-Grèves
Department Côtes-d'Armor
Postal Code 22310
Map 1 B5
Tel 02-96356215
Fax 02-96350975
e-mail campingmunicipalplestin@wanadoo.fr
Open 01 Apr – 30 Sep
From Lannion take D786 towards St-Michel-en Grève. After 2 km turn left. After 200mtrs site on right (E of Plestin).
Size (hectares) 4
Touring pitches 181
Sanitary facilities rating 8.2
inexpensive • sanitary facilities are good • located on a slope • Seven island excursion • historical buildings • Saint-Michel-en-Grève (2 km)
Electric hook-ups/amps 115/7

Le Saint Efflam is a municipal campsite set right next to the beach, and because of its location, it does not offer its own swimming pool. The campsite is on a hillside, but is divided up into a number of terraces. Pitches are of a reasonable size, but offer little privacy or shade. The sanitary facilities are modern and kept clean. Musical entertainment and themed evenings are put on in the bar and recreation area, and sports tournaments are organised for the older children. For the younger kids, there are daily programmes of activities throughout July and August.

There is also plenty to do in the local area around Plestin-les-Grèves. A number of beautiful churches and towns are well worth a visit, an excursion to Les Sept Îles is also likely to be rewarding. The islands are very green and teeming with colourful flowers and plants, a good variety of birds and an interesting history. You should not miss the beautiful nearby town of Saint-Michel-en-Grève. The campsite is simple, but is well located and the surrounding area provides everything you need for a great holiday.

Brittany

Domaine de Keravel

Rating	8.3
Tariff range	€€€€
Town	Plouha
Department	Côtes-d'Armor
Postal code	22580
Map	1 B5
Tel	02-96224913
e-mail	keravel@wanadoo.fr
Open	15 May – 30 Sep

From St-Brieuc D786 junct Plouha. Turn right in Plouha, immediately after church, then left past cemetery. After 2.5 km follow signs to site, NE of Plouha.

Size (hectares) 5
Touring pitches 104
Sanitary facilities rating 8.6
on an estate with ruins • in the shade of old trees • every tent has its own terrace • beach at 1,000 m • Kermaria chapel • Plouha (2 km)
Electric Hook-ups/amp 104/16

The Domaine de Keravel is set around a fine 'maison bourgeoise', dating from 1870, a perfectly quiet place surrounded by nature and historic relics. All over the estate there are ruins of chapels and other Gothic monuments. There is no evening entertainment on the campsite to disturb the silence, and as it is located outside the village, day time sounds are those of nature.

Put up your tent or place your caravan on your own terrace in the park, between old trees where woodpeckers, tree-creepers and owls will be your neighbours. The trees bring shade, and the terraces guarantee your privacy. There is a large swimming pool and tennis courts on site, and the beach is only 1,000m away. Early in the season it is surprisingly quiet, while in summer the intimacy of the park is reflected in the cosy little bar with its open-air section and the atmosphere around the swimming pool.

Close to the site rises the Pointe de Plouha (104m), one of the highest capes along the coast of Brittany. Other sights are the 15th-century chapel of Kermaria, and the ruins of Beauport Abbey near Paimpol.

Le Châtelet

Rating	8.1
Tariff range	€€€€
Town	St-Cast-le-Guildo
Department	Côtes-d'Armor
Postal code	22380
Map	1 C5
Tel	02-96419633
Fax	02-96419799
e-mail	chateletcp@aol.com
Open	28 Apr – 10 Sep

Site W of St-Cast-le-Guildo (signed).

Size (hectares) 8.4
Touring pitches 120
Sanitary facilities rating 7.7
view of the bay • paddling pool with attendants • rest and privacy • close to beaches • cape with sea bird colonies • St-Cast (1 km)
Electric Hook-ups/amp 120/6-8

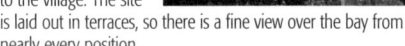

The village of Saint-Cast-le-Guildo and the campsite Le Châtelet are both located on the Baie de la Fresnaye, where they enjoy direct access to two of the seven beaches that belong to the village. The site is laid out in terraces, so there is a fine view over the bay from nearly every position.

On the opposite side of the water lies the 15th-century Fort de la Latte. Not far from there the colonies of sea birds on Cap Fréhel are a favourite destination for a day trip. In case the sea water is too cold, you can use the attended swimming pool which has a sunbathing terrace and a paddling pool. The perfect setting and the good facilities are often deciding factors for campers, who also enjoy its closeness to the towns of Saint-Malo, Dinan and Dinard. Golfers find that the course at Pen-Guen is another good reason to spend at least a few days in Saint-Cast-le-Guildo.

The campsite was laid out against the slopes of the hill, and much of the original vegetation has been preserved. The meals in the restaurant and the entertainment in the bar are distinctively British, as are the majority of the campers.

Les Capucines

Rating 8.5
Tariff range €€€€
Town St-Michel-en-Grève
Department Côtes-d'Armor
Postal Code 22300
Map 1 B5
Tel 02-96357228
Fax 02-96357898
e-mail les.capucines@wanadoo.fr
Open 15 Mar – 30 Sep
From Guingamp take D767 through Lannion and D786 to St-Michel. Then follow site signs. Site 1.5 km NE of St-Michel.
Size (hectares) 4
Touring pitches 87
Sanitary facilities rating 8.9
beautiful trees and flowers • breathtaking views • each pitch has its own water tap • Seven island excursion • beautiful churches • Saint-Michel-en-Grève
Electric hook-ups/amps 74/7

The campsite has been tastefully planted with respect for nature, and you can feel that the place is well loved. The site is about 1.5 km from the beautiful beach and the sea-front boulevard. There are many châteaux and churches in the local area within easy reach by bike or on foot, and the seven islands just off the coast also make for a popular excursion. These islands are covered in woodland that provides the habitat for a great variety of bird life.

The pitches are spacious and the hedges offer a high degree of privacy, while the sanitary facilities are decent and kept clean. You will not be disturbed by loud disco music at night and there is no entertainment programme for the kids. A tennis court, swimming pool and mini golf are sufficient to keep them entertained. It does not have its own restaurant, but the owner's wife can provide tasty takeaway meals. This is a great place to wind down in the evenings, while you sit outside your tent or caravan admiring the views over the valley. Dogs are not allowed.

Les Mouettes

Rating 8.7
Tariff range €€€€
Town Carantec
Department Finistère
Postal Code 29660
Map 1 B5
Tel 02-98670246
Fax 02-98783146
e-mail camping@les-mouettes.com
Open 17 May – 07 Sep
From Morlaix take D58 towards Carantec. Site is well signed.
Size (hectares) 15
Touring pitches 127
Sanitary facilities rating 9.1
attractive, illuminated swimming pool • a variety of sports and leisure activities • spacious pitches • delightful harbour towns • beautiful footpaths for walks • Carantec (2 km)
Electric hook-ups/amps 127/6-10

Life at Les Mouettes centres around the enormous swimming complex, the games room, the bar, the half-size tennis courts, the football pitch and the lake. It has a definite air of luxury, enhanced by its well looked after appearance. There's a variety of walks in the surrounding area, and good facilities in the nearby town of Saint-Pol-de-Léon. Spacious pitches offer the right level of privacy. The swimming pool is always busy, and once a week it provides the setting for an evening of fun on the waterslides when the fairytale lighting is switched on.

Other activities include archery, mini-golf, volleyball, a disco (twice a week) and much more. In the summer, the entertainment programme is extensive, ranging from local folklore groups and karaoke to tennis competitions on the half-size courts. The beautiful, child-friendly beach at Carantec is only 2 km away; the small beach on the island near the campsite is also suitable for sunbathing, but can only be reached when the tide is out. Brittany's coastal road, the GR34, passes close to the campsite.

Les Embruns

Rating	8.7
Tariff range	€€€€
Town	Clohars-Carnoët
Department	Finistère
Postal code	29360
Map	1 B4
Tel	02-98399107
Fax	02-98399787
e-mail	camping-les-embruns@wanadoo.fr
Open	04 Apr – 13 Sep

In centre of Le Pouldu; towards beach.

Size (hectares) 5
Touring pitches 75
Sanitary facilities rating 8.6
indoor and outdoor pools • beach suitable for children • snack bar and barbecue • interesting towns nearby • plenty of walking opportunities • Quimperlé (13 km)
Electric Hook-ups/amp 75/6-10

Only 250m from the beach, in the pleasant seaside resort of Le Pouldu not far from Clohars Carnoët, lies the family campsite of Les Embruns. Boats, buoys, anchors, lighthouses and references to the fishing history of the village, mark the entrance to this floral site. The true focal point is the indoor swimming pool with a roof that can be opened when the weather is hot and dry; there is also an outdoor pool with a water slide.

The snack bar serves simple meals like 'fruits de mer' and pizzas that you can take to your tent or caravan. Once a week in summer the bartender organises entertainment such as karaoke, soirées and folk music concerts, with barbecue parties from time to time. The sanitary facilities are acceptable. Returning campers praise the beautiful location, clean facilities and cheap prices.

The most interesting sights in the area are the town of Lorient, the Ile de Groix, Pont-Aven and the Maison Marie-Henry (with murals by Gauguin and other artists). The whole region is rich in churches, chapels, calvaries and abbeys. Fresh vegetables and fish are sold at the many markets: Le Pouldu (Wednesdays), Clohars-Carnoët (Saturdays) and Quimperlé (Fridays).

Le Kerleyou

Rating	8.4
Tariff range	€€
Town	Douarnenez
Department	Finistère
Postal Code	29100
Map	1 A4
Tel	02-98741303
Fax	02-98740961
e-mail	campingdekerleyou@wanadoo.fr
Open	01 May – 23 Sep

From Douarnenez towards Poullan-sur-Mer, follow site signs. Site on SW outskirts of Douarnenez.

Size (hectares) 3.5
Touring pitches 42
Sanitary facilities rating 8.6
plenty of privacy • close to the beach • well-equipped playground, swimming pool • many religious monuments • picturesque fishing ports • Douarnenez town centre (0.3 km)
Electric hook-ups/amps 42/10

Le Kerleyou is a family campsite located a mere kilometre away from the Plage des Sables Blancs beach in Tréboul, a suburb of Douarnenez. The site lies hidden among tall pine trees with plenty of privacy for all. It has modern sanitary facilities and a convivial bar with outdoor terrace. Although there's no restaurant, you can order pizzas and French fries. For children, there's a playground and a small but well-equipped recreation area.

The site is an excellent base from which to explore Douarnenez and the surrounding areas, including the westernmost point of the French mainland: the Pointe du Raz. The port of Douarnenez is home to many old churches and chapels, while many of its neighbouring towns – including Kerlaz, Le Juich, Poullan-sur-Mer and Pouldergat – boast other fine examples of church architecture. The town of Locronan, arguably one of the prettiest in France, is close-by, as are the picturesque fishing ports of Audierne and Le Guilvinec. Should you prefer the hustle and bustle of the city, Brest and Quimper are within easy reach.

L'Atlantique

Rating	8.2
Tariff range	€€€€
Town	Fouesnant
Department	Finistère
Postal code	29170
Map	1 A4
Tel	02-98561444
Fax	02-98561867
e-mail	sunelia@latlantique.fr
Open	25 Apr – 07 Sep

From Fouesnant take D145 towards Mousterlin. Then follow signs to site (4 km S of Fouesnant).

Size (hectares) 9
Touring pitches 88
Sanitary facilities rating 7.9

large, luxury campsite • partly covered water park • sauna and fitness suite • close to child-friendly beach • near the exotic Îles de Glénan • Fouesnant (4 km)

Electric hook-ups/amps 88/10

L'Atlantique near Fouesnant is a large campsite with all the luxuries a camper could wish for, including a very popular water park. Founded 20 years ago, it now occupies 22 acres of the attractive south coast of Brittany. Only 400m from the child-friendly beach that can be reached by a path through the nature reserve of Marais de Mousterlin, L'Atlantique guarantees swimming fun whatever the weather. The patrolled beach is 6 km long and is cleaned every day. On the inland side, the site borders the Mousterlin polder, a piece of low-lying land reclaimed from the sea. In the high season, you can make an excursion into the nature reserve with a biologist, and footpath GR34 runs along the coast here.

The site is neatly divided into pitches which are separated by hedges. The planting includes colourful flowers and exotic trees, adding to the feel of luxury, and the sanitary facilities are all modern. There are plenty of interesting days out to be had nearby, including the beautiful Îles de Glénan (departing from Beg-Meil), and the historic towns of Concarneau with its old city walls, as well as Quimper and Audierne.

Brittany

Les Abers

Rating 8.5
Tariff range €€€
Town Landéda
Department Finistère
Postal Code 29870
Map 1 A5
Tel 02-98049335
Fax 02-98048435
e-mail camping-des-abers@wanadoo.fr
Open 01 May – 30 Sep
From Brest (airport) take D67 then D13 to Lannilis. Left towards Landéda. In Landéda follow site signs. Site NW of Landéda.
Size (hectares) 5
Touring pitches 158
Sanitary facilities rating 8.7
located on beautiful coastline • tasteful facilities • local Breton flavour • the beautiful island of Ouessant • beach volleyball • Landéda (3 km)
Electric hook-ups/amps 158/5-10

Les Abers campsite is located right next to the beach. This friendly site was established over 35 years ago, and named after the many sea inlets which are known locally as 'abers'. Apart from excellent sunbathing and swimming, there is also good windsurfing in the bay, which provides some shelter from the Atlantic. The beach is also ideal for beach volleyball and kite flying. Because of its coastal location, there is a lack of tall trees on the site, and some of the pitches therefore have little shade. The hedges do make up for this to a certain extent, however.

A lot of effort has gone into careful planting and other features that reflect the local maritime tradition. Although the site does not have its own restaurant, cooking courses are available in high season, with the emphasis firmly on fruits de mer and other Breton specialities. There are also Breton dance and music evenings, and talks on the history of Brittany. The Île de Ouessant is not too far away and can be reached by boat from Le Conquet and Lanildut.

Yelloh! Village Le Manoir de Kerlut

Rating 8.4
Tariff range €€€€
Town Lesconil
Department Finistère
Postal Code 29740
Map 1 A4
Tel 02-98822389
Fax 02-98822649
e-mail info@yellohvillage-manoir-de-kerlut.com
Open 26 Apr – 30 Sep
Pont-l'Abbé - D102 - Plobannalec towards Lesconil. Site approx 1 km S of Plobannalec (on left).
Size (hectares) 12
Touring pitches 139
Sanitary facilities rating 8.5
located on château grounds • space, tranquillity and luxury • exceptionally well-suited to children • near Locronan and Quimper • ample opportunity to surf • Pont-l'Abbé (5 km)
Electric hook-ups/amps 139/5-10

The owner of this country estate - Madame Furic - decided to convert the château grounds to a campsite in 1990. Her objective was to create a children's paradise, and she's certainly succeeded. Children can spend all day enjoying the site's large swimming pool, exploring the play apparatus or participating in the various children's clubs. Adults have plenty of opportunity to play tennis, work out, or tour the beautiful surroundings on a (rented) bicycle. The estate, which borders the River Ria, is home to a large number of very old trees. The nearby capes, which extend far into the sea, are ideal for surfing or fishing. And if you enjoy long walks, the beaches won't disappoint. The beautiful Baie de Audierne can be dangerous, though, and anyone wishing to swim should head for a patrolled section. There's a safe beach within two kilometres of the campsite, near Lesconil. The village of Locronan, considered by some to be the most beautiful village in France, and the city of Quimper with its Roman remains, have plenty in store for those interested in history.

Le Ty Nadan

Rating	8.1
Tariff range	€€€€
Town	Locunolé
Department	Finistère
Postal code	29310
Map	1 B4
Tel	02-98717547
Fax	02-98717731
e-mail	infos@camping-ty-nadan.fr
Open	28 Mar – 04 Sep

Plouay-D2-Arzano to Locunolé. Over small bridge. Site S of Locunolé, on left.

Size (hectares) 20
Touring pitches 115
Sanitary facilities rating 8.3
lots of activities • swimming pool and survival track • restaurants • angling and swimming • surrounded by woodlands • Quimperlé (8 km)
Electric Hook-ups/amp 115/10

This must be one of the most beautiful campsites in France: located in the Ellé Valley, surrounded by extensive woodlands and with all the facilities you could wish for. You could stay here for weeks without getting bored, and the children will share your sentiments.

They will love the large swimming pool, the survival track, the riding centre, the tennis court, and the canoes on the river. Entertainment for all ages with competitions, disco nights and excursions are provided throughout the day, so few young people will find anything to complain about. The facilities are excellent, especially the toilets and washing rooms. There is no need to go out for a visit to a snack bar or restaurant, as there is even a crêperie opposite the site. Pitches are spacious, and there is sufficient shade.

The Ellé river is rich in trout and salmon, and you can go fishing directly from the site. With a little bit of luck you might even see otters swimming around. The trees in the forests are home to many wood owls, and you will hear them hooting during the night. It is not only the children who call this place a little paradise!

International Le Raguenès Plage

Rating	8.6
Tariff range	€€€€
Town	Névez
Department	Finistère
Postal Code	29920
Map	1 B4
Tel	02-98068069
Fax	02-98068905
e-mail	info@camping-le-raguenes-plage.com
Open	09 Apr – 01 Oct

From Pont-Aven, take D783 westbound. Take D77 to Névez, through village towards Raguenés. Site on left near village and beach.

Size (hectares) 6
Touring pitches 183
Sanitary facilities rating 8.8
good service • shady, private pitches • bar with music and dancing • close to child-friendly beach • the artistic village of Pont-Aven • Névez (2 km)
Electric hook-ups/amps 183/2-10

Yvonne Guyader established Le Raguenès Plage in 1965 and since then, it has grown into a fully-fledged campsite with around 300 pitches. A private road gives easy access to the child-friendly beach. The owners and their daughter and son still play a full role in making their guests feel welcome, in offering personal attention and excellent facilities for the less able.

The site is home to more than 100 different species of tree, which provide the pitches with plenty of shade and privacy. It boasts a large swimming pool, and there is plenty of equipment for the children to play on. In the high season, the restaurant serving seafood specialities and the bar are open until 11pm for music and dancing. Beach volleyball competitions are held, and there is a play area near the beach. In the local area, Concarneau, Quimper and the artist's colony of Pont-Aven, are all popular destinations. Markets are held in Concarneau (Monday and Friday), Pont-Aven (Tuesday) and Rospoden (Thursday).

Brittany

L'Océan

Rating 8.5
Tariff range €€€
Town Névez
Department Finistère
Postal Code 29920
Map 1 B4
Tel 02-98068713
Fax 02-98067826
e-mail campingocean@orange.fr
Open 15 May – 15 Sep
From Pont-Aven, take D783 westbound. Take D77 to Névez, through village towards Raguenés-Plage. Turn left towards site. Site north of Raguenés.
Size (hectares) 2.5
Touring pitches 136
Sanitary facilities rating 9
friendly family campsite • the beach and a swimming pool are available • recreation room and playing field • the artistic village of Pont-Aven • bicycle rides along the coast • Névez (3 km)
Electric hook-ups/amps 136/3-10

This friendly site is only 300m from the beach, and it also has its own heated swimming pool. At the centre of the campsite is a playing field for volleyball and other games, and recreation area for the kids to play table football or table tennis. People return year after year from all over Europe, attracted by the atmosphere, the clean sanitary facilities and the spacious pitches. The latter are bounded by hedges, while the trees provide sufficient shade and the flowers give the place a happy, summery feel. The campsite shop sells freshly-baked bread, but for fresh vegetables and fish you will need to venture out to one of the many local markets. The surrounding area is picturesque, and here and there you will find a country house or a ruined abbey. The most interesting sights are the artistic village of Pont-Aven (museum) and the fortress town of Concarneau. There are plenty of walking and cycling routes along the coastline of southern Brittany. It is also worth driving to Lorient, where the ferry will take you across the water to the beautiful island of Groix (bike rental available on the island).

International de Kervel

Rating 8.3
Tariff range €€€€
Town Plonévez-Porzay
Department Finistère
Postal Code 29550
Map 1 A4
Tel 02-98925154
Fax 02-98925496
e-mail camping.kervel@wanadoo.fr
Open 28 Apr – 30 Sep
From Châteaulin take D107 towards Douarnenez then Plonévez. After 4 km turn right towards Kervel, follow signs to site. Site SW of Plonévez.
Size (hectares) 7
Touring pitches 120
Sanitary facilities rating 8.4
varied sports facilities • well-suited to children • bar and disco • beach within walking distance • close to the medieval town of Locronan • Douarnenez (8 km)
Electric hook-ups/amps 120/10

The International de Kervel is set on the Baie de Douarnenez, offering all the conveniences and facilities that a holidaymaker could wish for. Despite the spacious layout, some spots offer limited privacy. It is nevertheless an ideal place from which to explore Brittany by bicycle, car or on foot.

There is plenty to keep you busy, including a large swimming pool with water slide, a multipurpose sports field, mini golf, table tennis and tennis facilities, and a recreation room. Night time entertainment (in the bar) includes karaoke, dancing and music. One of the main local attractions is Locronan, considered by some to be the most beautiful village in France. Exaggerated though that claim may be, the medieval houses around the old church have retained their former glory, and are extraordinarily pretty. Sandwiched between fields, the site is a mere 500 metres away from a sandy beach, which is well suited to children.

Castel L' Orangerie de Lanniron

Rating 8.9
Tariff range €€€€
Town Quimper
Department Finistère
Postal Code 29336
Map 1 A4
Tel 02-98906202
Fax 02-98521556
e-mail camping@lanniron.com
Open 15 May – 15 Sep
Do not drive into Quimper – follow ring road clockwise and follow signs. Site S of Quimper on River Odet.
Size (hectares) 27
Touring pitches 180
Sanitary facilities rating 8.8
located on château grounds • heated swimming pool • restaurant in orangery • opportunity to play sports • tranquillity, nature and culture • Quimper (0.5 km)
Electric hook-ups/amps 180/10-10

L'Orangerie de Lanniron is located in the grounds of a château (formerly a Bishop's palace), and offers all the amenities that the discriminating camper could wish for. The jewel in the crown is the château gardens which are being returned to their former (18th-century) glory following a ferocious storm in 1987. The site is owned by the Count and Countess De Massol de Rebetz, who go to every length to make their guests as comfortable as possible. You'll often find them in the reception area, or giving a tour of the château gardens.

L'Orangerie de Lanniron offers several levels of luxury (electricity only, water/electricity, and water/electricity/drains and sewerage).The sanitary facilities are excellent and you can also make unlimited use of the heated swimming pool. The orangery houses a quality restaurant, where the fish comes highly recommended. The bar hosts a variety of evening activities, including karaoke and folk music. Sports-minded campers can enjoy tennis, golf, horse riding, canoeing and cycling - rental facilities are available on or in the vicinity of the campsite.

Armorique

Rating 8.2
Tariff range €€€
Town Telgruc-sur-Mer
Department Finistère
Postal code 29560
Map 1 A4
Tel 02-98277733
Fax 02-98273838
e-mail contact@campingarmorique.com
Open 01 Apr – 30 Sep
From Châteaulin towards Crozon follow on D877, at Telgruc-sur-Mer junct, through village and follow signs; site S of Telgruc on right.
Size (hectares) 2.5
Touring pitches 100
Sanitary facilities rating 8.2
heated swimming pool • restaurant with special dishes • fitness room • outdoor activities • good shopping in towns • Crozon (10 km)
Electric Hook-ups/amp 100/6-10

This campsite lies on a slope overlooking Plage de Trez-Bellec. After a short drive over a steep road with some hairpin bends you enter a level camping area. Telgruc may not be exactly located 'sur Mer', but the beach is only 750m away. Guests can also use the heated swimming pool where there is a breathtaking view. The restaurant is run by the ever-smiling chef-cuisinier Jean-Pierre Pen Houët. Try his favourite dish on the menu: 'Andouillettes de Crabe façon Compagnie des Indes' is a curry-flavoured creation. For your dessert the 'tarte aux trois fromages' is highly recommended.

The sanitary facilities are modern, and there is a good fitness room to keep you in condition. Sports fans have a wide choice of outdoor activities: canoeing, kayaking, climbing, windsurfing, walking, cycling, angling and scuba diving. Shopping is available in a number of small towns nearby: Morgat, Camaret, Crozon, Argol. There is a market in Telgruc on Tuesdays and Wednesdays and in Crozon on Thursdays. In the summer time there are occasionally disco parties and folk music performances in the campsite bar.

Brittany

Le Bois Pastel

Rating 7.9
Tariff range €€€
Town Cancale
Department Ille-et-Vilaine
Postal code 35260
Map 1 C5
Tel 02-99896610
Fax 02-99896011
e-mail camping.bois-pastel@wanadoo.fr
Open 01 Apr – 01 Oct

From Cancale take D201 to St-Malo via Pointe du Grouin. Left after 4.5 km; site 300mtrs on right (signed).

Size (hectares) 4
Touring pitches 114
Sanitary facilities rating 8

beautiful young plantation • good sanitary facilities • no entertainment • fortified town Saint-Malo • Cancale (2 km) • Dinard

Electric Hook-ups/amp 114/6

A beautiful and well-tended campsite is how people describe Le Bois Pastel. It is set in an attractive and gently-sloping landscape, 2 km from the centre of Cancale. There is no organised entertainment because the owner prefers peace, so you will not hear music blaring over the site in the evening or during the day. Instead you can enjoy a quiet drink in the bar, or perhaps buy a snack.

There is no real restaurant at the moment, but the shop stocks the basic necessities. The sanitary facilities are clean and well maintained, and the whole site is attractively kept. Pitches are sufficiently spacious for comfort, and though planting is still young, one part of the site does offer more shade than the rest. There is a pool with a separate section for children, surrounded by beautifully tiled terraces with deck chairs and parasols.

About one and a half kilometres away lies the beach of Cancale, well known for its harbour, oysters and picturesque streets. Not far from Cancale is Saint-Malo, the fortified town with a beautiful cathedral, the same picturesque streets and delicious mussels. Dinard – known as 'Nice of the North' - is not far away either, and you will see why it owes its reputation to the fine beaches.

Le Vieux Chêne

Rating 8.1
Tariff range €€€€
Town Dol-de-Bretagne
Department Ille-et-Vilaine
Postal code 35120
Map 1 C4
Tel 02-99480955
Fax 02-99481337
e-mail vieux.chene@wanadoo.fr
Open 05 Apr – 21 Sep

Site on D576, E of Baguer-Pican, 3 km E of Dol-de-Bretagne.

Size (hectares) 12
Touring pitches 158 **Static pitches** 2
Sanitary facilities rating 8.3

quiet all over • good and cheap food • fine swimming pool • beautiful farm houses • Mont-Saint-Michel • Dol-de-Bretagne (3 km)

Electric Hook-ups/amp 130/5-10

The owner of Le Vieux Chêne is proud of his campsite and he has many reasons to be. The reception desk is in a 17th-century farmhouse set in extremely well kept grounds with many colourful flowers and trees. The pitches offer enough room to move around, but are a bit lacking in privacy and shade. The sanitary facilities are clean though rather old fashioned.

But on the plus side there is a great swimming pool, particularly suitable for children, and two ponds where you can go fishing in summer without needing a licence. You can eat and drink in the restaurant or take something lighter from the snack bar - try the mussels, all bearing the official label, which are delicious!

There are lots of facilities for sport and recreation, and an entertainment programme during the high season. Singers, bands, disco, karaoke, riding, games – there is always something to do for all ages. If you are going exploring, then call at one of the many farmhouses that still make cheese in a traditional way, and where you can get wonderful souvenirs or presents to take back. Or take a day trip to Saint-Malo, the fortified town with its massive walls and picturesque streets, or Mont-Saint-Michel.

Le P'tit Bois

Rating 8.2
Tariff range €€€€
Town St-Jouan-des-Guérets
Department Ille-et-Vilaine
Postal code 35430
Map 1 C5
Tel 02-99211430
Fax 02-99817414
e-mail camping.ptitbois@wanadoo.fr
Open 07 Apr – 08 Sep
From St-Malo S to Dol-de-Bretagne (N137); turn right after few km (rdbt), take D5 to La Passagère; then follow signs.
Size (hectares) 6
Touring pitches 120   **Static pitches** 12
Sanitary facilities rating 8
fine swimming pool • beautiful pitches • lots of activities • Saint-Malo • eating oysters in Cancale • Saint-Jouan-des-Guérets
Electric Hook-ups/amp 120/6

Though the name may not sound too promising, Le P'tit Bois is a large and well-equipped campsite with something for everyone. It is a children's paradise, but adults will find plenty to entertain them here too.

There is a swimming pool with a number of water slides, and even a hammam (Turkish bath) and a solarium. During the day there is a kids' club for the youngest guests, while older children can join the various sports competitions that are organised for their entertainment. In the evening campers of all ages can go to the disco or hear live music and karaoke. The pitches are very spacious with a lot of privacy and shade, and the sanitary facilities are excellent and very clean.

If none of this is what you are seeking, you can go and explore the region. Take a day trip to Saint-Malo, the fortified town that is famous for its mussels. Or to Cancale, where you should sample the local delicacy to which the village owes its reputation: oysters. Dinard is another popular destination for day-trippers, known as 'The Nice of the North' thanks to its large harbour and beaches. Le P'tit Bois is not a 'Little Forest', but a perfect place for a holiday where boredom is simply unheard of.

Le Bel-Event

Rating 7.5
Tariff range €€€
Town St-Père
Department Ille-et-Vilaine
Postal code 35430
Map 1 C4
Tel 02-99588379
Fax 02-99588224
e-mail contact@camping-bel-event.com
Open 22 Mar – 12 Oct
Rennes N137. Near Neufchâteau take D74 to St-Père. Site 2 km on left, 1.5 km S of St-Père.
Size (hectares) 3
Touring pitches 37
Sanitary facilities rating 7.7
activities for children • not a dull moment • yet very quiet • Cancale: fish restaurants • Dinard • Saint-Père (2 km)
Electric Hook-ups/amp 37/10

As soon as you enter Le Bel Event, you will feel at home. That is certainly the impression the owner sets out to give, and he is generally successful. Many guests come here for only a week, but after three weeks they are still here, and it is easy to see why.

One reason is the many activities which are organised for campers. Once a week a pig is roasted on the spit, and parties are frequently given. The owner's daughter, a trained nanny, takes care of the smallest children giving their parents some freedom. The pitches are spacious, and offer both privacy and shade, while the sanitary facilities are excellent. To go to the beach you will need your car or bicycle – it is 5 km away. But there is a pleasant swimming pool with tables, deck chairs and parasols. The bartender takes orders for snacks, and there is a snooker table, table football and video games to while away the hours.

There is plenty to see and do in the area as well. You could take a day trip to the fortified town of Saint-Malo, the port of Cancale, famous for its delicious mussels, or the port of Dinard, also known as 'Nice of the North'. The owner may be of British origin, but this is undoubtedly France, as you can tell by the wonderfully fresh home-made croissants which are sold for breakfast!

Brittany

Les Druides

Rating	8.1
Tariff range	€€€€
Town	Carnac
Department	Morbihan
Postal code	56340
Map	1 B3
Tel	02-97520818
Fax	02-97529613
e-mail	contact@camping-les-druides.com
Open	01 May – 13 May, 23 May – 13 Sep

From Auray follow D768 to Quiberon. Turn left after 6 km and take D119 to Carnac; then La Trinité-sur-Mer. Right after 1 km (Chemin-de-Beaumer); site on right (1 km).

Size (hectares) 2.5

Touring pitches 100

Sanitary facilities rating 8.3

very well tended • swimming pool and jacuzzi • sports grounds • alignments of Carnac • beach fit for children • Carnac (2 km)

Electric Hook-ups/amp 70/6

Les Druides is more than thirty years old, and is constantly being improved and extended including the addition of a swimming pool with paddling pool and jacuzzi; and the pride of the owners are the extensive sports grounds where you can play football, volleyball and many other games.

The toilets and washing rooms easily meet with modern demands, but the other facilities are a bit limited. There is no shop, but you can buy bread or croissants at reception. The pitches are spacious though, and there is a separate section for transit guests. The oldest part of the site offers plenty of shade, but the newer pitches will have to wait a few more years until the planting matures.

As on all sites in and around Carnac, people come here to see the famous alignments of standing stones. But the beaches of Carnac-Plage are equally attractive, especially for children. Dozens of megalithic monuments, menhirs or dolmens can be found around Carnac, as you will see on a walking or cycling tour to Locmariaquer or the Ile de Gavrinis. The nature reserve around the Golfe du Morbihan is not far from Carnac.

Du Lac

Rating	7.7
Tariff range	€€€
Town	Carnac
Department	Morbihan
Postal code	56340
Map	1 B3
Tel	02-97557878
Fax	02-97558603
e-mail	campingdekerleyou@wanadoo.fr
Open	12 Apr – 20 Sep

In Auray take D768 to Quiberon. Turn left after 4 km, follow D186 to La Trinité-sur-Mer. Turn left again after 3 km, and 2 km to lake. Site NE of Carnac.

Size (hectares) 2.5

Touring pitches 103

Sanitary facilities rating 8.1

situated near a tidal lake • spacious pitches • quiet and intimate atmosphere • ports and alignments • boating, windsurfing, golf • Vannes (32 km)

Electric Hook-ups/amp 103/4-10

Du Lac - Le Kerleyou was named after the nearby lake that dries up from time to time, due to the influence of a tidal river that runs close to the campsite. The effects of high and low tide are easily visible, even this far inland.

Years ago a bend in the river was blocked off, and a water mill was built on the dam; at the ebbing tide the flowing water worked the mill. Two decades ago the owners of the old mill, which still stands on the opposite side of the lake, started a campsite on this scenic location. It is laid out in terraces, and from nearly every pitch there is a view over the lake.

Bernard and Rachel Audic insist on welcoming their guests personally, and have created a pleasant atmosphere. Satisfied campers remark on the site's special setting, the tidal lake, and the wonderful views. The intimate atmosphere is another factor that is frequently mentioned, and the delightful absence of frills that draw the holiday crowds at other sites. The pitches are spacious and separated by hedges, and all around there are trees and flower beds. Le Lac lies close to La Trinité-sur-Mer with its fishing port. Going to Carnac you cannot miss the standing stones of Kerlessan, Kermario and Ménec.

Les Bruyères

Rating 8.3
Tariff range €€€
Town Carnac
Department Morbihan
Postal code 56340
Map 1 B3
Tel 02-97523057
Fax 02-97523057
e-mail camping.les.bruyeres@wanadoo.fr
Open 01 Apr – 15 Oct

From Auray follow D768 to Quiberon. Turn left 2 km beyond road to Carnac (D119), and take C4; site on right (500mtrs).

Size (hectares) 2
Touring pitches 93
Sanitary facilities rating 8.6

simple, tidy • enough room and privacy • in a forest • alignments in Carnac • diving, sailing, windsurfing • Auray (10 km)

Electric Hook-ups/amp 87/4-10

Les Bruyères lies just across the border of the municipality of Carnac. The pitches are spacious, and high hedges guarantee privacy, with old trees providing the necessary shade. Flowers grow everywhere and contribute to the pleasant atmosphere.

The sanitary facilities are reasonable, and kept very clean. Les Bruyères owes its reputation mainly to its quiet location in the middle of a forest. There is no swimming pool, but you can use the recreation room and the tennis court. During the high season there are table tennis and pétanque competitions, and young guests will appreciate the many playing facilities.

From this site the thousands of megalithic monuments of Carnac are only a short distance away. To reach the beaches of Carnac-Plage you will have to walk, ride or drive a mere 4 km. The beaches on the Quiberon peninsula, like La Grande Plage, are also 4 km from the site. Quiberon and Belle-Ile-en-Mer are worth a day trip, and so is the splendid nature reserve around the Golfe du Morbihan. Bird lovers can watch the thousands of birds that nest here, such as the herons with their silver coloured plumage – a truly exotic touch.

Le Bas de la Lande

Rating 8.5
Tariff range €€
Town Josselin-et-Guégon
Department Morbihan
Postal code 56120
Map 1 C4
Tel 02-97222220
Fax 02-97739385
e-mail campingbasdelalande@wanadoo.fr
Open 01 Apr – 31 Oct

From Ploërmel take N24 to Josselin (do not enter town). Exit N24 at junct Guégon/Camping Le Bas de la Lande, turn left, follow signs. Site on left (900 mtrs).

Size (hectares) 2
Touring pitches 49
Sanitary facilities rating 8.8

sober transit camp site • clean and modern sanitary facilities • mini golf, table tennis • picturesque villages • close to main road • Josselin (2 km)

Electric Hook-ups/amp 36/6-10

The chief attraction of this municipal campsite is that it lies close to the main N24, so is convenient for transit guests. Though it is quite a sober place with traffic noise constantly in the background, it does have all the necessary facilities. During the high season there is a snack bar, and the toilet facilities are relatively new. On the opposite side of the road there is a mini golf course with free admission for guests.

The site is laid out on terraces on the slope of a hill near the village of Guégon, not far from Josselin. This modest town offers many attractions, with the central point of interest being the mighty 14th-century castle, inhabited by the Rohan since the 15th century. It also houses the Musée de Poupées (dolls museum). Part of the castle was demolished in the 16th century, but it is still an impressive building with fine Gothic walls. The centre of Josselin is well preserved; you can see the 15th-century basilica of Notre-Dame du Roncier, and the many half-timbered houses from the 16th and 17th centuries. Around Josselin there are a number of castles, witnesses to the War of Succession that was fought between England and France after the death of John III in 1341. Of the many picturesque villages in the locality, Lizio is certainly worth a visit.

Brittany

Municipal Beg Er Roch

Rating	7.5
Tariff range	€€
Town	le Faouët
Department	Morbihan
Postal code	56320
Map	1 B4
Tel	02-97231511
Fax	02-97231166
e-mail	camping.lefaouet@wanadoo.fr
Open	15 Mar – 15 Sep

Site on D769, 2 km SE of Le Faouët.

Size (hectares) 3.5
Touring pitches 49
Sanitary facilities rating 7.6

simple but attractive • mini golf, tennis, bowling • trout and salmon fishing • rich in monuments • walking, canoeing • Le Faouët (1 km)

Electric Hook-ups/amp 49/3-5

A municipal campsite in a beautiful setting, near the picturesque village of Le Faouët in the heart of the Morbihan region. It has all the necessary facilities as well as a mini golf course, a tennis court and even a bowling alley. The sanitary facilities are simple but clean.

One of the attractions is its location on the river Ellé, where anglers are sure to catch a trout or salmon in spite of the strong competition from the otters that swim here. There are lots of historic monuments in the vicinity: here King Morvan of Armorica (ancient Brittany) unsuccessfully fought the armies of Louis the Pious, son and successor to Charlemagne. There are no traces left of these battles, but there are ruins of settlements dating from prehistoric times. You can admire the architecture of the 12th century and later churches and chapels.

The bizarre appearance of Les Roches du Diable rocks – thrown into the river by the devil so they say – is interesting. You can go walking along this river that is also suitable for rafting or slalom canoeing. A fine relic of the past is the old market hall in Le Faouët, where a market is held every first and third Wednesday of the month.

Le Bordenéo

Rating	8.1
Tariff range	€€€
Town	le Palais
Department	Morbihan
Postal code	56360
Map	1 B3
Tel	02-97318896
Fax	02-97318777
e-mail	camping.bordeneo@wanadoo.fr
Open	01 Apr – 20 Sep

From Le Palais ferry terminal take D30 to Sauzon, over harbour bridge. Turn right. Site on left (1.5 km), approx 2 km NW of Le Palais.

Size (hectares) 3
Touring pitches 136
Sanitary facilities rating 8.3

swimming pool and tennis court • electricity connection on pitches • diversity in plantation • coastal foot paths • diving, windsurfing, sailing • Le Palais (2 km)

Electric Hook-ups/amp 100/5

One of the most beautiful spots in France is the island of Belle-Ile-en-Mer off the southern coast of Brittany. It is very popular, both among French holidaymakers and foreigners, so booking in advance is essential. It is also advisable to book your ferry ticket to the island, especially when travelling by car and towing a caravan. To reach the mainland terminal you will have to cross the Quiberon peninsula – not easy on a busy day in summer.

This campsite is equipped with swimming pool, tennis court, clean sanitary facilities and spacious pitches with electricity. One of the reasons for going to Belle-Ile-en-Mer (there is also a Belle-Ile-en-Terre elsewhere in Brittany) is to enjoy its natural beauty and the history of the island. Fort Vauban in Le Palais (the island's only port) has a museum dedicated to the military history. The best way to explore this small island is on bicycle. Bird colonies, caves, beautiful bays and white sandy beaches – all are numerous here. Walkers can use the coastal footpath, divers can go to Sauzon and Le Palais, and windsurfers should head for the beaches on the NE coast.

Le Haras

Rating 8.2
Tariff range €€€
Town Monterblanc
Department Morbihan
Postal code 56250
Map 1 C3
Tel 02-97446606
Fax 02-97444941
e-mail camping-vannes@wanadoo.fr
Open All year

S from Monterblanc, cross D126 towards Kermoël. Left after military barracks. Site approx 3.5 km to W of Monterblanc, near small airport.

Size (hectares) 14
Touring pitches 50
Sanitary facilities rating 8
small and intimate • swimming pool with three pools • very clean and well maintained • parachuting • mountain bike trails • Vannes (10 km)
Electric Hook-ups/amp 30/4-10

Three years ago, Françoise and Patrick Danard transformed part of their stud farm ('haras') into a campsite. The stud farm, built around buildings that the Germans used as garages for tanks in the Second World War, covers 40 hectares, 1 hectare of which is now the campsite. Although there is room for expansion, Campsite Le Haras will remain small and intimate for the time being. In addition to horse riding, you can go parachuting at the airport next door (no night flights).

The area is also perfect for mountain biking. Because the campsite is relatively new, there are not many high hedges or tall trees. The sanitary facilities are good. There is a swimming pool with three pools, a big slide and running water. Only the basic necessary provisions can be bought at the campsite, but there is a snack bar nearby; more facilities are planned over the next few years. In the summer, table tennis and handball contests are organised for the guests.

Sights worth seeing include Vannes (an old city with partially preserved ramparts), the countryside around the Golfe du Morbihan and the Musée de la Compagnie des Indes in the citadel at Port-Louis (opposite Lorient). This is not a campsite for those who enjoy the beach because the nearest one is 15 km away.

Domaine d' Inly

Rating 7.5
Tariff range €€€€
Town Pénestin
Department Morbihan
Postal code 56760
Map 1 C3
Tel 02-99903509
Fax 02-99904093
e-mail inly-info@wanadoo.fr
Open 14 Apr – 24 Sep

From La Roche-Bernard on D34, left at rdbt before Pénestin, then left again. After 1 km turn 1st right, 2nd left. Entrance in 2 km.

Size (hectares) 30
Touring pitches 100
Sanitary facilities rating 6.9
(partly) indoor swimming pool • own riding centre and fishing water • entertainment programme • beach at 1,500 m • Guérande (30 km)
Electric Hook-ups/amp 100/10

Twenty years ago the mayor of Pénestin opened D'Inly Campsite, and in the following years it became one of the finest in the region. Sadly it fell into disrepair, but Christophe Vigneron is now the owner, and thanks to his investment is returning to its former high quality.

The pitches on this huge site are grouped in circles which offer a lot of privacy, and there is also plenty of space between the tents. Shade is provided by the many old poplars and hedges, and green woodpeckers searching for ants in the grass are a constant source of interest. Apart from the usual facilities there is a riding centre on the campsite, as well as a fishing lake, a football pitch and a large swimming pool, partly indoors, with water slides. At the lakeside you can rent canoes and pedalos, but swimming is not permitted.

There is a restaurant, a snack bar, a bar with a terrace and a recreation room, while during the high season guests are entertained by an extensive amusement programme. The beach of La Mine d'Or is only 1,500m away, and there are plenty of choices for a day trip.

Brittany

Les Iles

Rating	8.4
Tariff range	€€€€
Town	Pénestin
Department	Morbihan
Postal code	56760
Map	1 C3
Tel	02-99903024
Fax	02-99904455
e-mail	contact@camping-des-iles.fr
Open	01 Apr – 01 Oct

From Pénestin S over D201. Turn right after 3.5 km, left just before beach. Site close to Pointe du Bile, 5 km S of Pénestin.
Size (hectares) 4
Touring pitches 183
Sanitary facilities rating 8.5
good restaurant • special kids' club • cosy bar • beach within walking distance • nature reserve • Saint-Nazaire (40 km)
Electric Hook-ups/amp 183/6-10

The village of Pénestin lies on the banks of the Vilaine. You will find Les Iles a few kilometres south of the village, close to the Pointe du Bile, the beach and the sea. There are a number of tiny islands off the coastline that can be reached on foot at low tide. The campsite is split in two by a road, and most campers stay on the part that is facing the sea. The other side is occupied by mobile homes, and most of the sport and recreation facilities are also located there.

Due to exposure to the sea, trees cannot grow very high, though the willows give sufficient privacy and shade. Apart from a beach, Les Iles also offers the luxury of a large swimming pool with a terrace, next to the inviting bar. The restaurant serves delicious fish and meat dishes, as well as a take-away service for complete meals, pizzas and snacks. From Monday to Saturday there is a kids' club for guests between the age of 4 and 12.

The most important sight in the area is a nature reserve: Parc Naturel Régional de Brière is a vast swamp with a unique flora and fauna and a number of cultural features as well. For something completely different try a visit to the dockyards of Saint-Nazaire.

La Vallée du Ninian

Rating	8.4
Tariff range	€€
Town	Taupont
Department	Morbihan
Postal code	56800
Map	1 C4
Tel	02-97935301
Fax	02-97935727
e-mail	infos@camping-ninian.com
Open	15 Apr – 15 Sep

From Taupont N on D6. Just outside village turn left at site sign (2.5 km NW of Taupont).
Size (hectares) 2.7
Touring pitches 91
Sanitary facilities rating 8.3
fruit trees all around • quiet, intimate atmosphere • bar and shop • beach at Lac-au-Duc • swimming, windsurfing, angling • Ploërmel (5 km)
Electric Hook-ups/amp 91/3-10

Paul 'the Druid' Joubaud, his wife Marylène and his son Mickael own a special campsite that counts as one of the finest in Brittany. This site is hidden deep in the countryside, far from the noise of the town. Tents and caravans, with fruit trees all around, surround the farm house. The apples are used for apple cider, a process that takes place locally. The peaceful rural atmosphere is much commented on by visitors.

There is a heated swimming pool (July-August), and while the beach is quite a way away, you can go swimming, windsurfing and fishing in the Lac-au-Duc near Taupont with its supervised beach. The town of Ploërmel also has a 25m pool. In July and August a pizza van visits the site and the bar serves French fries. There is a weekly dance party in the same bar where owner Paul plays his accordion. You can also play 'quilles' (bowling), pétanque and a Dutch game named 'sjoelen' on an imported shuffleboard. The small shop sells basic articles, and of course the home-made apple cider. Shopping is available either in Ploërmel or Josselin (souvenirs), or the Friday morning market in Ploërmel and the Saturday market in Josselin.

Les Cent Vignes

Rating 7.2
Tariff range €€€
Town Beaune
Department Côte-d'Or
Postal code 21200
Map 3 F1
Tel 03-80220391
Fax 03-80220391
Open 15 Mar – 31 Oct

A6, junct Beaune follow 'Centre Ville' signs, Boulevard Circulaire (ring road). Towards Dijon, Rue du Faubourg-St-Nicolas, then 1st on left.

Size (hectares) 2
Touring pitches 117
Sanitary facilities rating 7.4

quiet city campsite • good starting point for trips • very clean sanitary facilities • well-known villages in the vicinity • Burgundy wine region • Beaune (0.5 km)

Electric hook-ups/amps 102/6

In France you occasionally find a campsite within the town limits, which is the case in Beaune. It is not just the town that is so attractive – the whole area, with its many famous vineyards is worth sticking around to see in a few day trips; an unusual place to visit is the old city hospital. It is a fairly simple site, but does have all the necessary facilities. There is no swimming pool of its own here, but there is one in the town about 800m away.

In spite of being set in the middle of Beaune this is above all a quiet campsite, which comes as a relief after a busy day of sightseeing. High trees and hornbeams separate the pitches (grass for tents, pebbles for caravans) and provide enough shelter from the sun. The shower cubicles are rather narrow, but the sanitary facilities are often praised by guests as being 'spick-and-span'. The only campers who may be disappointed are children because of the lack of swimming pool and games or entertainment. This will certainly be true for transit guests, although this campsite is often crowded as early as the start of the season.

Les Sources

Rating 7.7
Tariff range €€€
Town Santenay
Department Côte-d'Or
Postal code 21590
Map 3 F1
Tel 03-80206655
Fax 03-80206736
e-mail info@campingsantenay.com
Open 15 Apr – 31 Oct

From Beaune follow N74 to Châlon-sur-Saône, then take D974. In Santenay take D113a to Cheilly-les-Maranges. Right before rail crossing; site on right after 200mtrs.

Size (hectares) 3.1
Touring pitches 100
Sanitary facilities rating 8.2

simple and quiet • beautiful setting • brand new sanitary facilities • walking and cycling • extensive vineyards • Santenay (1 km)

Electric hook-ups/amps 100/6

On the outskirts of the neat winegrowers village of Santenay can be found this large and beautifully laid out campsite of Les Sources. It was modernised, and the washing and toilet complex is very well maintained. The friendly staff allow visitors to choose their own pitch, and there are sufficient trees all around to provide as much shade as necessary. The view over the vineyards is wonderful from every position. There is plenty of space for children to play, and though there is no swimming pool, guests can use the local pool free of charge.

No special entertainment is offered on the site, but children will enjoy the small sandy playground. Food in the restaurant is based on well known dishes like steak and chicken; there is also a take-away service with pizzas, chips, hamburgers and salads. A small shop sells bread, fresh produce and canned food. The tennis courts next to the site can be hired for a reasonable fee, and other games include bowling, table tennis and volleyball. The whole region is ideal for day trips through the vineyards by car, bicycle or on foot.

Le Lac de Panthier

Rating 7
Tariff range €€€
Town Vandenesse-en-Auxois
Department Côte-d'Or
Postal code 21320
Map 3 E1
Tel 03-80492194
Fax 03-80492580
e-mail info@lac-de-panthier.com
Open 06 Apr – 12 Oct
A6, junct Pouilly-en-Auxois. D18 to Créancey/ Vandenesse. Turn left, D97, left again after 2.5 km; follow signs. Or take A38 from Dijon, junct Pouilly-en-Auxois.
Size (hectares) 5.2
Touring pitches 207
Sanitary facilities rating 7.4
ideal for families • plenty of entertainment • on the border of a lake • water sport facilities • wine cellars and châteaux • Créancey (3 km)
Electric hook-ups/amps 205/6

The Lac de Panthier is a perfect campsite for watersport enthusiasts, and with its sand and pebble beaches it is also very suitable for swimming (under supervision) and sunbathing. Boating attracts lots of followers, so Lac de Panthier is a large and crowded site. One popular activity is to hire a canoe at the site and explore the lake by paddle-power. The site offers a perfect holiday for children, who can go boating, running, cycling, pony riding or dancing. There is always live music in the evening, produced by local bands or singers.

If the lake doesn't appeal to you particularly you can use the swimming pool. The pitches on this somewhat chaotic campsite are reasonably spacious, and surrounded by trees that provide the necessary shade and hedges to guarantee some privacy. There is a rather small shop and a restaurant for a quick meal. Washing and toilet facilities are adequate and clean. If you are interested in exploring more of the surrounding countryside, you are right in the heart of the wine region of Burgundy, the Côte d'Or. Large numbers of wine cellars and châteaux are crying out to be visited.

Les Mésanges

Rating 8.1
Tariff range €€
Town Montsauche-les-Settons
Department Nièvre
Postal code 58230
Map 3 E1
Tel/Fax 03-86845577
Open 01 May – 15 Sep
From N6 near Saulieu take D977 via Montsauche to Les Settons. Site on left.
Size (hectares) 5
Touring pitches 100
Sanitary facilities rating 8.1
ideal for families • quiet and spacious • in the middle of nature • Lac des Settons • Parc du Morvan • Montsauche-les-Settons (5 km)
Electric hook-ups/amps 100/4-16

Les Mésanges is set in the middle of the tourist bustle on the banks of the Lac des Settons in the Parc du Morvan, but offers an unexpected amount of space to move around and relax. Both boating types and lovers of nature are sure to enjoy it here. The lake, only 150m away, is suitable for swimming and all kinds of watersports. Most of all it is a great place for children.

The woods of the Morvan region are ideal for a good walk or a bicycle ride. There are plenty of pleasant spots for a family picnic, or you can try your luck as an angler. The friendly staff will show you where to camp on the spacious and well kept grounds. Trees provide the necessary shade (although not that much in the new section), and hedges prevent your neighbours from watching your every move. The washing and toilet facilities are decent and clean, but children may find it difficult to operate the showers. A snack bar and a small shop are all that is provided in the way of food. There may be many rules and regulations here, but that just makes this a well-organised campsite.

Municipal Les Feuilles

Rating	7.5
Tariff range	€€
Town	Chauffailles
Department	Saône-et-Loire
Postal code	71170
Map	5 G6
Tel	03-85264812
Fax	03-85265502
e-mail	st.mairie.chauffailles@wanadoo.fr
Open	01 May – 30 Sep

From D985 into village. Site just S of village and signed.

Size (hectares) 4

Touring pitches 60   **Static pitches** 10

Sanitary facilities rating 7.8

pleasant atmosphere • cosy and quiet • spacious • castles and abbeys • nature, walking • Chauffailles (1 km)

Electric hook-ups/amps 60/5-10

Camping Municipal Les Feuilles is certainly not a place for campers who demand the sort of facilities and entertainment that turn a campsite into a leisure park. But anyone looking for silence, clean sanitary facilities and a pleasant atmosphere will feel at home. The majority of people who stay here are walkers and wine lovers who want to taste the famous wines of the Beaujolais region right on the spot. Others may prefer a visit to the many castles and abbeys in the area. The site is well maintained and attractive with its high trees and neatly trimmed hedges, and some really spacious pitches.

There is no swimming pool, but guests may use the municipal pool (200m away). It has a paddling pool and there is an attendant who keeps an eye on the swimmers. The river that runs through the camping grounds is not suitable for swimming, but paddling in it can be fun on a hot day. Most importantly, there are plenty of shady places for when the temperature rises. With nothing much in the way of entertainment apart from playing pétanque and wine tasting, this is primarily a campsite where silence should be respected.

Village des Meuniers

Rating	8.2
Tariff range	€€€€
Town	Dompierre-les-Ormes
Department	Saône-et-Loire
Postal code	71520
Map	5 H6
Tel	03-85503660
Fax	03-85503661
e-mail	contact@villagedesmeuniers.com
Open	01 May – 30 Sep

A6, junct Mâcon, then N79. From centre of Dompierre-les-Ormes follow site signs.

Size (hectares) 4

Touring pitches 113

Sanitary facilities rating 8

laid out on a slope • quiet family camp site • plenty of sports and games • Cluny, Clayette, Charolles • good walking area nearby • La Clayette (19 km)

Electric hook-ups/amps 113/16

Well kept and spacious are two descriptions that apply well to the Village des Meuniers in Dompierre-les-Ormes. Guests are treated to a musical welcome by a pianist at a special newcomers' party, and lots of flowers and plants contribute to the pleasant appearance of the site. Good, clean and spacious washing facilities are another plus here, along with a fine swimming pool with lockers and changing rooms.

The site is laid out on the slope of a hill with a wonderful view. Basic necessities are on sale in the shop, like bread, milk and some canned food. Lots of entertainment including cabaret, live music, a kids' club and competitions (a daily pétanque championship for example). For a change you could try a game of basketball or volleyball, relax beside the fish pond or compete in a game of water polo. The pitches are surrounded by bushes and offer a lot of much-needed privacy.

Pretty villages like Cluny (site of the famous monastery), La Clayette and Charolles are not far away, and neither are the extensive vineyards that spread throughout the countryside.

Burgundy

Château de l' Épervière

Rating 9
Tariff range €€€€
Town Gigny-sur-Saône
Department Saône-et-Loire
Postal code 71240
Map 5 H6
Tel 03-85941690
Fax 03-85941697
e-mail info@domaine-eperviere.com
Open 29 Mar – 30 Sep

A6, junct Châlon-Sud, follow N6 to Sennecy-le-Grand. E over D18 to Gigny; route signed.

Size (hectares) 7
Touring pitches 125
Sanitary facilities rating 9

situated in a castle garden • plenty of luxury • perfect for families • it's the entertainment that does the trick • vineyards all around • Sennecey-le-Grand (5 km)

Electric hook-ups/amps 125/10

Le Château de l'Épervière is located in the gardens of a picturesque 16th-century castle. Trees which are more than 200 years old add to the beauty of the setting. There are two swimming pools, a jacuzzi and a sauna to add a touch of luxury to the amenities.

In the excellent restaurant there is a choice of regional specialities, and the food is of a very high standard. The genuine foie gras well worth sampling. For those who prefer to make their own meals there is a wide selection of fresh produce in the shop. You stand little chance of getting bored here: wine tasting events, a disco, live performances, children's playgrounds, sports competitions and a fish pond are all there to provide entertainment.

You can also rent a bike for a day trip over the relatively flat roads through the vineyards. A special team of entertainers is even employed to amuse the kids, so you can relax in the knowledge that they are in good hands. The owners are very proud of their clean new sanitary facilities, and they have every reason to be.

Le Lac

Rating 8.5
Tariff range €€
Town Palinges
Department Saône-et-Loire
Postal code 71430
Tel 03-85881449
e-mail camping.palinges@hotmail.fr
Open 01 Apr – 30 Oct

On N70, S of Montceau, to Palinges. Pass village church and turn left. Site on right, 800mtrs from centre and 4 km from N70.

Size (hectares) 1.6
Touring pitches 44
Sanitary facilities rating 8.6

quiet and pleasant • very clean sanitary facilities • friendly owner • biking and walking • boat trips on the canal • Paray (15 km)

Electric hook-ups/amps 36/8-20

Jean Bernard takes every opportunity to make life easy and pleasant for his guests. He takes the initiative whenever necessary and has a fair knowledge of English. But Le Lac has more to offer than a kind and concerned owner. Its limited size guarantees a quiet and relaxed atmosphere, reinforced by its charming location in a hilly landscape beside a small lake. The trees have not yet fully grown, but mature hedges separate the pitches and offer adequate privacy. A modest meal can be bought from the snack bar.

For the energetic there is always a game of volleyball to be enjoyed, or you can go horse riding or take a bike for a tour along the canal. Part of the lake is marked as a swimming area. Entertainment for children is limited to a playing room with a TV set, but they can also go fishing or swimming in the lake. Teenagers can go horseriding or learn to play golf. There is not much going on in the evening, but this is one of the reasons for this site being so popular with holidaymakers. What strikes visitors most are the extremely clean and well kept sanitary facilities.

Parc des Loisirs le Val Fleuri

Rating	7.5
Tariff range	€€€
Town	Cloyes-sur-le-Loir
Department	Eure-et-Loir
Postal code	28220
Map	2 C2
Tel	02-37985053
Fax	02-37983384
e-mail	info@parc-de-loisirs.com
Open	15 Mar – 15 Nov

From N10 take D35 to junct Parc de Loisirs (right), W of Cloyes.

Size (hectares) 6
Touring pitches 83
Sanitary facilities rating 7.6
quiet family camp site • spacious lay-out • large play- ground • beautiful castles • Grottes du Foulon • Cloyes (1 km)
Electric Hook-ups/amp 83/6-10

Parc des Loisirs, the spacious municipal campsite at Cloyes, is set on the banks of the River Loir (not Loire!). It lies at the foot of a wooded hill, and the grounds are filled with trees and shrubs. Pitches offer sufficient privacy, and the sanitary facilities are perfectly acceptable. Swimming in the Loir is not allowed, but next to the site is a swimming pool which has a number of water slides. The many activities during the high season are organised with the motto: 'Fun for the kids, relaxation for the parents'. Children can use the playground and the play garden, ride ponies, use pedalos, go canoeing, play mini golf or jump on the trampoline.

There is a pleasant restaurant as well as a cosy bar with take-away meals, but eating out means going to the nearby village of Cloyes. You can take enjoyable day trips to the many castles in this region, like Château de Châteaudun and the superb Château Monitgny-le-Gannelon, and there are plenty of parks and gardens which can be discovered in a special brochure. If you fancy a day in a cave, head for the Grottes du Foulon in Châteaudun.

Municipal du Pré de l'Église

Rating	7.9
Tariff range	€€
Town	St-Rémy-sur-Avre
Department	Eure-et-Loir
Postal code	28380
Map	2 C3
Tel	02-37489387
Fax	02-37488015
Open	07 Apr – 30 Sep

From Evreux take N154 to Dreux. A few km past St-Lubin-des-Joncherets take road to St-Rémy-sur-Avre; then follow signs.

Size (hectares) 0.7
Touring pitches 38   **Static pitches** 7
Sanitary facilities rating 8
not expensive • good transit camp site • located in a small town • interesting towns • angling • Dreux (10 km)
Electric Hook-ups/amp 38/10

The calm and peaceful municipal campsite in Saint-Rémy-sur-Avre is located on the main route connecting Paris with Alençon, making it a good transit site for those who are on their way to the south. Only French is spoken at reception, so brush up on some useful phrases first! The pitches are spacious, and the sanitary facilities well kept and clean, though there are only a few trees and hedges around the campsite. A small playground and a table tennis table are the only recreational facilities, but if you like fishing, you can try your luck in the nearby river or in a little lake.

Saint-Rémy-sur-Avre may be just a small town, but there are sports grounds, tennis courts and of course shopping here. There is even a small railway station! For a relaxing stroll after a hard day's driving you can go to the library, walk along the promenade or saunter past the picnic spots. The bridge in the Rue du Vieux-Pont that crosses the River Avre is a peaceful place on a summer afternoon, and here you will find a number of restaurants and hotels. The town of Dreux lies 10 km to the east, and Paris is less than an hour away.

Central France

Municipal La Ruelle aux Loups

Rating 7.7
Tariff range €€
Town Vatan
Department Indre
Postal Code 36150
Map 2 C1
Tel 02-54499137
Fax 02-54499372
e-mail tourisme@vatan-en-berry.com
Open 26 Apr – 14 Sep
Take exit 10 off A20 (Vierzon-Châteauroux). At town hall in Vatan, take road towards Guilly. Site on left after 200mtrs.
Size (hectares) 2
Touring pitches 52
Sanitary facilities rating 6.9
well-tended transient campsite • countryside atmosphere • inexpensive • Valencay château • Lentil festival in Vatan • Issoudun (20 km)
Electric hook-ups/amps 46/6-16

Municipal la Ruelle aux Loups is an easy-to-access municipal campsite, located alongside the A20, between Vierzon and Châteauroux, and surrounded by the hills of Indre and de Berry. The rural atmosphere with the rustic pond to the side of the site gives it a park-like ambience. Different types of camping areas range from large, open spaces (on the main field) to enclosed spots offering plenty of privacy. It also features several courtyards-cum-playing areas. The municipality of Vatan keeps the sanitary facilities exceptionally clean.

Although bread is sold (daily deliveries at 8.15am), groceries are only available from the village shop just around the corner. The municipal pool alongside the campsite offers facilities for children, who will also find playing apparatus near the pond, and a table-tennis table in the recreation room; the gravelled paths are ideal for a game of pétanque. Special children's entertainment programmes are arranged during the high season. The region is well-known for its gastronomy, and the local products, which include honey, goat's cheese and green lentils (from Berry), are well worth a try.

Les Grands Pins

Rating 7.6
Tariff range €€€
Town Velles
Department Indre
Postal Code 36330
Map 2 C1
Tel 02-54366193
Fax 02-54361009
e-mail contact@les-grands-pins.fr
Open 01 Mar – 30 Dec
A20 (N to S), take exit 14. Onto D920 (previously N20) towards 'Les Maisons Neuves'. Site approx 4 km from exit 14, directly E of A20 fly-over.
Size (hectares) 6
Touring pitches 52
Sanitary facilities rating 7.5
tranquillity and nature • free use of tennis court • good restaurant • medieval châteaux • Parc Mini-Châteaux • Velles (7 km)
Electric hook-ups/amps 52/10

Les Grands Pins is a spacious and exceptionally quiet campsite located in woody surroundings in the middle of the countryside. The free tennis court, shaded terrace, bar and restaurant are among its attractions. The restaurant caters for foreign guests who want to dine in typically French surroundings and it also sells ice-cream and French fries to take away. The pitches are scattered across a large open field though if you prefer a little more shade, ask for a spot underneath the large trees at the back of the site. The sanitary facilities are good and cleaned twice a day.

On the edge of the site you'll find a swimming pool, a mini golf course, a table-tennis table and a large recreation area, but there are no organised activities for children. The surrounding countryside – a combination of woods, gently sloping hills and fields – is a joy to explore, either on foot or by bicycle. The area boasts innumerable châteaux, including the La Ruelle and Le Château d'Azay-le-Ferron. Miniature versions of some of the most prominent châteaux are to be found at the Parc Mini-Châteaux in Amboise.

La Mignardière

Rating	8.3
Tariff range	€€€
Town	Ballan-Miré
Department	Indre-et-Loire
Postal code	37510
Map	2 B2
Tel	02-47733100
Fax	02-47733101
e-mail	info@mignardiere.com
Open	22 Mar – 19 Sep

From Tours take N10 S. Over River Cher bridge and turn right (D751 to Chinon). Right again at Campanile Hotel just before Ballan, follow signs.

Size (hectares) 3.5
Touring pitches 131
Sanitary facilities rating 8.5

family campsite • privacy and seclusion • good location • Loire châteaux • amusement park • Tours (5 km)

Electric Hook-ups/amp 131/6

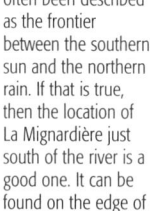

The Loire River has often been described as the frontier between the southern sun and the northern rain. If that is true, then the location of La Mignardière just south of the river is a good one. It can be found on the edge of a forest outside Ballan-Miré, where there are plenty of trees to provide the necessary shade. Pitches are surrounded by high hedges, making this site ideal for those who enjoy privacy and seclusion. It has an aquatic complex with three full-size pools and a large pool for children, a restaurant, and opposite the campsite is an amusement park which will keep the children happily occupied for hours. The playground and entertainment programme are intended for children aged up to 12.

It is not only the entertainment that counts here, as it is also a good starting point for a tour of the Loire châteaux. The Vallée des Rois (Valley of the Kings) with so many châteaux worth seeing, has made this region world famous. The most important ones are Chambord, with its decorative stairs, and Chenonceau, built over the River Cher. Château Villandry has extensive gardens that should be visited. The old town of Tours is only 5 km away, overlooking the Loire, where narrow streets, squares, restaurants, open-air cafés and a cathedral attract thousands of visitors.

Le Moulin Fort

Rating	8.5
Tariff range	€€€
Town	Chenonceaux
Department	Indre-et-Loire
Postal code	37150
Map	2 C1/2
Tel	02-47238622
Fax	02-47238093
e-mail	lemoulinfort@wanadoo.fr
Open	01 Apr – 30 Sep

Site 600mtrs from N76 (Vierzon-Tours); at Chenonceaux/Chisseaux junct take D80, and turn right just before bridge over River Cher. From N, turn left just after the bridge.

Size (hectares) 3
Touring pitches 137
Sanitary facilities rating 8.8

quiet and beautiful location • balloon rides • many activities • Château de Chenonceau • wine tasting • Montrichard (6 km)

Electric Hook-ups/amp 110/6

Le Moulin Fort is set on the banks of the River Cher, right in the middle of the French countryside. A corn mill was built 150 years ago for Château de Chenonceau, a castle that straddles the broad river just 1 km away. The mill now serves as the campsite restaurant where, for a reasonable price, you can order a 'salade tourangelle' or other speciality dish of the Touraine region. The pitches are spacious and you can choose either a place in the sun or a shady spot near the river, from where you can immediately launch your canoe. The children will certainly enjoy playing in the paddling pool next to the swimming pool, or in the playground.

In peak season there is a full programme of activities for 4 to 14 year olds, and for adults there are entertainment evenings, wine tastings, moonlit walks, and canoe trips to the château. The nearby Parc Mini-Châteaux has an exhibition of models of the most famous castles in the Loire Valley; children will also enjoy the aquarium.

Le Jardin Botanique

Rating 7.8
Tariff range €€€
Town Limeray
Department Indre-et-Loire
Postal code 37530
Map 2 C2
Tel 02-47301350
Fax 02-47301732
e-mail info@camping-jardinbotanique.com
Open All year
Site (signed) S of Limeray, (N152 on side of Loire embankment).
Size (hectares) 1.5
Touring pitches 50
Sanitary facilities rating 8.3
casual atmosphere • trees and flowers • many activities • many large châteaux • cave dwellings • Amboise (6 km)
Electric Hook-ups/amp 50/10

As the name suggests, there are lots of trees and flowering shrubs at Le Jardin Botanique, and the flower pots and roses in bloom give this campsite a very colourful appearance. The owners, Bertrand and Chrystèle, who live on the site with their children, greet their guests by welcoming them at reception with refreshments. Most of the spacious pitches are surrounded by high hedges and have their own picnic table, and sanitary facilities are good and kept very clean.

Bertrand and Chrystèle organise all sorts of activities for every age: karaoke, a beauty contest for little girls, volleyball competitions, sangria tasting on Sundays, and a weekly 'minimarché' selling regional products, to name just a few. You can play tennis or table tennis and go swimming, while children will enjoy the toys provided in the recreation room. Or just relax under the trees, a popular occupation here. From Limeray (famous for its cave dwellings) you can tour the many châteaux in the area, such as Chenonceau, Blois and Amboise. Le Clos Lucé, where Leonardo da Vinci lived and died, is also worth a visit. And don't forget the Loire itself, where you can go angling, canoeing or kayaking.

Domaine Les Bois du Bardelet

Rating	8.6
Tariff range	€€€€
Town	Gien
Department	Loiret
Postal Code	45500
Map	2 D2
Tel	02-38674739
Fax	02-38382716
e-mail	contact@bardelet.com
Open	01 Apr – 30 Sep

From Gien towards Bourges on D940 (SE direction). Turn left after approx 4 km, take D53 towards Autry-le-Chatel. Follow site signs.

Size (hectares) 18

Touring pitches 130   **Static pitches** 45

Sanitary facilities rating 8.6

strict rules • plenty of sports activities • entertainment • hunting museum in Gien • walks and cycling trips • Gien (6 km)

Electric hook-ups/amps 130/10

Sunêlia Les Bois du Bardelet is located near the River Loire, in one of the more popular regions of France where many families spend their summer holidays. As the campsite is very busy during the high season, the proprietors have come up with a number of rules, which are strictly enforced. As a consequence, the site is quiet after 11pm. The large pitches offer sufficient privacy, while the sanitary fittings are kept reasonably clean.

Children tend to have a great time here: the swimming pool – there is no pool attendant, so you'll have to keep an eye on them – is Mickey Mouse shaped and there are also several learners' pools, surrounded by a large sun terrace, and a new aquatic centre. Small children will enjoy the entertainment programmes (handicraft, dancing and sports), and teenagers and adults can take part in a variety of sports. Food and drinks are available from the bar, and the site has its own supermarket. If you fancy a day trip, why not visit the witchcraft museum in Blancafort? There are plenty of great walks in the area, and if you enjoy cycling and visiting châteaux you're in for a real treat.

Le Château des Marais

Rating	8.5
Tariff range	€€€€
Town	Muides-sur-Loire
Department	Loir-et-Cher
Postal code	41500
Map	2 C2
Tel	02-54870542
Fax	02-54870543
e-mail	chateau.des.marais@wanadoo.fr
Open	16 May – 30 Sep

Site 1 km S of Muides. Take D112 to Chambord, then turn right.

Size (hectares) 8

Touring pitches 130

Sanitary facilities rating 8.6

quiet and spacious • entertainment for children • spotless sanitary facilities • châteaux • cycling tours • Blois (19 km)

Electric Hook-ups/amp 130/6-10

Le Château des Marais is the sort of fairy tale castle for which the Loire Valley is famous. In its park you will find this campsite of the same name, close to the small town of Chambord. There are some 200 pitches, some of which are reserved for tour operators, and quite a few people use it as a transit site on their way south. Many tourists choose to explore the Loire region and stay here for their whole holiday. This luxurious campsite is set between meadows and forests so, no matter whether you prefer shade or sunshine, there is always a place to suit your taste. Fittingly, the sanitary facilities are outstanding, and the shop sells delicious home-made croissants and baguettes.

The partly-covered swimming pool complex, which features six pools and a paddling section, is not attended, so you will need to keep an eye on your children. They won't want to leave the large playground either, unless they are attracted by the morning entertainment programme, with one show for children aged 4 to 12, and the Magic Show for over-12s. The surrounding area is very attractive and famous for its châteaux, and the historic town of Blois with its Musée d'Histoire Naturelle is just 19 km away. South of Blois are the many forest lakes of Sologne.

Central France

Sologne Parc des Alicourts

Rating	8.5
Tariff range	€€€€
Town	Pierrefitte-sur-Sauldre
Department	Loir-et-Cher
Postal code	41300
Map	2 C2
Tel	02-54886334
Fax	02-54885840
e-mail	parcdesalicourts@yellohvillage.com
Open	30 Apr – 09 Sep

Site NE of Pierrefitte. On A71 turn off at Lamotte-Beuvron, take D923 E to Le Coudray.

Size (hectares) 8
Touring pitches 150
Sanitary facilities rating 8.7

quiet and spacious • fantastic swimming pool • especially child-friendly • beautiful castles • good walking and cycling • Orléans (45 km)

Electric hook-ups/amps 150/6

The Sologne Parc des Alicourts campsite is situated alongside a beautiful lake in the middle of the woods. The large pitches offer plenty of privacy and the sanitary facilities are brand new, with everything geared towards the family. The lake is open for swimming and fishing, but smaller children will prefer the swimming pool, with its areas all linked together. One of them has a wave machine, and the others have slides. Once the children are ready to get out of the water, a programme of activities awaits. Golf fanatics are well catered for here with a large golf course right next door.

Other sports fans are not left out as the site has its own mini golf, tennis, table tennis, volleyball court and football pitch. It is just as well that the campsite has its own supermarket because the nearest town with shops and restaurants is Orléans, 45km away. The surrounding area is perfect for long walks or cycle rides, and the area is dotted with beautiful châteaux which make for an excellent day out; the historic towns of Blois and Orléans, home of Joan of Arc, are worth a visit too.

Château de la Grenouillère

Rating	8.8
Tariff range	€€€€
Town	Suèvres
Department	Loir-et-Cher
Postal code	41500
Map	2 C2
Tel	02-54878037
Fax	02-54878421
e-mail	la.grenouillere@wanadoo.fr
Open	26 Apr – 06 Sep

A10 junct 16 (Mer-Chambord), then to Blois over N152. Site on right, 2 km beyond Mer, 2 km E of Suèvres.

Size (hectares) 11
Touring pitches 100
Sanitary facilities rating 8.7

beautiful setting • fine swimming pool • mobile homes for rent • castle routes • underground museum • Blois (16 km)

Electric Hook-ups/amp 100/6-10

Château de la Grenouillère is a luxurious campsite in the grounds of a château near the historic town of Blois on the Loire. It is a member of the 'Les Castels' chain that has been developing state of the art campsites around old buildings and on estates since 1959. History and modern comfort are combined here, where the large pitches provide a lot of privacy and the sanitary facilities are spacious and spotless. Next to the château is the swimming pool complex, with its extraordinary small bridges, exotic palm trees and rock gardens.

Naturally there is also a good restaurant and a shop. But though it is comfortable here, there is much to draw you away from the site. The surrounding area on the banks of the Loire, and especially around Blois, is beautiful, and there are wonderful châteaux, some of which are open to the public. You can also get maps with marked and unmarked walking and cycling routes, and just to the south of Blois there are dozens of tiny lakes in a vast woodland. Golfers will relish the course at Cheverny. Further away, in Bourré, is the fascinating underground museum 'Caves Champignonnières Ville Souterraine'.

Lac de Bairon

Rating 8
Tariff range €€
Town le Chesne
Department Ardennes
Postal code 08390
Map 3 E/F4
Tel 03-24301166
Fax 03-24301166
Open All year
From Sedan follow D977 until 2.5 km before Le Chesne. Turn right to Lac de Bairon; site signed.
Size (hectares) 6.8
Touring pitches 145   **Static pitches** 25
Sanitary facilities rating 7.9
rural environment • lake(side) recreation • quiet • rich in history • biking and hiking • Vouziers (20 km)
Electric hook-ups/amps 141/6-10

Breathtaking views over the lake and hills make Lac de Bairon a popular holiday choice for many. This jewel of a campsite can be found in the typical landscape of rural France that has barely changed over the centuries. Run by Dutch Antoinette and her French husband Jean-Luc Beaumont, it has plenty to offer besides gorgeous scenery. Guests of every generation will find pleasant recreational choices centred on the lake. A sailing school offers interesting opportunities for adults and children alike, and canoes and kayaks are available at the site. There are places to swim a short distance away, and there are ample facilities for the angler.

Away from the water you can ride a bike (your own or a rented one) through the hills of the French Ardennes. Privacy on site is limited, as the lakeside has an open aspect, but there is enough room for everyone. The grassy area is for longstay campers only, and those just passing through are directed towards hard standings. Washing facilities are constantly monitored and cleaned. Every morning the local baker visits the site, and during high season a mobile cafeteria serves meals.

Lac des Vieilles Forges

Rating 7.8
Tariff range €€
Town Les Mazures
Department Ardennes
Postal code 08500
Map 3 E5
Tel 03-24401731
Fax 03-24401731
Open All year
N51 to Givet-Fumay. Then take D988/D40 to Les Mazures. Follow signs to Lac des Vieilles Forges. Site 4 km SW of Les Mazures.
Size (hectares) 12
Touring pitches 277   **Static pitches** 10
Sanitary facilities rating 7.8
recreation on the lake • quiet site surrounded by nature • good facilities • walking and cycling • in the footsteps of Rimbaud • Charleville (15 km)
Electric hook-ups/amps 225/6-10

Lac des Vieilles Forges is a good example of what provincial authorities have done to make a lakeside as attractive as possible to visitors. Apart from a number of trees that disappeared to give more room for tents and caravans, nature has remained virtually untouched. The terraced campsite is set on a slope filled with old trees, so there is lots of greenery between the pitches. Toilet facilities are of an excellent standard. A children's playground keeps young ones happily occupied, and during the high season there are entertainment programmes for them as well.

The hills of the French Ardennes offer an irresistible invitation for long hikes or tough bicycle and mountain bike rides, while rowing equipment for use on the lake is available for hire on site. Even if the weather is disappointing, there is plenty here to entertain visitors, especially outdoor types. Ham from the Ardennes, tarte au sucre, quails with fresh mushrooms and blackberry cakes are all found on the menus of the local restaurants.

Champagne-Ardenne

Municipal

Rating 8
Tariff range €€€
Town Châlons-en-Champagne
Department Marne
Postal code 51000
Map 3 E4
Tel 03-26683800
Fax 03-26683800
e-mail camping.mairie.chalons@wanadoo.fr
Open 01 Apr – 31 Oct
On A4 take junct 27 and N44 to Châlons. From St.-Memmie site is well signed.
Size (hectares) 7.5
Touring pitches 148
Sanitary facilities rating 8.1
suitable for transit campers • cheap • friendly caretakers • wine museum • champagne tasting • Châlons-en-Champagne (3 km)
Electric hook-ups/amps 100/10

The municipal campsite at Châlons-en-Champagne is popular with British, German and Dutch campers travelling to and from the south. The site offers small pitches without any frills, but the washing and toilet facilities are good, and there are washing machines and tumble dryers.

Facilities for angling, tennis, table tennis and volleyball can all be found here, as well as a small playground, and there is a swimming pool in Châlons-en-Champagne (3 km). If your stay is a longer one you will certainly want to taste some local champagne, and there are many wine cellars in and around Epernay and Reims.

The Phare de Verzenay is also well worth a visit, where an exhibition shows the history of the production of sparkling wines; from this lighthouse you can overlook 'a sea of Champagne'. The local authorities of Châlons-en-Champagne offer an extra service to anyone wanting to stay at the campsite outside the normal season. Visitors should warn of their intended arrival one working day in advance by telephone.

Hautoreille

Rating 7.8
Tariff range €€
Town Bannes
Department Haute-Marne
Postal code 52360
Map 3 F2
Tel 03-25848340
Fax 03-25848340
e-mail campinghautoreille@orange.fr
Open All year
Site lies 500m S of Bannes. From N: A31, junct 8, D74 to Langres, just after Bannes turn left. From S: A31, junct 6, D428 to Langres. In Langres take D74 to Montigny-le-Roi.
Size (hectares) 3.5
Touring pitches 100
Sanitary facilities rating 8.2
well tended transit site • heated washing facilities • fine view • water sport • many lakes • Langres (10 km)
Electric hook-ups/amps 100/6

Hautoreille is a fine site hidden away in the hills, overlooking farmland with grazing cattle. Many campers choose it in order to visit the town of Langres, or as a transit site on the way south, and end up staying longer than originally planned. The washing and toilet facilities are decent and well maintained, while pitches are spacious and offer fine views. The little café and restaurant are pleasant places to linger in (or outside – this is France!), and make friends with people of many other nationalities.

As the washing facilities are heated in winter, many campers who are heading south to Spain use this site en route. Langres itself is a pleasant place for shopping, strolling along the city walls or visiting a local museum. Children will enjoy the small beaches of the reservoirs nearby that offer good facilities for swimming, angling and water sport. You can also explore the area on foot or mountain bike, and nearby Chalindrey is known for its interesting fortresses. Opportunities for sports and games might be limited, but this will not affect your enjoyment of the campsite.

Du Château

Rating	7.3
Tariff range	€€
Town	Montigny-le-Roi
Department	Haute-Marne
Postal code	52140
Map	3 F2
Tel	03-25873893
Fax	03-25873893
e-mail	campingmontigny52@wanadoo.fr
Open	15 Apr – 15 Oct

Site E of Montigny-le-Roi. On A31 take junct 8 (Montigny-le-Roi). In village follow signs. Please note – steep hill, sharp bend to the left.

Size (hectares) 6
Touring pitches 75
Sanitary facilities rating 7
good transit site • clean and well tended • view from the hilltop • good possibilities for walking • lake district nearby (20 km) • Langres (25 km)
Electric hook-ups/amps 75/5

Du Château is idyllically located on the top of a hill where a castle once stood, with sheltered pitches (you can stay either downhill or on a terrace) that offer marvellous views. The whole place is very well maintained, with a fine lawn and good, clean toilet facilities. Small children will find a neat playground, and there are two tennis courts for their older relatives. There is also a small bar at reception where canned drinks are sold.

Like most mainly-transit sites, this one is full of life early in the morning and late in the afternoon, and very quiet during the day. From the grounds you can walk straight into a centuries-old small town, where you will find a bakery and a small supermarket. For a special treat buy a 'pain cuit au feu de bois' - a loaf of bread baked on a charcoal fire right behind the counter. On your way back from a holiday further south this is an ideal spot to prepare for the journey home. Many campers decide to do this, and then take a walk to L'Arcombelle restaurant for a good meal and a last taste of France. The owner speaks some English, which is always a help.

Le Val de Bonnal

Rating	8.1
Tariff range	€€€€
Town	Rougemont
Department	Doubs
Postal code	25680
Map	3 G2
Tel	03-81869087
Fax	03-81860392
e-mail	val-de-bonnal@wanadoo.fr
Open	08 May – 07 Sep

In village of Bonnal, 4 km N of Rougemont; signed from D9 and D50.

Size (hectares) 15
Touring pitches 170
Sanitary facilities rating 7.7
lakeside location • good swimming pool • varied plantation • all kinds of water sport • route through flower villages • Villersexel (12 km)
Electric hook-ups/amps 170/5

The entrance to Le Val de Bonnal looks inviting, with its large terrace, épicerie, snack bar with chairs and take-away service, and a restaurant with a wide choice of menus. Selecting your pitch can be a bit of a dilemma: do you choose to be near the river that runs alongside the site, in one of the shady parts, or at the rear of the park where the hedges allow the sun in? The children will make a beeline for the pool with its terrific water slides. There is also a lake, with swimming (under supervision), pedalos, windsurfing, sailing, waterskiing, angling - in fact everything geared towards the watersports enthusiast.

On the campsite you can play table tennis, boules (with competitions) or go to the disco. The latter may be noisy, but is well policed by the staff. The sanitary facilities are acceptable and clean, though they lack any luxury. Day trips can be made to Besançon for a boat tour through the old town, and the Thursday morning market in Vesoul is the best in the region, and highly recommended. The Route des Villages Fleuris (through villages with an abundance of flower decorations) is fascinating.

Franche-Comté

La Broche

Rating	6.5
Tariff range	€€
Town	Fresse
Department	Haute-Saône
Postal code	70270
Map	3 G2
Tel	03-84633140
Fax	03-84633140
e-mail	contact@camping-broche.com
Open	15 Apr – 15 Oct

From Lure follow D486 N to Mélisey. 2.5 km beyond village turn right & take D97 to Fresse. Site on right (signed).

Size (hectares) 2.7
Touring pitches 44
Sanitary facilities rating 6.8

situated on a lake • helpful owner • playground, table tennis • walking area • Ballon d'Alsace • Lure (19 km)

Electric hook-ups/amps 30/10

Owner Alain Ferretti welcomes everyone with a message on the notice board: 'Dear camper, you can select your own pitch. If you need any advice, for instance about walking or sightseeing, or whenever there are any problems, like a puncture, do come to me. I shall do my best to help you.' At La Broche there is a large, partly open space with simple dishwashing facilities, a refrigerator with a freezing compartment for general use, and a large table covered with a plastic cloth where you can eat and read. This is the nucleus of the campsite, with its clean and well-maintained sanitary facilities.

From one of the terraces you can enjoy a good view over the pond, where fishing is allowed on the condition that any fish you catch are thrown back in. Another popular area is at the back of the site where the high pine trees give plenty of shade, and a number of picnic tables can be found for campers' use. Table tennis, a small playground and the paddling pond are provided for the children. Importantly, there is a bakery in the village. Some suggestions for a day trip include a visit to Belfort with its citadel, museums and shops, to Luxeuil-les-Bains, to the top of the Ballon d'Alsace, or to the Peugeot Museum in Sochaux.

L'Abbaye

Rating	7.8
Tariff range	€€
Town	Bonlieu
Department	Jura
Postal code	39130
Map	6 B6
Tel	03-84255704
Fax	03-84255082
e-mail	camping.abbaye@wanadoo.fr
Open	01 May – 30 Sep

1.5 km E of Bonlieu on N78.

Size (hectares) 4.5
Touring pitches 77
Sanitary facilities rating 8.4

spacious, open, quiet • many young families • own restaurant • Cascades de l'Hérisson • walking and cycling • Clairvaux-les-Lacs (10 km)

Electric hook-ups/amps 49/6

Once the site of an abbey beside the lake you will now find L'Abbaye, a quiet campsite in the heart of the Parc Naturel Régional du Haut-Jura. Lake Bonlieu is an ideal spot for peace and meditation. Swimming in the lake is not allowed, though the quieter sport of angling is. A beautiful footpath leads around the lake in the shade of the pine forest. The spectacular waterfalls of Hérisson are only a few kilometres away. This oasis of calm is very popular with young families who don't need to be entertained here, but prefer to explore the area on their own.

The campsite's spacious restaurant with its sunny terrace serves good regional dishes; morilles, a mushroom dish, is a house speciality. Every Monday Madame Roz organises a 'dégustation', a wine-tasting ceremony to get new visitors acquainted with Jura wines. The tent pitches are located around a small playground where parents can easily keep an eye on their children. Further away, along pretty lanes, are the caravan pitches. The site is open and light, and though some pitches are well sheltered, others are not.

Franche-Comté

Fayolan

Rating 8.1
Tariff range €€€€
Town Clairvaux-les-Lacs
Department Jura
Postal code 39130
Map 6 B6
Tel 03-84252619
Fax 03-84252620
e-mail reservation@RS139.com
Open 30 Apr – 14 Sep
From Clairvaux-les-Lacs follow D118 to Châtel-de-Joux. Turn right at town outskirts; site 500mtrs ahead.
Size (hectares) 17
Touring pitches 468 **Static pitches** 3
Sanitary facilities rating 8
friendly reception • lots of fun • swimming pool with attendants • Parc naturel régional du Haute-Jura • Cascades de l'Hérisson • Clairvaux-les-Lacs (1 km)
Electric hook-ups/amps 468/6

As a guest of Camping Fayolan you will be welcomed with a free drink. This large family campsite on the banks of Lake Fayolan offers a wide variety of amenities so it would be hard to be bored here.
There's a shop selling a good range of products, and a restaurant serving excellent pizzas. You won't even have to leave the site to find a cash dispenser (ATM), an internet point or a place to play boules or go for a stroll in the late afternoon.

There are music shows and dance parties every evening; or you can see a fakir perform, or take part in aquagym. Archery, beach volleyball, water polo and table tennis are all available, and the forest is a delightful place for a walk. After such strenuous activities you can relax on the sunbathing platform with a fine view over the lake. The children's swimming pool with supervised water slide is highly popular. The pitches are separated by hedges or the odd pine tree, which allows for plenty of sunshine but not a lot of privacy. Some of the best pitches can be booked through a booking agency that offers complete camping arrangements.

Beauregard

Rating 8
Tariff range €€€
Town Clairvaux-les-Lacs
Department Jura
Postal code 39130
Map 6 B6
Tel 03-84483251
Fax 03-84483351
e-mail reception@juracampingbeauregard.com
Open 01 Apr – 30 Sep
From Lons-le-Saunier follow N78 towards Geneva. In Thuron take D151 to Mesnois. Site on left (1.5 km).
Size (hectares) 6
Touring pitches 181 **Static pitches** 6
Sanitary facilities rating 8.1
rural setting • suitable for children • good restaurant • caves • Cascades de L'Hérisson • Clairvaux-les-Lacs (2 km)
Electric hook-ups/amps 181/6

Camping Beauregard, situated in the hills of the Jura region, is quiet, open, smallish and easy to explore. Broad, straight lanes lead to the pitches that are separated from each other by low hedges.
Everything is well looked after, and the sanitary facilities are extremely clean. From your tent or caravan you can watch the cows grazing between the green hills, and it comes as no surprise to learn that Beauregard started out as a 'camping à la ferme' for only six tents. It has a good restaurant of its own, serving not only pizzas and French fries, but also regional dishes.

The site is frequented by families with children under the age of 14, since there is not much for teenagers to do. The greatest attractions are the tennis courts and the large swimming pool. For the safety of the youngest swimmers there is a fence separating the paddling pool from the main pool. A stay at this site would not be complete without a visit to the Jura lakes and the waterfalls of Hérisson, where the river comes thundering down in six stages. A river nearby is suitable for canoeing, swimming or building dams.

Le Pasquier

Rating 8
Tariff range €€€
Town Dole
Department Jura
Postal code 39100
Map 3 F1
Tel 03-84720261
Fax 03-84792344
e-mail lola@camping-le-pasquier.com
Open 01 Mar – 30 Oct
Site S of Dole (S of Doubs River). In Dole follow signs.
Size (hectares) 1.8
Touring pitches 120   **Static pitches** 1
Sanitary facilities rating 8.2
international site • well situated • both vivid and quiet • wine route and caves • Louis Pasteur Museum • Dole (1 km)
Electric hook-ups/amps 120/6-10

On entering Dole you will be immediately struck by the town's pleasant setting near the river. At the reception desk you can register with Nathalie or Dominique and choose a place in the shade on this well laid out campsite. The pleasant international atmosphere is conducive to making friends with fellow campers from all over Europe. Le Pasquier is both lively and quiet at the same time, and appeals to all kinds of people. The washing and toilet facilities are acceptable and clean, and there is beautiful lawn and a nice open-air café where you can enjoy a simple meal or a drink.

Walking to Dole is a pleasant five-minute stroll with much to see on the way: boats moored in the river by their skippers, and a colourful collection of local people and campers playing football add to the interest. Once across the bridge you can visit the house where Louis Pasteur was born. There are quite a few shops and cafés to discover, plus a market which is held here three times a week. Children will enjoy being taken to the Aquapark with its water slides and playgrounds.

Domaine de Chalain

Rating 8
Tariff range €€€€
Town Doucier
Department Jura
Postal code 39130
Map 3 F1
Tel 03-84257878
Fax 03-84257006
e-mail chalain@chalain.com
Open 25 Apr – 23 Sep
Site 2 km E of Doucier. From village centre follow signs to Domaine de Chalain.
Size (hectares) 30
Touring pitches 565   **Static pitches** 30
Sanitary facilities rating 7.8
lakeside location • indoor and outdoor pools • suitable for all ages • excursions to lakes and waterfalls • walking and biking • Lons-Le-Saunier (27 km)
Electric hook-ups/amps 480/7

Domaine de Chalain is idyllically set on the banks of a lake, offering lots of opportunities for swimming, boating, windsurfing and playing. Children will enjoy the swimming pool, and will quickly find the places to hang around and play video games. Little children will want to spend hours in the indoor or outdoor pool (with water slides, waterfalls and bridges). You can choose a pitch near the lake, on the hill, or in between the two, either in the shade or partly in the sun. Sanitary facilities are reasonable, and there is a small shopping centre next to the site. Other amenities include a restaurant, a snack bar, a pleasant café with a typical French interior and terrace, and a table tennis centre.

You can play beach volleyball or enjoy the entertainment: the peace can be disturbed when the disco closes, though security staff take measures to reduce the noise. Try a tour round the lakes and to the caves and waterfalls, see the sights in Lons-Le-Saunier, hike in the Cirque de Baume or travel as far as Switzerland (25 km). You can use the campsite as a starting point for walking, cycling or embarking on a mountain bike tour.

Trélachaume

Rating 7.9
Tariff range €€€
Town Maisod
Department Jura
Postal code 39260
Map 6 B6
Tel 03-84420326
Fax 09-59737470
e-mail info@camping-trelachaume.com
Open 19 Apr – 06 Sep
Site S of Maisod, 800mtrs from east bank of Lac de Vouglans. Follow signed route from D470.
Size (hectares) 3.5
Touring pitches 164
Sanitary facilities rating 7.9
quiet area • personal approach • good entertainment • Jura lakes • Cascades de l'Hérisson • Moirans-en-Montagne (6 km)
Electric hook-ups/amps 105/6-16

Camping Trélachaume is a great place for boating fans and hikers who want to avoid the overcrowded banks of Lac de Vouglans. The site lies on a hill overlooking the lake, but it is still a long walk down to the shoreline. La Mercantine, a modest beach where you can buy an ice cream or a pizza from an old Citroen van, is the nearest place to go. You also have to go a long way to do your daily shopping, but on the other hand Trélachaume is the perfect spot for those who are seeking some peace and silence.

Its charm lies in its twisting tracks, higgledy-piggledy pitches, strewn rocks and plentiful hedges. If you want some privacy, you can find a spot on the higher grounds under the shelter of the bushes. Down by the busy pitches where you can play boules, the atmosphere is more like that of a bustling village. In a number of places camp fires are permitted in the late evening. On Mondays the owner invites her guests to share a glass of sangria, and she offers unusual entertainment on Trélachaume: hypnosis for adults, and magicians performing for the children.

La Pergola

Rating 8.9
Tariff range €€€€
Town Marigny
Department Jura
Postal code 39130
Map 3 F1
Tel 03-84257003
Fax 03-84257596
e-mail contact@lapergola.com
Open 01 May – 15 Sep
From Doucier follow D27 to Pont-du-Navoy. Site 3 km, on right, SE of Marigny.
Size (hectares) 10
Touring pitches 98
Sanitary facilities rating 8.9
terrace shaped and on a lake • swimming pool and playground • nice restaurant with open air section • all kinds of water sports • caves and waterfalls • Lons-Le-Sanier (25 km)
Electric hook-ups/amps 98/10

As soon as you enter La Pergola, the children will start to get excited. They will spot the table tennis centre where youngsters all hang out and friendships are quickly made. And then there is a lake with a beach, a great place for water sports. The climbing frame will also be a magnet for the younger kids.

You will probably have spotted the restaurant with its inviting open-air section. On the hillside there is a large swimming pool with deck chairs, a buffet with drinks and pancakes, and a view over the lake. Even higher up there is an open air theatre for evening entertainment, and where everyone goes dancing in the evening.

The pitches themselves are spacious and well kept, with some in the sun and some in the shade, and here and there a glimpse of the lake. The sanitary facilities are of a good standard and clean. Having dinner here is a great experience, both indoors and outside. The special menu is called the Franc-Comtois – put together by Gicquaire, her two brothers and friend Marco, who run the site together.

Franche-Comté

Les 3 Ours

Rating 7.7
Tariff range €€€
Town Montbarrey
Department Jura
Postal code 39380
Map 3 F1
Tel 03-84815045
Fax 03-84717754
e-mail camping.les.3.ours@free.fr
Open 01 May – 30 Sep
From Mont-sous-Vaudrey N over D11 to Montbarrey. Cross bridge over River Loue, site on left.
Size (hectares) 3
Touring pitches 100
Sanitary facilities rating 7.9
on a river • good restaurant • clean and well kept • Forêt de Chaux • Aquapark in Dole • Dole (20 km)
Electric hook-ups/amps 90/6-16

'The Three Bears' is the name of both the campsite and restaurant, called after a man who once trained two bears here, and reputedly had the strength of a bear himself. The current owner, Monsieur Joel, is more interested in cooking than bears. His restaurant is a lovely place for wining and dining after an aperitif in the small and cosy bar. The pitches are spacious and partly shady, with some sunny ones at the rear. Two neat and very clean buildings house the sanitary facilities, and there is a small tidy playground.

The river looks spectacular, and there is a very challenging passage for canoes that leads to a reservoir; when the water level is low you can swim and float in the sunshine. To the north lies the vast Forêt de Chaux, closed to motor cars but open to cyclists. A visit to Dole and its museums makes an interesting day trip, and its Aquapark is a children's paradise with its water slides and playground. In Arc-St-Senans you can see the Salines Royale, an example of innovative 18th-century architecture.

La Plage Blanche

Rating 8
Tariff range €€€
Town Ounans
Department Jura
Postal code 39380
Map 3 F1
Tel 03-84376963
Fax 03-84376021
e-mail reservation@la-plage-blanche.com
Open 01 Apr – 15 Oct
Site N of Ounans on River Loue. In Ounans (D472) take D71 to Montbarrey. Cross bridge (3 km) and turn left.
Size (hectares) 7
Touring pitches 211   **Static pitches** 6
Sanitary facilities rating 8.1
river and beach • swimming and paddling pool • there's something for everyone • Aquapark in Dole • Arc-et-Senans • Dole (20 km)
Electric hook-ups/amps 211/6

Even before you enter the campsite the children will have spotted a steeplechase course and a booking desk for raft or canoe trips. And there's more to come: in the evening they can sit by a camp fire on the pebble beach with fellow teenagers from all over Europe – all organised at their own initiative.

La Plage Blanche lies in an agricultural region in the Val d'Amour, stretching along the Loue River. When the water level is low, you can use the pebble beach to go swimming or sunbathing, or take a kayak or canoe; there is also a fine swimming pool with a paddling pool. The pitches are spacious and shady, and the sanitary facilities are clean.

The cosy restaurant offers a view of the river and good meals, and there is a small café for a drink and a sing-song in the evening. The weekly jazz sessions are not to be missed. Day trips can be made to Dole and its museums, Arbois, the Grotte de Planches and Arc-et-Senans. No cars are allowed in the vast Forêt de Chaux, which makes it pleasant to go cycling without being bothered; there is even a rather difficult mountain biking course.

Franche-Comté

Les Bords de la Loue

Rating 7.4
Tariff range €€
Town Parcey
Department Jura
Postal code 39100
Map 3 F1
Tel 03-84710382
Fax 03-84710342
e-mail contact@jura-camping.com
Open 15 Apr – 15 Sep

A39, junct Dole-Sud then N5 towards Genève. Turn right near Parcey, follow signs to site near sports ground.
Size (hectares) 17
Touring pitches 200
Sanitary facilities rating 7.8
quiet family site • on a river (beach) • swimming and paddling pool • Aquapark (Dole) • the town of Arbois • Dole (6 km)
Electric hook-ups/amps 200/6

Les Bords de la Loue is an elongated piece of land stretching along the river in the Val d'Amour. Depending on the level of the water, you can find a pebble beach for sunbathing, angling or watching the children swimming. Not far from the campsite you can take a canoe or kayak, and daredevils can book a guided river safari. You can even cycle through the Forêt de Chaux without being bothered by cars. The pitches themselves are spacious and shaded.

Two small buildings with adequately maintained sanitary facilities are provided, one of them better than the other. The swimming pool has a paddling pool for small children, and you can play tennis, table tennis, boules and volleyball (competition). Once a week there is a mobile discotheque with a popular karaoke. Because most people come here for a rest, the owner is reluctant to bring in anything else that would create noise. A visit to Dole, with its market, museums and the birthplace of Louis Pasteur is a good option for a day out. Take the children to the Aquapark in Dole. Salines Royale, an example of visionary 18th-century architecture (in Arc-et-Senans), has a good educational animation programme for young visitors.

L'Étang des Forges

Rating 8.3
Tariff range €€€
Town Belfort
Department Territoire de Belfort
Postal code 90000
Map 3 G2
Tel 03-84225492
Fax 03-84227655
e-mail contact@camping-belfort.com
Open All year

Site 1.5 km N of Belfort centre; follow signed routes from town centre.
Size (hectares) 3.4
Touring pitches 176 **Static pitches** 3
Sanitary facilities rating 8.5
on the border of a lake • overlooking a fortress • spacious stands • Ballon d'Alsace • Peugeot Museum in Sochaux • Belfort (1.5 km)
Electric hook-ups/amps 90/6

L'Étang des Forges with its international clientele is set between a residential area and a lake. The pitches are spacious, and rather open thanks to the young trees which allow fine views. In particular you can see over the Fort de la Miotte, part of a group of fortifications around Belfort that is waiting to be explored on bicycle.

The washing and toilet facilities are good and well maintained, but don't expect any entertainment or playing facilities on a site right in the middle of a town. A small playground, table tennis and volleyball, are all there is. If you want to keep fit you can join French holidaymakers on a 4-km run around the lake.

One of the main reasons for coming here is to visit Belfort, with its musical and theatre performances all through the summer. Take a stroll through the old town or the shopping streets, visit a museum, or take a trip to the Ballon d'Alsace. Luc, who runs the site with his partner Cyril, recommends the Peugeot Museum in Sochaux as the highlight of a visit; Cyril is also an author, whose books are on sale in reception.

Club Le Parc de Paris

Rating 8.1
Tariff range €€€€
Town Villevaudé
Department Seine-et-Marne
Postal code 77410
Map 2 D4
Tel 01-60262079
Fax 01-60270275
e-mail camping.leparc@club-internet.fr
Open 01 Jan – 31 Dec
From N on A104 take junct 6b near Francilienne; from Villeparisis follow D105 to Villevaudé. Site 200mtrs E of Montjay.
Size (hectares) 9
Touring pitches 168   **Static pitches** 162
Sanitary facilities rating 8.2
view over the Marne Valley • quiet and rural • comfort • close to Paris • Lake Jablines • Claye Souilly (5 km)
Electric hook-ups/amps 148/6

The incredible quiet of the woods and the Marne Valley are the first thing you notice on arrival at this very rural campsite. It is definitely not the sort of place for those seeking excitement and evening entertainment, but country lovers will find it hard to tear themselves away. One of its attractions is that you can cycle from the site along the Ourcq Canal to Notre Dame in the centre of Paris, as well as Disneyland or Parc Astérix. The same option for the less energetic is available by public transport from Porte de la Villette. Free parking for your car or bike at the station of the RER suburban railways is available.

The valley of the Marne River is a delightful place to explore whether on foot, by bike or by car. The pitches have been laid out against the terraced slope of a hill, and there are old broad-leaved trees here and there, though they don't offer much shade. Modern toilets with special facilities for young children are a welcome feature. There is a paddling pool and a playground, but swimmers go to Lake Jablines, some 5 km away.

Le Martinet Rouge

Rating 7.4
Tariff range €€€
Town Brousses-et-Villaret
Department Aude
Postal Code 11390
Map 5 F2
Tel 06-19344160
Fax 04-68265198
e-mail campinglemartinetrouge@orange.fr
Open 15 May – 08 Sep
On A61 take Carcassonne-Ouest exit onto western ring road then D118 to Pezens. In Pezens, turn right immediately after bridge. Take D48 towards Broussens-et-Villaret. Site outside village on left.
Size (hectares) 2.7
Touring pitches 47
Sanitary facilities rating 7.3
easy going family campsite • green and hilly • countless sporting activities • caves and monasteries • cycling and hiking routes • Carcassonne (9 km)
Electric hook-ups/amps 47/6

Le Martinet Rouge is a cosy, easy-going campsite situated in hilly surroundings, where seekers of peace and quiet will feel at home. A lot of building is going on – including a beautiful gazebo full of climbing plants behind the campsite. Once a week, long trestle tables are set for a menu that varies from paella to cassoulet de Castelnaudary (white beans, pâté, garlic and bacon). Needless to say, the wine flows freely.

The French guests come here specifically for the peace and quiet, while foreign guests often seem to prefer some action. In addition to the swimming pool, there are countless other sporting activities on offer, including: basketball, volleyball, badminton and billiards and a gym next to the swimming pool. You will find plenty to do away from the campsite as well. The medieval citadel of Carcassonne with its impressive city walls and beautiful castle is worth a visit, as is the Château de Saissac, or perhaps a monastery or some caves. The Montagne Noir is easily accessible, and the forests have marked hiking and cycling routes.

Domaine d'Arnauteille

Rating	7.8
Tariff range	€€€€
Town	Montclar
Department	Aude
Postal Code	11250
Map	5 F2
Tel	04-68268453
Fax	04-68269110
e-mail	arnauteille@mnet.fr
Open	30 Mar – 03 Oct

Follow D118 towards Carcassonne-Quillan. 15km S of Carcassonne take D43 towards Montclar. Narrow, steep road to site (well signed).
Size (hectares) 7
Touring pitches 99
Sanitary facilities rating 7.9
very large grounds • sportive programme for children • stables • a variety of water sports • Cathar forts • Limoux (8 km)
Electric hook-ups/amps 99/6-16

The extremely large Domaine d'Arnauteille campsite lies in the Malepère Massif. The site offers very spacious, terraced pitches with a feel of luxury, and excellent sanitary facilities. Forests stretch out as far as the eye can see - from the Corbières to the Montagne Noir, an ideal spot for active campers. The site has its own stables for horse riding as well as its own instructors. In addition to excellent bridle paths, there are marked hiking and cycling routes, and you can hire a mountain bike at reception. Once a week, campers can travel by van to the river for a raft trip.

For children aged between 4 and 12, there are organised sports activities every morning. There are table tennis tables, a volleyball court and a lovely swimming pool, and 5km away you'll find a beach suitable for windsurfing. You can discover the ruins of Cathar forts in the near vicinity and visit historic towns and cities like Carcassonne. A visit to the markets of Limoux is well worthwhile: the town lies 8 km away from the campsite and is home to the blanquette de Limoux, a sparkling wine that is older than champagne.

Les Mimosas

Rating	7.8
Tariff range	€€€€
Town	Narbonne
Department	Aude
Postal Code	11100
Map	5 F2
Tel	04-68490372
Fax	04-68493945
e-mail	info@lesmimosas.com
Open	21 Mar – 01 Nov

From A9 take Narbonne-Sud exit. Left at rdbt towards La Nautique, follow signs. Site in Mandirac, 6 km S of Narbonne.
Size (hectares) 9
Touring pitches 250   **Static pitches** 30
Sanitary facilities rating 8.2
three luxurious swimming pools • sauna and library • surrounded by vineyards • close to sandy beaches • fishing and windsurfing • Narbonne (6 km)
Electric hook-ups/amps 220/6

Les Mimosas family campsite has a fantastic location, and with so many on-site activities, you will hardly want to leave. There are three swimming pools with four slides, a waterfall and a separate toddler's pool with a water mushroom. A club card gives you access to the mini golf, tennis courts, gym, sauna and library for the duration of your stay. The card also gives access to organised sports, games and dancing.

You can fish and windsurf in an adjacent lake (Etang de Bages), and there are delightful sandy beaches at Narbonne-Plage and Gruissan (7 km). From the pitches, which are separated by hedges, you will barely notice any of the busy activity around the disco and the karaoke. The complex is surrounded by vineyards, and you can discover for yourself whether the local wines of L'Aude justify their reputation. Visit Narbonne, with its Archbishop's Palace, or take a boat trip on the Canal du Midi or the Canal de la Robine. On the other hand, you can also walk or cycle alongside them.

Languedoc-Roussillon

La Nautique

Rating	8.2
Tariff range	€€€€
Town	Narbonne
Department	Aude
Postal Code	11100
Map	5 F2
Tel	04-68904819
Fax	04-68907339
e-mail	info@campinglanautique.com
Open	15 Feb – 15 Nov

From A9 take Narbonne-Sud exit. Left at rdbt, follow 'La Nautique' signs. Site on right after sharp bend.

Size (hectares) 16
Touring pitches 273
Sanitary facilities rating 7.8

aerobics and aqua gym • restaurant with top chef • private sanitary facilities • close to the Mediterranean Sea • rafting, surfing and sailing • Narbonne (6 km)

Electric hook-ups/amps 273/10-16

Over the past ten years, the Schutjes family have transformed a very basic overnight campsite into a luxurious holiday park. Advance booking is now definitely recommended if you want to stay here in the high season. This beautiful, park-like site with its tall cypresses lies next to a Mediterranean lagoon which offers fishing and excellent windsurfing. Surfboards and canoes can be hired at the campsite, and you will see flamingos on the Etang de Bages.

If you want a refreshing dip in the Mediterranean, you will have to go to Narbonne-Plage or Gruissan (12 km), which have wonderful long, sandy beaches. The swimming pool has a long slide, and there is a water mushroom in the toddler pool. You can also take lessons in aerobics or aqua gym, or use the mini golf and tennis courts – all for no extra charge. You could also try mountain biking, sailing, rafting, horse riding, or canyoning, and there are weekly orienteering exercises in the high season. The pitches are spacious and have individual sanitary facilities. The restaurant has a first-class chef, or try the snack bar and pizza parlour.

La Royale

Tariff range €€€€
Town Villardonnel
Department Aude
Postal Code 11600
Map 5 F2
Tel 04-68775113
e-mail info@laroyale.net
Open 25 May – 24 Aug

Take D118 towards Carcassonne-Mazamet to exit for Villardonnel. In village follow Salsigne sign. After 3 km, take 1st paved road on left.

Size (hectares) 2
Touring pitches 10
around an old farmhouse • ecological garden • magnificent view • castles of the Cathars • medieval Carcassonne • Carcassonne (20 km)

Electric hook-ups/amps 6/4

'Since I was six years old, I've been a backpacker, and having my own small campsite was always my cherished dream', says Luuk Leenarts, the Dutch owner of La Royale. He had intended to own a campsite in the Pyrénées, but since his site is on a 400-metre plateau that offers magnificent views of this southern French mountain range, he is more than happy. The centre of the campsite is the old farmhouse with an inner courtyard where you will find the excellent sanitary facilities, and a large dining table. There is a table d'hôte menu every day, which you can book a day in advance. As the farm has its own herd of goats, there is sometimes goats' cheese on the menu. An ecological vegetable garden is also part of the farm. The pitches at La Royal are spacious and most of them have good views.

Carcassonne is a city that is definitely worth a visit, as are the less well-known castles of the Cathars at Lastours. Swimming in a lake with a sandy shore is possible in Les Monagnès, about 20 km away. Fresh and appetising regional products are on display at the market in Revel.

Campin Das Pinhiers

Rating 7
Tariff range €€
Town Villemoustaussou
Department Aude
Postal Code 11620
Map 5 F2
Tel 04-68478190
Fax 04-68714349
e-mail campindaspinhiers@wanadoo.fr
Open 01 Mar – 31 Oct

On A61 take Carcassonne-Ouest exit onto D118 from Mazamet to Villemoustaussou. After several rdbts turn right at last rdbt (near yellow filling station). Site well signed from here.

Size (hectares) 2
Touring pitches 61
Sanitary facilities rating 6.5
centrally situated • recreation room with bar • pitches with ample shade • vineyards • monasteries and castles • Carcassonne (2 km)

Electric hook-ups/amps 46/10

Das Pinhiers is just 5 km from Carcassonne and 2 km from the Canal du Midi. This simple campsite serves as a good home base for day trips into the surrounding area. The grounds are reminiscent of dune areas, hilly with a great deal of sand and scattered stones, with trees and bushes to provide protection from the sun. During the day, the cool swimming pool is a popular attraction for the guests, with its small paved area for sunbathing, and showers and toilet facilities close by. You will also find a recreation room with a pinball machine, table tennis table and a bar.

In the evenings there is little to do, but you will find plenty of entertainment and culture in the near vicinity. The region is well known for its wines so a visit to the many vineyards is worthwhile. You can also explore castles – particularly those left by the Cathars – fine examples of which can be seen at Saissac and Lastours. Other attractions include monasteries and prehistoric caves. The highpoint is undoubtedly the medieval citadel of Carcassonne that has seemingly remained untouched through the centuries.

Languedoc-Roussillon

Château de Boisson

Rating	8.2
Tariff range	€€€€
Town	Allègre-les-Fumades
Department	Gard
Postal Code	30500
Map	5 G3
Tel	04-66248561
Fax	04-66248014
e-mail	reception@chateaudeboisson.com
Open	12 Apr – 30 Sep

On A7 take Bollène exit to Pont-St-Esprit. Then N86 to Bagnols & D6 towards Alès. After 35 km, follow Fumades signs. After 10 km follow site signs.

Size (hectares) 7.5
Touring pitches 100
Sanitary facilities rating 8.4
the château • excellent facilities • much to do in the low season • the caves of La Cocalière • Cascades de Sautadet • Barjac (16 km)
Electric hook-ups/amps 100/6

The lovely village of Allègre lies on a hillside between sunflower fields, where the beautifully restored château forms the entrance to the campsite. The pitches are somewhat small, but the château grounds offer you everything you need for a relaxing holiday. The large swimming pool with its twisting slide might catch your eye, and the children won't be able to get enough of it. If you prefer to stay out of the sun, you can swim in the covered pool. The restaurant offers a selection of delicious dishes, and the terraces have a pleasant atmosphere. Outside the peak season, this is the perfect spot to take drawing lessons or participate in a bridge drive. The campsite shop lies outside the gates in an idyllic lane – one of many such lanes just waiting to be discovered. There are dance and ballet clubs for younger children, and on special evenings, families and guests can enjoy a performance. You can search for gold under the supervision of a professional gold digger, and for a day out, you can visit the waterfalls of Sautadet or take a ride on the steam train from Anduze to Saint-Jean-du-Gard.

Cévennes Provence

Rating	8
Tariff range	€€€
Town	Anduze
Department	Gard
Postal code	30140
Map	5 G3
Tel	04-66617310
Fax	04-66616074
e-mail	marais@camping-cevennes-provence.com
Open	20 Mar – 01 Nov

Site 4 km N of Anduze (D907) on D284 towards Corbès.

Size (hectares) 15
Touring pitches 220
Sanitary facilities rating 7.9
beautifully situated • peace and quiet • hidden away • steam train to St-Jean-du-Gard • bamboo forest at Anduze • Anduze (4 km)
Electric hook-ups/amps 180/3-15

Cévennes Provence was the first campsite to open in this area nearly 50 years ago, and the same owner is still in charge. The family has put its heart and soul into running the campsite and pleasing its guests. The grounds are peaceful and spacious, the natural surroundings are lovely and there is something to please everyone.

The area around the Gardon River is flat, but the pitches stretch over a mountain with spectacular views across valleys through which rivers flow like silver snakes. The narrower parts of the river are circled by rocks, but where it broadens it is ideal for swimming and aquatic games. In addition to a large playground for younger children, at the entrance to the river there is a large playing field for volleyball, football, basketball and badminton.

The sanitary facilities are strategically distributed across the grounds, and there is a special area for bathing dogs. The campsite has its own shop, and three times week the local butcher drops by. Once a week there is live music in the restaurant, but at 10.30pm it's lights out.

Languedoc-Roussillon

Le Bel Été

Rating 8.4
Tariff range €€€€
Town Anduze
Department Gard
Postal code 30140
Map 5 G3
Tel 04-66617604
Fax 04-66617604
e-mail contact@camping-bel-ete.com
Open 02 Apr – 25 Sep
Site on D982 1.5 km SE of Anduze.
Size (hectares) 2.6
Touring pitches 85
Sanitary facilities rating 8.3
abundant water and electricity • quiet and clean • close to Anduze • walking and cycle tours • steam train to Saint-Jean-du-Gard • Anduze (1 km)
Electric hook-ups/amps 85/6

In winter the sun barely rises above the mountain ridges. Luckily, in the summer there is plenty of sun, and you can enjoy it to the full from the shade of this family campsite. Le Bel Été lies on the Gardon River, strategically located between the Cévennes, the Ardèche, the Alpilles and the Camargue; the sea is only an hour away. The pitches are not overly large, and the layout offers little privacy, but the sanitary facilities are spacious and modern. Fresh bread, croissants, milk and camping gas are available in the shop.

You can take a steam train from Anduze to Saint-Jean-du-Gard – but beware: you will be completely blackened by smoke! It stops at the Bambouseraie, an exotic park, unique in Europe and famous for its giant bamboo. Back on site, a special supervised activities programme is organised for young children. Swimming enthusiasts can choose between the swimming pool and the Gardon where the sun-warmed rocks attract sunbathers. Volleyball and table tennis competitions are organised for everyone, plus a biathlon – a combination of running and swimming events.

Le Fief d'Anduze

Rating 8.2
Tariff range €€€
Town Anduze
Department Gard
Postal code 30140
Map 5 G3
Tel 04-66618171
Fax 04-66618780
e-mail lefief@wanadoo.fr
Open 01 Apr – 30 Sep
Take N110 towards Alès-Montpellier. In St-Cristol turn onto D910 towards Anduze, then immediately S onto D24 towards Lézan. Before Lézan take D982 towards Attuech. Site 2 km on right, to E of Attuech.
Size (hectares) 5
Touring pitches 83
Sanitary facilities rating 8.8
peace and quiet and natural surroundings • friendly atmosphere • activities • many places of interest • the sea • Anduze (5 km)
Electric hook-ups/amps 83/6

The seven brothers and sisters who established Le Fief d'Anduze have succeeded in making a very homely campsite. This site is peacefully set beside the Gardon River, offering very spacious pitches and ample shade. Two sanitary blocks with more than enough showers stand on a central section, and they are spotlessly clean and brightly painted. The facilities are surrounded by grape vines and magnificent hibiscus bushes. Right at the back of the site you will find large playing fields and a playground. It also has a swimming pool, and a restaurant with many charming seating arrangements, completely encircled by geraniums and petunias. The menu offers a wide range of delicious salads, fish and meat dishes and home-made pasta.

The rear exit takes you towards the river where you will find a lovely fishing lake. The paths between the reeds lead to the river, and the water at the pebble beaches is so shallow that children can amuse themselves safely for hours on end. Take note though: above the dam the water is at least two metres deep. The open-air cinema – where everyone brings their own chair – is a delightful extra.

Languedoc-Roussillon

L'Arche

Rating	8.7
Tariff range	€€€€
Town	Anduze
Department	Gard
Postal code	30140
Map	5 G3
Tel	04-66617408
Fax	04-66618894
e-mail	camping.arche@wanadoo.fr
Open	15 Mar – 30 Sep

From D907 towards St-Jean-du-Gard. At Anduze take 2nd drive (not 1st via Castel Rose campsite); 2.9 km from bridge over the Gardon. Site NW of Anduze.
Size (hectares) 5
Touring pitches 210
Sanitary facilities rating 8.4
pebble beaches • shade and peace and quiet • no evening entertainment • bamboo • steam train to St-Jean • Anduze (2 km)
Electric hook-ups/amps 210/6-10

L'Arche is situated just past Anduze in the lovely setting of mountains, rock faces and the winding Gardon River. When you arrive at the impressive, luxurious reception area, you will find a great deal of tourist information and Internet access. The sanitary facilities are excellent: light and spacious, with separate baby areas. The pitches range in size from spacious to huge, with ample shade from poplars, pines, acacias and weeping willows. Those on the first section have paths bordered by arched, pruned privet hedges – idyllic.

The ace in the hole at L'Arche is the river with its wide pebble beaches and gorges where diving is possible in several places. In the summer, a bouncy castle is set up on the beach for smaller children, and on the site is a delightful playground. You can enjoy delicious food at the restaurant, like stuffed veal à la Provence or squid in Armoricaine sauce. L'Arche has a babysitting service. For young people there are plenty of sports activities: archery, handball volleyball and basketball. Campsite L'Arche has no entertainment programme for the evenings.

La Buissière

Rating	7.6
Tariff range	€€€
Town	Barjac
Department	Gard
Postal Code	30430
Map	5 G/H3
Tel	04-66245452
Fax	04-66245452
e-mail	camping.labuissiere@wanadoo.fr

From Barjac take D176 NE towards l'Aven d'Orgnac. Site 3 km on left.
Size (hectares) 1.6
Touring pitches 70
Sanitary facilities rating 7.3
child-safe and child-friendly • clean facilities • helpful owners • Gorges d'Ardèche • caves (l'Aven d'Orgnac) • Barjac (3 km)
Electric hook-ups/amps 70/2-10

The small campsite of La Buissière, run by the friendly Ginestière family, is set in the middle of the area that surrounds Barjac. The landscape is densely packed with green oak and conifer-like bushes with a delightful fragrance. During World War II, the Resistance used the area to hide in, and that is where its name comes from. In the 16th and 17th centuries, at the time of the religious wars, the area also offered a safe haven to fleeing Huguenots. The pitches get ample shade from the fragrant trees – vital given the heat of the sun.

This site is ideal for youngsters as in addition to the activities programme, there is a children's pool (next to the swimming pool) and a delightful playground with a jungle gym, a slide and a see-saw. High swings and rings have been set up on an open playing field with a volleyball court. Mini golf is popular (and free of charge). The sanitary facilities are extremely clean, and include a baby-changing room and facilities for the less able. The atmosphere around the central barbecue next to the swimming pool is very friendly.

Languedoc-Roussillon

La Croix Clémentine

Rating 8.2
Tariff range €€€€
Town Cendras
Department Gard
Postal code 30480
Map 5 G3
Tel 04-66865269
Fax 04-66865484
e-mail clementine@clementine.fr
Open 31 Mar – 10 Sep
Take D916 from Alès towards Cendras-Mende (W of Gardon). After 4 km (at La Blaquière) turn onto D32. Site 1 km on left.
Size (hectares) 10
Touring pitches 195
Sanitary facilities rating 7.7
densely wooded and hilly • activities at the entrance • many facilities • mountains and sun • centrally situated • Alès (5 km)
Electric hook-ups/amps 195/6-10

The road to La Croix Clémentine offers stunning views of mountains and the picturesque village of Cendras. This large campsite is set in the shade of a tranquil oak forest, with play areas, tennis courts, a restaurant, outdoor cafés and three swimming pools – the largest of which is 25m. It lies in a hilly area so you can choose a pitch on high or low ground. However, the former means a long walk to the swimming pool. The good quality sanitary facilities have unique arched doorways and each section is painted a different colour. The campsite shop in the restaurant section sells a wide range of products including meat.

Every morning you can go on a guided walk, in the afternoons you can take part in a swimming competition and in the evenings – after a delicious meal in the restaurant – it's time for chess, or tarot cards. Smaller children have their own walks, pétanque or swimming competitions as well as board games, and a crèche two mornings a week. Young campers have their own clubhouse that stays open all night under supervision, with six table-tennis tables, and a weekly disco.

Les Amarines II

Rating 8.8
Tariff range €€€
Town Goudargues
Department Gard
Postal Code 30630
Map 5 H3
Tel 04-66822492
Fax 04-66823864
e-mail les.amarines@wanadoo.fr
Open 01 Apr – 15 Oct
Take D980 from Bagnols towards Barjac. After Cornillon turn onto D23 towards Goudargues. Site immediately on left.
Size (hectares) 5
Touring pitches 104
Sanitary facilities rating 9.3
sun and peace and quiet • petanque and karaoke evenings • spotlessly clean sanitary facilities • caves and waterfalls • many places of interest • Bagnols-sur-Cèze (14 km)
Electric hook-ups/amps 104/6-10

Les Amarines II is a typical French family campsite. It is set on the Cèze River with a magnificent view of the village of Corneillon. The pitches on the left side of the campsite are very sunny, while those on the right are extremely shady. All are very spacious, and guests like the neatly trimmed hedges that provide ample privacy. The sanitary facilities are modern and are kept spotlessly clean, with the useful addition of a special baby-changing room with bath.

At the far end of the expansive grounds you will find tranquil parklands with playing fields and a small playground, with access to the Cèze. The river is shallow here, and ideal for paddling or floating in a rubber boat. For those who really want to swim, there is the campsite pool, complete with sunbathing area. Twice a week the guests gather to play pétanque in front of the restaurant, and this is always a good opportunity to meet your fellow campers. The karaoke evenings are a lot of fun, and are preceded by a meal that features dishes like coq au vin, leg of lamb in a creamy garlic sauce and salmon steak with basil.

Languedoc-Roussillon

Le St-Michelet

Rating	7.9
Tariff range	€€
Town	Goudargues
Department	Gard
Postal Code	30630
Map	5 H3
Tel	04-66822499
Fax	04-66823443
e-mail	camping.st.michelet@wanadoo.fr
Open	01 Apr – 30 Sep

Take D980 from Bagnols towards Barjac. In Goudargues N on D371. After 1.5 km site on right.

Size (hectares) 5
Touring pitches 145
Sanitary facilities rating 8
simple with a pleasant atmosphere • friendly owners • clean grass beaches • the village of Goudargues • caves • Bagnols-sur-Cèze (15 km)
Electric hook-ups/amps 145/3-6

In the patois of the south of France, the place where thyme grows (la frigoule) is known as 'le frigoulet'. In the area around Le Saint-Michelet you will find it growing wild - hence the name of the campsite road. The lovely surroundings, beautiful landscape, magnificent river and the simple cosiness of the site are all plus points for Le Saint-Michelet. The sanitary facilities are spacious and are kept clean. The higher pitches are uniformly laid out, neatly demarcated by hedges, while the lower pitches are more haphazardly spaced. There is ample shade, sometimes from ancient trees with gnarled trunks, apart from the small section reserved for hikers where the trees are newly planted.

The Cèze River has grassy beaches that are cleaned every morning. The waters are shallow in many areas so that children can play with the pebbles. The campsite has a large playground for younger children but their favourite activity is the weekly pony ride – free of charge! A get-together evening is held every week.

La Sousta

Rating	8.1
Tariff range	€€€
Town	Remoulins
Department	Gard
Postal code	30210
Map	5 H3
Tel	04-66371280
Fax	04-66372369
e-mail	info@lasousta.com
Open	01 Mar – 31 Oct

From A9 exit 23 follow N100 to Remoulins. Then take D981 to Pont du Gard. After 1.5 km site W of Remoulins.

Size (hectares) 12
Touring pitches 236
Sanitary facilities rating 8.5
attractive pitches • many activities for children • access to the river • the Pont du Gard • village festivals • Remoulins (2 km)
Electric hook-ups/amps 236/6

A picturesque route along a road lined with sycamores leads to La Sousta, close to the famous Pont du Gard. The landscape is hilly with enormous pine trees and green oaks, and the pitches are scattered across the grounds and have no fixed shape. The Gardon River flows below the campsite, and at this point it is broad and shallow with several sandy beaches. La Sousta also has a swimming pool with a fountain and a separate paddling pool, and the sanitary facilities are excellent.

Behind the hedgerows that surround the swimming pool you will find grassy fields where you can sunbathe. Beyond these fields are the tennis and volleyball courts, the football pitch, two playgrounds and a big empty field where you can learn archery, and where kite-flying competitions are held. Younger campers can learn hip-hop dancing, and attend disco evenings, enjoy live music next to the pub, and all kinds of sports activities. A visit to the Pont du Gard, the famous Roman aquaduct, is a must and only 800m from the campsite! Nîmes is worth seeing, with its Roman buildings, flea markets and the night market on Thursdays.

Les Sources

Rating	8.2
Tariff range	€€€
Town	St-Jean-du-Gard
Department	Gard
Postal code	30270
Map	5 G3
Tel	04-66853803
Fax	04-66851609
e-mail	camping-des-sources@wanadoo.fr
Open	01 Apr – 30 Sep

From St-Jean-du-Gard take D983 N towards St-Etienne-Vallée-Française. Then take D50 towards Mialet. After 4.5 km site on right.

Size (hectares) 2.7
Touring pitches 80
Sanitary facilities rating 8.7
nature, sun and space • all mod-cons • quiet family campsite • Gardon River • cycling and walking tours • Anduze (14 km)
Electric hook-ups/amps 80/6-10

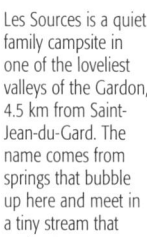

Les Sources is a quiet family campsite in one of the loveliest valleys of the Gardon, 4.5 km from Saint-Jean-du-Gard. The name comes from springs that bubble up here and meet in a tiny stream that snakes its way across the land. The many flowers and blossoming bushes add an attractive touch, and there is ample shade. The campsite has a relatively large group of regular visitors, and the friendly owners try and ensure that they encounter something new each time they visit.

As a result, there are super-modern, spotlessly clean sanitary facilities, built-in rubbish bins, and hidden toilet-roll holders. The restaurant and outdoor café have been renovated, and the former also houses a small shop. The renovation of the swimming pool is the next big project on the agenda, but even swimming here is still a pleasure. The surrounding area is well suited to walking or touring by bike or on horseback, while for children there is a playground and a paddling pool. In the off-peak seasons you can enrol for pottery and ceramics courses. A musical evening is held once a month, and every week you can book a place at a communal meal.

Mas de la Cam

Rating	8.4
Tariff range	€€€
Town	St-Jean-du-Gard
Department	Gard
Postal code	30270
Map	5 G3
Tel	04-66851202
Fax	04-66853207
e-mail	camping@masdelacam.fr
Open	27 Apr – 20 Sep

Site 3 km NW of St-Jean-du-Gard on D907 towards l'Estrechure.

Size (hectares) 6
Touring pitches 175
Sanitary facilities rating 8.9
perfectly maintained • many places to swim • Mont Aigoual • pleasant villages • Anduze (13 km)
Electric hook-ups/amps 150/6-10

Mas de la Cam is beautifully situated on a river in the Cévennes and it offers peace and quiet, natural beauty, a river with broad, grassy banks, a large swimming pool and lovely playing fields. The restored farmhouse at the entrance is very pretty. The sanitary facilities are clean, spacious and modern, and though the pitch sizes vary, you will not actually be spending much time there. The children simply can't get enough of the large playground, the paddling pool and the river – the waters are shallow and irresistible.

In the off-season, you can take part in boules competitions, bridge evenings and painting courses, while sports activities and a music evening once a week make up the fixed programme in the peak season. The restaurant (with adjacent bar) has only a few main courses on its menu, but there are take-away meals as well. For young campers, every Wednesday evening is party night, alternating between outdoor disco night and live music. The surrounding area is ideally suited to hiking, and St-Jean-du-Gard has lots of shops and restaurants.

Languedoc-Roussillon

Domaine de Labeiller

Rating 7.8
Tariff range €€€€
Town St. Victor-de-Malcap
Department Gard
Postal Code 30500
Map 5 G3
Tel 04-66241527
Fax 04-66241408
e-mail campinglabeiller@wanadoo.fr
Open 01 May – 30 Sep
On A7 take exit 19 (Bollène) onto D51 past Pont-Saint-Esprit & Barjac towards St-Ambroix. Site on right before small bridge.
Size (hectares) 5.3
Touring pitches 146
Sanitary facilities rating 8.2
huge aqua centre • extremely child-friendly • good restaurant • caves at La Cocalière • waterfalls at Sautadet • Saint-Ambroix (3 km)
Electric hook-ups/amps 146/6

Domaine de Labeiller is like an oasis in the desert because of the large number of swimming pools. Younger children can enjoy a magnificent pool with slides and water parasols, while older children can use air beds on the larger slides or fight their way through the rapids. Terraces have been beautifully laid out between the pools, decorated with olive trees and fragrant lavender bushes. The entire pool complex is open until 10pm, and beautifully lighted in the evenings.

Apart from all the fun of the swimming pools, this is a quiet campsite, with organised activities only once a week. The pitches on the newer sections are very spacious, but the lack of shade (the plants are still growing) makes things uncomfortable in hot weather. Oaks, poplars, acacias and olive trees provide ample shade for the other pitches. The view of the region from the grounds is spectacular. The sanitary facilities are well equipped. The restaurant boasts its own chef and a 3-course meal offers very good value, with main courses like entrecôte, salmon steak, and chicken with mushroom sauce.

L' Ile des Papes

Rating 8.6
Tariff range €€€€
Town Villeneuve-lès-Avignon
Department Gard
Postal Code 30400
Map 5 H3
Tel 04-90151590
Fax 04-90151591
e-mail ile.papes@wanadoo.fr
Open 01 Apr – 31 Oct
On A9 take exit 22 (Roquemaure) onto D976. Then take D980 towards Villeneuve-lès-Avignon. Turn right at Barrage de Villeneuve, follow site signs.
Size (hectares) 20
Touring pitches 196
Sanitary facilities rating 8.8
luxurious facilities • situated on an island • expansive grounds • theatre festival of Avignon • historic towns and villages • Avignon (6 km)
Electric hook-ups/amps 196/10

L'Ile des Papes is a large, quiet campsite situated on an island between the Rhône and the Rhône Canal, directly behind a large weir. The grounds are large and the pitches offer more than enough space for your tent and a table and chairs. The trees are somewhat young so that the shade is minimal. Sanitary facilities are modern and located in three red and blue buildings – painted in the typical style of Provence. The site has a number of luxury facilities including a TV room where you can also play electronic games.

Two swimming pools have large sunny terraces, and you will find lovely playing fields with two playgrounds for smaller children. An excellent restaurant with an outdoor café holds swinging musical evenings several times a week. You can visit the Pont du Gard, Avignon – the historic city of the Popes, try wine tasting at Châteauneuf-du-Pape, or visit the beach that lies 90 km from the campsite. Sport-loving campers may like to canoe on the Gorges du Gardon or take part in a trip to the Camargue.

Le Neptune

Rating 7.6
Tariff range €€€€
Town Agde
Department Hérault
Postal Code 34300
Map 5 G2
Tel 04-67942394
Fax 04-67944877
e-mail info@campingleneptune.com
Open 01 Apr – 30 Sep
On D32 from Agde to Le Grau-d'Agde (1.5 km). Site S of Agde, on left after viaduct.
Size (hectares) 2.5
Touring pitches 120   **Static pitches** 40
Sanitary facilities rating 7.9
beautiful greenery • heated swimming pool • Night security • boat trips on the Canal du Midi • cycling trips • Agde (2 km)
Electric hook-ups/amps 120/6-10

The beautiful greenery, very wide paths and generous pitches mark out quiet Le Neptune campsite. The umbrella pines and exuberantly blossoming oleanders give off a delightful scent, and every pitch is screened by a large fern or small palm tree as well as hedges and oleander bushes. The sanitary facilities are excellent. The swimming pool is heated, which in spring and autumn is no extravagant luxury. The bar also has a tiny shop for those items that slipped your mind. Fresh bread and croissants are available every day (delivered to your tent in spring). From July onwards, cheese, eggs and vegetables are sold.

An activities supervisor entertains the children with games and gymnastics, with swimming and diving lessons available in the swimming pool. Apart from two pleasant social evenings each week, there is little entertainment. The sea and Le Grau d'Agde are only 1.5 km away, and you can even hire small, open-topped, two-seater cars to get there. A boat trip on the Canal du Midi is also most enjoyable. Look out for the round lock in Agde.

Le Boisseron

Rating 6.6
Tariff range €€€
Town Boisseron
Department Hérault
Postal Code 34160
Map 5 G3
Tel 04-66809430
Fax 04-66930121
e-mail info@campingdomainedegajan.fr
Open 01 Apr – 30 Sep
W from Boisseron. On N110 (towards Montpellier-Sommières), over bridge 250mtrs on left
Size (hectares) 3
Touring pitches 69
Sanitary facilities rating 6.9
friendly atmosphere • many activities • large swimming pool • country festivals (with bulls) • caves and wine cellars • Sommières (3km)
Electric hook-ups/amps 69/10

'Abrivados', 'bandidos', 'encierros' and 'concours de manades' are words often heard at this camp site. You might think you are in Spain because these terms all refer to bulls! In summer in Boisseron and the surrounding areas, bulls are very much the focus of the festivities. The camp site is situated on the outskirts of the village, and the pitches are under the oaks trees, and happily, in the shade. The sanitary facilities are adequate. Due to the dry conditions it is forbidden to barbecue by your tent or caravan, but in the central open field there are barbecues for public use.

There are regular, supervised activities for children, and in and around the swimming pool there is always something interesting to do for young and old alike. Tuesday night is party time at Le Boisseron: after an open-air communal meal that includes local speciality dishes you can dance in the bar-cafeteria. Mucat, the local sweet white wine, and the red wines from Lunel and Nîmes are readily available. The nearby wine cellars are certainly worth a visit.

Les Rivières

Rating	7.1
Tariff range	€€€
Town	Clermont-l'Hérault
Department	Hérault
Postal Code	34800
Map	5 G2
Tel	04-67967553
Fax	04-67965835
e-mail	camping-les-rivieres@wanadoo.fr
Open	07 Apr – 15 Sep

After Montpellier take A9 towards Millau. In Gignac, follow signs to Canet. In Canet follow site signs. Site 1.5 km E.

Size (hectares) 3
Touring pitches 78   **Static pitches** 32
Sanitary facilities rating 7.5

family atmosphere • quiet and secure • Philippe's pizzas • Lac de Salagou • Cirque de Navacelles • Clermont-l'Hérault (6 km)

Electric hook-ups/amps 78/6

Just outside the village of Canet by the River Hérault lies Les Rivières campsite, a peaceful, shady, place where everyone seems to enjoy themselves. Some campers have been coming here for twenty years and have known each other since they were children. The pitches are spacious and the sanitary facilities are good, though apart from the swimming pool, there is only a volleyball court and a large pétanque pitch. An activities supervisor entertains the children, and there is also a Native American Indian evening, with a big campfire by the river and a picnic. There is a combined bar/restaurant, with a covered terrace right next to the swimming pool.

Delicious grills are prepared at the large open hearth, but the kitchen is famous for its pizzas. In the summer, the gypsy band 'Los Allegros' gives eight performances when you can be sure of a lively evening of dancing. Convivial social evenings are organised twice a week, accompanied by somewhat quieter music. There is excellent swimming in the Hérault, where the water quality is checked regularly, and there are enough fish to make it worthwhile baiting a hook.

Les Tamaris

Rating	8.3
Tariff range	€€€
Town	Frontignan
Department	Hérault
Postal Code	34110
Map	5 G2
Tel	04-67434477
Fax	04-67189790
e-mail	les-tamaris@wanadoo.fr
Open	02 Apr – 18 Sep

Site 6 km E of Frontignan on D50 to Les Arlesquiers. Follow 'Frontignan-Plage' signs.

Size (hectares) 4.5
Touring pitches 150
Sanitary facilities rating 8.2

numerous activities • excellent swimming pool and sea bathing • good restaurant • nature reserve • Montpellier • Frontignan (5 km)

Electric hook-ups/amps 150/10

The remarkably attractive Les Tamaris campsite is 4.5 km from Frontignan next to a quiet coastal path in a protected nature reserve. As its name indicates, numerous tamarisk trees grow here, a species for which the Mediterranean area is renowned. They surround most of the pitches, allowing soft, filtered light to penetrate. Les Tamaris is divided into 'camemberts', each of which contains six sections. This results in a triangular pitch that gives you plenty of privacy. Behind the site is a clean, peaceful beach where you can swim, dive and surf; on the campsite itself there is a huge swimming pool with a waterfall and water jets that are illuminated at night.

The restaurant has an excellent, inexpensive menu including many fish and seafood dishes. For the children, there is a large playground and a daily painting club. If you want peace and sunshine, select a pitch at some distance from the swimming pool and restaurant, because the fun goes on until midnight every evening here.

Languedoc-Roussillon

Eden

Rating	7.4
Tariff range	€€€€
Town	Lattes
Department	Hérault
Postal Code	34970
Map	5 G2
Tel	04-67151105
Fax	04-67151131
e-mail	edencamping@wanadoo.fr
Open	01 Apr – 03 Sep

On A9 take exit 30 (Montpellier-Sud/Les Plages-Palavas), follow D986 towards Palavas until 500mtrs S of Lattes. Site on left.

Size (hectares) 6

Touring pitches 160   **Static pitches** 102

Sanitary facilities rating 7.1

good transit campsite • close to the sea • various activities in the evenings • beach bus service • Montpellier • Palavas (5 km)

Electric hook-ups/amps 160/10

Eden lies slightly to the south of Montpellier, not far from the A9-E15. The sea is 3 km away, and the beach bus service will get you there in just a few minutes. Palavas is an old fishing village with a lively centre including a casino, nice shops, good restaurants, and many sandy beaches. Montpellier – the Paris of the south – is well worth visiting.

The pitches are large and most are well shaded by high poplars. Tamarisks provide the newer pitches with privacy. The sanitary facilities are spotlessly clean and spacious, though the toilets and showers are on the first floor which makes access difficult for some people. However, there is a modified toilet for the less mobile on the ground floor. The swimming pool is a good place to relax, and after your swim you can spoil yourself with a delicious meal 'faites maison' (the lasagne is excellent!). In the evenings, the large covered canteen is the venue for entertainment ranging from live music, karaoke, discos and Brazilian dancing to a beauty pageant.

La Créole

Rating	7.5
Tariff range	€€€€
Town	Marseillan-Plage
Department	Hérault
Postal Code	34340
Map	5 G2
Tel	04-67219269
Fax	04-67265816
e-mail	campinglacreole@wanadoo.fr
Open	01 Apr – 12 Oct

From Marseillan-Plage centre towards sea and follow site signs.

Size (hectares) 1.6

Touring pitches 110   **Static pitches** 14

Sanitary facilities rating 7.5

right by the beach • good sanitary facilities • at pleasant seaside resort • authentic fishing villages • sun, sea and sand • Agde (5 km)

Electric hook-ups/amps 110/6

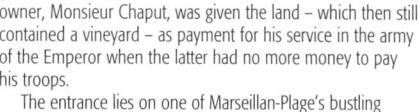

La Créole is a peaceful campsite by the beach, its name commemorating Joséphine de Beauharnais, Napoleon's mistress who later became his wife. The great-great-grandfather of the owner, Monsieur Chaput, was given the land – which then still contained a vineyard – as payment for his service in the army of the Emperor when the latter had no more money to pay his troops.

The entrance lies on one of Marseillan-Plage's bustling streets. The site is small and well laid-out, with medium-sized pitches and adequate shade. Luxurious sanitary facilities (including a shower for dogs) are provided. You can find the daily essentials in the village, and the site's rear exit gives direct access to the beach. The sea is calm and shallow here – ideal for small children, and beach games are organised by the campsite staff. A pleasant social evening is held once a week, with sangria and a DJ. A trip to Agde (5 km) or Sète (11 km) is definitely worth the effort. In these authentic fishing villages, you can find delightful fish restaurants and all kinds of interesting little shops.

Languedoc-Roussillon

Le Paradis

Rating	8.3
Tariff range	€€€
Town	Sérignan
Department	Hérault
Postal Code	34410
Map	5 G2
Tel	04-67322403
Fax	04-67322403
e-mail	paradiscamping34@aol.com
Open	01 Apr – 30 Sep

A9 exit 35 (Béziers-Est). Follow D64/D19 for approx 7 km to rdbt near supermarket, just outside Sérignan. Site near rdbt.

Size (hectares) 1.5
Touring pitches 85
Sanitary facilities rating 8.6

quiet and secure • open-air disco • 3 km to beach • flower market in Béziers • archaeology in Ensérune • Béziers (8 km)

Electric hook-ups/amps 85/6-10

Monsieur Zonta, the owner of Le Paradis, has created an atmosphere at his campsite in which everyone feels happy. He has drawn up a number of rules to ensure that harmony is preserved between campers, and he makes sure that people follow them. The most valued things here are peace, safety and quality, though the busy road and roundabout next door are quite noisy.

The pitches are adequate and separated by trees. At the centre of the campsite is the supervised swimming pool. Next to it is a terrace with a snack bar, where simple meals are served, and you can also order food to take away. The campsite has a small shop selling the bare essentials, but there is a large supermarket on the other side of the roundabout. There are few significant tourist attractions in the immediate area though most campers are not bothered by this; they come here for the sunshine, and there is plenty of that in this part of the world.

Aloha

Rating	8.2
Tariff range	€€€€
Town	Sérignan-Plage
Department	Hérault
Postal Code	34410
Map	5 G2
Tel	04-67397130
Fax	04-67325815
e-mail	info@yellohvillage-aloha.com
Open	29 Apr – 17 Sep

Leave A9 at exit 35 (Béziers-Est). Turn right in Sérignan-Plage at Centre Commercial. Site 6 km SE of Sérignan.

Size (hectares) 10
Touring pitches 280
Sanitary facilities rating 8.3

right by the sea • big water slides • very child-friendly • good mountain biking • Canal du Midi • Sérignan (6 km)

Electric hook-ups/amps 280/10

The first water slide ever built in France can be found on this campsite. Since then many campers, young and old, have sped down the two 75-metre slides and there is also a large children's swimming pool, a normal pool where you can swim up and down, and the sea is close by. A great deal of attention is clearly devoted to younger children here, and the activities are partly oriented towards this age group.

However, apart from the beach there is not a lot here for children of twelve and over. On Wednesday mornings, adult campers can hire a mountain bike for a guided tour of the surrounding area. Through the flat landscape, rough tracks pass by small lakes where you can see flamingos. The pitches on the campsite are quite big enough, and shaded by tall trees. The service here is also very good; on arriving, someone accompanies you to your pitch and helps you to uncouple your caravan or trailer tent. Fish lovers should definitely pay a visit to Les Délices des Dunes.

Languedoc-Roussillon

Centre Naturist Le Clos de Ferrand

Rating 7.5
Tariff range €€€€
Town Sérignan-Plage
Department Hérault
Postal Code 34410
Map 5 G2
Tel 04-67321430
Fax 04-67321559
e-mail centrenaturiste.closferrand@wanadoo.fr
Open 10 May – 20 Sep
Leave A9 at exit 35 (Béziers-Est). Take D64-D37. 700mtrs before beach turn right, follow signs.
Site 7 km SE of Sérignan.
Size (hectares) 1.4
Touring pitches 90
Sanitary facilities rating 7.5
naturist campsite • right by the sea • secure and clean • windsurfing • Canal du Midi • Sérignan (5 km)
Electric hook-ups/amps 90/2-6

After the great storm of 1953 devastated the vineyards, Clos de Ferrand was opened as a campsite. Because the French government had designated the beach near Clos de Ferrand as a naturist beach, the campsite was also organised for naturists. The owner aims to provide a site in which the campers show mutual respect and can enjoy themselves in quiet surroundings. There are no organised activities because the campers are quite capable of having fun without any outside help!

The tall poplars on the site provide adequate shade, and although the trees do not provide a screen, the fact that the caravans all have their doorways on the same side serves to create a degree of privacy. It is an orderly campsite, as can be seen from the way the cars are neatly parked alongside the paths. Other special points about the site are its small scale and its direct access to the beach of fine sand. The sanitary facilities are modern and spotlessly clean. There is not much for young people of around 18 years of age so families with children of 14 or under form the main client group.

L'Occitanie

Rating 8
Tariff range €€€€
Town Valras-Plage
Department Hérault
Postal Code 34410
Map 5 G2
Tel 04-67395906
Fax 04-67325820
e-mail campingoccitanie@wanadoo.fr
Open 31 May – 06 Sep
From A9 take Béziers-Est exit onto D19 towards Valras-Plage. Turn left at rdbt and left again just before Valras-Plage. Site by rdbt N of Valras-Plage-Est.
Size (hectares) 6
Touring pitches 300   **Static pitches** 30
Sanitary facilities rating 8.4
spacious pitches • varied greenery • swimming pool and shop • 1 km to beach • Canal du Midi • Sérignan (5 km)
Electric hook-ups/amps 300/6

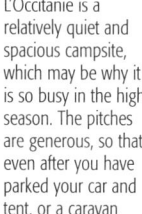

L'Occitanie is a relatively quiet and spacious campsite, which may be why it is so busy in the high season. The pitches are generous, so that even after you have parked your car and tent, or a caravan with an awning, there is still enough room to sit out comfortably. The pitches are screened off by trees, and also by high hedges in many cases. Because the vegetation here is quite luxuriant, there is plenty of shade, especially in the lower part of the campsite. The higher part contains the amenities such as the swimming pool, the shop and the restaurant, plus the pitches with the best view.

Part of the restaurant is on a terrace where the tables are arranged around a flower display. In the evenings it is great fun here, as some kind of entertainment is arranged every day. By midnight the campsite reverts to its former peaceful state. The beach is just over 1 km away, though you can also swim and sunbathe at the swimming pool. The campsite shop is a fairly modest affair, but that does not really matter as there is a large supermarket only 3 km away.

Languedoc-Roussillon

Domaine de la Yole

Rating 8.2
Tariff range €€€€
Town Valras-Plage
Department Hérault
Postal Code 34350
Map 5 G2
Tel 04-67373387
Fax 04-67374489
e-mail layole34@aol.com
Open 28 Apr – 20 Sep

From A9 take Béziers-Ouest exit onto D64 towards Vendres. After 10 km right at rdbt towards La Yole. Right again immediately after 2nd rdbt. Site 2 km SW of Valras-Plage on D37.

Size (hectares) 20
Touring pitches 680
Sanitary facilities rating 7.9

shady pitches • lots to do for the children • well-stocked shops • beach 400 m away • canoes • Sérignan (6 km)

Electric hook-ups/amps 680/6

If you are looking for a campsite where there is plenty for the children to do, then the extensive La Yole is just the place. Here youngsters of up to about 16 will find plenty to keep them amused. Twice a week there is a disco on the terrace; on other evenings, there are performances by professional entertainers, or karaoke. The entertainment, including the disco, always finishes by 11.30pm. There is a mini-club and some fairground attractions for the younger children, and very nice children's pool with a small slide. On the other hand, you can also swim just outside the campsite, as the beach is only 400m away.

The site is well shaded by the tall poplars, which also mark out the pitch boundaries, and some are separated by low hedges. In general, the pitches are quite spacious, and you can park your car next to your tent. A number of the sanitary buildings are modern. You do not need to do your own cooking at Domaine de la Yole because the restaurant has a special menu at an affordable price. With the well-stocked supermarket and a couple of other small shops, you don't even have to brave the high season traffic to do your shopping.

La Plage et du Bord de Mer

Rating 8
Tariff range €€€
Town Valras-Plage
Department Hérault
Postal Code 34350
Map 5 G2
Tel 04-67373438
e-mail daniel.coumelongue@wanadoo.fr
Open 01 May – 13 Sep

From A9 take Béziers-Ouest exit onto D64 towards Vendres. After 10 km turn right at rdbt towards La Yole. Straight on at next rdbt. After 400mtrs site on right (2 km SW of Valras-Plage).

Size (hectares) 13
Touring pitches 620
Sanitary facilities rating 7.8

right by the sea • pleasant restaurant • various shops • Gorges d'Heric • Sérignan (6 km)

Electric hook-ups/amps 550/6-10

This is the only campsite in Valras with direct access to the beach, and families with children of all ages delight in this, as it means they do not have to cross a busy road. The sea is so close to the campsite that the trees do not flourish here, and as a result the pitches, though quite spacious, are somewhat lacking in shade. However, the sea breeze usually ensures that you can stay cool enough.

Because dogs are not allowed on the beach, they are also barred from the campsite. There are shops on site, and the pleasant restaurant offers an extensive menu, especially fish. You can also eat well in Sérignan, 5 km further on where, beside a large square surrounded by plane trees, there are numerous restaurants with terraces. Next to the campsite restaurant some kind of entertainment is held every evening. To ensure that everyone gets a good night's sleep, it ends at 11.30pm. The only thing missing at La Plage et du Bord de Mer is a swimming pool, but the proximity of the sea more than makes up for this.

Camping Yelloh! Village le Club Farret

Rating	8.4
Tariff range	€€€€
Town	Vias-Plage
Department	Hérault
Postal code	34450
Map	5 G2
Tel	04-67216445
Fax	04-67217049
e-mail	farret@wanadoo.fr
Open	24 Apr – 11 Oct

From A9 exit 34 follow N312 to Vias, then take D137 to Vias-Plage. Site at end of road on left.

Size (hectares) 12
Touring pitches 344   **Static pitches** 71
Sanitary facilities rating 8.9
situated on the sea front • many sports activities • restaurant and take-away counter • Agde and Pézenas • canoeing at Roquebrun • Vias (2 km)
Electric hook-ups/amps 344/6

   EUROTOP

Farret was the family name of the founder of this site – and the father-in-law of the current owner, Robert Giner. A "farret" is also a thatched hut found along beaches in Polynesia, and Monsieur Giner likes to see his site as a temporary home at the seaside. You can easily stay here for a week without ever leaving the grounds. If you don't feel like lying on the beach, you can relax in a deck chair by the pool.

There are plenty of sports activities here, like football, archery, and a beach volleyball court with artificial grass. In the evenings, the take-away meals counter is very busy, or you can choose to eat in the restaurant, with its terrace and views of the swimming pool and the sea. The campsite has many different types of trees and feels like a park, while the grounds and facilities are kept very clean. It is not possible to reserve a pitch here, which is a pity because you can set your caravan or tent up almost on the beach itself if there are spaces. Many of the pitches are larger than usual. The owners do their best to keep the noise down, but in the evenings you can hear the music from the cafés along the beach road.

Méditerranée Plage

Rating	7.2
Tariff range	€€€€
Town	Vias-Plage
Department	Hérault
Postal Code	34450
Map	5 G2
Tel	04-67909907
Fax	04-67909917
e-mail	contact@mediterranee-plage.com
Open	02 Apr – 30 Sep

Leave A9 at exit 35 (Béziers-Est) towards Portiragnes-Plage. Before Portiragnes-Plage, turn left over bridge.

Size (hectares) 10
Touring pitches 240   **Static pitches** 120
Sanitary facilities rating 7
genuine family campsite • close to the sea • quiet surroundings • plenty of opportunities for cycling • Vias (2 km)
Electric hook-ups/amps 240/6

One of the advantages of this campsite is that it lies away from all the noise and bustle of Vias. The area around the campsite is flat, with a varied landscape of cornfields, vineyards and fallow ground – excellent for cyclists. However, while it is true that you can tour along the Canal du Midi to your heart's content, you should not expect any smooth cycle paths.

The canal has an interesting arrangement of locks by the River Libron, and runs through delightful countryside. At the campsite, quite a few of the trees find it hard to grow because of the location so close to the sea. There are some poplars and tamarisks, though, that flourish reasonably well on this type of soil. The pitches are open and of various sizes, and they are marked out by trees that do their best to provide some shade. Otherwise, Mediterrannée Plage is a real family campsite. Families with older children can also enjoy themselves here, as there is a disco at night from 11.30pm to 2am. Other campers will not be disturbed very much by this, because the disco is held in an enclosed hall.

Languedoc-Roussillon

Le Napoléon

Rating 7.1
Tariff range €€€€
Town Vias-Plage
Department Hérault
Postal Code 34450
Map 5 G2
Tel 04-67010780
Fax 04-67010785
e-mail reception@camping-napoleon.fr
Open 07 Apr – 01 Oct

Take Pézenas/Agde exit from A9, then follow N112 towards Vias. Follow to Vias-Plage towards Côte Sud. Site 2 km S of Vias, signed.

Size (hectares) 3
Touring pitches 132
Sanitary facilities rating 7.3

plenty to do in the evenings • next to seaside boulevard • sauna and gym • Agde and Pézenas • Europark amusement park • Vias (2 km)

Electric hook-ups/amps 132/10

At the end of the road to the sea, hidden behind little shops and restaurants… it would normally be the last place you would expect to find a campsite. One advantage of this is that the sounds from the road do not penetrate. The pitches are marked out by tall poplars, which also provide the necessary shade. The centre of the campsite is the terrace and stage, on which there is some kind of performance every evening.

Young people are welcome, and in the evening they can have a good time at the discothèque near the entrance, also frequented by teenagers outside. The younger children are also catered for, with the 'mini-club'. Alain Grazian, the campsite owner, recommends the fish restaurant next door (it just happens to belong to him!) where they do an excellent seafood meal. In the daytime, those who feel daring and have no fear of heights can get a rush of adrenaline at the breathtaking attractions in the Europark.

Club Californie Plage

Rating 7.5
Tariff range €€€€
Town Vias-Plage
Department Hérault
Postal Code 34450
Map 5 G2
Tel 04-67216469
Fax 04-67215462
e-mail californie.plage@wanadoo.fr
Open 01 Apr – 30 Oct

Leave A9 at exit 34, follow N312 towards Vias. At junct with N112 turn off to Vias-Plage. Follow Vias-Plage 'Côte-Ouest' signs. Pass Europark amusement park S over small bridge.

Size (hectares) 5.8
Touring pitches 276
Sanitary facilities rating 7.5

right by the sea • various swimming facilities • restaurant and entertainment • Europark amusement park • Art and culture • Vias (2 km)

Electric hook-ups/amps 276/3-10

If you book early enough, you may be able to get a splendid, elevated pitch right by the rocky coast and close to a small bay with a sandy beach. The campsite owner, Monsieur Goubet, has tried to make the most of this wonderful location. He does offer some entertainment in the evening, but campers mainly come here for the beach, and are not very bothered about anything else. There is also a swimming pool with a retractable roof for when it is not quite warm enough on the beach.

If you find the swimming pool at Club Californie Plage too basic, you can also use the splendid pool at the campsite on the other side of the road. The pitches, which are spacious enough, are shaded by tall poplars on part of the campsite, and these also mark out the pitch boundaries. The part of the campsite by the beach is somewhat less shady, though these pitches are surrounded by bushes. For culture lovers there is plenty to see in the surrounding areas. Fans of the French playwright Molière will appreciate a visit to Pézenas. Apart from the small swimming pool, the play area and the mini-club, there are few special facilities for children.

Languedoc-Roussillon

Chon du Tarn

Rating 8.2
Tariff range €€
Town Florac
Department Lozère
Postal code 48400
Map 5 G3
Tel 04-66450914
Fax 04-66452291
e-mail info@camping-chondutarn.com
Open 01 Apr – 20 Oct
Site on D988, 2 km from N106 near Florac and well signed.
Size (hectares) 2.1
Touring pitches 96
Sanitary facilities rating 8
attractive beach • pleasant atmosphere • good home base •
Parc National des Cévennes • caves • Florac (2 km)
Electric hook-ups/amps 75/6

Chon du Tarn lies under the watchful eye of the collégiale of Bédouès (a church dating from the 14th century that is beautifully lit at night). The campsite was once an orchard, and the remaining apple trees bear witness to this fact. Grape vines hanging under a wooden roof separate some of the pitches from others. The sanitary facilities are more than adequate in number and are kept clean. You can go swimming in the Tarn River where you will find some sandy and some pebble beaches, and plenty of delightful spots just waiting to be discovered.

The shop at reception sells cool drinks, dairy products, fresh fruit and vegetables and fresh bread every day. There are no organised activities apart from the traditional pétanque, but there is a large playground for children. However, in Florac – only 2.5 km away – you will find a wealth of shops and restaurants, and a market every Thursday morning. Chon du Tarn is an excellent home base for hikes or those touring on horseback or mountain bike, or going canoeing, kayaking, rafting, canyoning, rock climbing and abseiling.

Le Capelan

Rating 8.3
Tariff range €€€
Town Meyrueis
Department Lozère
Postal code 48150
Map 5 G3
Tel 04-66456050
Fax 04-66456050
e-mail camping.le.capelan@wanadoo.fr
Open 30 Apr – 15 Sep
Site 800mtrs W of Meyrueis.
Size (hectares) 4.5
Touring pitches 69
Sanitary facilities rating 8.8
excellent facilities • spotlessly clean • peace and quiet • Gorges de la Jonte • Dargilan caves • Meyrueis (0,5 km)
Electric hook-ups/amps 69/4-10

Le Capelan is surrounded by towering rocky mountains at the beginning of the Gorges de la Jonte. It stretches out along the Jonte River, and its heated swimming pool – high up on the other side of the quiet road – has magnificent views that makes swimming even more enjoyable than usual. Many of the low-lying pitches are very close to the river (25m), so cooling off during the day is easy, and privacy guaranteed. The sanitary facilities are of top quality: new, modern and spotlessly clean, complete with baby bath, disabled cubicles and a shower for washing dogs or cleaning shoes. There is a road to be crossed, which is not ideal for those with small children.

The facilities for youngsters are excellent, however: there are playing fields and table tennis tables on the other side of the river which can be reached via a rope bridge. Sports outings are organised from the site, and include hikes across the plateau to several farms, or to the Chaos de Nîmes (with an à la ferme meal) or a canoe or kayak trip complete with picnic. There is twice weekly entertainment in the bar alternating between folk music and a disco.

Languedoc-Roussillon

Le Dauphin

Rating 7.5
Tariff range €€€€
Town Argelès-sur-Mer
Department Pyrénées-Orientales
Postal Code 66701
Map 5 F1
Tel 04-68811754
Fax 04-68958260
e-mail info@campingledauphin.com
Open 20 May – 20 Sep
Take exit 10 on N114 , then C2 towards Taxo d'Avall and on to Agulle. Site on right.
Size (hectares) 8
Touring pitches 85
Sanitary facilities rating 7.2
many facilities • individual sanitary facilities • sheltered pitches • beach train • Pyrenees • Argelès (3 km)
Electric hook-ups/amps 85/10

A pitch with individual sanitary facilities provides the ultimate in comfort here. The pitches are spacious and bordered by hedges which provide all the privacy you need; the shade comes from the numerous trees. The restaurant, which is renowned for its delicious paella, has a large terrace that looks out on the swimming pool. Next to the terrace is the spacious recreation area, where campers can have fun in the evening with a wide variety of organised entertainment.

The centre of attention is the swimming pool, a large-scale affair with three pools, one of which is for small children. Younger children can also have great fun in the play area, where the assault course will provide them with a real challenge. Older children have lots of fun on the trampoline near the swimming pool. If you want to go to the beach, you can leave your car at the site and take the tourist train instead. This can also take you to Argelès centre.

Les Marsouins

Rating 8
Tariff range €€€€
Town Argelès-sur-Mer
Department Pyrénées-Orientales
Postal Code 66702
Map 5 F1
Tel 04-68811481
Fax 04-68959358
e-mail marsouin@campmed.com
Open 07 Apr – 23 Sep
Leave N114 at exit 10. At next rdbt follow signs for Pujols. At next rdbt follow signs for Plage des Pins. Site on left in 800mtrs.
Size (hectares) 10
Touring pitches 397
Sanitary facilities rating 7.7
plenty of entertainment • swimming pool with terrace for sunbathing • beach 800m away • Argelès boulevard • beautiful beaches • Collioure (10 km)
Electric hook-ups/amps 397/6

Many people are attracted to this campsite by the entertainment which is provided in the evenings. In addition to the discothèques for the younger campers, there is plenty for the parents too. Children from six to twelve are not forgotten either as there is a club for this age category. During the day, many campers congregate on the large sun terrace next to the beautiful swimming bath. A number of exercise machines stand here for those who want to keep in trim.

The pitches at Les Marsouins are spacious and most are separated by hedges or greenery, with tall poplars to provide the necessary shade. It is never completely quiet here, due to all the activities and the road that runs by. If you do not feel like cooking, there is a simple restaurant and a pizza takeaway. The latter has an extensive menu, and you can also order hot pasta dishes. The beach is just a short stroll away, and the lively shopping area of Argelès is also definitely worth a visit. Once a week in July and August, the campsite organises a boat trip from Argelès harbour to the picturesque fortified town of Collioure. The campsite also has an agreement with a local business for free use of canoes.

Paris Roussillon

Rating 7.9
Tariff range €€€€
Town Argelès-sur-Mer
Department Pyrénées-Orientales
Postal Code 66702
Map 5 F1
Tel 04-68811971
Fax 04-68816877
e-mail contact@parisroussillon.com
Open 15 May – 30 Sep

Leave N114 at exit 10. At next rdbt follow signs for Pujols. At next rdbt follow signs for Plage Nord. Site in 500mtrs.
Size (hectares) 3.5
Touring pitches 151
Sanitary facilities rating 7.7
close to the beach • spacious and shady • enclosed play area • Collioure • Gorges de la Fou • Argelès (1 km)
Electric hook-ups/amps 138/6-10

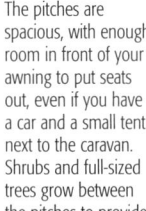

The pitches are spacious, with enough room in front of your awning to put seats out, even if you have a car and a small tent next to the caravan. Shrubs and full-sized trees grow between the pitches to provide privacy. Small children can play in the attractive enclosed play area while their parents watch from a bench, and you can walk to the beach in about fifteen minutes via a footpath.

The Pyrénées are just a stone's throw away, and a trip to the Gorges de la Fou, some of the narrowest gorges in the world, is not to be missed. Apart from table tennis, there is not much at the campsite for sports enthusiasts. However with the sunshine, beach and beautiful surroundings, there is enough to guarantee an enjoyable stay.

La Coste Rouge

Rating 8
Tariff range €€€€
Town Argelès-sur-Mer
Department Pyrénées-Orientales
Postal Code 66701
Map 5 F1
Tel 04-68810894
Fax 04-68959417
e-mail info@lacosterouge.com
Open 20 Apr – 30 Sep

From N114 take exit 13 to Port-Argelès. At 2nd rdbt take D114 to Argelès-Racou. Site 200mtrs on left.
Size (hectares) 3.7
Touring pitches 75
Sanitary facilities rating 8
beautiful view • child-friendly • 2 km to beach • mountain hiking • pleasant fishing villages • Collioure (6 km)
Electric hook-ups/amps 75/6-10

Most people come here for a quiet time, and for that reason it offers only a limited schedule of entertainments. The majority of campers are families with children from one to twelve years of age who can have an excellent time playing in the swimming pool and the play area. Otherwise a ping-pong table and a boules green are the only things available here. The pitches are of average size, and most of them have sufficient shade, provided by cork oaks. Some pitches also have a beautiful view of the mountains and the sea.

The beach is within easy reach, but for walkers the Pyrénées provide another attraction. If you want a quick meal at your tent or caravan, the campsite snack bar is quite adequate. For a stylish meal go to the centre of Collioure about 6km away. If you like anchovies, you will have another reason to visit Collioure, which is famed for this fish.

Languedoc-Roussillon

Brasilia

Rating	8.9
Tariff range	€€€€
Town	Canet-en-Roussillon
Department	Pyrénées-Orientales
Postal Code	66140
Map	5 F1
Tel	04-68802382
Fax	04-68733297
e-mail	camping-le-brasilia@wanadoo.fr
Open	26 Apr – 27 Sep

Leave A9 at exit 41 onto D83 towards Le Bacarès/Canet. Take D81 to Canet. In Canet follow signs to Zone Technique du Port. Site 2km N of Canet-Plage between harbour & River Têt.

Size (hectares) 15
Touring pitches 523
Sanitary facilities rating 8.7
swimming pool with reclining chairs • Catalan shopping centre • extensive programme of activities • sea and sandy beach • Perpignan • Canet (3 km)
Electric hook-ups/amps 526/6-10

Le Brasilia campsite is very well cared for and caters for every convenience. The pitches are well screened off, with most in a wooded area. If you do not feel like cooking, you can go to the spacious dining hall for a tasty meal; at peak times the service is buffet-style. A good alternative is a visit to the caterer, who has a wonderful selection of hot and cold dishes. There are also various shops on site.

The main attraction, however, is the beautiful swimming pool with its inviting reclining chairs where you can relax with a book or newspaper. If you prefer to swim in the sea and sunbathe on warm sand, the campsite has direct access to the beach. Young campers have no reason to be bored at Le Brasilia; there are adequate sports facilities and, in the evening, they can enjoy themselves at the campsite disco. If you own a boat, there is a yachting marina next door. Surfers can simply carry their surfboard from the tent to the beach. Except for Mondays, Canet has a daily market.

Ma Prairie

Rating	8.2
Tariff range	€€€€
Town	Canet-en-Roussillon
Department	Pyrénées-Orientales
Postal Code	66140
Map	5 F1
Tel	04-68732617
Fax	04-68732882
email	ma.prairie@wanadoo.fr
Open	05 May – 25 Sep

From Canet-Plage take D617 to Canet-en-Roussillon, then D11 to St.Nazaire. After approx 500mtrs site signed at rdbt.

Size (hectares) 5
Touring pitches 210
Sanitary facilities rating 8.2
soothing peace and quiet • separate recreation area • child-friendly • day trip on the Yellow Train • 3 km to beach • Canet-Plage (3 km)
Electric hook-ups/amps 180/10

A peaceful campsite that is aimed at older people as well as families with young children. Just across a reasonably quiet road is the swimming pool which invites you to take a dip, and the tennis courts, play area and restaurant are also in this section. The attractive toddler pool incorporates all kinds of extra attractions, and the play area includes a climbing wall. For older children there are two electronic dartboards. Because the recreation area is across the road, the campsite's peace is only disturbed occasionally by traffic on the road. The site is also quite wooded.

The restaurant looks simple but well cared-for, and once a week there is a lamb spit-roast, served up with grilled escargots. Some entertainment is organised on the terrace during evenings in the high season. If you have had enough of the beach and you don't mind a long ride, a day trip on the "Yellow Train" is highly recommended. This departs from Villefranche-de-Conflent, winds through the mountains and crosses high viaducts to arrive in Latour-de-Carol on the Spanish border.

Languedoc-Roussillon

Las Closas

Rating 8.1
Tariff range €€
Town Err
Department Pyrénées-Orientales
Postal code 66800
Map 5 E/F1
Tel 04-68047142
Fax 04-68040720
e-mail reception@camping-las-closas.com
Open All year
Site in centre of village of Err.
Size (hectares) 2
Touring pitches 34   **Static pitches** 6
Sanitary facilities rating 8.2
located in the centre of the village • good, grassy pitches • simple and clean • cycling and hiking • close to Andorra • Puigcerda (10 km)
Electric hook-ups/amps 34/3-10

This campsite offers magnificent grassy pitches where you can easily set up your tent or park your caravan. Even if your car is parked on the pitch, you will still have enough room to set up a table and chairs. Some sections of the sanitary facilities are relatively new and they are kept very clean. The campsite has no restaurant, but there is the occasional Fideoa evening when a type of communal paëlla is served using pasta instead of rice. The owner of Las Closas is a cycling enthusiast, and if you have your mountain bike with you, he will gladly take you on a tour of the area. His wife organises hiking trips through the foothills twice a week.

If you stay here you will have every opportunity to mix with the local residents. The campsite itself has very few facilities, but you don't have to go far for your bread etc because you will find everything you need within a radius of 200m. The local butcher also supplies take-away meals, and opposite the campsite there is a simple café. You will not find any organised activities at Las Closas, but this is not a problem for most campers who come here simply to relax in the evening after a strenuous, active day.

L'Enclave

Rating 7.5
Tariff range €€€
Town Estavar
Department Pyrénées-Orientales
Postal code 66800
Map 5 E1
Tel 04-68047227
Fax 04-68040715
e-mail contact@camping-lenclave.com
Open 01 Jan – 30 Sep and 25 Oct – 31 Dec
Site on D33 on E outskirts of Estavar.
Size (hectares) 3.5
Touring pitches 148
Sanitary facilities rating 7.2
bisected by a small river • tennis and golf • entertainment for children • many hiking routes • Four Solaire in Font-Romeu • Bourg-Madame (8 km)
Electric hook-ups/amps 143/3-10

At L'Enclave they specifically target campers who love hiking, and owner Thérèse Botet organises guided hikes two or three times a week. In addition to walking day trips, you can go on a two-day hike and spend the night in a cabin. Sport-loving campers visiting L'Enclave will find plenty to suit their tastes. You can take tennis lessons, or learn the basics of golf. For the less sports-minded there is a swimming pool with an area for sunbathing – and the sun shines here an average of 300 days a year! Reason enough for the world's largest solar panel to be located in the area. The Four Solaire stands in Font-Romeu, 6 km away from the campsite, and it's definitely worth seeing.

The campsite grounds are long and narrow and are bisected by a river with waterfalls and a small section of rapids. Many of the pitches border the river. You will find a restaurant adjacent to the site, and for any emergency supplies, you can visit the shop some 100m away. However, it's not all sunlight and warmth at an altitude of 1200m: at night, it cools off significantly and you may find you need an extra blanket!

Languedoc-Roussillon

California

Rating	7.5
Tariff range	€€€
Town	Le Barcarès
Department	Pyrénées-Orientales
Postal Code	66423
Map	5 F1
Tel	04-68861608
Fax	04-68861820
e-mail	camping.california@wanadoo.fr
Open	01 Apr – 15 Sep

Leave A9 at exit 41, follow D83 towards Les Bararès. Take D81 towards Canet, immediately turn off at 'Campings Sud' sign. Site on left in 400mtrs.

Size (hectares) 5
Touring pitches 102
Sanitary facilities rating 7.2

water slide • Miniclub every day • Aqualand in St-Cyprien • harbour with museum • Perpignan (30 km)

Electric hook-ups/amps 102/10

Despite appearances, the coast at Le Barcarès is not just there for sun worshippers and pleasure cruisers. Every evening the fishermen sail out, returning the next morning between 7 and 8am with anchovies, sardines and other fish. If you want fresh fish for your barbecue, it is sold on the spot, directly to the consumer. The campsite only allows the use of gas barbecues because of the number of trees and shrubs growing there. Most of the spacious pitches get adequate shade from this greenery, and the campsite is reasonably quiet, particularly towards the back.

In the swimming pool, the children can have great fun on the water slide, and also they have a play area, tennis court, volleyball court, and a ping-pong table. The mini-club is open every day for them, and some evenings there is entertainment for adults on the terrace, such as live music, a dance troupe or a bingo evening. There is no restaurant but some simple food is available at a table under an awning. If you want something more sumptuous you will have to go to the village centre.

Les Bruyères

Rating	7.6
Tariff range	€€€
Town	Maureillas-las-Illas
Department	Pyrénées-Orientales
Postal Code	66480
Map	5 F1
Tel	04-68832664
Fax	04-68835131
Open	01 Feb – 30 Nov

From N9, S of Le Boulou, take D618 to Maureillas, then onto D618 to Céret. Site on left in 1km.

Size (hectares) 4
Touring pitches 68   **Static pitches** 25
Sanitary facilities rating 7.6

small-scale and peaceful • swimming pool and children's pool • shady pitches • museum in Céret • Mont Canigou • Céret (6 km)

Electric hook-ups/amps 68/6-6

Les Bruyères is owned by Madame Viguier, who is the epitome of friendliness, concern and courtesy. Her family turned this oak wood into a quiet, family campsite. An evening of entertainment is held only once every two weeks on the small terrace by the snack bar. The small swimming pool doesn't have any extra facilities such as slides, but that does give you the opportunity to swim up and down in peace. There is a round, shallow pool for small children, who can also have fun in the modest play area.

The pitches have sufficient shade and are distributed through the wood, next to paths, in a natural way. Only the road beside the site disturbs the soothing quiet. There is no elaborate restaurant, so to eat out you will have to go to the small town of Céret. While there, you can also visit the museum of modern art, which houses works by Picasso, Braque, Matisse and other artists. Walkers have plenty of opportunity to explore the area along marked footpaths.

Domaine La Clapère

Rating 7.9
Tariff range €€€€
Town Maureillas-las-Illas
Department Pyrénées-Orientales
Postal Code 66480
Map 5 F1
Tel 04-68833604
Fax 04-68833444
e-mail clapere@aol.fr
Open 01 May – 30 Sep

From Le Boulou take N9 towards Le Perthus. After approx 3 km take D618 to Maureillas, then D13 to Las Illas. Turn right over small bridge.

Size (hectares) 50
Touring pitches 192
Sanitary facilities rating 7.2

large naturist campsite • privacy and shade • good restaurant • good area for walking • museum in Céret • Céret (6 km)

Electric hook-ups/amps 150/3-10

Everything the naturist camper could want is provided here including a wooded, hilly site for families with children of up to about 14 years of age, in which people can play sports and games or just quietly enjoy the surroundings. The pitches are spacious and generally provide sufficient privacy and shade. And if you want complete peace and quiet, there are some pitches towards the back of the site where you can be alone.

Next to the swimming pool there is a good-sized play area, and sports and games are organised on a regular basis. The restaurant has a good menu, though no organised entertainment is provided in the evening as this would disturb the peace and quiet too much. A cabaret-type evening once a week is organised by the campers. The campsite lies among the foothills of the Pyrénées, and is therefore an excellent base for walking trips. For culture lovers there is a museum of modern art in Céret. A trip to the Gorges de la Fou is also highly recommended, as they are thought to be the narrowest in the world.

Cala Gogo

Rating 8.5
Tariff range €€€€
Town St-Cyprien-Plage
Department Pyrénées-Orientales
Postal Code 66750
Map 5 F1
Tel 04-68210712
Fax 04-68210219
e-mail camping.calagogo@wanadoo.fr
Open 10 May – 20 Sep

From D81 turn off towards St-Cyprien-Sud. Site in Les Capellans.

Size (hectares) 12
Touring pitches 400
Sanitary facilities rating 8.9

right by the sea • swimming pool with terrace for sunbathing • disco and restaurant • 500 m from Aqualand • surfing beach and yachting marina • St-Cyprien (1 km)

Electric hook-ups/amps 400/6

People come here for the sun and the beach, and they generally find no reason to spend their time anywhere else. It is quiet in the middle of the day when people relax by the pool or stroll onto the beach, and offers plenty of facilities. The site is supervised, in an unobtrusive way: both the entrance and the gateway to the beach are guarded, and visitors feel safe as a result. The sanitary facilities are modern and quite luxurious. The site's latest attraction is the new swimming pool, designed with fun in mind, has a large amphitheatre-like sunbathing area with reclining chairs. The swimming pool is also bordered by a large terrace with shady straw umbrellas.

The pitches at Cala Gogo are so roomy that you can pitch a small tent next to your caravan with little effort. The campsite also has a stylish restaurant, a pizzeria and a takeaway food outlet. In the daytime there is an arts and crafts club for children of six and over. Entertainment is available for adults in the evenings.

Languedoc-Roussillon

La Pergola

Rating 8.5
Tariff range €€€€
Town Ste. Mairie-la-Mer
Department Pyrénées-Orientales
Postal code 66470
Map 5 F1
Tel 04-68730307
Fax 04-68730240
e-mail info@campinglapergola.com
Open 1 Jun - 30 Sep

In S suburb of Ste. Marie-Plage. A9, exit 41 towards le Barcarès via D83. In 10km right towards Canet via D81. 6km left at rdbt towards Ste. Marie-Plage. Follow signs. Right in 400mtrs; at road end turn left. Site 150mtrs on left.

Size (hectares) 2.7
Touring pitches 150
Sanitary facilities rating 8.3
beautiful beach • Roman history • good washing facilities •
Electric hook-ups/amps 150/10

Campsite La Pergola is located in Sainte-Marie 15 km from Perpignan. A magnificent area with a sandy beach running for 3km from the harbour of Ste. Marie to the mouth of the Agly, and with the beautiful le Canigou in the distance. An exceptional location, ideal for a wonderful holiday with family or friends. The regions has Cathar castles, Roman abbeys and Catalonian villages such as Collioure de Castelnou.

The grounds are located is divided into two areas by a quiet road, and the pitches are separated by hedges. This well maintained campsite enjoys the shade cast by the trees. La Pergola has basins for laundry and dishwashing as well as a washing salon. There is a bathroom for children. There is also a campsite shop (bread, butter, drinks, ice cream, take-away meals), a restaurant and a room with electronic games.

Le Palais de la Mer

Rating 8.2
Tariff range €€€€
Town Ste-Marie-la-Mer
Department Pyrénées-Orientales
Postal Code 66478
Map 5 F1
Tel 04-68730794
Fax 04-68735783
e-mail contact@palaisdelamer.com
Open 10 May – 27 Sep

Leave A9 at exit 41. Follow D83 towards Le Barcarès. Onto D81 towards Canet. At the Ste-Marie rdbt, turn left to Ste-Marie-Plage. After approx 250mtrs turn left. Follow to rdbt then turn left again.

Size (hectares) 3
Touring pitches 128
Sanitary facilities rating 8.3
right by the sea • spacious and shady • petting zoo • windsurfing • The Castillet • Perpignan (15 km)
Electric hook-ups/amps 128/10

Le Palais de la Mer really is a palace among campsites. Thanks to rows of poplars and pine trees, the pitches have abundant shade, while oleanders and other shrubs ensure that there is adequate privacy and screening. It was no easy matter to grow all that greenery, as the soil is saline and its takes a lot of effort to get everything to grow well on it. The salt in the soil comes from the sea, which is separated from the campsite only by the sandy beach.

If you do not feel like swimming in the sea, there is a pool at the campsite, and reclining chairs where sunbathers can while away the hours pleasantly. In the gym there are about a dozen professional-standard exercise machines to help keep your muscles in tone. You must be older than fourteen to use these, and there is no supervision. Next to the restaurant there is a takeaway and meal delivery service, and you need only call to have the meal delivered to your table. Le Palais de la Mer is mainly oriented towards families. There is a disco for the younger campers every evening which finishes at midnight, as the owners want their guests to have a peaceful, undisturbed night.

Le Gibanel

Rating 8
Tariff range €€€
Town Argentat
Department Corrèze
Postal Code 19400
Map 5 E4
Tel 05-55281011
Fax 05-55288162
e-mail contact@camping-gibanel.com
Open 01 Jun – 06 Sep
Site on D18 (Argentat-Égletons), approx 4 km to NE of Argentat.
Size (hectares) 8
Touring pitches 224
Sanitary facilities rating 8.3
château grounds • lake-side location • plenty of activities • old châteaux • waterfalls and reservoirs • Argentat (8 km)
Electric hook-ups/amps 224/6-10

You can see the 13th-century Château Le Gibanel as you drive down the wooded mountainside. It dominates the campsite, which is both large and inviting. The television and recreation rooms are located in charming old buildings, while the pétanque court is in the shadow of the huge beech trees that line the drive. The pitches are set on a field between the reservoir and the château, and though small, they offer a lovely view across the Dordogne Valley. The sanitary facilities are in good condition and cleaned regularly.

If you want to go for a swim, you have two options: either the large swimming pool or the lake, though the latter is rather cold. The campsite boasts a volleyball field, a basketball field and a recreation area, where you can play table tennis or table football. There's an organised entertainment programme for children several times a week, with performances by clowns among others. The lake is used for canoeing and kayaking contests and offers excellent fishing. The château houses the restaurant.

Europe

Rating 7.2
Tariff range €€€
Town Argentat
Department Corrèze
Postal code 19400
Map 5 E4
Tel 05-55280770
Fax 05-55281960
e-mail camping-europe@wanadoo.fr
Open 01 Apr – 31 Oct
From Argentat S on D12 towards Beaulieu-sur-Dordogne. Site on left.
Size (hectares) 2
Touring pitches 97
Sanitary facilities rating 7.1
on the banks of the Dordogne • peace and quiet in a natural setting • water recreation • many sights • good walking and cycling • Argentat (1.5 km)
Electric hook-ups/amps 97/5-10

Europe campsite is set in the middle of natural countryside in a rugged part of the Dordogne. The tranquil tributary was originally built to allow the wood transporter ships to navigate this rough section of the Dordogne without getting into difficulties. These days, the river is filled with canoeists who love the thrill of struggling with raging torrents.

You can watch the events on the water from the campsite, on the pebble beaches along the river or sitting outside your caravan or tent beneath the tall oaks that line the riverbanks. It has a friendly atmosphere, and the pitches are generous and private, especially those along the water. The sanitary facilities are good and clean. The river is fine for swimming, if a little cold, and the temperature of the water in the swimming pool is much more pleasant; smaller children have got their own pool. Volleyball and boules are played on site. The surrounding area offers all sorts of beautiful walking and cycling opportunities, and there are plenty of great days out to be had.

Limousin

Le Vaurette

Rating 8.1
Tariff range €€€
Town Argentat
Department Corrèze
Postal Code 19400
Map 5 E4
Tel 05-55280967
Fax 05-55288114
e-mail info@vaurette.com
Open 01 May – 21 Sep
From Argentat take D12 towards Beaulieu. Site 10 km on left.
Size (hectares) 5
Touring pitches 118
Sanitary facilities rating 8.5
surrounded by nature • good sports facilities • mountains and reservoirs • medieval villages • Argentat (10 km)
Electric hook-ups/amps 118/6

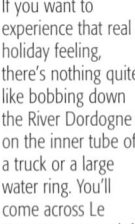 

If you want to experience that real holiday feeling, there's nothing quite like bobbing down the River Dordogne on the inner tube of a truck or a large water ring. You'll come across Le Vaurette on your left and wooded mountainsides on your right. The campsite itself features many beautiful flowerbeds, and the largest pitches are to be found on the central field, with smaller places underneath the trees or along the river. The sanitary facilities are brand-new and exceptionally clean. Le Vaurette also has washing and drying facilities.

The grounds boast a good swimming pool and a well-manicured terrace. For small children, there's a special Children's Club, which organises different activities. The shop stocks a reasonably large assortment of products, including vegetables, fresh bread and bottles of gas. If you want to spend a day away from the site, there's the dam at Le Chastang, Beaulieu Abbey with its superb portal, or one of the 'plus beaux villages de France'. A visit to the beautiful medieval port of Argentat is also recommended.

Le Vianon

Rating 8.4
Tariff range €€€
Town Palisse
Department Corrèze
Postal code 19160
Map 5 E4
Tel 05-55958722
Fax 05-55959845
e-mail camping.vianon@wanadoo.fr
Open All year
From N89, 20 km beyond St-Angel, take D47 to Palisse & Neuvic. 7 km to site (N of Palisse).
Size (hectares) 5.5
Touring pitches 50
Sanitary facilities rating 8.6
rest and privacy • pleasant atmosphere • many activities • wonderful nature • volcanoes, lakes, gorges • Neuvic (9 km)
Electric Hook-ups/amp 50/16

Over winding mountain roads through silent forests, passing rolling fields and tiny hamlets, you reach the top of the hill where Le Vianon is located. Tents and caravans are spread over the camping areas, carefully pitched among shady broad-leaved trees and pines. You will immediately spot the wooden bungalows under the trees, painted in bright colours. The buildings with the pointed roofs that almost reach to the ground contain the clean sanitary facilities. The owners, Patrick and Isabelle Calens, have an eye for cleanliness, and also know how to create a pleasant family atmosphere.

For the little ones there is a special entertainment programme and a large playground with a climbing castle. Teenagers will easily make friends and never get bored. To relax you can cool off in the large swimming pool (with paddling pool), or take a nap in your deck chair. The area around Le Vianon is very inviting for hikers, and the large pond next to the site will challenge the ambitious angler. You might make a day trip to the volcanoes of Auvergne, the lake near Neuvic, the Plateau de Millevaches or the Gorges de la Dordogne. And if you're fed up with cooking, order a pizza on the terrace by the snack bar.

La Plage

Rating	7.6
Tariff range	€€
Town	Treignac
Department	Corrèze
Postal code	19260
Map	5 E5
Tel	05-55980854
Fax	05-55981647
e-mail	camping.la.plage@wanadoo.fr
Open	01 Apr – 30 Sep

Site on D940, 3 km N of Treignac.

Size (hectares) 4
Touring pitches 117
Sanitary facilities rating 7.4
an oasis of rest • well tended • tunnel to the beach • Lac de Bariousses • mountain range at Monédières • Treignac (4 km)
Electric Hook-ups/amp 116/6

La Plage is located along a minor road just outside Treignac and, like almost everywhere in the rural Corrèze region, it is an oasis of calm. Traffic noise is limited anyway, and hardly reaches the campsite.

The 130 spacious pitches are spread over three terraces and offer sufficient privacy. Trees give plenty of shade, and through the various species of hedges and rose bushes there are beautiful views over the lake near Bariousses.

You can reach the lakeside through a tunnel under the road; there is plenty of room for watersports, but motor boats are not allowed on the lake. Part of it is fenced off for a supervised swimming area. Under the trees on the white beach is a snack bar with a terrace, and this is also the place for parties, musical performances, and water polo competitions. Because of this the campsite itself is very quiet.

By taking day trips on foot, by bicycle or by car you can explore the Haut-Corrèze, the nearby mountain range of Monédières, and the famous Plateau de Millevaches 30 km further east. Every morning (weekdays only) there is an entertainment programme for the children at La Plage.

Le Château de Poinsouze

Rating	8.9
Tariff range	€€€€
Town	Boussac-Bourg
Department	Creuse
Postal code	23600
Map	5 F6
Tel	05-55650221
Fax	05-55658649
e-mail	info@camping-de-poinsouze.com
Open	12 May – 15 Sep

A20 (Toulouse), junct 12 Châteauroux. D943 towards Montluçon. 5.5 km beyond La Châtre D917 to Boussac. Site 2.5 km before Boussac.

Size (hectares) 22
Touring pitches 145
Sanitary facilities rating 8.8
beautiful swimming pool • rest and order • Aubusson (tapestry) • potteries • Montluçon (38 km)
Electric Hook-ups/amp 145/6-25

From his turret room the Count de Poinsouze runs this campsite which, among other delights, boasts a terrace with a magnificent view, close to the swimming pool. An artificial lake was created for recreational purposes and on this you can sail your dinghy or any other small boat, go windsurfing or take a pedalo. Swimming is not permitted as there is no supervision, though angling is allowed.

Wherever you choose to pitch camp, the lake is always in sight. The surrounding area is a mixture of sweeping fields and woodlands; after a devastating tornado a few years ago when many old trees were uprooted, new trees and bushes were planted and are gradually maturing. Pitches are open, but privacy is guaranteed thanks to their large size.

Maintenance and cleaning of the luxurious sanitary facilities and the swimming pool is excellent. Children under the age of 12 will probably enjoy being here, although there is only limited organised entertainment. There are many restrictive regulations controlling the use of this campsite, which means it is well run and peaceful.

Limousin

Municipal les Grèves

Rating 7.8
Tariff range €€
Town Aixe-sur-Vienne
Department Haute-Vienne
Postal code 87700
Map 5 E5
Tel 05-55701298
e-mail camping@mairie-aixesurvienne.fr
Open 01 Jun – 30 Sep

From Limoges take N21 to Aixe-sur-Vienne (follow the river). Right 200mtrs after crossing bridge. Route signed from both directions.

Size (hectares) 2.9
Touring pitches 80
Sanitary facilities rating 7.7

flowery and cosy • by the riverside • very clean sanitary facilities • medieval Aixe • many activities • Limoges (9 km)

Electric Hook-ups/amp 65/10-16

Camping Municipal les Grèves is a pretty site that appeals to all ages, with a striking floral appearance thanks to the many hanging baskets. Old oak trees and poplars on the shady central lawn create a casual and typically French atmosphere where pétanque players gather. The sanitary facilities are clean and simple. If you choose a riverside pitch, you can savour the wonderful view of the medieval town of Aixe-sur-Vienne. On site there is a football pitch and a tennis court, but no other sport facilities.

The surrounding area, however, offers lots of opportunities for an active holiday. You can go fishing in the Vienne, or stroll along the many beautiful Romanesque and Neogothic monuments in historic Aixe. Marked walking routes of any distance between 8 and 23 km can be explored in the surrounding hills. Not far from the campsite is an indoor swimming pool offering a reduced entrance fee for campers. Or you can use the climbing wall, or rent a canoe or kayak for a river trip. Local decorative art is on display in various museums, and in Aixe there is an exhibition of enamel work from Limoges. In Limoges itself you can join a guided tour of the famous chinaware factory (with a shop), and visit the Maison de la Porcelaine.

Le Pas de l'Ours

Tariff range €€€
Town Aston
Department Ariège
Postal Code 09310
Map 5 E1
Tel 05-61649033
Fax 05-61649032
e-mail contact@lepasdelours.fr
Open 31 May – 13 Sep

Follow N20 (Foix-Andorre) past Tarascon-sur-Ariège; turn right after Sinsat towards Les Cabannes. Just before this village turn right towards Aston and follow signs. Site S of village.

Size (hectares) 3.5
Touring pitches 32

chalets for rent • entertainment team for children • free mountain bikes • walking and cycling • visit to Andorra • Les Cabannes (1 km)

Electric hook-ups/amps 26/6

This small campsite, located in a valley, is not just a fine place in summer. When the weather is cold or wet you can exchange your tent for a rented chalet. The River Aston runs beside the campsite, but swimming is not permitted in it. Sun-bathing is no problem, but you need a parasol and sun cream as this is an exposed space.

On the bank of the river is a covered barbecue, where once a fortnight a grill party is organised. These parties are particularly popular because you can taste delicacies from the region, like 'assiette de charcuterie de montagne' and 'coustellous grillés'. The sanitary facilities are clean and spacious. An entertainment team organises activities for children, like craftwork, tennis, volleyball and table tennis. A day trip to Andorra could be a bargain hunt, although prices are not as low as they used to be. Take a walk through the mountains to beautiful spots like the Carrière de Talc de Trimouns.

Le Lac

Rating 7.6
Tariff range €€€
Town Mercus-Garrabet
Department Ariège
Postal Code 09400
Map 5 E1
Tel 05-61059061
Fax 05-61059061
e-mail info@campinglac.com
Open 05 Apr – 18 Oct

From Foix follow N20 S to Mercus/Téléski Nautique junct. Site between Mercus & Bompas. Turn left after crossing rail line and follow narrow road for approx 100mtrs.

Size (hectares) 1
Touring pitches 51
Sanitary facilities rating 8

riverside location • spacious, shady • close to railway and motorway • mountains and caves • cheese farms • Tarascon-sur-Ariège (4 km)

Electric hook-ups/amps 51/6-10

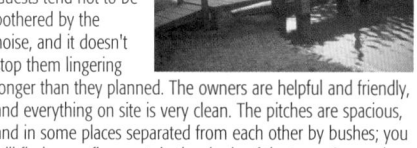

The green campsite of Le Lac lies on the bank of the River Ariège, but is also close to a railroad and a motorway. Guests tend not to be bothered by the noise, and it doesn't stop them lingering longer than they planned. The owners are helpful and friendly, and everything on site is very clean. The pitches are spacious, and in some places separated from each other by bushes; you will find many fine spots in the shade of the trees. Sun seekers also get what they want, especially close to the river.

Swimming in the river is not allowed, and for the safety of small children there is a fence between the campsite and the river. About 1 km from the site you can rent a small boat. There is a table tennis table and boules area, and you can buy ice creams and canned soft drinks beside the inviting swimming pool. Le Lac is not an ideal place for young children, as there are hardly any facilities or activities for them. The nearest town is Tarascon-sur-Ariège, about 4 km away, and if you are interested in French cheese, visit one of the cheese farms in the neighbourhood.

Midi-Pyrénées

Parc d'Audinac les Bains

Rating 8.3
Tariff range €€
Town St. Girons
Department Ariège
Postal Code 09200
Map 5 E2
Tel 05-61664450
Fax 05-61664450
e-mail accueil@audinac.com
Open 01 May – 30 Sep

From St-Girons follow D117 to Foix. Turn left after 3 km at Elf petrol station. Keep to right on rdbt. Site 3 km on right.

Size (hectares) 8
Touring pitches 86
Sanitary facilities rating 8.2

vast camp grounds • many sports facilities • sauna and jacuzzi • rafting and canoeing • prehistoric caves • Saint-Girons (3 km)

Electric hook-ups/amps 86/10

Parc d'Audinac les Bains covers a vast area between the hills, and offers lots of space to all its guests, aiming mainly at families with children. There is enough room to play football or badminton. The size of the grounds and the number of bushes, trees and lawn make Parc d'Adinac les Bains look like a park. Swimming is not allowed in the pond or the river, but there is a swimming pool.

The natural beauty of the valleys is the main attraction of this area, and exploring the neighbourhood is easy when you rent a bike at the campsite. Those who prefer a bit of adventure have a choice of mountaineering, rafting or canoeing. On the site itself you can play a game of tennis or volleyball. There is an entertainment programme for children, which includes a weekly disco party between 9 and 11pm. The mountains offer a challenge to hikers, and all peaks are of a similar height. Combine your walking tour with a visit to one of the many caves with prehistoric paintings, a cheese farm or one of the neighbouring towns like Saint-Girons, Foix or Saint-Gaudens.

Le Sédour

Rating 7.9
Tariff range €€€
Town Surba
Department Ariège
Postal Code 09400
Map 5 E1
Tel 05-61058728
Fax 05-61014933
e-mail info@campinglesedour.com
Open All year

Leave N20 (Tarbes-Ax-les-Thermes) on rdbt just before Tarascon, turn right towards Col de Port/Saurat. Right again after 100mtrs, follow narrow road to site.

Size (hectares) 1.5
Touring pitches 40
Sanitary facilities rating 8.1

mountains and woodlands • quiet and simple • relatively cheap • prehistoric caves • walking and angling • Tarascon-sur-Ariège (2 km)

Electric hook-ups/amps 40/10

At the foot of the Calamès, in the woodlands and near a mountain stream and a farm, lies the simple and above all quiet camp site Le Sédour. There is a large grass area for tents and a section with a great number of site caravans, mainly occupied by older people. The former is the most lively part of the campsite, but generally this is a very quiet place. During the day most campers – many French though a few British – leave the site; in the evening everybody enjoys the sounds of the birds in the trees and the rippling water in the river.

For real relaxation you can take a rod and try your luck by the riverside. There are a few more facilities, including a field for boules, a table tennis table, a slide, a swing – and that's all. The sanitary facilities are equally simple but good and they are kept perfectly clean. The whole area is a hiker's paradise, and you can walk into the mountains straight from the campsite and spend hours without meeting anybody. There are many prehistoric caves, like those in Niaux and Bédeilhac, and all of them are well worth a visit.

Le Pré Lombard

Rating	8.2
Tariff range	€€€€
Town	Tarascon-sur-Ariège
Department	Ariège
Postal Code	09400
Map	5 E1
Tel	05-61056194
Fax	05-61057893
e-mail	leprelombard@wanadoo.fr
Open	22 Mar – 11 Nov

In Tarascon take D23 to Ussat. Cross bridge after 1.5km past bridge, site on right.

Size (hectares) 3.5
Touring pitches 120
Sanitary facilities rating 7.8

perfect family campsite • central location • extensive internet connections • prehistoric cave • walking • Tarascon-sur-Ariège (1 km)

Electric hook-ups/amps 120/10

CCI

Le Pré Lombard is the perfect family campsite, with its wide choice of activities for kids of all ages as well as adults. The site covers a large area, bordered by the River Ariège on one side and mountains on the other. Tents and caravans are pitched along both sides of long, straight lanes. Although this is often a crowded place, it looks very pleasant, in part because of the many trees and other vegetation that lend it a lush appearance. There are the usual facilities like a swimming pool and a recreation room with pin ball machines and a tennis table, but there is also a special entertainments team that keeps the guests, and especially the young ones, busy: archery, aqua gymnastics, karaoke and the Miss Pré Lombard competition.

All of the other facilities are excellent too, and the supermarket only 400m away solves your shopping problems. For an evening out in a bar or discotheque you only have to walk 2 km to Tarascon. Some small villages in the neighbourhood are worth a visit too, and less than 500m from the campsite there is a cave with prehistoric drawings.

Les Terrasses du Lac

Rating	8.1
Tariff range	€€€
Town	Pont-de-Salars
Department	Aveyron
Postal code	12290
Map	5 F3
Tel	05-65468818
Fax	05-65468538
e-mail	campinglesterrasses@wanadoo.fr
Open	01 Apr – 30 Sep

From N88 S of Rodez take D91 then D523 to Le Vibal. Site on right.

Size (hectares) 6
Touring pitches 135
Sanitary facilities rating 8.5

good privacy • splendid location • friendly welcome • Roquefort and gastronomic delights • castles and villages • Rodez (25 km)

Electric hook-ups/amps 135/6

CCI

Les Terrasses du Lac lies in the ever-verdant Aveyron district, and the grounds on either side of the entrance look out over the extensive Lac de Pont de Salars. You will not find anyone directly opposite your tent, as the spacious pitches are arrayed in rows on hillside terraces and separated by hedges. On the left-hand section is a splendid view over the rolling landscape. The view from the right-hand section is much more confined due to the tall trees.

You can only reach the lake itself after an exciting walk along steep footpaths, but it is a paradise for anglers who can catch fresh trout or perch for the grill. On the public beach, just outside the campsite, a lifeguard watches over swimmers. As well as the two play areas and the paddling pool there is a special club for young children. The sanitary facilities are very good; spacious, cheerful and brightly coloured. The surrounding area is rich in old trades and crafts: at the market in Pont-de-Salars, where local products are mainly sold, you can visit workshops and see the potter or the wood turner at work.

Midi-Pyrénées

Le Caussanel Lac de Pareloup

Rating 7.7
Tariff range €€€€
Town Canet-de-Salars
Department Aveyron
Postal code 12290
Map 5 F3
Tel 05-65468519
Fax 05-65468985
e-mail info@lecaussanel.com
Open 28 Apr – 13 Sep
Take D911 W towards Pont-de-Salars. Approx 2.5km before Pont-de-Salars take D992 on left. At junct with D535 turn right, immediately left to site. Site SE of Canet-de-Salars.
Size (hectares) 10
Touring pitches 135
Sanitary facilities rating 7.8
quiet and spacious • beautiful location by lake • many facilities • Lac de Pareloup • Roquefort cellars • Salles Curan (10 km)
Electric hook-ups/amps 135/6

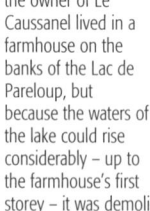 

The grandparents of the owner of Le Caussanel lived in a farmhouse on the banks of the Lac de Pareloup, but because the waters of the lake could rise considerably – up to the farmhouse's first storey – it was demolished in the 1950's. The attractive barns now house the reception, table tennis room, sanitary facilities, bar and restaurant. The pitches are spacious (though there is little privacy) and the sanitary facilities are reasonable.

The rolling ground provides splendid views of the lake, which swarms with small boats and people engaged in watersports. You can jog along the sandy beach or play a game of tennis. For the younger children there is a small swimming pool and a delightful play area; every morning, the kids' club meets in the tepee. The shop is well stocked, and the butcher visits three times a week. Mainly local specialities are served in the restaurant, such as smoked breast of duck, duck confit or Salade Aveyronnaise, or you could just order a pizza. More adventurous activities are available outside the site: canyoning, bungee jumping, caving, hang gliding, mountain climbing or an exciting tour by mountain bike.

Les Rivages

Rating 8.5
Tariff range €€€€
Town Millau
Department Aveyron
Postal code 12100
Map 5 F3
Tel 05-65610107
Fax 05-65590356
e-mail campinglesrivages@wanadoo.fr
Open 01 Apr – 15 Oct
Site 2 km E of Millau, on D991 to Nant.
Size (hectares) 7
Touring pitches 286
Sanitary facilities rating 8.5
plenty of activities • close to the town • beautiful walking routes • Tarn River • Millau (0.5 km)
Electric hook-ups/amps 286/6-10

Surrounded by the high mountains of Millau with their steep cliffs, Les Rivages is set idyllically beside the River Tarn. There is a large tent for children up to 13, plus play areas, ping-pong tables, tennis courts, two swimming pools, terraces, a restaurant, a snack bar and an open air theatre. The activities include sports, games, trips to explore the surrounding area and other open-air activities. Then there is evening entertainment in the form of plays, dancing, cabaret, carnivals, circuses or musical entertainment while you dine! However, the activity area is so placed that it will not disturb you.

The restaurant has an extensive and delicious menu at affordable prices. The pitches are shady and the sanitary facilities are luxurious and clean, with a children's section with toilets in various sizes, baby baths, a nappy changing table and a small wash basin. You can go swimming in the Tarn, where a number of footpaths give direct access to the river and its gravel beaches. Most children (and adults) prefer the river to the swimming bath, where they can build dams and paddle about in a rubber boat, though the current can be strong.

Val de Cantobre

Rating	8.5
Tariff range	€€€€
Town	Nant
Department	Aveyron
Postal code	12230
Map	5 G3
Tel	05-65584300
Fax	05-65621036
e-mail	info@rcnvaldecantobre.fr
Open	12 Apr – 11 Oct

Follow N9 Millau/Millau-Centre signs. After 2nd rdbt follow Montpellier signs. Then signs for Gorges de la Dourbie/Nant. Site 4 km N of Nant on D991.

Size (hectares) 7.5
Touring pitches 99
Sanitary facilities rating 9.1
wonderful view • swimming pool and sports field • good restaurant • Roquefort village, famous for cheese • L'Aven Armand Cave • Millau (25 km)
Electric hook-ups/amps 99/4-8

Because this campsite is set on a terraced hillside, nearly every pitch has a splendid view of the village of Cantobre on the other side of the valley. The terraces are wide and provide enough space to park your car next to the tent or caravan. This campsite is a favourite of families with children of up to twelve years old, who can have the time of their lives in the swimming pool and on the beautiful playing field.

The sanitary facilities are modern and spotlessly clean. The restaurant offers a set menu that changes daily, and often includes regional products. Just thinking about Roquefort can set gastronomic enthusiasts' mouths watering, but even if your tastes are less sophisticated it is worth visiting this small village to see the production of its world-famous cheese. But there is much more here. Even if you have seen almost all the caves, L'Aven Armand is so unique that you really have to see it. The Templars' citadel at La Couvertoirade should not be missed, either. Evening entertainment is only provided a couple of times per week, but nobody minds that.

Les Peupliers

Rating	8.4
Tariff range	€€€
Town	Rivière-sur-Tarn
Department	Aveyron
Postal code	12640
Map	5 F3
Tel	05-65598517
Fax	05-65610903
e-mail	lespeupliers12640@wanadoo.fr
Open	01 Apr – 30 Sep

Site 150mtrs S of Rivière-sur-Tarn, 11 km N of Millau.

Size (hectares) 2
Touring pitches 102
Sanitary facilities rating 8.7
family campsite • sports facilities • peace and quiet • canoe trip through caves • Vautours (birds of prey) • Millau (12 km)
Electric hook-ups/amps 102/6

This is an old-fashioned family campsite beside the River Tarn where more sunshine days are enjoyed than the rest of the French mid-south. The owner drove around the most beautiful parts when he was a lorry driver forty years ago: nowadays the only route that he still drives frequently is to the starting point for the canoe trip through the Gorges du Tarn, where he drops his campsite guests.

At the site there are several table tennis tables, but if you are feeling active and prefer something else, you can sign up for pony trekking, caving or climbing. Every week there is an organised evening walk to the illuminated Peyrelade. The bird-of-prey park in Vautours and the caves of Roquefort must also be classed among the 'compulsory' sights to see.

According to an old story, a drover left his bag of bread and cheese nearby, and weeks later, he found it had turned into a delicious blue cheese - now called Roquefort! Good takeaway meals are served here. If you want to cool off, there is the Tarn (where you can also fish) and the swimming pool. There are plenty of activities, such as karaoke and shuffleboard.

Les Tours

Rating	8.1
Tariff range	€€€€
Town	St-Amans-des-Cots
Department	Aveyron
Postal code	12460
Map	5 F4
Tel	05-65448810
Fax	05-65448307
e-mail	camping@les-tours.com
Open	20 May – 07 Sep

Site 6 km SE of St-Amans-des-Cots. Then take D97 & D599 to lake.

Size (hectares) 15
Touring pitches 153
Sanitary facilities rating 8.5
recreational lake • beautiful view • peace and quiet • Lot Valley • Château de Calmont-d'Olt • Laguiole (16 km)
Electric hook-ups/amps 153/6

There are breathtaking views from this campsite, and where the owner's parents used to graze cattle fifty years ago there is now a glittering reservoir. On its banks, almost all the spacious pitches can look out on the windsurfers as they skim across the water. There is plenty of privacy, due to the site's layout on hillside terraces with numerous trees, which in turn attract lots of birds. On the highest pitches, static caravans are available to rent. The sanitary facilities are state-of-the-art; you can enjoy the view even as you wash. A shop sells a wide range of goods, and simple meals are served in the bistro.

The terrace next to the swimming pool is a delightful spot for an aperitif. Older children will find table tennis and other amusements, and there is a play area for younger children. A campfire is lit once a week next to the football field. If you are celebrating, you can try one of the local restaurants 16 km away in Laguiole. You can also go on delightful day trips to Bez-Bedène, Conques, Espalion and Estaing. The Lot valley is an excellent place for challenging walking and cycling.

Campéole La Boissière

Rating	8
Tariff range	€€€
Town	St-Geniez-d'Olt
Department	Aveyron
Postal code	12130
Map	5 F3
Tel	05-65704043
Fax	05-65475639
Open	25 Apr – 25 Sep

In Laissac (via D45 & D95) turn right at crossroads towards site. Try to avoid town centre.

Size (hectares) 5
Touring pitches 125   **Static pitches** 5
Sanitary facilities rating 8.2
beautiful riverside scenery • generous pitches • swimming and fishing • numerous places to visit • walking and cycling routes • Saint-Geniez-d'Olt (0.5 km)
Electric hook-ups/amps 120/6-10

Campéole La Boissière is a tranquil campsite beside the River Lot, right on the edge of the village of Saint-Geniez-d'Olt. It offers abundant shade and generously-sized pitches which, because of the gently rolling terrain, mostly look out over the river. Apart from a few simple items, only fresh bread is sold at the campsite; for your daily shopping you can go to the centre of Saint-Geniez, only 500m from the site. Here it is always pleasantly busy, with some nice shops and good restaurants that serve local specialities.

There are three large tennis courts on site which are run by the council, and a large swimming pool and a separate pool for children. Activities are organised in the morning and afternoon, and there are also volleyball and table tennis facilities. Two sanitary blocks with clean facilities serve all the campers well. The site is a favourite with a core of regular visitors who organise many activities for themselves, among them fishing and boules. A number of places in the surrounding area are well worth visiting, like Laissac, where France's fourth largest cattle market is held every Tuesday.

La Grange de Monteillac

Rating 8.5
Tariff range €€€€
Town Sévérac-l'Église
Department Aveyron
Postal code 12310
Map 5 F3
Tel 05-65702100
Fax 05-65702101
e-mail info@la-grange-de-monteillac.com
Open 01 Apr – 15 Oct
Site N of Sévérac-l'Eglise, 300mtrs off N88, and approx 20 km W of A75.
Size (hectares) 4.5
Touring pitches 70
Sanitary facilities rating 8.7
hearty welcome • nice activities • clean and spacious • visits to cheese factories • sports activities • Rodez (25 km)
Electric hook-ups/amps 70/6

The luxurious campsite La Grange de Monteillac lies at the approach to the rural village of Séverac, where the houses are decorated with flower boxes and the farmers still herd their cattle along the street. The modern reception building also houses a small shop and luxurious washing facilities, and pitches are reasonably spacious. An old country manor and a wonderful barn built in the local style of Aveyron houses a youth club, a restaurant and bar, and you can look up at the original wooden roof beams.

The terraces lead to the swimming pools and the children's paddling pool with its small slide. Every week, a musical evening or an Apéro (cocktail party) is organised, with a disco for children. During the day, clubs are held for youngsters; among other things, they might be initiated in the art of juggling, and later they can show what they have learned in a special performance. You can take part in activities outside the campsite under qualified supervisors, like abseiling from a château, or a two-hour trip from treetop to treetop, without touching the ground, using pulleys, rope bridges and lianas.

Les Cantarelles

Rating 7.5
Tariff range €€€
Town Villefrance-de-Panat
Department Aveyron
Postal code 12430
Map 5 F3
Tel 05-65464035
Fax 05-65464035
e-mail cantarelles@wanadoo.fr
Open 01 May – 30 Sep
Site 4 km NE of Villefranche-de-Panat on D25.
Size (hectares) 3.5
Touring pitches 158
Sanitary facilities rating 7.3
abundant water sports facilities • spacious and green • high (727 m) • hiking • medieval villages • Requista (15 km)
Electric hook-ups/amps 140/6

Les Cantarelles lies by the Lac de Villefranche-de-Panat, one of three lakes on the Plateau du Lévezou. Most pitches have a splendid view over the water, and by comparison with the other lakes, this one is wonderfully tranquil. The site is high up (727m), and as a result the days are warm and the nights cool. The sanitary facilities are spotless. Everyone is welcome in the bar/cafeteria, and you can shop in the village, 3 km away, as only bread, milk and hot snacks are available on the site. For younger children there is a play area and an entertainments supervisor.

You can fish or swim in the lake, and there are canoes, kayaks and surfboards for hire: or sign up for rafting in the Gorges du Tarn, or a guided 'randonnée' (hike) along narrow footpaths. Briand, the campsite owner, has mapped out all the local sights for his guests and is happy to explain them for you (in French, of course). Castelnau-Pegayrolles is a medieval walled town built of pink sandstone, with no fewer than five historic monuments, including a hydraulic system that is among the top one hundred protected world monuments.

Midi-Pyrénées

Les Lacs de Courtès

Rating 7.3
Tariff range €€€
Town Estang
Department Gers
Postal Code 32240
Map 4 D3
Tel 05-62096198
Fax 05-62096313
Open 27 Mar – 30 Sep
E from Mont-de-Marsan on D1 to Estang (35 km). Site S of village, just behind church.
Size (hectares) 3.5
Touring pitches 80
Sanitary facilities rating 7.4
quiet in spring and autumn • entertainment programme • sports facilities • visit to an Armagnac factory • cycling and walking tours • Estang (5 km)
Electric hook-ups/amps 80/6-16

[CCI]

Two decades ago the current owner bought this hilly piece of land to build a 'centre de loisir'. It has a wonderful layout, with a very large fish pond, some small 'étangs' and a modern swimming pool. There are also facilities for archery, angling and boating, and extensive entertainment programmes for all ages. The thoughtful owner has improved the sanitary facilities, and there are attractive chalets for hire. For the smallest visitors there is a special programme that includes treasure hunts, building huts in the forest, and playing on the small sandy beach by the pond. Older children and adults can play water polo, volleyball, basketball or bowling.

Parents can join the aquagymnastics or pay a visit to the factory nearby where Armagnac is produced. In the evening people tend to gather on the dance floor with a glass of wine. If you want you can show off your talent as an actor or singer. You don't have to travel far for a night in the casino in Barbotan-les-Thermes, or a day in the 'marché aux puces' in Cazaubon or Eauze. Everything is within easy reach, for the very young, the young and the older guests.

Camp de Florence

Rating 7.6
Tariff range €€€€
Town la Romieu
Department Gers
Postal Code 32480
Map 4 D3
Tel 05-62281558
Fax 05-62282004
e-mail info@lecampdeflorence.com
Open 01 Apr – 11 Oct
A64, junct Agen-Auch. Then take D931 to Condom. Turn left in Ligardes (D36), then right. Follow D166 to La Romieu. Site 500mtrs NE of La Romieu (signed).
Size (hectares) 15
Touring pitches 100   **Static pitches** 50
Sanitary facilities rating 7.4
fine swimming pool • historic site • many facilities • castles, antique markets • lots of cultural sights • La Romieu (0.5 km)
Electric hook-ups/amps 100/6-10

Dutchman Mr Mijnsbergen started this campsite in 1983 in Gascogne, on a historic site where mercenaries from Florence had been quartered (which explains the name of the site). He was a cook on a passenger ship and had already seen a lot of the world before he came to this place. His son and his English daughter-in-law are now running the site. La Romieu is a small town 500m away that earned a place in the UNESCO World Heritage List. Here you can find a bakery, a restaurant, a supermarket and a doctor.

On the campsite there are many sports facilities: a tennis court, boules alleys, table tennis tables, football, volleyball and basketball pitches. There is also a room with pool tables, a TV set and games. Around a field, where either sunflowers or wheat is growing, are the spacious pitches. Children can play games under the guidance of an instructor, and there is a kids' club for the youngest where they can take part in a pancake party. If one is celebrating a birthday, a clown will ride them around the campsite in a decorated car. Elsewhere there are facilities for flying in microlight planes, kart racing or angling. The fine swimming pool has a jacuzzi that is also accessible for wheelchair users.

Le Talouch

Rating 7.6
Tariff range €€€€
Town Roquelaure
Department Gers
Postal Code 32810
Map 4 D2/3
Tel 05-62655243
Fax 05-62655368
e-mail info@camping-talouch.com
Open 01 Apr – 30 Sep
Site signed on N21. Follow D272 to Roquelaure and turn left (D148). Site on left (SW of Roquelaure).
Size (hectares) 9
Touring pitches 110
Sanitary facilities rating 7.7
interesting excursions • relatively unknown area • helpful owners • picturesque villages and châteaux • white-water canoeing • Auch (8 km)
Electric hook-ups/amps 110/4-6

In 1981 a young married couple from Holland gave up their jobs and started removing all the blackberry bushes and birches from an old and abandoned campsite. With an 18-month-old child and another one on the way, Hetty and Arnold Bil took the plunge. It takes some time to attract people to a new campsite, but an article by a journalist friend drew more than fifty guests in the first year.

The site is full of activities. You have a choice of numerous excursions ranging from white-water canoeing to a family day trip by coach to the stages of the Tour de France or a visit to Lourdes. A much shorter trip could bring you to a jazz or country music festival, the cathedral of Auch, or the 370 steps of the Tour d'Armagnac. The Gers region is still relatively unknown, but it has a lot to offer, and so has the campsite: games for young children, survival training, ghost hunts and shows are all on offer. Teenagers can play tennis, water polo and volleyball, or meet at a place where hanging around is the best way of relaxing. A night watchman guarantees a quiet night.

Soleil du Pibeste

Rating 7.4
Tariff range €€€
Town Agos-Vidalos
Department Hautes-Pyrénées
Postal Code 65400
Map 4 D2
Tel 05-62975323
e-mail info@campingpibeste.com
From Lourdes on N21 site on right, just before Agos-Vidalos.
Size (hectares) 1.5
Touring pitches 60   **Static pitches** 1
Sanitary facilities rating 7.2
wonderful view • entertainment programme • multilingual staff • canoeing, rafting • pilgrim city of Lourdes • Argelès-Gazost (5 km)
Electric hook-ups/amps 60/3-15

This beautiful terraced campsite lies at the foot of the Pibeste, and whether you are swimming in the pool or using the washing-room, you always have that wonderful view of the mountains. During the day there are many outdoor activities, so it is rather quiet on the campsite itself, with the exception of the swimming pool of course.

The owners invite village people in to teach guests the skills needed for the traditional game of boules, and every day there is some kind of entertainment for all ages. Once a week the library becomes a dance hall! Sports fans have a wide choice on offer: horse riding, cycle racing, archery, canoeing, and rafting. Should you prefer a day of rest acquiring some knowledge, go the library which is an oasis of silence (except on that special dance evening). There is a supermarket opposite the campsite, but you might prefer to do some shopping on the farm that belongs to the family of the owner, where you can buy dairy products. For a day trip you can go to nearby Spain or historic Lourdes and Toulouse. Argelès-Gazost, much smaller, is 5 km away.

Midi-Pyrénées

Le Lac

Rating	8.3
Tariff range	€€€
Town	Arcizans-Avant
Department	Hautes-Pyrénées
Postal Code	65400
Map	4 D2
Tel	05-62970188
Fax	05-62970188
e-mail	campinglac@campinglac65.fr
Open	15 May – 30 Sep

From Argelès-Gazost take D21 south. At rdbt at end of own, follow St.-Savin sign. Keep to caravan route via D13. Follow site signs in town.

Size (hectares) 4
Touring pitches 90
Sanitary facilities rating 8.3

extensive green areas • partially covered swimming pool • disco & party hall in 100m • close to national park • delta kiting & hang-gliding • St.-Savin (2 km)

Electric hook-ups/amps 70/5-10

Le Lac campsite is especially suited to people who are looking for a mix of rest, countryside and sports but who also want to stay near a town. The site is surrounded by woods and is clean and well-maintained. The pitches differ greatly from one another - large, small, protected or unprotected. Le Lac owes its name to the nearby storage reservoir, where swimming is strictly prohibited.

The campsite is located in an undulating area in the middle of the mountains, and you can walk directly into the Parc National de Pyrénées. There is a small shop, a partially covered swimming pool with a meadow for sunbathing, a jeu-de-boules court and very clean sanitary facilities. Although the campsite itself does not offer any evening entertainment, there is a disco and party hall just 100 metres away. The surrounding area provides ample opportunity to go fishing, delta kiting, hang-gliding, white water rafting, canoeing and to play tennis. And after all that activity guests can in the bar in the evening.

The campsite is centrally located for day trips, such as to the busy Cirque de Gavarnie or to the much quieter Cirque de Troumouse; and, of course, a visit to the pilgrimage site of Lourdes is a must. Closer still are St. Savin, Argeles and Tarascon, with their attractive restaurants and cafés.

Les Trois Vallées

Rating	7.2
Tariff range	€€€€
Town	Argelès-Gazost
Department	Hautes-Pyrénées
Postal Code	65400
Map	4 D2
Tel	05-62903547
Fax	05-62903548
e-mail	3-vallees@wanadoo.fr
Open	07 Mar – 12 Nov

From Lourdes follow N21 to just before Argelès-Gazost; turn left after Champion supermarket.

Size (hectares) 14
Touring pitches 250
Sanitary facilities rating 7

rich vegetation • sauna and jacuzzi • entertainment programme for children • Funiculaire du Pic du Jer • picturesque towns • Argelès-Gazost (1 km)

Electric hook-ups/amps 250/3-6

This large campsite offers excellent facilities, with spacious pitches well separated from each other, and bushes, trees and flowers to form an attractive landscape. The sanitary facilities are luxurious, clean and easily accessible for less able guests. The large indoor and outdoor pools attract many campers, as do the sauna and the jacuzzi. The indoor pool is chiefly meant to be used in winter, though all the bathing facilities will be extended in due course.

With all these attractions Les Trois Vallées is a perfect destination for families with children. There is an entertainment programme for small children, and musical evenings and theatre performances for all ages. On the N21, which leads to the campsite, you will find the Champion supermarket. With so many facilities at hand it is possible to almost forget about the Pyrénées, and picturesque towns in the neighbourhood like Argelès-Gazost, Auch, Tarbes and Lourdes. A ride on the Funiculaire du Pic du Jer is a great experience, when the electric train rises to an altitude of more than 1,000m to some caves.

Les Fruitiers

Rating 7.1
Tariff range €€
Town Bagnères-de-Bigorre
Department Hautes-Pyrénées
Postal Code 65200
Map 4 D2
Tel 05-62952597
Fax 05-62952597
e-mail danielle.villemur@wanadoo.fr
Open 01 May – 31 Oct
From Tarbes take D935; turn left after 300mtrs (towards Toulouse). At road end turn right (motorway sign to Toulouse); site on left (250mtrs).
Size (hectares) 1.5
Touring pitches 109
Sanitary facilities rating 6.8
quiet, cosy • panoramic view • cheap and clean • mountain passes • pilgrims destination of Lourdes • Bagnères-de-Bigorre (1 km)
Electric hook-ups/amps 85/2-6

Just a short distance from the well-known health spa Bagnères-de-Bigorre is this simple campsite offering a panoramic view of the Pyrénéan mountain ranges. The vicinity of so many mountain passes that are famous among cyclists makes Les Fruitiers extra attractive. You need to be in perfect physical condition to conquer these 'cols' of Tour de France fame, with a 24-speed bike since differences in altitude are considerable. The camping fees are low, and there's a supermarket and restaurants nearby. The bustle in Bagnères does not affect the campsite, which is quiet with a pleasant atmosphere.

Between the spacious pitches there is always a tree or bush to maintain boundaries. The sanitary buildings are simple though clean, and recreational facilities are limited, so Les Fruitiers is hardly suitable for children. The municipal swimming pool is only 200m away, and elsewhere you can play tennis or ride a horse. Most guests spend their time cycling or walking in this splendid mountain area. Day trips can be made to mountains with well-known names like Tourmalet or Col d'Aspin, and Lourdes, the world famous pilgrim's destination, is only 20 km away.

Hélio Nature L'Eglantière

Rating 7.2
Tariff range €€€€
Town Castelnau-Magnoac
Department Hautes-Pyrénées
Postal Code 65230
Map 4 D2
Tel 05-62398800
Fax 05-62398144
e-mail info@leglantiere.com
Open 01 Apr – 30 Sep
From N on D929, turn left 6 km beyond Castelnau, follow small signs 'L'Eglantière'; turn right after 3 km near church.
Size (hectares) 45
Touring pitches 91
Sanitary facilities rating 7.3
nudist camp site • green oasis • swimming pool and river • historic villages • canoeing on the Gers • Castelnau-Magnoac (6 km)
Electric hook-ups/amps 87/10

The first nudist campsite in the Hautes Pyrénées is a small paradise. This site, situated near the village of Castelnau-Magnoac is often described as a green oasis, and high old trees, bushes and narrow lanes are responsible for this reputation. All over the grounds you can see wild flowers, like orchids and roses. You can take a refreshing dive into the crowded swimming pool or the River Gers, where you can relax on the banks and sunbathe, undisturbed by traffic noise. Although this is often a crowded campsite, service at the reception desk and in the bar is friendly and helpful.

The sanitary facilities are simple but clean, and the restaurant and the snack bar look cosy and inviting. Children can join the miniclub every day to play or do craftwork. There are all sorts of activities for older children like a treasure hunt, archery or a volleyball competition. No wonder that so few guests leave the site, although there is enough to do and to see in the neighbourhood. You can rent a canoe for a tour on the Gers or make a full day trip to the olive trees of Alto Aragón in nearby Spain. This site is also a good starting point for long or short walks to the many historic villages.

Airotel Pyrénées

Rating	8.1
Tariff range	€€€€
Town	Esquièze-Sère
Department	Hautes-Pyrénées
Postal Code	65120
Map	4 D1/2
Tel	05-62928918
Fax	05-62929650
e-mail	airotel.pyrenees@wanadoo.fr
Open	01 Jan – 30 Sep, 01 Dec – 31 Dec

From Lourdes take N21 to Pierrefitte, then D921 to Luz-Saint-Sauveur. Site on left, just before village.

Size (hectares) 2.8
Touring pitches 80
Sanitary facilities rating 8.3

sauna, fitness training • outdoor and indoor swimming pools • climbing wall and cycling paths • mountain area • rafting, canoeing • Luz-Saint-Sauveur (1 km)

Electric hook-ups/amps 80/3-10

Airotel Pyrénées is a modern campsite in a mountain area in the Parc National des Pyrénées. It aims mainly at sports enthusiasts, and has a climbing wall as well as a sauna, an indoor and an outdoor swimming pool and a fitness centre. There is also table tennis and – in keeping with French tradition – a place to play boules.

For children there is an entertainment programme twice a week. It is an open place where there are relatively few trees, so don't forget to bring a parasol for protection against the burning sun. The sanitary facilities are simple but good and very clean.

There is a lot to do outside the campsite – walking, cycling, horse riding, rafting and canoeing. The wonderful Cirque de Gavarnie is nearby, and if you like stretching yourself you can climb the Tourmalet on your bicycle as if you were a Tour de France superstar. Half a kilometre away lies the interesting town of Luz-Saint-Sauveur that has a few shops, restaurants and a real castle ruin rising high over the houses.

International

Rating	7.7
Tariff range	€€€
Town	Esquièze-Sère
Department	Hautes-Pyrénées
Postal Code	65120
Map	4 D1/2
Tel	05-62928202
Fax	05-62929687
e-mail	reception@international-camping.fr
Open	20 Dec – 20 Apr, 01 Jun – 30 Sep

From Argelès-Gazost S to Pierrefitte, follow D921 to 1 km before Luz-Saint-Sauveur. Site on left.

Size (hectares) 4
Touring pitches 140
Sanitary facilities rating 7.5

casual atmosphere • grand view • entertainment programme for children • walking in the mountains • castle ruins • Luz-Saint-Sauveur (1 km)

Electric hook-ups/amps 140/2-6

This site in the Pyrénées is a very simple one, and the casual atmosphere attracts people back year after year. The owners are very friendly and speak English. Their site has been laid out on terraces with many trees and other vegetation, and from every position you have a grand view of the Pyrénées, where birds of prey circle around the mountain tops. The shop is well stocked, and the sanitary facilities, although rather small, are in excellent condition. During the day quite a few campers leave for long walks in the mountains, where a tour of the magnificent Cirque de Gavarnie is very popular. Other possibilities include mountaineering, rafting, hang-gliding and horse riding.

The ruins of the castle near Luz are worth a visit, and a procession in the evening in nearby Lourdes is an unforgettable experience. For the youngest children there is an extensive entertainment programme. The evenings are for the teenagers and adults, but in general it is a quiet campsite. There is, however, some noise from the traffic on the nearby road. If you want more entertainment, you can walk to Luz-Saint-Sauveur, where you will find a lot of restaurants and bars.

Pyrénées Natura

Rating 9
Tariff range €€€€
Town Estaing
Department Hautes-Pyrénées
Postal Code 65400
Map 4 D2
Tel 05-62974544
Fax 05-62974581
e-mail info@camping-pyrenees-natura.com
Open 01 May – 20 Sep
From Tarbes & Lourdes (N21) turn right in Argelès-Gazost and take D918. Left after 8 km (towards Lac d'Estaing), over D13 & D103 to Estaing and site.
Size (hectares) 2.5
Touring pitches 52
Sanitary facilities rating 9.2
nature camp site • bird watching • good library • municipal swimming pool (free) • walking in the mountains • Argelès-Gazost (11 km)
Electric hook-ups/amps 52/3-10

Pyrénées Natura can be found at an altitude of about 1,000m in an unspoilt valley where numerous birds, chamois, marmots and other animals live, surrounded by a ring of mountains. The site is planted with trees, bushes and lawns, and split in two by a murmuring river. Between the tents and caravans you can see chickens and chicks walking around. An observation post attracts many bird watchers, eager to get a glimpse of the vultures.

A qualified naturalist can take you on a walking tour through the mountains, and other experts can teach you white-water canoeing or trout fishing. There are few facilities for children, apart from a pool table and a gigantic chess board in the open air. Above the reception desk and bar is a large room with comfortable couches and chairs, and guests can borrow books from the well stocked library. For more entertainment you can go to Arrens (3 km) where you can have free use of the municipal swimming pool, or try the mini golf and the tennis courts. Good shops and restaurants can be found in Argelès-Gazost, a pleasant bicycle ride of 11 km.

Relais Océan Pyrénées

Rating 8.1
Tariff range €€
Town Poueyferré
Department Hautes-Pyrénées
Postal Code 65100
Map 4 D2
Tel/Fax 05-62945722
Open 01 May – 30 Sep
From Tarbes follow N21, turn right before rail viaduct (towards Pau from Soumoulou, D940). Site 3.5 km on left.
Size (hectares) 1.2
Touring pitches 86
Sanitary facilities rating 7.8
amazing trees • quiet • central location • walking in the mountains • Grotte de Massabielle • Lourdes (2 km)
Electric hook-ups/amps 86/4-10

In the vicinity of the Pyrénées, 2 km from Lourdes, is this camp site with its many trees, bushes and lawns. The conifers that separate the pitches have been trimmed to a perfect height so that they guarantee the privacy you need. The site is laid out in terraces on the slope of a hill, and the most striking aspect is the trees whose fluffy red blossoms form a colourful roof. The guests are generally older people who are offered a wide choice of facilities including a small snack bar, a shop, a television room, a swimming pool, and even a trampoline!

If fun is what you are looking for, this may not be the place for you. But the area is a perfect location for those who like walking or riding, rafting or hang-gliding. The Pyrénées are an ideal destination for day-trip lovers, or those who dream of climbing the Tourmalet on a bicycle. One of the world's most famous places of pilgrimage, Lourdes, lies within walking distance. A visit to the Grotte de Massabielle or the Basilique du Rosaire should not be missed either. Relais Océan Pyrénées is a pleasant site without too much fuss.

Midi-Pyrénées

Les Chalets sur la Dordogne

Rating 7.7
Tariff range €€
Town Bretenoux
Department Lot
Postal Code 46130
Map 5 E4
Tel 05-65109333
e-mail contact@camping-leschalets.com
Open 01 May – 30 Sep
Site on D703, approx 3 km W of Bretenoux towards Vayrac.
Turn left just before bridge over Dordogne.
Size (hectares) 2.5
Touring pitches 39   **Static** 7
Sanitary facilities rating 7.9
private beach on a river • not too large • entertainment for
children • the Dordogne river • Rocamadour • Bretenoux (3 km)
Electric hook-ups/amps 39/6-10

This campsite, which is not too large, lies under trees right on the bank of the Dordogne River. These trees offer ample shade to all of the pitches, and despite being located on a busy road, the site is known for its quiet atmosphere. Guests who do not want to sleep in a tent can rent one of the chalets in the grounds. There is a limited programme of entertainment for children on some days, including grilling fish, playing water polo or participating in jeu-de-boules contests; but they do have fun just playing in the river and on its banks, where canoeing, fishing, swimming and sunbathing are among the possibilities. There are even barbecue pits along the Dordogne. There is a small swimming pool near the patio. The modern sanitary facilities are clean and fresh.

The reasonably priced restaurant offers traditional French meals and has an extensive wine list. You can order fresh bread or buy a newspaper or ice cream at the shop. Those who want more can go 3 km further along to Bretenoux with its attractive shops and restaurants. The Dordogne is famous for its many caves with prehistoric cave drawings, a number of which can be visited. And locations such as Rocamadour and the larger Sarlat are also perfect for a day out.

Rivière de Cabessut

Rating 8.3
Tariff range €€€
Town Cahors
Department Lot
Postal Code 46000
Map 5 E3
Tel 05-65300630
Fax 05-65239946
e-mail contact@cabessut.com
Open 01 Apr – 30 Sep
Follow N20 Brive-Montauban; in Cahors take D911 to Rodez.
Site NE of Cahors on river (signed).
Size (hectares) 5
Touring pitches 113
Sanitary facilities rating 8.4
quiet • tidy • fine mini golf course • Pont Valentré • historic
railway • Cahors (1 km)
Electric hook-ups/amps 113/10

In 1991 a market garden on the bank of the Lot was turned into a campsite, and ever since then the owners and their son have been running it as a popular place for older people who enjoy a quiet holiday. In summer the number of families with young children rises; they come here to enjoy the sights and attractions of the neighbourhood. Cahors is worth a visit because of its gastronomy, and also for its widely-appreciated 18th-century architecture and wide promenades.

A special attraction is the historic railway line between Cahors and Cajarc; you can combine a ride on the train with a return trip by boat. Château de Cénevières in Cajarc should not be missed. The level pitches on the campsite are separated by high hedges; broad-leaf trees offer shelter to both campers and birds. Although the site is located at the end of a road and on the riverside it is a quiet place. There is a swimming pool, a small playground and a mini golf course. The pizza and snack van that visits the site five days a week does good business, even in this region of gourmet products like truffles and foie gras. Some regional foods and basic necessities are on sale in the little shop.

Les Trois Sources

Rating 8.2
Tariff range €€€
Town Calviac
Department Lot
Postal code 46190
Map 5 F4
Tel 05-65330301
Fax 05-65330301
e-mail info@les-trois-sources.com
Open 26 Apr – 31 Oct
From St-Céré take D673 & D653 to Sousceyrac. After 5 km left onto D25. Then 2 km, past Calviac. Site on right, NE of Calviac.
Size (hectares) 7.5
Touring pitches 120
Sanitary facilities rating 8.5
lots for children to do • sports facilities • water slide • pleasant area for walking or cycling • prehistoric caves • Saint-Céré (25 km)
Electric hook-ups/amps 120/6

Located in a forested area, this campsite is very popular with families with young children. Most visitors come here for the peace and natural surroundings, like the babbling brook that runs past and offers a wonderful place to play. Next to it lie a restaurant, and a swimming pool with a double water slide, which is supervised until 7pm. The restaurant serves simple meals, chips (French fries) and a variety of snacks, while a mobile pizza service visits six times per week. Many activities are organised for older children, such as karaoke, talent shows and discos. The younger children are also well catered for with exciting games, while orienteering competitions, a woodland safari and canoeing are some of the possible sporting activities.

The nearest town for shopping and eating out is Saint-Céré, 25 km away. Recreation facilities in the surrounding area are too numerous to mention. The highly acclaimed hiking and cycling trips, organised from Les Trois Sources, are very rewarding. In the area's limestone strata there are abundant caves, in which paintings bear witness to habitation in prehistoric times. A little further is the River Dordogne, where you can indulge in many water sports.

Château de Lacomté

Rating 8.5
Tariff range €€€€
Town Carlucet
Department Lot
Postal code 46500
Map 5 E4
Tel 05-65387546
Fax 05-65331768
e-mail chateaulacomte@wanadoo.fr
Open 15 May – 30 Sep
From N20 (S of Payrac), take Peyrebrune exit, follow D1 to junct with D677. Turn left, take 1st left to site. Carlucet is S of Rocamadour.
Size (hectares) 12
Touring pitches 89
Sanitary facilities rating 8.3
château campsite • Little England • refrigerator hire • canoes • Rocamadour • Gramat (10 km)
Electric hook-ups/amps 89/10

This splendid campsite, located in the grounds of a château, is very popular with British campers. The château and the other buildings have been extensively restored, and the former stable building now accommodates the reception and restaurant. From here you can look out on the simple but attractive swimming pool, which offers plenty of space too for sun worshippers. Children can enjoy the many activities offered by the Kids' Club, and live music is played on the terrace twice weekly. The site is in the middle of natural surroundings and is rich in trees, bushes and isolated clearings.

The restaurant, which is rather expensive, serves English cuisine with lamb as its speciality, though snacks are also available. The nearest village, Gramat, is 16 kilometres away. The Dordogne region is one of unrivalled beauty where water has carved innumerable caves from the limestone hills inhabited, thousands of years ago, by our ancestors. You can still visit some of these prehistoric caves. Other attractive options are canoeing on the River Dordogne or cycling to the towns of Rocamadour and Cahors.

Midi-Pyrénées

Club de Vacances Duravel

Rating	8.1
Tariff range	€€€€
Town	Duravel
Department	Lot
Postal code	46700
Map	5 E3
Tel	05-65246506
Fax	05-65246496
e-mail	info@clubdevacances.eu
Open	28 Apr – 22 Sep

From A20 (Souillac-Cahors) take Francoulès exit (Cahors-Nord), then N20 to Cahors. Then take D911 towards Villeneuve-Lot. In Duravel turn left at rdbt. Site in 3 km.

Size (hectares) 8
Touring pitches 198
Sanitary facilities rating 8.5
extensive facilities • excellent food • wonderful service • Rocamadour • Padriac (caves) • Puy-l'Évêque (6 km)
Electric hook-ups/amps 198/10

One of the best campsites in Europe where you can be sure of a royal welcome and excellent facilities. You can even have your own sanitary facilities at your pitch. The service is even better than you might expect in many French châteaux! At this holiday paradise, you can swim (in two pools equipped with slides), play tennis and other ball sports, or even use the facilities for climbing and mountain biking. Boules matches are regularly held, and in the low season there are matches for older guests (50+). Special packages for watercolourists and bridge players are also organised.

In the high season, the activities are mainly oriented towards children and include a children's theatre, talent shows and dance evenings (until 11pm). The charming Place Henri is bordered by the restaurant, the bar and the covered terrace, where major events can be viewed on a large-screen TV. The high-quality restaurant has an extensive menu (plus special selections for children), and the snack bar is also very good. The shop is of the same high standard and supplies a wide range of products, including fresh bread. For a change you can go fishing in the River Lot where the campsite has jetties and mooring points.

Le Rêve

Rating	8.6
Tariff range	€€€
Town	le Vigan
Department	Lot
Postal code	46300
Map	5 E4
Tel	05-65412520
e-mail	info@campinglereve.com
Open	25 Apr – 21 Sep

Siet NE of Le Vigan. From Souillac (N20) take 1st exit to Le Vigan (D673) after passing Payrac. 1km to site.

Size (hectares) 3
Touring pitches 56
Sanitary facilities rating 8.9
quiet and friendly • delicious food • Rocamadour • caves • Gourdon (8 km)
Electric hook-ups/amps 56/6

Many people look for a quiet campsite, and they find it at Le Rêve. This friendly place lies in hilly, wooded country, and although many families come here, it is delightfully peaceful between 11pm and 8am. The pitches are of a generous size, and the site is well endowed with trees and grassy fields. The sanitary facilities are extremely clean. By way of amusement, there are two simple swimming pools, one for toddlers, table tennis and boules. Otherwise the recreational facilities are rather limited, and there are no organised activities.

The restaurant serves excellent food, including a "tourist specialities" menu as well as traditional dishes. If you prefer to cook for yourself, basic groceries and fresh bread are sold in the small shop. More shopping facilities are available in Gourdon, 8 km from Le Rêve. You can visit the bird-of-prey show in Rocamadour, the caves of Padirac or the town of Sarlat with its many attractions. Swimming is allowed in a lake near Gourdon, and other watersports are available on the River Dordogne, which is very popular with canoeists.

Moulin de Laborde

Rating	8.1
Tariff range	€€€
Town	Montcabrier
Department	Lot
Postal Code	46700
Map	5 E4
Tel	05-65246206
Fax	05-65365133
e-mail	moulindelaborde@wanadoo.fr
Open	25 Apr – 08 Sep

Take A20 (Limoges-Brives-Souillac), then N20 to Peyrac. Beyond Peyrac S over D673 for approx 40 km. Site just before Montcabrier (NE of village).

Size (hectares) 12
Touring pitches 90
Sanitary facilities rating 8.3
suitable for children • many facilities • Château de Bonaguil • vineyards • Puy-l'Evêque (8 km)
Electric hook-ups/amps 86/6-10

While on holiday in France, the Dutch couple Van Bommel got the opportunity to buy a piece of land by a 17th-century water mill. Since 1987 they have been running a campsite, and by doing so have made their dream come true.

Angling and sailing on the river, swimming in the pool, a fine playground for the children or a treasure hunt are just some of the attractions. You can practise on the climbing wall just outside the campsite, use the free tennis court in the village 1 km away, and a little bit further on ride a horse or pony, or paddle away in a canoe. You are always free to organise your own table tennis or volleyball competitions, a good way to make friends. The spacious pitches are marked by low bushes; trees give enough shade, but some pitches are open. The sanitary facilities are not new, but in good condition.

The old water mill and the annexes surround a central court with a terrace, bar and restaurant. Mrs Van Bommel is a good cook, and she serves the regional specialities based on 'canard'. Most campers bring a tent, so caravans are a minority.

Les Chênes

Rating	8.1
Tariff range	€€€€
Town	Padirac
Department	Lot
Postal code	46500
Map	5 E4
Tel	05-65336554
Fax	05-65337155
e-mail	les_chenes@hotmail.com
Open	15 Apr – 29 Sep

Site NW of Padirac, not far from Gouffre. 1 km before village on left of D90.

Size (hectares) 5
Touring pitches 61 **Static** 47
Sanitary facilities rating 8.3
plenty of facilities for children • plenty of evening entertainment • central location • Aquaparc • Gouffre de Padirac • Gramat (12 km)
Electric hook-ups/amps 61/6

In a beautiful oak forest in the Dordogne region lies this pleasant family campsite, which has a wide range of activities for children. Les Chênes is not far from the A20, making it a good place to spend the night on your way south. The swimming pool is small, but that is no problem, with the Aquaparc swimmers' paradise part of the campsite, and free to guests at Les Chênes. The individual pitches are spacious and the modern sanitary facilities are kept spotlessly clean and perfectly maintained.

Every evening, children can look forward to talent shows, disco dancing, drama performances and table tennis tournaments. There is plenty to do in the morning, especially for the younger children. The restaurant offers a simple tourist menu at a reasonable price, while the shelves of the small shop are filled with bread, a variety of fruit and vegetables, and other basic commodities. The prehistoric caves in the surrounding area are definitely worth visiting. On the River Dordogne you can take part in numerous water sports, including canoeing. Highly recommended for children is the Gouffre de Padirac dinosaur park, just 1 km away.

Midi-Pyrénées

Flower Camping Les Pins

Rating	8.8
Tariff range	€€€€
Town	Payrac
Department	Lot
Postal code	46350
Map	5 E4
Tel	05-65379632
Fax	05-65379108
e-mail	info@les-pins-camping.com
Open	05 Aug – 13 Sep

Site 1km S of Payrac. From Souillac take N20 southbound.

Size (hectares) 4
Touring pitches 55   **Static pitches** 37
Sanitary facilities rating 8.9

clean with plentiful sanitary facilities • swimming pool with 3 slides • very suitable for children • caves of Padirac • Reptiland • Payrac (1 km)

Electric hook-ups/amps 55/6-10

A hilltop setting with marvellous views of the surrounding area distinguishes this campsite. The site consists of woods and grassy fields, while at its centre are the restaurant, bar and swimming pool complex with various pools and a double slide. Many pitches are separated by hedges which provide privacy. The reception staff speak English and the managers are extremely friendly and helpful. Most of the campsite's clients are families with young children, and the facilities are oriented towards them. The extensive sanitary facilities are kept very clean.

There is an extensive programme of entertainments for the children, with the list of activities including disco dancing, tennis, a casino evening and bingo. The youngest children are well catered for in the morning. Close by is Rocamadour, which is listed as the second most important historic monument in France. The caves of Padirac deserve a visit, and the Dordogne valley with its fantastic châteaux is not far away.

La Truffière

Rating	7.7
Tariff range	€€€
Town	St-Cirq-Lapopie
Department	Lot
Postal Code	46330
Map	5 E3
Tel	05-65302022
e-mail	contact@camping-truffiere.com
Open	01 Apr – 30 Sep

From Cahors follow D911 to Rodez. Turn left in Concots and take D26 & D42 to site. Please note road via St-Cirq-Lapopie (D662) is unsuitable for caravans (very steep with sharp bend).

Size (hectares) 4
Touring pitches 87
Sanitary facilities rating 7.8

natural site • quiet • no-nonsense atmosphere • Quercyrail • open-air museum in Cuzals • Cahors (25 km)

Electric hook-ups/amps 87/6

La Truffière occupies a large field next to a former farmhouse. The number of pitches is limited, so this is the perfect place for those who appreciate silence and simplicity without any organised entertainment. The swimming pool, the sanitary facilities and the simple meals are all perfectly acceptable. In the old days pigs used to root for 'the black gold', truffles that grow so well under oak trees. If you would like to know more about this region's way of life, you should visit the open-air museum in Cuzals. There you get a good impression of everyday life on farms from the Middle Ages to the 19th century, and the role of the animals, machinery and craftsmen.

On your way to Cuzals you pass the prehistoric caves of Pech-Merle with an exhibition on man's existence thousands of years ago. St-Cirq-Lapopie (2.5 km from the campsite) is a station on the Quercy railway line. This is an historic route along the River Lot between Cahors and Capdenac, passing through interesting places that are good for a stop-over. The area is also suitable for pony trekking, walking and mountain biking.

La Paille Basse

Rating	8.5
Tariff range	€€€€
Town	Souillac
Department	Lot
Postal code	46200
Map	5 E4
Tel	05-65378548
Fax	05-65370958
e-mail	info@lapaillebasse.com
Open	10 May – 15 Sep

Site NW of Souillac. From Souillac take D15-D62 towards Salignac. After Bourzoles turn right and uphill to site.

Size (hectares) 80
Touring pitches 180
Sanitary facilities rating 8.5
luxurious with plentiful facilities • on a country estate • various catering facilities • Rocamadour • cycling and walking • Souillac (8 km)
Electric hook-ups/amps 180/3-6

This campsite was established in the grounds of a château some 25 years ago when there was nothing here; now it looks like a small village with lots of central facilities. The site is circled by an extensive forest, and it blends into the natural surroundings. In the restaurant, traditional French dishes are served in combination with specialities from the Périgord region, such as duck and goose liver. Eating here can be quite expensive, but as an alternative, you can order pizzas or other snacks. The site also has a crêperie, a café and a discotheque.

Rustling up a healthy meal of your own is no problem. The shop is larger than average and stocks fresh bread, vegetables and fruit. If you need more ingredients, you can always go to Souillac, which is 8 km away. A great variety of activities is organised every evening, and in the morning the youngest children head for the miniclub, while there are numerous sports facilities on offer for other age groups as well. Small villages such as Rocamadour or the towns of Brive and Sarlat are attractive destinations for day trips, and everything that goes to make France attractive is within reach.

Le Ventoulou

Rating	8.7
Tariff range	€€€
Town	Thégra
Department	Lot
Postal code	46500
Map	5 E4
Tel	05-65336701
Fax	05-65337320
e-mail	contact@leventoulou.com
Open	08 Apr – 30 Sep

Site on D60 to SE of Padirac. From N140 N of Rocamadour take Alvignac exit. After Alvignac take D11.

Size (hectares) 2
Touring pitches 36
Sanitary facilities rating 8.7
helpful management • beautiful flowers and shrubs • quiet; good, central base for surrounding area • canoeing on R. Dordogne • Rocamadour • Loubroussac (8 km)
Electric hook-ups/amps 36/10

Le Ventoulou is set in the countryside not far from the River Dordogne. It is fairly quiet, but that is how most guests prefer it. The owners are always ready to help, and as they have only been running the campsite for a few years they appreciate the importance of a reputation for hospitality. Countless plants and flower tubs decorate the entrance, terrace and restaurant. Some parts of the site are open to the sun, while other parts are quite shady. The sanitary facilities are good and are cleaned several times each day. There is a simple swimming pool surrounded by an area where you can sunbathe and keep an eye on the children.

The restaurant serves straightforward meals, and snacks are available in the bar-cum-cafeteria. Among other items, the small shop sells fresh bread for breakfast. The nearest place with bigger shops and restaurants is Loubroussac, 8 km away. Le Ventoulou is a good central base for a number of day trips, such as to the River Dordogne or the picturesque village of Rocamadour. The prehistoric caves for which this region is famous are also well worth visiting.

Midi-Pyrénées

Moulin de Julien

Rating	7.2
Tariff range	€€€
Town	Cordes-sur-Ciel
Department	Tarn
Postal Code	81170
Map	5 E3
Tel	05-63561110
Fax	05-63561110
e-mail	tassellifaurie.eric@neuf.fr
Open	01 May – 30 Sep

Site 1.5 km S of Cordes on D922.

Size (hectares) 8
Touring pitches 116
Sanitary facilities rating 7
luxurious sanitary facilities • swimming pools • spacious, quiet pitches • medieval Cordes • many wine châteaux • Cordes (1 km)
Electric hook-ups/amps 90/5

Thirty years ago cattle grazed on the banks of the river where nowadays campers gather to go fishing. Le Moulin de Julien, situated on a green plain less than 1 km away from medieval Cordes, is a quiet and comfortable campsite where the spacious pitches and luxurious sanitary facilities go down well. One of the pools has a curved water slide that comes down from an old tower, and boules is played on a field with artificial light for a thrilling late evening game.

There is not much for sale apart from ice cream, ice cubes and bread, so there are good reasons to walk into Cordes where you will find numerous small restaurants, shops and some museums. The national holiday on July 14th is celebrated in medieval style with historic costumes, street musicians, parades, performances, good food and regional wine. On a normal day wine châteaux and manor houses offer the opportunity to taste and appreciate the Gaillac wines. If you follow the Bastide route, which also runs through Cordes, you will reach Castelnau-de-Montmiral, Bruniquel, Puycelci and Penne, some of the most beautiful old villages in France.

Camp Redon

Rating	8.3
Tariff range	€€€€
Town	Cordes-sur-Ciel
Department	Tarn
Postal Code	81170
Map	5 E3
Tel	05-63561464
Fax	05-63561464
e-mail	info@campredon.com
Open	1 Apr - 30 Oct

From Cordes take D600 to Albi. Turn left after 6 km (D107 to Virac) to site entrance.

Size (hectares) 2
Touring pitches 44
Sanitary facilities rating 8.5
old wine farm • great views • spacious, sheltered pitches • walking and cycling • canoeing through gorges • Cordes (1 km)
Electric hook-ups/amps 44/6-16

This was once a wine farm, and the owners, Jacques and Marjo Tjaarda, have preserved the old tradition of wine producing. Being Dutch, they serve some typical Dutch snacks like 'kroketten' and 'frikandellen' on the menu in the take-away restaurant. They plan to renovate older parts of the campsite such as the sanitary facilities.

There are marvellous views over the valley. The pitches are spacious with bushes, high trees and hedges that fit very well into the natural environment. There is a swimming pool, and drinks and ice creams are available on the terrace. Tap water comes from a natural source and is safe to drink. Young children like the garden and the playground, though opportunities for older children are limited to a recreation room and a volleyball pitch.

Needless to say, the quiet atmosphere is the most important attraction. Camp Redon is a good starting point for walking and cycling tours in the area around the famous Gorges de l'Aveyron and Gorges du Tarn.

Les Clots

Rating	7.7
Tariff range	€€€
Town	Mirandol-Bourgnounac
Department	Tarn
Postal Code	81190
Map	5 F3
Tel	05-63769278
Fax	05-63769278
e-mail	campclots@wanadoo.fr
Open	01 May – 01 Oct

From Rodez follow N88 to Carmaux. Then take D905 to Mirandol, follow signs. Site 5 km NE of village.

Size (hectares) 7
Touring pitches 48
Sanitary facilities rating 7.8

18th-century farm • variety in pitches • riverside beach • excellent walking routes • canoeing through gorges • Cordes (20 km)

Electric hook-ups/amps 48/6

Les Clots, situated on the banks of the crystal clear River Viaur, is a fine place to stay if you are looking for a quiet campsite in a beautiful setting. Badgers, foxes and deer feel equally at home in the surrounding forests. Follow the Grande Randonnée (long distance route) or other footpaths along rivers and through hidden hamlets.

You get a quite different view when canoeing through the gorges of the Viaur and the Aveyron. The tent pitches in the forest offer a lot of privacy, and there's plenty of room everywhere. There are also modern sanitary facilities, washing machines and dryers and a shop that sells fresh bread in the morning. If you want to rent a large tent or a caravan, you should book early. Young children will love the swimming pool or the mini golf course, and there is a small beach by the riverside where older children can spend the summer nights sleeping by a camp fire.

The main building is an authentic 18th-century farmhouse, and in the old barn you will find a table tennis table, a shuffle board and a box with LEGO toys. There is also a bar for your afternoon or evening drink, like a glass of gaillac, the wine of the Tarn region.

Indigo Rieumontagne

Rating	8.2
Tariff range	€€€
Town	Nages
Department	Tarn
Postal code	81320
Map	5 F2
Tel	05-63372471
Fax	05-63371542
e-mail	rieumontagne@camping-indigo.com
Open	16 Jun - 14 Sep

Approx 3 km S of Nages. A75 (Clermont-Ferrand-Beziers), exit 57 towards Castres. Continue N of Bedarieux (D922). In Murat (D162) towards Rieu Montagne.

Size (hectares) 8.3
Touring pitches 121 **Static pitches** 6
Sanitary facilities rating 8.3

Child friendly • many activities • sports and games • aquatics •
Electric hook-ups/amps 121/10

Located on a large peninsula 250mtrs from the Lac de Lauzas, Indigo Rieumontagné campsite covers 9 hectares and has spacious, shady terraced pitches. You can relax under a parasol around the heated pool (with a wading pool) or swim at the lake beach (with games for children, a wading pool and water sports, plus volleyball, table tennis and boules). Younger guests can entertain themselves in a room with video games, table football and board games.

Not far from the campsite, there is tennis, horseriding and fishing. Between 10 and 12 on eachweekday morning in the high season, the children can partake in outdoor games and arts and crafts. In addition, you can go for walks or hikes (if wished, with a guide), join in with the exercises and aqua gymnastics, enjoy one of the frequent theme evenings (dance parties, barbeques) or participate in water activities organized on the lake.

Midi-Pyrénées

Relais de l'Entre Deux Lacs

Rating	7.6
Tariff range	€€
Town	Teillet
Department	Tarn
Postal Code	81120
Map	5 F3
Tel	05-63557445
Fax	05-63557565
e-mail	contact@campingdutarn.com
Open	01 Apr – 31 Oct

Site 22 km SE of Albi, just outside Teillet on D81 to Lacaune.

Size (hectares) 4
Touring pitches 48
Sanitary facilities rating 7.3

pleasant family campsite • pool, children's farm • quiet, spacious pitches • between two lakes • Albi • Teillet (0.5 km)
Electric hook-ups/amps 40/6-10

Every guest between the ages of 2 and 99 is kept busy at Relais de l'Entre-Deux-Lacs, owned by two Belgians who may have emigrated to France but have not forgotten their home country; Flemish fries and Belgian beers are some of the delights on their menu. There's a large swimming pool, a children's farm, playgrounds and table tennis tables. The campsite is located on a hill, where pitches are spacious and the sanitary facilities are good.

Three kilometres away is Lac de Rassisse, one of the two lakes after which the campsite was named, and where you can see the towers of the mysterious château of Grandval. The lake is a good place for canoeing, though children will prefer to play on the beach and by the creeks. The other lake, Lac de Bancalie, 7 km further away, offers greater opportunities for watersports. Higher up in the mountains you can walk on the Grande Randonnée no.36 (long distance footpath) or use the paths laid out for mountain bikers. Close to the site is a climbing wall. For a day trip you can choose from a number of lovely French villages or visit one of the regional markets. The most important attraction is the 'pink' city of Albi with its Toulouse-Lautrec museum.

Village de Loisirs le Lomagnol

Rating	7
Tariff range	€€
Town	Beaumont-de-Lomagne
Department	Tarn-et-Garonne
Postal Code	82500
Map	5 E3
Tel	05-63261200
Fax	05-63656022
e-mail	villagedeloisirslelomagnol@wanadoo.fr
Open	15 Apr – 30 Sep

From Beaumont follow 'camping/plan d'eau/centre de loisirs' signs. Site E of Beaumont.

Size (hectares) 36
Touring pitches 100
Sanitary facilities rating 6.8

safe and quiet • suitable for children • water sports • close to a lake • historic towns • Montauban (38 km)
Electric hook-ups/amps 100/10

Because of the location near a lake, this campsite is geared for watersports enthusiasts. One of its advantages is the strict supervision at the swimming pool, jacuzzi, sauna, lockers and the lake. It gives a feeling of safety, especially for families with children, and there is also a night watch service. Guests tend to be quiet and respect each other here, and the peaceful atmosphere, lacking a discotheque, is relished by all.

The centre of all activities is the lake, where you can go swimming, canoeing, windsurfing and sailing. The part of the lake that is reserved for swimmers is marked by a rope with floats (only in July and August). The lake bed gradually slopes down from the shore, so the shallow water near the edge is perfectly safe for little children. An entertainment team organises all sorts of activities for children under the age of 12. You can enjoy long walks in sunflower fields in summer, and there are a number of historic towns nearby where farmers sell local produce such as wine, cheese or pâté. Beaumont, about 800m away, has a few shops. A visit to Lourdes, the famous pilgrimage site, or Toulouse and Auch, are highly recommended.

Château du Gandspette

Rating 8.6
Tariff range €€€€
Town Éperlecques
Department Pas-de-Calais
Postal code 62910
Map 2 C6
Tel 03-21934393
Fax 03-21957498
e-mail contact@chateau-gandspette.com
Open 01 Apr – 30 Sep
Site N of Éperlecques on D22, between Watten and N43 (or between St-Omer and Calais).
Size (hectares) 11
Touring pitches 100
Sanitary facilities rating 8.7
hospitality • swimming and playing • quiet • walking area with bunker • fine golf links • Saint-Omer (12 km)
Electric hook-ups/amps 100/6

At the Gandspette estate you can expect the sort of complete tranquility enjoyed through the centuries by its aristocratic owners. The site is quietly situated at the edge of the castle grounds, close to Éperlecques village. If you head out in the opposite direction you will find a forest with marked walks, and a 'log cabin' which is actually a concrete bunker built by the Germans. There are guided tours complete with an explanation of the bunker's original function, and the events that took place here during World War II.

The newer part of the campsite, which is located on a hill, offers plenty of room to pitch your tent and enjoy the fine views; nearby are the spotless sanitary facilities. The older part of the site is closer to the stately château, where old trees attract plenty of bird life. Good views can be had over the playing area. Nearby is the swimming pool with separate paddling pool, and tennis courts that can be used by guests free of charge for an hour per day (bookings one day ahead). The restaurant offers take-away facilities, but you can also order one of the region's specialities: 'Potje Vleesch' or 'Carbonade Flamande'.

La Bien Assise

Rating 8.4
Tariff range €€€€
Town Guînes
Department Pas-de-Calais
Postal code 62340
Map 2 C6
Tel 03-21352077
Fax 03-21367920
e-mail castel@bien-assise.com
Open 15 Apr – 24 Sep
In Guînes take D231 to Marquise. Site on left.
Size (hectares) 12
Touring pitches 146
Sanitary facilities rating 8.4
camping on castle grounds • swimming pool, sports and games • spacious • walking and cycling itineraries • beach and sea • Calais (10 km)
Electric hook-ups/amps 146/6-10

La Bien Assise is a splendid campsite located in the grounds of the château. The complex has a stylish entrance through spacious château gardens, with camping areas located on different levels. Each grassy pitch is surrounded by hedges and bushes affording plenty of privacy. At the square, dominated by the round tower in the middle, is a restaurant with indoor and open-air tables. Here you can book a table for a classic French dinner, or there is a more modest restaurant on site. Children will enjoy exploring the park, with its playgrounds with climbing nets, table tennis, mini golf and a tennis court.

The main attraction is undoubtedly the heated indoor swimming pool with water slides and paddling pool. Calais is just 10 km away, and this is a perfect place to spend your first night after (or your last night before) crossing the Channel. But there are plenty of good reasons to add a few more nights. It is not just the good facilities (for disabled campers as well) that make this site so attractive. Think of the war memorial museums nearby, the lovely sandy beaches and the wild sea.

Normandy

La Vallée

Rating 8.7
Tariff range €€€€
Town Houlgate
Department Calvados
Postal code 14510
Map 2 B4
Tel 02-31244069
Fax 02-31244242
e-mail camping.lavallee@wanadoo.fr
Open 29 Mar - 2 Nov

On southern edge of Houlgate on the Route de la Valée towards Lisieux. From A13 & D513 follow rail line until it crosses road. At lights, turn right D24 towards campsites. Follow campsite sign.

Size (hectares) 11
Touring pitches 140
Sanitary facilities rating 8,6
Beautiful views • Norman history • swimming pool
Electric hook-ups/amps 140/4

The campsite dominates the attractive coastal town of Houlgate, and offers a swimming pool, a wading pool and a beach only 900mtrs away. The grounds gradually slope upwards from the entrance to a steep incline. Hedges, trees and numerous flowers separate the pitches but do not provide much shade. The most popular pitches are usually level and are centrally located. In the high season, concerts and performances are given in the evenings, making the summer nights under the starry skies a true delight.

Children can ride ponies. Houlgate, a spa town dating from around 1900, is only within a few minutes' walk, and has small streets with lovely houses and shops; coach rides through the centre and horseriding on the sandy beach can be enjoyed. The area offers magnificent views of the sea and buildings that are typical of the architecture of Normandy.

Château de Martragny

Rating 8.5
Tariff range €€€€
Town Martragny
Department Calvados
Postal code 14740
Map 2 A4
Tel 02-31802140
Fax 02-31081491
e-mail chateau.martragny@wanadoo.fr
Open 01 May – 12 Sep

From Caen to Bayeux follow N13 to Martragny. Then right and follow signs.

Size (hectares) 6
Touring pitches 160
Sanitary facilities rating 8.8
in the garden of a castle • golf course • stylish restaurant • Bayeux tapestry • sea and beaches • Bayeux (10 km)
Electric hook-ups/amps 150/6

This campsite in the gardens of the Château de Martragny is approached by a long and truly impressive drive. The site is surrounded by trees and a magnificent English-style garden.

On one side of this garden you will find a swimming pool with a view of the stately mansion. As well as the main pool there is a separate paddling pool and a small fishpond. The pitches are spacious, and though the washing and toilet facilities are a bit small they are quite acceptable. On site are a restaurant, a snack bar and a café, and you can enjoy the luxury of a stylish breakfast in the castle.

Sports fans can play football, mini golf or the full 18 holes. The shop takes orders for fresh bread but for daily shopping you will have to go to Bayeux. In this charming town you can visit the world-famous tapestry. The Normandy beaches which were the scene of the Allied invasion in 1944 are still full of atmosphere and worth a visit, and a number of museums (e.g. in Caen) tell the story of this turning point in the Second World War.

Normandy

Château Le Colombier

Rating 8.6
Tariff range €€€€
Town Moyaux
Department Calvados
Postal code 14590
Map 2 B4
Tel 02-31636308
Fax 02-31631597
e-mail info@camping-lecolombier.com
Open 01 May – 21 Sep
Rouen (N175)-Pont Audemer (D139), Cormeilles (D810)
St-Jean-d'Asnieres (D22). Then take D143 to Moyaux. 3 km NE
of Moyaux (signed).
Size (hectares) 10
Touring pitches 188
Sanitary facilities rating 8.7
friendly reception • ambiance, style, quiet • beautifully laid out •
Cerza Safari Park • ruins of abbey and castles • Lisieux (10 km)
Electric hook-ups/amps 188/10

Château le Colombier offers a great ambiance, plenty of style, and enough peace and quiet to truly chill out. The site was laid out on an estate, and from the spacious pitches you can see the round pigeon tower (colombier) that rises from the beautiful French garden. A fine and well-kept lawn covers the whole camping area, and apple trees grow all around. Pitches are not particularly marked out, so you can pick your own favourite spot to park your tent or caravan.

Inside the castle's sturdy walls you will find a grand restaurant that is often used for concerts. In the beautiful grounds there is also a heated swimming pool. The luxurious sanitary facilities are very clean, as you would expect in such a smart place. There is plenty of room for the youngest children to play, and they can visit Monsieur Pont the rabbit, or go to the weekly mini disco party. Teenagers will relish the proper disco. The Normandy coast with its reminders of the invasion by the allied forces is never far away. You can go on a day trip to Caen, Rouen, Lisieux or the museum with the famous Bayeux tapestry. Cerza has a safari park.

Le Brévedent

Rating 8.1
Tariff range €€€€
Town Pont-l'Évêque
Department Calvados
Postal code 14130
Map 2 B4
Tel 02-31647288
Fax 02-31643341
e-mail conact@campinglebrevedent.com
Open 01 Apr – 12 Nov
From Pont-l'Évêque follow D579 to Lisieux. Turn left after 5 km
(D51 to Blangy-le-Château); site 3 km.
Size (hectares) 7
Touring pitches 100
Sanitary facilities rating 8.1
on an estate • suitable for children • lots of activities • Bayeux
tapestry • history in Caen • Deauville (13 km)
Electric hook-ups/amps 100/10

Camping Le Brévedent is part of a beautiful estate on the edge of a lake, close to a 17th-century hunting lodge. Le Brévedent is very comfortable, with its spacious pitches which offer plenty of privacy, and sanitary facilities that are kept spotlessly clean. The shop is stocked with local delicacies, and there are plans to open a restaurant; in the meantime there is only a take-away service, and some snacks like panini.

The hunting lodge has a bar, and there are two swimming pools, one for children which also has a fenced-off playground. There is so much entertainment for the smallest children that they quickly feel at home, but dogs are not allowed on site. This area was the scene of the great invasion by the allied forces in 1944. Beaches, museums and cemeteries are all reminders of this dramatic period in history. Nearby Caen is the town dedicated to William the Conqueror, and you can visit the famous tapestry in Bayeux. His life, the crossing of the Channel and the Battle of Hastings in 1066 are all depicted on it.

Normandy

Les Vikings

Rating	8.4
Tariff range	€€€
Town	Barneville-Carteret
Department	Manche
Postal code	50270
Map	1 C5
Tel	02-33538413
Fax	02-33530819
e-mail	campingviking@aol.com
Open	15 Mar – 01 Nov

From Barneville to Barneville-Plage, then onto Plage; follow road signs.

Size (hectares) 6
Touring pitches 110
Sanitary facilities rating 8.3
good recreational facilities • good shop • spacious pitches • Jersey and Guernsey • Cherbourg: WW II • Barneville-Carteret (2 km)
Electric hook-ups/amps 110/6-20

A large and pleasant family campsite set close to the beach at Barneville, where plenty of activities and entertainments are always being organised. The staff are friendly and helpful, and the owner has a lot of time for her guests. The pitches are spacious though they don't offer much privacy, and nor are there many trees around to provide a bit of shade. The sanitary facilities are quite reasonable, however, and kept clean. You can go swimming in the pool or just lounge around it for some sunbathing.

A special attraction is the brand new recreation rooms which are painted in cheerful colours. There is a medium-size shop, and two restaurants, one with a take-away service. In the evening guests can attend the large discotheque, visit the separate bar, or try out the two halls that offer entertainment for young campers of all ages. From Barneville there are daily ferry services to Jersey and Guernsey in the Channel Islands. Cherbourg, one of the major ports of France, is only a short distance away, and is home to one of the greatest yachting clubs in the country.

Saint Michel

Rating	8.5
Tariff range	€€€
Town	Courtils
Department	Manche
Postal code	50220
Map	1 D4/5
Tel	02-33709690
Fax	02-33709909
e-mail	info@campingsaintmichel.com
Open	15 Mar – 15 Oct

Avranches D43, Mont-Saint-Michel D43. Beyond Courtils 1st site on left.

Size (hectares) 3.5
Touring pitches 64   **Static pitches** 9
Sanitary facilities rating 9.1
a sea of flowers • special shop • spacious lay-out, quiet • Mont-Saint-Michel • Dol-de-Bretagne • Courtils (3 km)
Electric hook-ups/amps 64/6

For the second year running Saint Michel has been awarded the special prize for the most beautiful display of flowers on a French campsite. Blooms of all colours grow in glorious flower beds, and there are little fountains to add interest. The shop has been stylishly decorated with hundreds of dried flowers that give off a lovely refreshing scent. The pitches are spacious and offer a lot of privacy thanks to the hedges all around.

In the toilets and washrooms you can listen to music when you take a shower. There is a good swimming pool with lots of deck chairs and parasols, but otherwise there is no river or lake swimming in the immediate vicinity. Saint Michel is a quiet campsite without entertainment or live music, where children can indulge in video games or let off steam in the playground. The famous Mont-Saint-Michel, a former pilgrim's sanctuary, is not far away, and neither is Dol-de-Bretagne, where you can see Brittany's most famous megalithic monument, the Champ Dolent.

Le Grand Large

Rating	8.9
Tariff range	€€€€
Town	les Pieux
Department	Manche
Postal code	50340
Map	1 C6
Tel	02-33524075
Fax	02-33525820
e-mail	le-grand-large@wanadoo.fr
Open	12 Apr – 21 Sep

From La Haye-du-Puits follow D903 and past Barneville-Carteret D904 to Les Pieux. Turn left (D4) after 2 km (towards Sciotot). Route signed.

Size (hectares) 4
Touring pitches 146
Sanitary facilities rating 8.7

fantastic swimming pool • close to the beach • lots of activities and games • Jersey and Guernsey • Cherbourg harbour • Les Pieux (2 km)

Electric hook-ups/amps 146/6

This site which is set close to the sea has just about everything to guarantee an unforgettable holiday. It is dominated by a large swimming pool with water slides, a sun terrace and a snack bar. The pitches are spacious, and surrounded on three sides by hedges that ensure there is plenty of privacy. The washing and toilet facilities are fairly new too, and always look very clean. A nice touch is that the central washing room is always filled with plants and flowers.

Children won't get bored here, as there are all kinds of activities to absorb them: drawing competitions and building sand castles for the youngest guests, sports competitions for teenagers, and live music for all ages. There are also numerous sports facilities on site that can be used by everyone. Day trips to Jersey and Guernsey on the Channel Islands make an interesting change, and Cherbourg, one of the major ports of France, is certainly worth a visit. It takes only a little more time to reach Mont-Saint-Michel.

L'Anse du Brick

Rating	8.8
Tariff range	€€€€
Town	Maupertus-sur-Mer
Department	Manche
Postal code	50330
Map	1 D6
Tel	02-33543357
Fax	02-33544966
e-mail	welcome@anse-du-brick.com
Open	01 Apr – 30 Sep

From Cherbourg take coast road (D116) to Barfleur. In L'Anse du Brick site on right.

Size (hectares) 17
Touring pitches 170
Sanitary facilities rating 8.8

splendid nature, quiet • good facilities • friendly staff • Cité de la Mer (aquarium) • D-day beaches and museums • Cherbourg (15 km)

Electric hook-ups/amps 160/10

L'Anse du Brick is a well-equipped campsite uniquely located in a hewn-out rock face. Boulders from here were used to pave the old road from Paris to Roubaix, which is still famous as the scene of the annual cycling race through Northern France. The pitches are spacious and well laid out on the slopes of a hill where there are plenty of trees to provide shade. The sanitary facilities are clean and inviting, with their neatly-tiled walls, though the showers are a little on the small side. The pool has a paddling pool and a water slide, with deck chairs and parasols strategically placed around the edge. For children there is a range of activities, including karaoke, sports competitions and disco parties; the young ones can learn how to make masks and build sand castles.

Other sports include mountain biking, archery and snooker. The major attraction in this area is the Cité de la Mer, a large aquarium and underwater museum in Cherbourg. The beaches of Normandy that were the scene of the D-day invasion in 1944 are not far away from L'Anse du Brick.

Normandy

Le Cormoran

Rating 8.6
Tariff range €€€€
Town Ste. Mère-Église
Department Manche
Postal code 50480
Map 1 D6
Tel 02-33413394
Fax 02-33951608
e-mail lecormoran@wanadoo.fr
Open 01 Apr – 28 Sep
NW from Carentan on N13. Turn right in Ste-Mère-Église towards Ravenoville (Bourg), 3.5 km to Ravenoville-Plage.
Size (hectares) 8.5
Touring pitches 95
Sanitary facilities rating 8.5
full service (even a hairdresser) • lots of activities • children's farm • D-day beaches and museums • Cité de la Mer (aquarium) • Sainte-Mère-Église (10 km)
Electric hook-ups/amps 95/6

A children's farm is a tremendous draw at the campsite at Le Cormoran with goats and horses, and many different kinds of birds. This collection of animals, along with the nearby beach, have established this site, above all, as a real family site. Every day except Saturdays there is some kind of entertainment: singers, karaoke, sports competitions for adults and older children, with sandcastle building and drawing contests for the youngest. The site has a good restaurant, serving not only snacks and pizzas but also local specialities like poulet Vallée-d'Auge and tripes au cidre – certainly worth trying!

The pitches are very spacious and offer some privacy as well as necessary protection against the sun. The toilet block is somewhat old-fashioned, but more than meets visitors' expectations. Sainte-Mère-Église was a landing place for paratroopers during the invasion of Normandy, and everywhere there are reminders of this historic episode. A special treat for all the family is a day trip to the Cité de la Mer in Cherbourg, which is now Europe's largest aquarium.

La Source

Rating 7.8
Tariff range €€€
Town Petit-Appeville
Department Seine-Maritime
Postal code 76550
Map 2 C5
Tel 02-35842704
Fax 02-35822502
e-mail info@camping-la-source.fr
Open 15 Mar – 15 Oct
On outskirts of Petit-Appeville across railway (towards St-Aubin-sur-Scie) over rail line.
Size (hectares) 3.5
Touring pitches 78   **Static pitches** 42
Sanitary facilities rating 8.2
absolutely quiet • helpful staff • spacious pitches • fishing village Le Tréport • castles • Dieppe (4 km)
Electric hook-ups/amps 50/6

La Source is located in a wooded area alongside a river within walking distance of the port of Dieppe and the sea. Nearly all the spacious pitches are accessible by car via a paved lane. There is a generous provision of sanitary facilities which are kept very clean. During the day most guests set off to explore the region, but even in the evening when everyone is back it is a remarkably quiet place. Children can use the garden or the playground, but there is nowhere to go swimming. For this you would need to go to Dieppe, where you will be able to cool off in one of the two swimming pools. The site shop sells basic items, including fresh bread, and next to the shop is a nice café.

As there is no restaurant here, most campers go into Dieppe where there are plenty of shops and eating places. A popular day trip, especially with children, is to the Cité de la Mer, the largest aquarium in Europe, or you could spend some time in Le Tréport, an old fishing village. On the way to Le Tréport you can take part in a guided tour of the Penly power station.

Municipal Les Mouettes

Rating 8.1
Tariff range €€€
Town Veules-les-Roses
Department Seine-Maritime
Postal code 76980
Map 2 B5
Tel 02-35976198
Fax 02-35973344
e-mail camping-les-mouettes@veules-les-roses.fr
Open 01 Mar – 30 Nov
Site E of Veules-les-Roses on D68 towards Sotteville.
Size (hectares) 3.6
Touring pitches 96   **Static pitches** 56
Sanitary facilities rating 8.3
tidy and well kept • English spoken • Cany-Barville: Château de
Cany • Benedictine museum in Fécamp • Dieppe (23 km)
Electric hook-ups/amps 67/6

Municipal Les Moulettes is just 300m from the Atlantic Ocean where the sunsets are breathtaking. Other sought-after factors here include the very clean sanitary facilities. There are not many amenities – no swimming pool for example, but children under 6 can use a playground, and there is a basketball court, and a recreation room with table tennis and a pinball machine plus a television room. The municipal football pitch and basketball court next to the campsite are open to everyone. In the evening it is very quiet, with no bar or restaurant, but the charming small village is only a 400-m stroll away.

You will find a swimming pool and tennis courts 7 km away. A little bit further on lies the town of Dieppe, a good place for shopping where the restaurants serve delicious mussels. The whole area is suitable for walking and cycling. Favourite destinations for a day trip are the 17th-century Château de Cany near Cany-Barville with its splendid garden, and the Benedictine museum.

Les Écureuils

Rating 8.1
Tariff range €€€€
Town la Bernerie-en-Retz
Department Loire-Atlantique
Postal Code 44760
Map 1 C3
Tel 02-40827695
Fax 02-40647952
e-mail camping.les-ecureuils@wanadoo.fr
Open 01 Apr – 30 Sep
Site 500mtrs N of La Bernerie-en-Retz, near station. Site signed
from D13.
Size (hectares) 5.3
Touring pitches 220
Sanitary facilities rating 8.6
free entertainment • near the sea • special barbecues • Planète
Sauvage (zoo) • several seaports • the town of Pornic (7 km)
Electric hook-ups/amps 220/10

Les Écureuils is a real family campsite located near the sea, offering plenty of entertainment and a large, heated swimming pool with two separate baby pools. Tennis tournaments, watersports and games, handicraft sessions, treasure hunts, bingo and a discotheque are just a few examples of the free entertainment on offer. The rear section of the site is very quiet, while the front section is somewhat noisy given the proximity of the swimming pool and bar. Although Les Écureuils does not have a restaurant, you're able to buy a reasonable selection of snacks.

You'll find a range of shops and restaurants in nearby La Bernerie-en-Retz and Pornic (7 km). Large stone communal barbecues are scattered around the site, and provide an excellent opportunity to meet your neighbours. The nearby beach, which borders on a lagoon, has plenty to offer watersports enthusiasts. Although children are unlikely to get bored at Les Écureuils, a day trip to Planète Sauvage is highly recommended. The campsite is less well-suited to older children and teenagers.

Pays de la Loire

Parc Ste-Brigitte

Rating	8.2
Tariff range	€€€
Town	la Turballe
Department	Loire-Atlantique
Postal code	44420
Map	1 C3
Tel	02-40248891
Fax	02-40233042
e-mail	saintebrigitte@wanadoo.fr
Open	01 Apr – 01 Oct

From Guérande follow D99 to La Turballe. Site after 3 km, E of La Turballe (take road beyond Clis).

Size (hectares) 10
Touring pitches 128
Sanitary facilities rating 8.1

on an estate • farm animals • extraordinary lay-out • sea and beach • harbour towns • Guérande (3 km)

Electric Hook-ups/amp 128/6-10

This campsite in the middle of a grand estate could not be more stylish, nor a better retreat after a day on the crowded beach. The name Parc Sainte-Brigitte comes from the patron saint who first appeared in the early Middle Ages when Irish monks founded a sanctuary here in honour of Sainte-Brigitte, daughter of an Irish druid. The park's image doesn't just come from the stylish 17th-century mansion, but also the donkey, goats, chickens, ducks and sheep that wander around. Hugging and feeding is allowed, as is fishing in the pond.

On the lawn and under the trees you will find a good choice of pitches, and the sanitary facilities are clean and luxurious. There is a large indoor swimming pool that can be turned into an outdoor pool, with a heated outdoor paddling pool. A visit to the attractive restaurant is recommended, with its good choice of dishes, including a children's menu; it stays open as long as there are guests. Once a week there is live music. During the day you can visit small harbour towns like La Turballe, La Baule, Piriac-sur-Mer and Le Croisic, or go hiking in the salt marshes or the Grande Brière wetlands. And of course there are the fine sandy beaches of the Côte d'Amour.

Soir d'Été

Rating	7.7
Tariff range	€€€
Town	Mesquer
Department	Loire-Atlantique
Postal code	44420
Map	1 C3
Tel	02-40425726
Fax	02-51739776
e-mail	info@camping-soirdete.com
Open	01 Apr – 31 Oct

From Guérande take D252 to Mesquer. Turn left after 6 km, take D52 to Quimiac. Turn right after 2 km; site 400mtrs NW of Mesquer on right.

Size (hectares) 1.5
Touring pitches 43
Sanitary facilities rating 7.9

small and often crowded • young people • shiny toilets • sea and beach • cycling • Guérande (10 km)

Electric Hook-ups/amp 43/6

Enjoy a lovely summer evening ('soir d'été' in French) on the lawn of Soir d'Été campsite, located opposite the salt basins of Mesquer. Most people spend the whole day on the beach just 800m away, though on Tuesdays and Fridays there is a market close to the site which is always well attended. The shop only takes orders for fresh bread, so you will have to do your shopping elsewhere. Sanitary facilities on this site are immaculate.

A good way to start the day is with a game of tennis on the court in the village 2.5 km away, or you can go to the riding centre for a spot of pony-trekking. Children over 5 will probably prefer the daily entertainment programme in the morning. There is a whole range of walking and cycling routes covering the coastal area and the salt marshes. Guided tours that start from the site are a good option. Another interesting day trip is a visit to the oyster banks, where the old traditions are still practised on a large scale. Naturally the fruits of the sea feature on the restaurant menu, but take-away meals like mussels and chips are equally popular. Many guests enjoy karaoke, disco dancing or playing boules in the evenings.

Armor Héol

Rating 8.3
Tariff range €€€€
Town Piriac-sur-Mer
Department Loire-Atlantique
Postal code 44420
Map 1 C3
Tel 02-40235780
Fax 02-40235942
e-mail info@camping-armor-heol.com
Open 05 Apr – 21 Sep
Site on D333, 1 km S of centre of Piriac (towards St-Sébastien), on right.
Size (hectares) 6
Touring pitches 100
Sanitary facilities rating 8.3
family camp site • free entertainment • relaxed atmosphere • fun on the beach • Océanium in Le Croisic • Piriac-sur-Mer (1 km)
Electric Hook-ups/amp 100/5

It is not unusual for families who spend their holiday at Armor Héol to come back year after year. In most cases the overriding attraction is the heated swimming paradise with paddling pool and water slides. The many deck chairs around the pool make it possible for parents to keep an eye on the youngsters, and it is only a few steps to get a cup of coffee, a cool drink or a snack. But even on dry land there is enough to do for people of all ages, especially if they like sports and games.

Joining the entertainment is completely free, and anyway the beach is only 700m away. In spite of all these advantages Armor Héol cannot be qualified as a luxury campsite. The sanitary facilities are well kept but a bit old fashioned now, and there is no shop, though fresh bread can be ordered through reception. No haute cuisine is available either, but the take-away snacks are acceptable. On the other hand the lack of commercial activities contributes to the casual atmosphere. It takes about 15 minutes to walk to Piriac, or you can take the little train (departure from site at 10am, and from Piriac at 12 noon). A popular day trip for the whole family is to the Océanium in Le Croisic.

Parc du Guibel

Rating 7.9
Tariff range €€€
Town Piriac-sur-Mer
Department Loire-Atlantique
Postal code 44420
Map 1 C3
Tel 02-40235267
Fax 02-40155024
e-mail camping@parcduguibel.com
Open 22 Mar – 30 Sep
From Piriac follow D52 for 3.5 km (NE towards Mesquer/Quimiac). Turn left at junct; site 500mtrs on right
Size (hectares) 14
Touring pitches 319
Sanitary facilities rating 7.8
in the woodlands • train to Piriac • located near the seaside • Marais de Grande-Brière • Côte Sauvage • Piriac-sur-Mer (3 km)
Electric Hook-ups/amp 242/3-10

Parc du Guibel is one of those family campsites where children who came here with their parents now come back with their own offspring. In the summer young visitors find plenty of freedom here, although they have to quieten down after midnight like everybody else. You can pitch camp right in the middle of the woods, under high pine trees with shrubs underneath and some broad-leaved trees. The spacious pitches are split in two by a road, and the sea is about 1 km away.

The large, heated swimming pool sits between the trees and flowering shrubs like an oasis with an almost tropical appearance. Every week there is a dance party, and drinks and snacks draw campers to the many terraces. The restaurant prepares various dishes for a reasonable price, while bread in the supermarket is baked on the spot. Teenagers gather in the recreation room, and there are playing facilities and a mini golf course. The Marais de Grande Brière 25 km away offers the chance to go punting through the wetlands with their exceptional flora and fauna – a treat for nature lovers. Young children will love a ride on the campers' train to Piriac, or to go searching for shells and crabs along the shoreline of the Côte Sauvage.

Pays de la Loire

Château du Deffay

Rating	8.3
Tariff range	€€€€
Town	Pontchâteau
Department	Loire-Atlantique
Postal Code	44160
Map	1 C3
Tel	02-40880057
Fax	02-40016655
e-mail	campingdudeffay@wanadoo.fr
Open	01 May – 30 Sep

From N165 exit at Herbignac. Then take D33 towards Ste. Reine-de-Bretagne. Site on right in 5 km, (2 km E of Ste. Reine-de-Bretagne).

Size (hectares) 13
Touring pitches 120
Sanitary facilities rating 8.6

lovely old buildings • pedal boats and fishing • tennis court and trampoline • attractive and quiet surroundings • the ocean • La Baule (15 km)

Electric hook-ups/amps 120/6

The name of this site might be deceptive, as this château campsite is more like a large 'camping à la ferme'. It is attractively situated in a 350-hectare estate that has been in the possession of the Count d'Espivent de la Villeboiset family since 1880. During the Second World War, the castle was used for military purposes, resulting in some damage to the buildings. In 1964 the parents of the present owner began to restore the buildings and the estate. The campsite was established in 1976.

The old mountain subsoil has only a small layer of humus, making the ground somewhat irregular, but the site has large pitches. The extensive sanitary facilities are located in a renovated barn.

There is ample opportunity for aquatic sports on the centrally located lake, and you can also play tennis or volleyball, or swim in the fenced-in pool which is safe for children - all of these activities are free. There is so much to see in the area, especially the beaches, the picturesque villages tucked away in the heart of the countryside and the well-known marsh area of Grande Brière.

Belle Rivière

Rating	8.2
Tariff range	€€
Town	Ste-Luce-sur-Loire
Department	Loire-Atlantique
Postal Code	44980
Map	1 D3
Tel	02-40258581
Fax	02-40258581
e-mail	belleriviere@wanadoo.fr
Open	All year

From Nantes-Ste-Luce-sur-Loire, take D68 towards Thouaré. Turn right at traffic lights just before Thouaré. Cross rail line. Site entrance on left (approx 500mtrs). Site 2 km SE of Ste-Luce.

Size (hectares) 3.5
Touring pitches 80   **Static pitches** 44
Sanitary facilities rating 8.2

tranquillity • landscape surroundings • fishing • châteaux • the Loire valley • Nantes city centre (8 km)

Electric hook-ups/amps 80/3-10

Whereas most campsites are a paradise for children, Belle Rivière is particularly well-suited to adults (and older people). Its popularity owes much to its location: the city of Nantes, which is surrounded (or traversed) by the rivers Erdre, Loire and Sèvre, is worth a visit, and you'll find a diversity of stately homes and châteaux in these picturesque watery surroundings. If you're planning a trip along one of the above rivers, either by boat or by bicycle, remember to head upstream along the elegant vineyards.

Anyone not embarking on a daytrip is likely to go fishing; the campsite borders on the River Loire, and there are organised excursions for anglers hoping to catch a pike, perch or eel; the proprietors also arrange riding tours. The campsite has a large playground and several recreation areas for children. The Belle Rivière grounds combine bamboo, mayflower and Scotch fir with butterfly-attracting shrubs and a diversity of trees and plants. As a result, there's sufficient privacy and plenty of shade. The sanitary facilities are excellent, and the site well tended. The cement works on the banks of the Loire can be noisy.

Lac de Maine

Rating	8.7
Tariff range	€€€
Town	Angers
Department	Maine-et-Loire
Postal code	49000
Map	2 A2
Tel	02-41730503
Fax	02-41730220
e-mail	camping@lacdemaine.fr
Open	21 Mar – 10 Oct

In Angers take N23 to Nantes over River Maine (800mtrs). Follow road to Lac de Maine (with many rdbts). Follow signs to Bouchemaine.
Size (hectares) 4
Touring pitches 142
Sanitary facilities rating 8.5
much privacy • well kept • for all ages • castles • bird watching with guides • Angers (1 km)
Electric Hook-ups/amp 142/10

CCI

Lac de Maine is a good, cheap campsite in the Loire Valley with a lot going for it. Ornithologists who enjoy an early start in the morning in pursuit of their hobby can hire a guide to find the best spots for birdwatching. Pitches are spacious, and surrounded by hedges on three sides to provide plenty of shade and privacy. Each one has its own water tap, and there are waste bins everywhere. The sanitary facilities are acceptable and kept very clean. A swimming pool with a terrace is just the place to go for a sun tan and a refreshing drink.

Food here is excellent, with delicious regional specialities: try the 'Filet de Sandre'. During the high season there is plenty of entertainment for all ages; once a week live music is played, and the rest of the week is filled with competitions and parties. Children can take part in daytime activities. Don't forget to bring your bike, as there is a whole range of cycling and walking routes around Angers. Brandy lovers will probably know that this is the home of the Cointreau, while some wine-producing châteaux can also be visited. A day trip to the cave dwellings of the troglodytes is a special experience, or you could take a boat trip on the Loire.

La Vallée des Vignes

Rating	9
Tariff range	€€
Town	Concourson-sur-Layon
Department	Maine-et-Loire
Postal code	49700
Map	2 A1
Tel	02-41598635
Fax	02-41590983
e-mail	campingvdv@wanadoo.fr
Open	01 Apr – 30 Sep

From Saumur follow D960 to Doué-la-Fontaine/Cholet. 3 km beyond Doué, over bridge, take 1st right.
Size (hectares) 3.5
Touring pitches 57
Sanitary facilities rating 9.2
safe for children • baby sitting service • thematic meetings • Doué Zoo • rose garden • Doué-la-Fontaine (4 km)
Electric Hook-ups/amp 57/10

An unforgettable holiday for your children is what La Vallée des Vignes promises, and the English owner does her very best to make them feel welcome. What is more, she does it in a special way by organising treasure hunts around the nearby village, and painting and drawing classes: afterwards she displays their efforts in the bar where parents and others can admire them. If you fancy a good meal without worrying about small kids, that can be arranged here as there is even a baby sitting service. Cars are not allowed on the grounds, allowing the children to play in safety.

The campsite is located just outside Doué-la-Fontaine in a particularly verdant landscape. Pitches offer sufficient room and privacy as well as some protection against the sun. The sanitary facilities are quite new but simple, and there is a swimming pool with a paddling pool for small children. A number of sights and attractions in the area are worth a visit: not far away is the zoo in Doué-la-Fontaine, while just a few kilometres away is a colourful rose garden. Cave dwellings can be seen in the Village Troglodytique. Though this is primarily a family campsite, older people travelling without children will feel equally at home.

Pays de la Loire

Le Chantepie

Rating	9.1
Tariff range	€€€€
Town	Saumur
Department	Maine-et-Loire
Postal code	49400
Map	2 B1
Tel	02-41679534
Fax	02-41679585
e-mail	info@campingchantepie.com
Open	01 May – 15 Sep

NW from Saumur on D751 to Gennes. Turn left in La Mimerolle, follow signs to site (3 km).

Size (hectares) 10
Touring pitches 123
Sanitary facilities rating 9.3

quite a few activities • handicapped staff • view over the Loire Valley • castles and wine châteaux • Saumur: historic city (4 km)

Electric Hook-ups/amp 123/6-10

Le Chantepie in Saumur is a rather unusual campsite in that throughout the year the staff are helped by mentally-handicapped people who do an excellent job. In June and July the site tends to be visited mainly by families, whereas in spring and autumn most of the guests are either older people or adults without children.

There is a lot to do in the area, especially for walkers and cyclists. Saumur is a picturesque town with beautiful buildings and fine restaurants. Wine tasting is a big draw in an area known for its many wine-producing châteaux. There are few dull moments on the campsite either, where quite a few activities are organised in summer: sports competitions, mask making, building sand castles, barbecue parties and mussel-tasting ceremonies all add to the daily fun.

But peace returns after 10pm, as this is mainly a quiet site in a tranquil environment. It is located on a hill overlooking the beautiful Loire Valley, just outside the town. The pitches are very spacious with plenty of privacy and shady spots, and the sanitary facilities are well maintained.

L'Étang de la Brèche

Rating	8.4
Tariff range	€€€€
Town	Varennes-sur-Loire
Department	Maine-et-Loire
Postal code	49730
Map	2 B1
Tel	02-41512292
Fax	02-41512724
e-mail	mail@etang-breche.com
Open	08 May – 15 Sep

SW from Tours on N152 until 6 km before Saumur. Site on right (signed).

Size (hectares) 24
Touring pitches 127
Sanitary facilities rating 8.6

spacious lay-out • many activities • very well equipped • zoo in Doué-la-Fontaine • wine tasting • Saumur (6 km)

Electric Hook-ups/amp 127/10

If you are looking for a large campsite where there is a lot to do, then you will be delighted with L'Etang de la Brèche. The site looks very elegant with its slate pillars, and it is surrounded by countryside with lots of trees, bushes and colourful flowers. Pitches are very spacious and offer a lot of privacy as well as those vital shady spots, while the sanitary facilities are excellent. A large swimming complex with four pools and a water slide are enough to keep everyone happy. The shop carries a large selection of goods, and there is a snack bar, a café, an ice cream parlour, and a restaurant (the special dish of 'Brochettes beurre blanc' is certainly worth trying).

In July and August you can spend your evenings watching (or joining) karaoke, quiz shows and talent competitions, and there is a weekly disco party. During the day there are lots of activities for sports enthusiasts, including pedal-karting and pony riding, plus loads of on-site entertainment for the children. Bird watching is another popular activity in these woodlands, and in nearby Doué-la-Fontaine there is a zoo. Tasting Touraine wines and visiting cave dwellings are another two ideas for day trips into the surrounding region.

Le Vaux

Rating	7.9
Tariff range	€€
Town	Ambrières-les-Vallées
Department	Mayenne
Postal code	53300
Map	2 A3
Tel	02-43040067
Fax	02-43089328
e-mail	otsiambrieres@wanadoo.fr
Open	01 Apr – 30 Sep

From Mayenne follow D23 to Ambrières; 12 km to site on right (S of Ambrières).
Size (hectares) 1.5
Touring pitches 36
Sanitary facilities rating 7.7
canoeing, water cycling • sunny • view over the riverbed • archaeological finds • weaving museum • Ambrières-les-Vallées (1 km)
Electric Hook-ups/amp 36/10

A medium-sized, very green campsite located on the Varenne River, which makes it a perfect destination for boating enthusiasts. Kayaking, canoeing and pedalos can be followed by a picnic at one of the tables on the banks (there is also a snack bar). In this wooded area there is always a shady spot for those who want to stay out of the sun. The high hedges around the spacious pitches offer a lot of privacy, and the sanitary facilities are in good condition. Unfortunately there is no shop, and fresh bread is only available in July and August.

But there is a fine swimming pool, and further sport facilities include pétanque, mini golf, archery, tennis and occasionally other games. For both children and adults there are music and theatre performances, and small children can join the special daytime activities organised for them, like sports, games and drawing contests. There is a lot to do in the area for those interested in walking, cycling, and visiting castles. A number of places where archaeological discoveries have been made can be found, among which are some megalithic monuments. For art and history lovers there are various museums in Mayenne.

Municipal La Chabotière

Rating	8.7
Tariff range	€€
Town	Luché-Pringé
Department	Sarthe
Postal code	72800
Map	2 B2
Tel	02-43451000
Fax	02-43451000
e-mail	lachabotiere@ville-luche-pringe.fr
Open	01 Apr – 15 Oct

From La Flèche follow N23 to Clermont-Créans; right and take D13 to centre of Luché-Pringé. Right before war memorial, then left. After 100mtrs site on right.
Size (hectares) 2
Touring pitches 65
Sanitary facilities rating 8.7
well kept and clean • suitable for children • no cars permitted on the grounds • castles • Le Mans • La Flèche (14 km)
Electric Hook-ups/amp 65/10

This municipal campsite, less than ten years old, is situated along the River Loir (not Loire) near the village of Luché-Pringé. There are 75 large touring pitches, and the site is run by a friendly Polish lady. With the playground occupying a central position, the site is particularly suitable for families with children, and the river is separated from the site by a large fence. Cars must be left behind at the entrance and the two large swimming pools are constantly supervised, with child safety given top priority here too.

The spotless sanitary facilities, tarmac lanes and well-tended grounds make an excellent impression on visitors. There is no restaurant or café, but you can find these in the village. Twice a week the local baker and the cheesemonger visit the site, but for full scale shopping you can go to the supermarkets in La Flèche or La Lude. For the smallest children there is also a municipal playground just outside the site where, every morning at 10, an entertainment programme starts. Adults have to wait until 8pm for their version. The river is a good place for canoeing, and walkers can use the many routes that can be found locally. If a limited number of not too steep hills doesn't daunt you, then this is also a perfect starting point for bicycle tours.

Pays de la Loire

Le Pin Parasol

Rating 8.5
Tariff range €€€€
Town La Chapelle-Hermier
Department Vendée
Postal Code 85220
Map 1 C2
Tel 02-51346472
Fax 02-51346462
e-mail campingpinparasol@free.fr
Open 25 Apr – 25 Sep
From La Chapelle-Hermier take D42 W for approx 5 km.
Turn left after La Faverie, then right after 1 km.
Size (hectares) 12
Touring pitches 279
Sanitary facilities rating 8.6
water sports • tranquillity • well-maintained • Lac du Jaunay •
cycling/walks • Saint-Gilles-Croix-de-Vie (15 km)
Electric hook-ups/amps 289/6-16

Le Pin Parasol is located in a quiet part of the Vendée, close to the beautiful Lac du Jaunay. The sanitary facilities are excellent, the sandy beach is a mere 15-minute drive, and the immediate surroundings offer plenty of interesting sights. As the campsite was only founded in 1994, the plants, trees and shrubs surrounding the spacious pitches are not yet fully grown. The view is fantastic, and the place radiates tranquillity and makes you feel completely at ease.

Children can often be found in the heated swimming pool or on the play apparatus. The site also has a recreation area with table football, a pool table and table tennis. Karaoke is a popular evening entertainment here. Although you're not allowed to swim in the reservoir, you can rent pedalos, canoes and rowing boats at the campsite. You can discover the surrounding areas on a (rented) mountain bike. Don't forget to ask the owner about the riding possibilities in the area – she'd be more than happy to explain your options. There's also a golf course approximately 5 km from the campsite.

Bel

Rating 8.4
Tariff range €€€€
Town La Tranche-sur-Mer
Department Vendée
Postal Code 85360
Map 1 D2
Tel 02-51304739
Fax 02-51277281
e-mail campbel@wanadoo.fr
Open 24 May – 06 Sep
Site N of La Tranche-sur-Mer, between D105 and village;
follow signs.
Size (hectares) 3.5
Touring pitches 100
Sanitary facilities rating 8.4
family camp site • close to beach and village • suitable for
children • sea and beach activities • many restaurants • La
Tranche-sur-Mer (0.5 km)
Electric hook-ups/amps 100/10

If you want to camp by the sea, come to Bel. You will find a fine beach only 500m away, a large supermarket and a pretty village, La Tranche-sur-Mer. In spite of all that, the site is remarkably quiet. For families with young children who are happy with sand and water, this is a perfect place to stay. There is a lot of room to play and run around, with playground equipment and even a section for the very youngest with baby toys. They might even meet a clown. The pitches are not particularly spacious, but offer enough privacy. The sanitary facilities are beyond all praise though, and hygiene is perfectly maintained.

Twenty years ago cattle grazed on the ground that is now occupied by a sheltered and heated swimming pool. An artificial lake near the beach provides even more swimming opportunities, though if you don't like swimming, you can watch all the activities from a quiet spot on the shoreline. From time to time there are sailing competitions and you can always see lots of windsurfers. This site is ideal for anyone with small children who prefers a quiet, clean setting and entertainment for everyone. To satisfy shoppers there are lots of stores and restaurants nearby.

Le Jard

Rating	7.9
Tariff range	€€€€
Town	la Tranche-sur-Mer
Department	Vendée
Postal Code	85360
Map	1 C2
Tel	02-51274379
Fax	02-51274292
e-mail	info@campingdujard.fr
Open	10 May – 15 Sep

On D46 about 4 km E of La Tranche-sur-Mer in village of La Grière. Site is signed.

Size (hectares) 6
Touring pitches 150
Sanitary facilities rating 7.6

family campsite • close to the ocean/beach • large complex of swimming pools • beach and ocean • Château de Terre-Neuve • La Tranche-sur-Mer (4 km)

Electric hook-ups/amps 150/10

Le Jard is a family site with a lovely playground, a basketball and volleyball court, miniature golf and attractive paths for roller-blading. Underneath a covered area is a table-tennis table and table football games. The average age on the tennis and jeu-de-boules courts is a bit higher though! There is also a swimming pool complex with heated indoor and outdoor pools, a slide, a bubble bath and comfortable deck chairs.

Just a ten-minute walk from the campsite will bring you to the beach, where there is ample opportunity to go windsurfing and sailing. Many guests use the fully equipped tents and caravans run by various specialised travel agencies, and Le Jard also rents caravans. Unfortunately there is not much privacy as most of the pitches are bordered by low, newly planted hedges. The sanitary facilities are good. Although the supplies in the shop and the restaurant are limited, you can buy groceries or dine not far from site in La Grière (1 km) and La Tranche-sur-Mer.

A special treat is a visit to Château de Terre-Neuve (1580) in Fontenay-le-Comte, where the writer Georges Simenon lived from 1940 to 1943. Although the location of Le Jard is not spectacular, recreation-minded campers will not mind, as there is the beach nearby and many other activities to enjoy.

Les Sorinières

Tariff range	€€€
Town	Nieul-le-Dolent
Department	Vendée
Postal Code	85430
Map	1 C2
Tel	02-51079158
Fax	02-51079478
e-mail	bouronp2@wanadoo.fr
Open	01 May – 30 Sep

D747 (La Roche-sur-Yon/La Tranche-sur-Mer), junct Aubigny. Take D36 to Les Sables-d'Olonne. Site 2 km W of Nieul-le-Dolent.

Size (hectares) 2
Touring pitches 25

farm camp site • simple • good for a short stay • fine beaches • Vendée region • La Roche-sur-Yon (15 km)

Electric hook-ups/amps 20/6

Simplicity has its charm, and nowhere more than on Les Sorinières. There is only room for 20 tents or caravans on the lawn of this 'camping à la ferme', but most of the time this number is not even reached. The view of the barns and rolling fields is nearly always clear. The narrow road that runs along the campsite doesn't cause any nuisance, and indeed the only sounds you will hear are farmyard ones: tractors and other agricultural machinery.

The owners, Patrick and Françoise Bouron, combine their farming activities with the courteous attention they pay to their guests. Electricity and water supply points are spread over the whole site. The toilet building is modern, and an unexpected surprise is the heated swimming pool with deck chairs. For your daily shopping you can go to the local supermarket, about 1.5 km away, but most visitors will spend the day elsewhere, exploring the Vendée region with its fine beaches, attractive harbour towns and fortified castles. You can also visit the wetlands of Poitevin, known as 'Green Venice', where you can take trips in a boat or by bicycle. Les Sorinières is a good place for those who like basic facilities and spend their time exploring the surrounding area.

Pays de la Loire

Les Écureuils

Rating 8.5
Tariff range €€€€
Town St-Hilaire-de-Riez
Department Vendée
Postal code 85270
Map 1 C2
Tel 02-51543371
Fax 02-51556908
e-mail info@camping-aux-ecureuils.com
Open 01 May – 15 Sep
Site 6 km NE of St-Hilaire-de-Riez on D123, halfway between La Pège & Les Mouettes.
Size (hectares) 4
Touring pitches 51
Sanitary facilities rating 8.5
swimming paradise • close to the sea • sports and games • soft sandy beaches • the Vendée • Saint-Jean-de-Monts (6 km)
Electric hook-ups/amps 51/6

Les Écureuils campsite is located in the dunes next to the main road to the beach, and you cannot get much nearer to the sea. It is one of many sites in the area, but its extensive swimming facilities make it really special. It is known as an 'Aquaticamp', which in this case means a covered swimming pool with a large slide. Sun loungers are available by the pool for those quiet moments between the fun and games in the water. Other activities include tennis, table tennis, boules and even a fitness centre where you can keep yourself in trim.

Water sports include surfing, long-boarding, sailing, sea fishing and diving. Only a few visitors will actually get round to the variety of tours and trips available in the area, and there are numerous beauty spots in the Vendée. There are busy harbour town and quiet marshes where you are more likely to see herons than people. Old castles and open-air museums for those looking to broaden their knowledge of the local area are plentiful. The local cuisine is delicious and involves lots of fruits de mer.

Aux Coeurs Vendéens

Rating 8.7
Tariff range €€€€
Town St. Jean-de-Monts
Department Vendée
Postal code 85160
Map 1 C2
Tel 02-51588491
Fax 02-28112075
e-mail info@coeursvendeens.com
Open 1 Apr - 20 Sep
From St. Jean-de-Monts N on D38. Site approx 4km on left, clearly signed.
Size (hectares) 8.9
Touring pitches 59
Sanitary facilities rating 8.9
Friendly atmosphere • sports • sea and beach fun • cycling tour Noirmoutier
Electric hook-ups/amps 59/10

What distinguishes Aux Coeurs Vendéens from the many other campsites in the immediate surroundings? Its small size and the married couple who own it; they are determined not to let their campsite grow so large that they would lose the personal contact they have with the guests. You won't find any of the complete and pre-erected tent arrangements here that are so commonly found in this area, but the small scale of this family campsite does not mean that it lacks facilities. The owners' son, a professional sports teacher, is in charge of entertainment; he organizes a triathlon, water polo, beach volleyball, horseriding and even diving lessons in the swimming pool. In addition to all this you can rent a bike or scooter to explore the surroundings, or visit the the sandy beach which is only 700mtrs away.

Le Bois Joly

Rating 8.4
Tariff range €€€€
Town St-Jean-de-Monts
Department Vendée
Postal code 85165
Map 1 C2
Tel 02-51591163
Fax 02-51591106
e-mail campingboisjoly@wanadoo.fr
Open 05 Apr – 27 Sep
Site on D38, 2 km N from St-Jean-de-Monts, on right.
Size (hectares) 7.5
Touring pitches 183
Sanitary facilities rating 8.3
quiet • sea bathing within walking distance • fine swimming pool • beaches • Marais Vendéen • St-Jean-de-Monts (1 km)
Electric hook-ups/amps 183/6

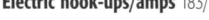

Le Bois Joly is a family enterprise in which the original proprietors are now helped by their two children with their spouses; together they create a friendly atmosphere and give a helping hand where needed. Although the area is heaving with busy campsites, peace and quiet can still be guaranteed at Le Bois Joly. The resort of Saint-Jean-de-Monts is within walking distance, so the lack of a shop is hardly a problem.

Most of the pitches are level and reasonably spacious, and the very clean sanitary facilities look as good as new. There is a large outdoor swimming pool with slides and deckchairs, and a beautiful indoor pool is a popular addition to the amenities. The sea is 1 km away, and there is a centre for thalassotherapy. From 1 July to the middle of September there is a team on site to entertain young and old. Various catering facilities are available but only during this high season. Given the location, Le Bois Joly is a reasonably quiet campsite with plenty to offer the whole family in the summertime.

Les Places Dorées

Rating 8.2
Tariff range €€€€
Town St-Jean-de-Monts
Department Vendée
Postal Code 85160
Map 1 C2
Tel 02-51590293
Fax 02-51593047
e-mail contact@placesdorees.com
Open 31 May – 31 Aug
From St-Jean-de-Monts follow D38 (northward); site on right (3.5 km).
Size (hectares) 7
Touring pitches 46
Sanitary facilities rating 8.1
large swimming pool • 800 m from the sea • sports facilities • beautiful sandy beaches • cycling to Noirmoutier • Saint-Jean-de-Monts (3 km)
Electric hook-ups/amps 46/10

Seaside fun is still number one on the list of priorities for most holiday makers. Close to the beach (800m) and equipped with a real swimmers' paradise – Camping Les Places Dorées is ideal. If you don't want to whoosh down the water slide, you may be attracted by spa bath therapy, so join the fitness club on L'Abri des Pins, the campsite facing Les Places Dorées.

If you are looking for peace and quiet you should avoid the high season. In summer all the camping sites in this area are overcrowded, while sports and playgrounds are constantly occupied. The entertainment team works hard, and the music plus the noise coming from the D38 can be loud. Cycling on the beautiful route to Noirmoutier is popular. In every season the site attracts different groups of guests, but the beautiful beaches are always there and so are the inland sights and – probably – the sun that is so often present.

Pays de la Loire

Les Amiaux

Rating 8.3
Tariff range €€€€
Town St-Jean-de-Monts
Department Vendée
Postal Code 85160
Map 1 C2
Tel 02-51582222
Fax 02-51582609
e-mail accueil@amiaux.fr
Open 01 May – 30 Sep
Site approx 3 km NW of St-Jean-de-Monts (left of D38).
Size (hectares) 16
Touring pitches 266
Sanitary facilities rating 7.9
located in wooded surroundings • near seaside resort • plenty of sports facilities • sea and beaches • Ile d'Yeu • Saint-Jean-de-Monts (3 km)
Electric hook-ups/amps 266/10

Camping Les Amiaux is a great place if you want to be near the sea, which is just 900m down a footpath. The old coniferous and deciduous trees not only look charming, but they also provide much-needed shade. However, the traffic on the D38 will soon remind you that you haven't wandered very far from the inhabited world. The campsite is cut in two by the road, and the two fields are connected by a tunnel. The huge swimming pool, which has four double waterslides and other features, is popular. An indoor pool is about to open.

You'll have plenty of opportunity to play sports or games – the campsite has a playground, a sports field and a recreation area with table tennis and table football. The small supermarket and restaurant make Les Amiaux seem more like a holiday village. A day trip can nevertheless be very appealing. If you've brought your own bicycles, you'll want to see Ile de Noirmoutier. The boat trip to Ile d'Yeu is also great fun. The swimming pool and nearby beach ensure that most guests enjoy a fun vacation.

Domaine de la Forêt

Rating 8.4
Tariff range €€€€
Town St-Julien-des-Landes
Department Vendée
Postal code 85150
Map 1 C2
Tel 02-51466211
Fax 02-51466087
e-mail camping@domainelaforet.com
Open 15 May – 15 Sep
Site on D55, just NE of St-Julien.
Size (hectares) 50
Touring pitches 148
Sanitary facilities rating 8.3
country estate • relaxed atmosphere • not over-organised • sea and beach • Jardins des Olfactions • Bretignolles-sur-Mer (10 km)
Electric hook-ups/amps 148/6

Domaine de la Forêt is the sort of place where a one-night stay could easily turn out to last a lot longer. It is a good base for exploring the surrounding area, and has spacious, sheltered pitches. Along with the many old trees with dense undergrowth and wooded banks, there are lots of birds and squirrels. It is a well-kept campsite and the swimming pool offers unique views of the castle and its formal gardens. An older swimming pool with a separate children's pool is situated at the back of the castle complex.

The fenced-off pitches offer plenty of privacy, and there are activities for all campsite guests, including the weekly triathlon. Those looking for peace and quiet will be content to throw out a line in one of the lakes. The Côte de Lumière is only 12 km away, but for aromas other than the salty sea air and mussels, you should visit the scent-filled gardens in nearby Coëx.

Village de la Guyonnière

Rating 8
Tariff range €€€€
Town St-Julien-des-Landes
Department Vendée
Postal Code 85150
Map 1 C2
Tel 02-51466259
Fax 02-51466289
e-mail info@laguyonniere.com
Open 12 Apr – 26 Sep
Site 3 km W of St-Julien-des-Landes on road off D12.
Size (hectares) 30
Touring pitches 200
Sanitary facilities rating 8
space • nature • tranquillity • beaches and sea (10 km) •
walking/cycling • Saint-Gilles-Croix-de-Vie
Electric hook-ups/amps 200/6-10

At La Guyonnière you're unlikely to trip over your neighbour's guy ropes or get bored. The exceptionally-spacious campsite, run by Dutch proprietors, has grown dramatically from a small-scale farm, though there are still goats' paddocks, which are clearly visible from most places. Lac du Jaunay, where you can rent rowing boats and pedalos, is within walking distance (500m). You can also rent canoes and mountain bikes at the campsite.

There is plenty of organised entertainment during the high season, ranging from football matches to six-event competitions for children. Older children can play football, volleyball or table tennis, and there's also a recreation room with a pool table and video games, and a library. The lakeside camp fire is exceptionally popular. The owners arrange excursions to, for example, Île d'Yeu during the early and late seasons. If you're not in the mood to cook, try the plat du jour, or put your name down for the weekly communal meal. Tenters can spend their last night in one of the campsite rooms, free of charge (sanitary facilities available).

Pays de la Loire

La Garangeoire

Rating	9.1
Tariff range	€€€€
Town	St-Julien-des-Landes
Department	Vendée
Postal Code	85150
Map	1 C2
Tel	02-51466539
Fax	02-51466985
e-mail	info@garangeoire.com
Open	26 Apr – 27 Sep

Site 2.5 km N of St-Julien-des-Landes on D21 (site signed).

Size (hectares) 18
Touring pitches 140
Sanitary facilities rating 9

country estate • sports facilities • natural surroundings • beaches and sea • walking/cycling • Saint-Gilles-Croix-de-Vie (15 km)

Electric hook-ups/amps 140/6-10

La Garangeoire forms part of a large country estate with oak forests, lakes and a beautiful river, and a stately home that is still occupied. The Gallo-Roman temple used to attract large numbers of people to the area many centuries ago. The spacious pitches come with or without shade, and the sanitary facilities are excellent and well-maintained. The site has a new – and very large – heated swimming pool, with several waterslides and more than enough deck chairs. There's also a tennis court, where you can get lessons from a professional.

La Garangeoire has six horses and six ponies, which are available for trips around the estate, or you can rent bicycles. There are plenty of sports and games facilities, and some of the entertainment is organised. The excellent and well-cared-for restaurant only uses fresh produce. Vegetarian dishes, a crêperie and a takeaway service are all available. The shop has a good selection of products. The stunning coast is 10 km away and there are five golf courses in the immediate vicinity.

Du Château de Bertangles

Rating 8.1
Tariff range €€
Town Bertangles
Department Somme
Postal code 80260
Map 2 D5
Tel 03-60656836
e-mail camping@chateaubertangles.com
Open 25 Apr – 08 Sep
On N side of village in no through road. From N25 follow D97 near Bertangles to château and site.
Size (hectares) 1
Touring pitches 33
Sanitary facilities rating 9.6
situated near a château • rural environment • simple and quiet • Amiens cathedral • memorial sites of WWI • Amiens (10 km)
Electric hook-ups/amps 33/5

With just a little imagination, this old château with its brooding stone walls and atmospheric presence easily conjures up an age of chivalry peopled by knights and ladies. The site is set close to the castle's park, where boar and partridge can be found running wild. The pitches are surrounded by hedges which combine to offer screening and privacy for visitors. The chief attraction here is the setting, and facilities and amenities are geared towards lovers of the countryside. The toilet building is perfectly adequate, and there is a modest playground. Table tennis is played in a dusty Great Hall. There is no restaurant in Bertangles, so campers who want to eat on site should be sure to bring their own food.

A baker arrives early every morning with his bread and croissants, but apart from wine, soft drinks and fruit there is nothing on sale at the site. For entertainment and evenings out you can visit nearby villages, or drive the 10 kilometres to the town of Amiens (look out for the towers of the splendid cathedral). Need more inspiration? Then join one of the daily guided tours of the château, from mid-June to mid-August daily at 5.30pm.

Le Val d'Authie

Rating 8.1
Tariff range €€€
Town Villers-sur-Authie
Department Somme
Postal code 80120
Map 2 C5
Tel 03-22299247
Fax 03-22299330
e-mail camping@valdauthie.fr
Open 01 Apr – 12 Oct
Leave N1 near Vron for Villers-sur-Authie. Site in S part of village. Accessible via D85 towards Rue.
Size (hectares) 7
Touring pitches 61
Sanitary facilities rating 8.2
spacious • swimming and sports facilities • perfect state of maintenance • cycling itineraries • beach • Rue (6 km)
Electric hook-ups/amps 61/6-10

Many visitors are pleasantly surprised by Le Val d'Authie, a site that well deserves its reputation. It has a quiet atmosphere, helped by hedges around all the pitches and trees that offer shade and shelter. The sanitary facilities are also excellent. Leisurely mornings here can start on the training circuit, followed by a few lengths in the swimming pool, and a visit to the jacuzzi. Breakfast baguettes and croissants taste much better as a result! You can complete the triathlon by taking a bicycle ride into the village of Rue (6 km) or to the beach (around 12 km); a different route for every day of the week makes the trip more interesting.

Picardy also has something to offer further inland, from monuments to the battles against Edward III and prominent personalities in the history of early aviation, to Gothic architecture and golf courses. Even the children will want to linger here, tempted by the swimming pool, the playgrounds, the tennis courts, the mini golf course, the basketball court, the fitness centre, the playing fields and the entertainment. The restaurant at Le Val d'Authie (partly open air) serves good meals at low prices, but no chips.

Poitou-Charentes

Les Gorges du Chambon

Rating 8.3
Tariff range €€€€
Town Montbron
Department Charente
Postal Code 16220
Map 4 D5
Tel 05-45707170
Fax 05-45708002
e-mail gorges.chambon@wanadoo.fr
Open 19 Apr – 20 Sep
From Montbron D699 eastward; outside town this road becomes D6. Turn left after 4 km in La-Tricherie (D163) and right after 2.5 km. Site 7 km E of Montbron.
Size (hectares) 7
Touring pitches 100
Sanitary facilities rating 8.6
quality camp site • lots of activities • breathtaking view • romanesque art • beautiful nature • Montbron (7 km)
Electric hook-ups/amps 93/6

Les Gorges du Chambon lies hidden in an unspoilt natural environment. Much has improved since the present owner bought the somewhat neglected campsite a few years ago, and the highest emphasis was placed on quality as the results clearly show. The spacious pitches are scattered all over the grounds, and surrounded by a reasonable number of trees and hedges. Toilets are clean and the washing rooms are well maintained.

The view from the campsite is really breathtaking – it is laid out against the slope of a hill and from every point campers overlook the hills on the opposite side of the valley. Special attention has been given to the reception hall, the little shop, the recreation and dance room and the terraces. There is a large swimming pool with deck chairs all around. An entertainment programme is not just aimed at small children, and older ones are invited as well. Crafts, drawing, games are for the young, with dancing lessons, karaoke, tennis, mini golf and volleyball for the teenagers. But that does not mean that Les Gorges is a fun factory, as all these activities take place on a modest scale. The region is very isolated, but the roads are in good condition and the natural beauty is unsurpassed.

Ostrea

Rating 8.1
Tariff range €€€€
Town Dolus-d'Oléron
Department Charente-Maritime
Postal Code 17550
Map 4 C5
Tel 05-46476236
Fax 05-46752001
e-mail camping.ostrea@wanadoo.fr
Open 15 Mar – 30 Sep
From Le Château-d'Oléron towards Dolus/St-Pierre. Then right and follow 'Route des Huitres'. Site on left (4 km), E of Dolus.
Size (hectares) 2
Touring pitches 60   **Static pitches** 7
Sanitary facilities rating 8.2
tidy and clean • genuine hospitality • unspoilt nature • good shellfish • St-Pierre-d'Oléron (8 km)
Electric hook-ups/amps 60/3-6

Some two decades ago Jean-Michel Dormeau gave up his job as a sports teacher to start this seaside campsite with his wife. The owners keep everything tidy and well maintained. The immaculate sanitary building is a sight in itself, with its baths, lavatories and showers especially for children. Pitches are fairly spacious, but they are not separated from each other, so there is hardly any privacy. During the day there is some traffic noise from the coastal road.

There is no swimming pool and the sea is not a good alternative; the mud flats only allow swimming at high tide, about two hours a day. A better option is the beach at St-Trojan-les-Bains or the east coast. Children can have fun on the large playground, and every morning except weekends there is an entertainment programme between 10 and 12pm. In the snack bar, chef/caterer Gérard Dupuy prepares regional specialities or a three-course menu to be served on the terrace in July and August, as well as the usual Moroccan couscous, pizza, and French fries. About 800m from the campsite there is another gourmet highlight, Chez Mamelou, where lunch consists of delicious fresh fish soup, mussels or oysters. Don't look for any cultural attractions – this is a place to relax.

Camping Sunêlia Interlude

Rating 8.2
Tariff range €€€€
Town Le Bois-Plage-en-Ré
Department Charente-Maritime
Postal Code 17580
Map 4 C6
Tel 05-46091822
Fax 05-46092338
e-mail infos@interlude.fr
Open 08 Apr – 05 Nov
Follow D201 past toll bridge to Le Bois-Plage. Turn left after 4.5 km (La Noue) and left again after 500mtrs. Site E of Le Bois-Plage.
Size (hectares) 7.5
Touring pitches 148
Sanitary facilities rating 8.6
park-like terrain • good and clean sanitary facilities • many amenities • beautiful beach • cycling routes • Saint-Martin (5 km)
Electric hook-ups/amps 148/6-10

Only a small section of Interlude, a campsite laid out in park style, is open to campers. The greater part is reserved for rental chalets and tents. This site is extremely popular, so there is no chance of finding a place in summer without booking ahead. By April it is full. A positive result of this popularity is the fact that some amenities, like the swimming pool and the restaurant, are already open in the early season.

The campsite is located by the seaside, in a partly wooded dune area. A storm in 1999 destroyed many trees, so some of the spacious pitches are not provided with shade. Unfortunately in many places the grass has disappeared as well. The sanitary facilities are simple but clean, and there is a nice playground for the children and daily entertainment. You can also play boules and many other games. Just 50m away there is a beautiful wide beach. You don't have to go to the village for shopping, as there is a shop on the site. The surrounding area is ideal for walkers and cyclists, and pretty villages with daily markets are within easy reach.

L'Estanquet

Rating 7.7
Tariff range €€€€
Town Les Mathes
Department Charente-Maritime
Postal Code 17570
Map 4 C5
Tel 05-46224732
Fax 05-46225146
e-mail contact@campinglestanquet.com
Open 01 Apr – 30 Sep
Site 3 km NW of Les Mathes on D141-E 4. Follow signs.
Size (hectares) 8.5
Touring pitches 130
Sanitary facilities rating 8
ideal for teenagers • fine swimming pool • many activities • Phare de la Coubre • oyster farms • Royan
Electric hook-ups/amps 130/10

L'Estanquet is the ideal place for those who enjoy cycling, walking and beach holidays. There is also plenty to do on the campsite itself, so there is no chance of getting bored. L'Estanquet is located in a pine forest, so most of the pitches offer enough shade. The modern swimming pool is fairly large and has a big, thrilling water slide. You can sit under cover in the afternoon and relax in French style with a glass of pastis, watching the swimmers.

In the evening there is an entertainment programme with disco, karaoke, bingo and a circus performance. During the day the entertainment team organises tennis tournaments, table tennis and volleyball. Small children are not forgotten; painting and other games will keep them busy. All these activities make this site very popular with teenagers and children, and as a consequence it can be boisterous and noisy. So if you prefer a really quiet holiday, you may find this site a bit overpowering. The highlights of a stay here are the sandy Atlantic beaches and the oyster farms, all within cycling distance.

L'Orée du Bois

Rating 7.9
Tariff range €€€€
Town Les Mathes
Department Charente-Maritime
Postal Code 17570
Map 4 C5
Tel 05-46224243
Fax 05-46225476
e-mail info@camping-oree-du-bois.fr
Open 23 Apr – 17 Sep
Site 3 km NW of Les Mathes on D268. Follow signs.
Size (hectares) 6
Touring pitches 101
Sanitary facilities rating 7.8
private sanitary facilities • ideal for families • good and spacious pitches • Phare de la Coubre • oyster farms • Les Mathes (2 km)
Electric hook-ups/amps 101/8

This is a super place for a beach or cycling holiday, only a few kilometres from the Atlantic coast and right in the middle of the Forêt Domaniale de la Coubre. It is a well-kept site in a pine forest with spacious pitches that offer plenty of privacy.

The general sanitary facilities are good, but guests can also make use of separate buildings with 'private' toilets. The fine swimming pool with its water slide is large enough for a campsite of this size; on the edge of the pool there are comfortable deck chairs for the sun worshippers. Small children have a paddling pool and playground to entertain them. In the Club d'Enfants experienced entertainers put on a special programme for the little ones, and this makes the site particularly suitable for families with children under the age of 12; older children can swim and play tennis.

L'Orée du Bois does have an evening programme with disco, bingo and karaoke. Cycling paths through the pine forest allow you to make trips to the oyster farms or the lighthouse at Phare de la Coubre.

Monplaisir

Rating 7.5
Tariff range €€€
Town Les Mathes
Department Charente-Maritime
Postal Code 17570
Map 4 C5
Tel 05-46225031
Fax 05-46225031
Open 01 Apr – 01 Oct
Site 300mtrs W of Les Mathes on D141-E1, just outside village.
Size (hectares) 2.3
Touring pitches 112   **Static pitches** 10
Sanitary facilities rating 7
close to the village centre • green surroundings • quiet place to stay • Forêt Domaniale de la Coubre • Royan • Les Mathes beach (4 km)
Electric hook-ups/amps 112/6

This is an area that is especially popular with campers – there are no fewer than 30 camp sites within the borders of this municipality. The local mayor owns this one at Monplaisir, located just outside the village near a forest with many opportunities for cycling and walking tours.

Trees and hedges offer enough shade to most caravans and tents as well as the necessary privacy. The central part is occupied by a swimming pool with a paddling pool, a playground, volleyball court, mini golf, and a small recreation room. In fact that is all there is; Monplaisir is not a place for people who want to be entertained all day. Families with small children and senior citizens are the target group for 'monsieur le maire'. The sanitary facilities are very clean and so are the pool and the rest of the buildings.

In spite of the location next to a major through-road, it is a quiet campsite. Royan, a small town nearby, is easily reached by bicycle, and so is the shore of the Atlantic Ocean.

Le Clos Fleuri

Rating	8
Tariff range	€€€€
Town	Médis
Department	Charente-Maritime
Postal Code	17600
Map	4 C5
Tel	05-46056217
Fax	05-46067561
e-mail	clos-fleuri@wanadoo.fr
Open	01 Jun – 15 Sep

A10, junct Saintes; then N150, junct Médis; follow signs to site, SE of Médis on D117 - E3.

Size (hectares) 3.5
Touring pitches 125
Sanitary facilities rating 7.9
park lay-out • friendly atmosphere • many playing facilities • beautiful beaches • pretty villages • Royan (6 km)
Electric hook-ups/amps 110/5-10

Le Clos Fleuri is a family campsite, laid out like a park around an old farm. There are many trees and hedges scattered over the area that bring shade and shelter to the pitches. The sanitary facilities are old-fashioned but very clean. Jean Devais and his son Christian, together with their wives, do everything they can to keep their customers happy. There is a lot to do for all ages. Children can play in a paddling pool or in the playground, and there is an entertainment programme specially for them. Twice a week a party is held with a barbecue, music or a sports competition. If you like you can use the sauna, and there are even lessons in archery.

To many guests, however, this is primarily a place of rest after previous activities elsewhere. One of the main attractions is the beach at Saint-George-de-Didonne, only 5 km away. Worth a visit are the village of Talmont, the port of La Rochelle and the zoo in La Palmyre. You can also shop or eat in Royan on the banks of the Gironde. The small pleasure airport near the campsite may be noisy, but most guests see the aerobatics and skydivers as just another attraction.

Les Moulins de la Vergne

Rating	7.5
Tariff range	€€
Town	Pons
Department	Charente-Maritime
Postal Code	17800
Map	4 C5
Tel	05-46905084
e-mail	uffelen@wanadoo.fr
Open	All year

A10, junct 35; then follow N137 to Pons. After 20 km Pons junct and straight on. After 100mtrs follow yellow sign (left) to Moulins de la Vergne; site 1 km N of Pons.

Size (hectares) 4
Touring pitches 51
Sanitary facilities rating 8
pleasant atmosphere • good service • excursions • Hennessey Cognac factory • canoe tours • Saintes (20 km)
Electric hook-ups/amps 51/10

Moulins de la Vergne occupies about one quarter of the recreation park that was created by a water mill dating from 1880. Good service and hygiene play an important role here, and there is enough room on every pitch to guarantee privacy. Most people who stay here are looking for social contact with fellow campers, and the many activities are the best way of doing this. Many guests join the group tours by canoe or the barbecue parties; the 'happy hour' in the bar is also a great success.

Excursions are made to the Hennessy cognac factory, wine tasting cellars, châteaux, churches, museums and nature reserves. In fact there is more to see and do than is possible in one holiday. Idle hours are spent by the swimming pool, on the terrace, by the riverside (the River Seugne runs through the grounds) and in the restaurant with its gourmet reputation. Children have enough room to play, but they are more attracted by the forest and the river. The pleasant atmosphere and the many sights in the region cause many campers to return. And of course this site is also a perfect stopover on your way to the South. It is situated only 4 km off the motorway A10 from Paris to Bordeaux, just south of Saintes.

Poitou-Charentes

La Campière

Rating	8.9
Tariff range	€€€€
Town	St-Georges-d'Oléron
Department	Charente-Maritime
Postal Code	17190
Map	4 C5
Tel	05-46767225
Fax	05-46765418
e-mail	lacampiere@orange.fr
Open	29 Mar – 15 Nov

Site 4 km W of St-Georges, near Chaucre. Enter village from D734, turn right, drive around village; after 400mtrs turn right again, continue 300mtrs to site on right.

Size (hectares) 1.7
Touring pitches 50
Sanitary facilities rating 9
excellent sanitary facilities • unpretentious • a pure haven • beach • St-Pierre • several bird sanctuaries
Electric hook-ups/amps 50/10

This quiet, well-known campsite is situated in a nature reserve on the island of Oléron off the west coast of France. It took the owner a long time to find this wonderful location, 400m from the beach. The site is surrounded by a pine forest, and some people say that in hot weather the trees exude resin. As soon as a guest leaves, the pitch is cleaned and rearranged. There is not much room between the pitches and in some places you can see into your neighbour's tent.

Although the sea and a lovely sandy beach are so near, the site has a small swimming pool. For youngsters it also offers a small playground, a table tennis table, and a bar-football table. There is no restaurant either, but on Mondays, Wednesdays and Fridays take-away meals are available, like paella and mussel dishes that are said to be delicious. The main attraction is the beach, where you can go swimming, surfing and sailing. There are a few nice ports on the island, with day trips to Saintes or La Rochelle quite popular.

Séquoia Parc

Rating	8.8
Tariff range	€€€€
Town	St-Just-Luzac
Department	Charente-Maritime
Postal Code	17320
Map	4 C5
Tel	05-46855555
Fax	05-46855556
e-mail	info@sequoiaparc.com
Open	08 May – 14 Sep

From Marennes take D728 to Saintes. Turn left after 2.5 km; leads to site.

Size (hectares) 45
Touring pitches 200
Sanitary facilities rating 9
château estate • entertainment for children • luxurious, many facilities • Ile d'Oléron • aquarium in La Rochelle • Marennes (5 km)
Electric hook-ups/amps 200/6

        EUROTOP

A wonderful campsite in one of the sunniest places in France, near the Atlantic coast. Séquoia Parc is a member of the Les Castels chain, which means that it is situated on the parkland of a château. There is no access to the main building, but you can visit the outbuildings. The renovated wine barn now serves as a restaurant and the dovecot is a shop selling souvenirs. There is a supermarket with a wide range of products, such as fruit, vegetables and ready meals.

The estate also has an exotic swimming pool, surrounded by palm trees. The campsite offers a good choice of sports, including diving lessons, while there is an entertainment programme for children. If you think that a tent is too simple, you can rent a static caravan or a chalet. Away from the site you can relax on the beach, or on the enchanting island of Oléron. Fishing and swimming is available in many nearby ponds and lakes. The nearest major towns are Rochefort and La Rochelle, the latter with an interesting saltwater aquarium.

L'Estuaire

Rating	8.3
Tariff range	€€€
Town	St-Thomas-de-Conac
Department	Charente-Maritime
Postal Code	17150
Map	4 C5
Tel	05-46860820
Fax	05-46860918
e-mail	lestuaire@wanadoo.fr
Open	01 May – 30 Sep

A10, junct 37; then follow D254 to St-Thomas village square. Follow signs onto narrow road, to site, 3.5 km SW of St-Thomas.

Size (hectares) 8

Touring pitches 120

Sanitary facilities rating 8

entertainment programme • many sports facilities • modern swimming pool • pretty villages • Gironde • Mirambeau (12 km)

Electric hook-ups/amps 120/10

A gate at the end of a long drive on the east bank of the Gironde marks the entrance to L'Estuaire. As you might expect in such a flat region, the campsite occupies a level terrain with straight lanes and spacious pitches, surrounded by numerous high trees and dense hedges. Wherever you camp there is always enough privacy.

On open ground there is a tennis court, and a multi-purpose sports complex is highly popular. The modern, luxurious swimming pool (with paddling pool) is large enough for a campsite of this size. There are no facilities for swimming or boating in the Gironde. For a quick bite there is a snack bar. Other facilities include a bar, a recreation room, a dance floor and a discotheque. An experienced team of entertainers provides a special programme: drawing and painting for the little ones, karaoke and disco for the teenagers.

Exploring the region, you can visit villages like Blaye and Mirambeau, both of which have a market on Saturdays, good shops and restaurants.

Poitou-Charentes

Le Courte Vallée

Rating 8.5
Tariff range €€€€
Town Airvault
Department Deux-Sèvres
Postal Code 79600
Map 2 B1
Tel 05-49647065
Fax 05-49941778
e-mail camping@caravanningfrance.com
Follow D938 (Thouars-Parthenay), from La Maucarrière to Airvault (D725). Turn left after 4 km (towards Airvault). After 500mtrs cross bridge and rail line (left); 2nd street on left, then approx 500mtrs to site.
Size (hectares) 8
Touring pitches 64
Sanitary facilities rating 8.8
relaxed atmosphere • quiet • friendly English owners • Poitiers - Futuroscope • Doué-la-Fontaine Zoo • Airvault (1 km)
Electric hook-ups/amps 60/8

'A nice campsite in a relaxed atmosphere' is what most people say when asked why they are staying on Le Courte Vallée. The very friendly English owners, who know every guest by name, are responsible for this positive opinion, and the weekly barbecue party held on Friday night also helps foster good relations. The recreational facilities are limited to pétanque, table tennis and table football.

The site lies on the outskirts of Airvault, not far from Poitiers, in the Thouet Valley. During the day you can sometimes hear sounds coming from the village, but in the evening everything is quiet. Airvault is within walking distance, which is a great advantage as there are no shops or restaurants on the site, although there are some snacks for sale and the baker brings fresh bread every morning. The village has some shops and restaurants, a municipal swimming pool and a number of historic monuments like a medieval bridge.

More history can be found in Poitiers, an interesting town 40 km away. Outside the town is the attraction park Futuroscope. Further away you can visit the magnificent châteaux of the Loire Valley.

Le Relais du Miel

Rating 7.7
Tariff range €€€€
Town Châtellerault
Department Vienne
Postal Code 86100
Map 2 B1
Tel 05-49020627
e-mail camping@lerelaisdumiel.com
Open 17 May – 01 Sep
A10 junct 26; turn left at rdbt; site on right, 2 km E of Châtellerault.
Size (hectares) 7
Touring pitches 80
Sanitary facilities rating 7.8
spacious lay-out • pleasant, rural atmosphere • telescope • Futuroscope (30 km) • Poitiers • Châtellerault (2 km)
Electric hook-ups/amps 80/10

A manor house with outbuildings and a grand estate are the setting for Le Relais du Miel. The present owner bought this former farm to turn the grounds into a campsite, and the stables and old barns were renovated to house the reception area, two apartments, the activities room, the snack bar, the bar and the sanitary facilities. But the rural atmosphere of the estate remains unchanged. Low shrubs and some scattered trees grow within the spacious layout. The campsite is handy for the motorway (A10) – which creates some background noise – but it is also a good place for a longer stay.

A swimming pool, a paddling pool, a playground and – as a special attraction – a genuine telescope make the site even more attractive. Not far from here you can visit Futuroscope, which illustrates the ideas people had about the future when it opened. Châtellerault is a small town with a quaint centre and a market on Wednesdays and Saturdays. Here there is also an interesting museum with vintage cars, motorbikes and bicycles. A few kilometres away lies Poitiers, a town with a number of beautiful churches.

Les Peupliers

Rating 8.4
Tariff range €€€€
Town Couhé
Department Vienne
Postal Code 86700
Map 4 D6
Tel 05-49592116
Fax 05-49379209
e-mail info@lespeupliers.fr
Open 02 May – 30 Sep
N10 (Poitiers-Angoulême), junct Couhé-Nord. Site 500mtrs on right.
Size (hectares) 16
Touring pitches 128
Sanitary facilities rating 8.5
family camp site • fine swimming pool • sports and games • Vallée des Singes • cycling and walking routes • Vivonne (11 km)
Electric hook-ups/amps 128/5-16

It all started with one shower and two toilets, but now you will find three sanitary buildings, one of which has very modern equipment. Everything here is clean and well kept.

Les Peupliers stretches along a river, partly in the forest and partly against a rock wall. Some pitches under the trees are blessed with shade, while others are right in the burning sun. Here and there you can find a place with a view of the river. The pitches are barely separated, so you find yourself camping back to back with your neighbours and privacy is lacking. There is a small shop where you can buy the basic necessities.

The aqua world with four swimming pools and a paddling pool looks great; it includes an 80m-long water slide. Deck chairs by the pool give you the opportunity to relax and doze off, or watch all the fun in the water. The campsite also has a fishing pond for anglers. During the day you can play a game of volleyball, water polo or tennis, and the entertainment programme has something for everyone. In the evening you can impress your fellow campers on the dance floor. The surrounding area is perfect for a long or short tour by bicycle or on foot.

Lac de St-Cyr

Rating 8.4
Tariff range €€€€
Town St-Cyr
Department Vienne
Postal Code 86130
Map 2 B1
Tel 05-49625722
Fax 05-49522858
e-mail contact@parcdesaintcyr.com
Open 01 Apr – 30 Sep
A10 (Paris-Bordeaux) junct 27 (Châtellerault-Sud). Then follow N10 to Poitiers. In La Tricherie take D82 to Bonneuil-Matours.
Size (hectares) 5
Touring pitches 180
Sanitary facilities rating 8.5
lots of entertainment • lakeside location • spacious lay-out • Futuroscope • water sports on the lake • Poitiers (17 km)
Electric hook-ups/amps 180/10

The layout of the campsite is very spacious and so are the pitches. High hedges provide enough privacy, and the lanes are wide. Its location by the side of a lake makes it extra attractive, and the site even has its own beach. The well-kept sanitary buildings are strategically placed, so there is always one within reach.

Part of the lake is reserved for swimmers, and this marked area is supervised so children can swim safely. There are several opportunities for practising water sports like windsurfing, sailing, angling and pedalos. On the campsite you will find tennis courts, a restaurant, a snack bar, terraces in the sun, a fitness centre with modern equipment and a very extensive entertainment programme. The lake is also open to the public, so from time to time the area is overrun by day trippers. Many campers go to see another major attraction; Futuroscope is a large theme park dedicated to the future, film and new media, and is a stone's throw away. A visit to the city of Poitiers with its churches is also recommended.

Rio Clar

Rating	8.1
Tariff range	€€€
Town	Barcelonnette
Department	Alpes-de-Haute-Provence
Postal code	04340
Map	6 C3/4
Tel	04-92811032
Fax	04-92811032
e-mail	rioclar@wanadoo.fr
Open	27 May – 09 Sep

Take D900 from Gap towards Barcelonnette. Site on right approx 10 km before Barcelonnette.

Size (hectares) 8
Touring pitches 167
Sanitary facilities rating 8
many activities yet peaceful • wooded grounds • situated in the mountains along a river • Mercantour National Park • Serre-Ponçon reservoir • Barcelonnette (10 km)
Electric hook-ups/amps 167/6-10

Rio Clar is situated in a beautiful Alpine landscape, and none of the pitches are far from the swimming pool and restaurant. The pitches are in a pine forest; each one different from the others, and privacy is excellent. Some tents are pitched along the Rio Clar stream – camping in the wild except for the electric hook-ups! The majority of pitches are very peaceful, so you can holiday without even noticing the entertainment programme.

And yet the organised activities – especially sporting ones – are numerous. There are tennis courts, mini golf, pétanque and archery as well as volleyball and basketball courts and six table tennis tables. The swimming pool is heated and well maintained, and there is a leisure pool where you can sail in a rubber boat. Introductory canoeing classes are run here before graduating to the nearby Ubaye River. The campsite rafting school is run by a former European professional, so you will be in good hands when you tackle the rapids. Cyclists are not an uncommon sight, as Barcelonnette is surrounded by seven mighty cols, and when you conquer them you are awarded a certificate.

Le Soleil

Rating	6.9
Tariff range	€€€
Town	Esparron-de-Verdon
Department	Alpes-de-Haute-Provence
Postal code	04800
Map	6 B3
Tel	04-92771378
Fax	04-92771045
E-mail	campinglesoleil@wanadoo.fr
Open	15 Apr – 01 Oct

Site S of Esparron. Take D82 in Esparron towards Quinson/Albiosq. Just before built-up area ends, turn right. Site 1 km on right.

Size (hectares) 2
Touring pitches 92
Sanitary facilities rating 7.3
situated on a reservoir • private beach • good restaurant • Gorges du Verdon • Musée de la Préhistoire • Esparron-de-Verdon (1 km)
Electric hook-ups/amps 92/6

At Le Soleil you can camp on terraced pitches above a reservoir, swim at a private beach and sunbathe on limestone plateaux along the water – and all this under the warm sun of Provence. You can hire canoes and small sailing boats on the other side of the lake, though power boats are forbidden as they disturb the peace and quiet at the campsite. The lower terraced pitches are smaller than the higher ones and cannot be reached by car. People who choose to be down here are mainly young couples who have a magnificent view of the lake but sometimes lack shade.

The paths between the pitches are excellent – no one ever has to walk past anyone else's tent. The high-lying pitches are larger and have ample shade – the down side being that the trees can obstruct the view. These mainly attract families with children and older couples, and they are just wide enough to cope with large caravans. On the upper terraces, the sanitary facilities are particularly good. The restaurant does not have a view of the lake but it offers good value for money, and the take-away pizzas are large. There are organised activities for children once a week as well as weekly dinner dances.

Provence-Alpes-Côte d'Azur

Domaine des Marmottes

Rating 8.1
Tariff range €€€
Town Larche
Department Alpes-de-Haute-Provence
Postal code 04530
Map 6 C4
Tel 04-92843364
Fax 04-92843364
e-mail georges.durand25@wanadoo.fr
Open 01 Jun – 20 Sep
From Gap take D900 towards Cuneo (Italy). Site on right, 50mtrs past former frontier post.
Size (hectares) 2
Touring pitches 50
Sanitary facilities rating 8
for hill walkers • pleasantly simple (has electricity) • good restaurant • Mercantour National Park • between several passes • Jausiers (18 km)
Electric hook-ups/amps 50/10

A campsite for hill walkers, nature lovers and those seeking peace and quiet, Domaine des Marmottes is set beside a stream among wonderful mountains. You don't have far to climb to see Alpine marmots (the site is named after them) because you start out at 1678m. If you have done all the local walks, a short car drive takes you into different mountain landscapes and important passes, just a stone's throw from Italy. The Mercantour National Park begins directly above the campsite.

If you come back tired out you don't need to cook, because there is a very good restaurant. The little shop is also very useful, offering more than just the basics – you can buy fresh fruit, for example. You are also welcome without a tent or caravan. Water, electricity and generous pitches are provided, and there is no noise – anyone creating a disturbance is turned off the site. Walkers like their night's rest and are often tucked up by 10 o'clock, so it is very peaceful apart from the sound of the stream. After a strenuous walk you can cool off in it, although it is not a place to swim. There are no activities except for table tennis.

Manaysse

Rating 7
Tariff range €€
Town Moustiers-Sainte-Marie
Department Alpes-de-Haute-Provence
Postal code 04360
Map 6 B3
Tel 04-92746671
Fax 04-92746228
e-mail camping.manaysse@free.fr
Open 15 Mar – 02 Nov
From Riez follow the D952 to Moustiers-Sainte-Marie. The campsite lies 900 m W of Moustiers-Sainte-Marie.
Size (hectares) 1.5
Touring pitches 87
Sanitary facilities rating 7.1
quiet home base • activities all around • fine views • Gorges du Verdon • Plateau de Valensole • Moustiers-Sainte-Marie (1 km)
Electric hook-ups/amps 87/5-10

There are quite a few campsites around Moustiers and Lake Sainte-Croix, at the entrance to the Gorges du Verdon. Manaysse is a small, quiet site without a swimming pool, but within walking distance of the village. There is a wonderful view of the mountain range with its famous gorges, and all the necessary entertainment and activities can be found locally. Sometimes people return out of season when the higher water levels in the Verdon river allow for spectacular canoe trips.

You can visit the gorges, the coastal region or the city of Aix-en-Provence, and the lavender fields on the Plateau de Valensole should be seen in July when they are in full bloom. The sanitary facilities are well kept by the owners, a young man and his elderly grandmother who like to keep in touch with their guests. There is a lot of shade, but it doesn't spoil the view. About one third of the pitches have uneven surfaces, so you will have to adjust your caravan supports and possibly sleep on a slope! But this is a fine campsite for those who like to be active in a quiet spot.

Provence-Alpes-Côte d'Azur

Lou Passavous

Rating 8.2
Tariff range €€€
Town Seyne-les-Alpes
Department Alpes-de-Haute-Provence
Postal code 04140
Map 6 B3
Tel 04-92351467
e-mail loupassavous@wanadoo.fr
Open 15 Apr – 01 Oct
Take D900B from Gap towards Barcelonnette. Then follow D900 towards Col-St-Jean & Digne. Past Seyne-les-Alpes and on for 10 km. Site before Le Vernet.
Size (hectares) 1.5
Touring pitches 61
Sanitary facilities rating 8.3
magnificent view • many children's activities • small, child-friendly beaches • Serre-Ponçon reservoir • Seyne-les-Alpes (10 km)
Electric hook-ups/amps 61/10

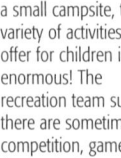

Lou Passavous is a small campsite with a magnificent, unobstructed view of the mountains. Surprisingly for such a small campsite, the variety of activities on offer for children is enormous! The recreation team supervises the youngsters and older children, there are sometimes events twice a day, like a volleyball competition, games with animal noises or a day out rafting on the nearby Ubaye River.

Parents can enjoy a barbeque night or a Provençal-themed evening on the terrace of the bar/pizzeria, and such evenings sometimes end up with dancing. At eleven o'clock, however, it is always quiet and this makes Lou Passavous a campsite where you can completely relax. Some of the walks start right on the campsite itself, and in the surrounding area your choice is even wider. Although the swimming pool is small and simple, some 50m away you will find the heated municipal pool, while 9 km away there is an indoor pool with stables next door. Hang-gliding and para-gliding enthusiasts sometimes stay at the campsite, because St-Jean and Seyne-les-Alpes are centres where you can take courses in both sports.

Les Prairies

Rating 8.3
Tariff range €€€
Town Seyne-les-Alpes
Department Alpes-de-Haute-Provence
Postal code 04140
Map 6 B3
Tel 04-92351021
e-mail info@campinglesprairies.com
Open 19 Apr – 13 Sep
Take D900 from Gap towards Barcelonnette/Digne. Site on D7 to S of Seyne towards Col du Fanget.
Size (hectares) 3.9
Touring pitches 92
Sanitary facilities rating 8.4
a true family campsite • various playing fields • swimming pool and snack bar • small, child-friendly beaches • Lac de Serre-Ponçon • Seyne-les-Alpes (1 km)
Electric hook-ups/amps 92/10

Les Prairies is bigger than it looks at first sight: behind it is a large open field where hikers pitch camp. Along the river – in which you cannot swim but you can paddle – you will see a number of expansive fields which look like open spaces in the woods until you notice the electricity connections. This section of the campsite – where you will see campers drying out after their paddle – looks totally different from the central grounds close to the sanitary facilities and snack bar.

The spacious pitches here are neatly ordered and screened off. The sanitary facilities at Les Prairies are clean and well maintained, and so are the reception area and the snack bar that tends towards being a restaurant without reflecting this in its prices! Guests come here for the peace and quiet, and to take trips and go hiking in the surrounding area. 300m away from the site you will find stables with a pony club. You can play tennis here as well as football, and try your hand at wall climbing, or go swimming in the indoor pool. However, most people prefer the swimming pool.

Provence-Alpes-Côte d'Azur

Les Prés Hauts

Rating	8.2
Tariff range	€€€
Town	Sisteron
Department	Alpes-de-Haute-Provence
Postal Code	04200
Map	6 B3
Tel	04-92611969
Fax	04-92611969
e-mail	camping.sisteron@wanadoo.fr
Open	05 Mar – 30 Oct

Follow N75 (Grenoble-Sisteron). On rdbt N of city centre take D951 and over bridge. Approx 3 km keep to left, continue 500mtrs. Site on right, on left bank of the Durance.

Size (hectares) 3
Touring pitches 135
Sanitary facilities rating 8

simple and quiet • ample privacy • a good transit stop • Gorges du Verdon • Lac de Sainte-Croix • Sisteron (3 km)

Electric hook-ups/amps 92/10

A clean, neat and tidy campsite, full of flowers and hedgerows. Out of season, Les Prés Hauts is the perfect spot to break a journey for a few days before continuing along the Route Napoléon. The same applies in summer – thanks to the nearby motorway running from the Alps on one side, to the coast of Provence on the other. There is plenty to see and do in Sisteron – a town bursting with restaurants, pavement cafés and shops. You can even walk into town (3 km) if you wish.

If you are seeking peace and quiet, this campsite is ideally suited to your needs. Children generally amuse themselves at the swimming pool or take part in organised activities. The entertainment arranges games for smaller children every morning, and towards evening – when it gets cooler – there are table tennis and boules competitions. There is no restaurant or snack bar, so that apart from relaxing there is actually not very much to do – certainly not for older children. There is a youth clubhouse of sorts, but it is intended more to keep the children off the campsite grounds than to entertain them.

L'Hippocampe

Rating	7.9
Tariff range	€€€€
Town	Volonne
Department	Alpes-de-Haute-Provence
Postal Code	04290
Map	6 B3
Tel	04-92335000
Fax	04-92335049
e-mail	camping@l-hippocampe.com
Open	22 Mar – 30 Sep

Follow N85, 7 km after Sisteron turn left over bridge towards Volonne. Right on D4. Site 500mtrs S of Volonne.

Size (hectares) 8
Touring pitches 248
Sanitary facilities rating 7.4

musicals and a concert stage • situated between the Alps • underground disco • Gorges du Verdon • Lac de Sainte-Croix • Sisteron (12 km)

Electric hook-ups/amps 248/10

If you have always wanted to take part in a musical, you can do just that at L'Hippocampe campsite. Guests are encouraged to participate in the musical extravaganzas performed here. The on-site theatre was specifically designed for this kind of activity, with two stages: one for the performers, and another for the band. The background sets are beautiful and the lighting professional. Musical concerts, cabarets and soirées are held regularly. Every evening you can dance till you drop at the underground disco.

L'Hippocampe is situated alongside the Durance river. Swimming is not allowed, but you can sail, and there is a quiet place to moor for those who want to sunbathe. The view of the reservoir from the boules greens, the handiwork tables and the mini-club is breathtaking. Thanks to the Gap-Côte d'Azur motorway you can reach many places of interest quickly and easily – whether it be the Gorges du Verdon, Aix-en-Provence, the seaside or the Écrins. This large, lively campsite has many hedgerows to provide all necessary privacy without obstructing the view of the mountains.

Provence-Alpes-Côte d'Azur

Le Rossignol

Rating 7.4
Tariff range €€€
Town Antibes
Department Alpes-Maritimes
Postal Code 06600
Map 6 C2
Tel 04-93335698
Fax 04-92919899
e-mail campinglerossignol@wanadoo.fr
Open 08 Apr – 30 Sep
On A8 take exit 44 towards Antibes. Take D35 to N7. At N7, left immediately into Avenue-Jules-Grec which becomes Avenue J-Michard-Pelissier. Site on right in 2nd road to NE of Antibes.
Size (hectares) 1.8
Touring pitches 111
Sanitary facilities rating 7.5
quiet, neat and clean • beach 1 km away • swimming pool and bar • Nice, Cannes and Monaco • adjacent to Marineland • Antibes (3 km)
Electric hook-ups/amps 58/6-10

Antibes is one of the most popular – and busiest – places along the Côte d'Azur. You will find Le Rossignol, a quiet, neat and tidy campsite with a lovely swimming pool, within walking distance (1km) of the seaside. Most guests come here for the sun, the proximity to the beach and the many interesting sights along the Côte d'Azur and in the nearby countryside. Campers particularly like the privacy and shade of Le Rossignol's pitches, as well as the spotless sanitary facilities. There is no lifeguard, but the owner himself keeps an eye on the pool – which is heated in the cooler months.

The owner has decided to limit the entertainment to the two lit swimming pools and a weekly dance night because the surrounding area offers an abundance of things to do. There is no restaurant or bar with snacks, and no shop – except for 'emergency' supplies – as you will find shops 800m away or can drive to a nearby hypermarket. Although youth groups and organised tours are excluded from this campsite you will still find quite a few young couples.

Parc des Monges

Rating 8.1
Tariff range €€€€
Town Auribeau
Department Alpes-Maritimes
Postal Code 06810
Map 6 C2
Tel 04-93609171
Fax 04-93609171
E-mail contact@parcdesmonges.fr
Open 05 Apr – 17 Sep
Follow D9 from Pégomas towards Grasse. Turn left onto D509 at Moulin-Vieux towards Auribeau. Right after approx 1 km towards Tanneron, 500mtrs turn right to site on left.
Size (hectares) 1.4
Touring pitches 45
Sanitary facilities rating 8.5
relaxed atmosphere • water sports and other recreational activities • delightfully cool at night • the Siagne River • river plains nature reserve • Grasse (8 km)
Electric hook-ups/amps 45/4-10

The Siagne River borders this beautiful campsite and has been widened here to enhance its natural beauty. Wooded hills rise above the waters, which are suitable for swimming but are too deep for young children. You can find narrow beaches 200m from the campsite. Away from the river is equally delightful: sun and shade, spotless sanitary facilities, and a lovely swimming pool. The owner and his wife have located the reception next to the swimming pool so that it can be partially monitored.

Their daughter will take you on guided walks free of charge. Every morning the owners lead the ladies in an aqua gym session, then set up water volleyball for the children on alternate mornings. Every ten days, a dance or special evening is held in the campsite restaurant. There is no obligation to buy food or drink, and at a quarter past eleven everything is quiet again. The restaurant owner is an independent operator, and every week he features a regional speciality – always a dish from Provence – that is very reasonably priced. At night the temperature drops significantly ensuring a good night's sleep.

Green Park

Rating	8
Tariff range	€€€€
Town	Cagnes-sur-Mer
Department	Alpes-Maritimes
Postal Code	06800
Map	6 C3
Tel	04-93070996
Fax	04-93143655
e-mail	info@greenpark.fr
Open	22 Mar – 15 Oct

On A8 take exit 47, follow N7 towards Nice. After 4.2 km turn left towards Val Fleuri. Continue, site on right (opp Le Todos site).

Size (hectares) 6
Touring pitches 63
Sanitary facilities rating 8

quiet and luxurious • separate youth section • many activities • Nice, Monaco and Cannes • St-Paul artists' village • Cagnes-sur-Mer (1 km)

Electric hook-ups/amps 63/6-20

Green Park is idyllically situated on the eastern slope of a small, tranquil valley. Although the beach is only 4 km away, the guests seem to stay on the site, drawn by the large swimming pool overlooked by a restaurant, the shady terrace and the many deck chairs. Another campsite, Le Todos, lies on the other side of the road and is run by the same family. Guests from Le Todos provide extra competitors for the inter-campsite swimming competition.

Green Park is more luxurious and better laid-out than its neighbour. The pitches are consequently larger (and less shady) and the sanitary facilities are extremely clean. Youthful guests – couples and small groups aged between 18 and 25, have their own section on the site, situated on a slope with a view. The pitches here are somewhat small but the younger guests don't seem to mind. The majority of campers – families with children – have pitches lower down in the valley, and are not bothered by any noise from the youth section.

Les Pinèdes

Rating	8.4
Tariff range	€€€€
Town	La Colle-sur-Loup
Department	Alpes-Maritimes
Postal Code	06480
Map	6 C3
Tel	04-93329894
Fax	04-93325020
e-mail	camplespinedes06@aol.com
Open	15 Mar – 30 Sep

Take D6 from La Colle-sur-Loup W towards Grasse. 2.5 km and site on right.

Size (hectares) 3.8
Touring pitches 136
Sanitary facilities rating 8.6

an oasis of greenery and tranquillity • pleasant restaurant • river suitable for swimming • Nice, Monaco and Cannes • organised hikes • La Colle-sur-Loup (2 km)

Electric hook-ups/amps 136/3-10

Les Pinèdes is a beautifully situated, terraced campsite with plenty of shade, a delightful swimming pool and a pleasant restaurant. The seaside is 7 km away, so you will need transport. However, the Loup River is only 200m away, where the waters in a bend in the river are even deep enough for diving and you will find several small beaches. The campsite with its sub-tropical plants is an oasis of peace along the hectic coast. The grounds are decorated with terracotta pots here and there, and the main sanitary facilities are designed in the typical style of Provence.

Along with your welcome drink, you will receive a pile of information about the region. In the high season, the majority of guests are families with children, and out of season mainly older couples. The organised hiking trips are free of charge and your guide is an enthusiastic hiker. For younger children, there is a children's club in the mornings and older children can play volleyball, basketball or water polo and learn archery. The introductory scuba diving course in the swimming pool is followed up by the real thing in the sea.

Provence-Alpes-Côte d'Azur

Les Merveilles

Rating 7.4
Tariff range €€€
Town Lantosque
Department Alpes-Maritimes
Postal Code 06450
Map 6 C3
Tel 04-93031573
Open 01 Jul – 15 Sep

From A8 take exit 52 towards Nice/ St-Isidore. Then take N202 towards Digne. At Plan-du-Var turn right onto D2565. Left onto D373 at Le Suquet (5 km before Lantosque). 5.5 km SW of Lantosque, site on left.

Size (hectares) 0.7
Touring pitches 44
Sanitary facilities rating 7.3

for hiking enthusiasts • tranquillity and space • complete caravan connections • Vallée des Merveilles • river with small beach • Lantosque (5 km)

Electric hook-ups/amps 36/3-6

The owner of Les Merveilles runs this campsite on his own, with a great deal of enthusiasm. As soon as 35 of his more than 50 pitches are occupied, he hangs up the 'No Vacancies' sign so that he can provide everyone with an equal amount of service and information. Les Merveilles is a campsite specifically for hikers; sometimes they move on the following day, but more often they stay. They may even arrive with a family-size tent and a caravan to spend an entire holiday here. The area surrounding Lantosque offers a wealth of hiking day trips.

A day out in Nice is equally easy, and the beach is only 50 minutes away. Although the site has no frills, caravanners will find everything they need. The pitches are large, with plenty of shade and the grounds are quiet. You will find the only motorhome service station in the Vésubie Valley here. There is no swimming pool, but 300m away is a river with a waterfall and a small beach alongside several pools surrounded by pebbles. The most popular (alpine) hiking destination is La Vallée des Merveilles, the valley of wonders, with its unique Bronze Age rock carvings.

Les Cigales

Rating 7.8
Tariff range €€€€
Town Mandelieu-la-Napoule
Department Alpes-Maritimes
Postal code 06210
Map 6 C2
Tel 04-93492353
Fax 04-93493045
e-mail info.lescigales@wanadoo.fr
Open All year

From A8 take exit 40 (Mandelieu). Turn right. Approx 200mtrs turn right towards Plages-Ports. Turn left at end of road. Site 200mtrs on left.

Size (hectares) 2
Touring pitches 75
Sanitary facilities rating 8

luxuriant trees and shrubs • good service • sandy beach within walking distance • centrally located • Cannes and St-Tropez • Cannes (8 km)

Electric hook-ups/amps 75/6

In the middle of a lively seaside resort, within walking distance of a sandy beach, you will find such a huge variety of subtropical trees and shrubs in bloom that you could forget you are on a campsite, let alone in a town. Even the sanitary facilities are housed in Mediterranean-style buildings. The swimming pool is another feast for the eye with its unusual shape. This campsite offers peace and quiet, with no entertainment or even a restaurant, but simply personal service and plenty of information.

There is a vast number of things on offer outside the site combined with the tranquility within it, because this is that hectic area between St-Tropez and the Italian border. Some couples come here in the summer with their children and then return on their own out of season to visit places of cultural interest. The combination of cheap flights and caravans for rent on a campsite that is open all year round makes this easy. Some people bring their boat: Les Cigales has its own little harbour on the Siagne, which flows into the sea. The campsite is not suitable for families with children over twelve.

Provence-Alpes-Côte d'Azur

Le Prieuré

Rating 7.5
Tariff range €€€
Town St-Martin-d'Entraunes
Department Alpes-Maritimes
Postal code 06470
Map 6 C3
Tel 04-93055499
Fax 04-93055374
e-mail le.prieure@wanadoo.fr
Open 01 May – 30 Sep
From Digne take N85/N202 towards Entrevaux. Approx 7 km after Annot turn left, take D2202 to St-Martin-d'Entraunes. Before bridge turn right to site. (NB: steep hills)
Size (hectares) 1.5
Touring pitches 35
Sanitary facilities rating 7.6
peaceful and green • roomy pitches • swimming pool and restaurant • Mercantour National Park • picturesque Péone • Guillaumes (12 km)
Electric hook-ups/amps 35/3-6

If you like peace and quiet, hill walking and nature you will enjoy Le Prieuré. It offers all the basic amenities plus a small swimming pool, a restaurant and an activities leader. The site merges nicely into the alpine meadows, and on three sides you look out onto the Mercantour National Park. Walking in this area you will come across chamois and alpine marmots, and perhaps even ibex.

Le Prieuré attracts families with children and walkers, and next door is a stopping place on a six-day donkey trek, which is an additional attraction for the children. The pitches offer sufficient space and privacy, and plenty of shade comes from the trees. The sanitary facilities are clean, but in the high season the toilets and showers can be stretched. The restaurant is more comparable to a local pub, and you can also get take-away pizzas and bruchettas, in which pain de campagne replaces the pizza dough and local cheese is used instead of the grated cheese. The last part of the approach road is single track, and those towing caravans are advised to walk to reception where the owner will then make sure that no one is coming in the opposite direction.

La Vieille Ferme

Rating 8.4
Tariff range €€€€
Town Villeneuve-Loubet
Department Alpes-Maritimes
Postal Code 06270
Map 6 C3
Tel 04-93334144
Fax 04-93333728
e-mail info@vieilleferme.com
Open All year
Take N7 towards Antibes. After 2 km turn right. Site 500mtrs on right.
Size (hectares) 2.8
Touring pitches 110
Sanitary facilities rating 8.6
seaside at walking distance • railway station 1 km away • luxurious swimming pool • Nice, Monaco and Cannes • parklands and wetlands • Antibes (5 km)
Electric hook-ups/amps 103/2-15

A relaxed atmosphere, generously large, shady pitches and a luxurious heated swimming pool – with a sliding roof – and all to be found within walking distance of the seaside! Biot Station is only 1 km away, which provides a good travel option to the busy coastal roads – and you will, of course, have no parking problems. You can visit Nice, Monaco, the lovely Menton, and even cross into Italy to Ventimiglia (with markets on Fridays). In the other direction, Cannes and Marseilles await you.

If you prefer to stay on the campsite, the swimming pool has a children's pool and bubble pool. The lifeguard makes sure that everyone behaves themselves, and on special mornings, children are given free rein under his watchful eye. Twice a week you can enjoy an evening dip in the illuminated pool. There is a shop for emergency supplies with an adjacent terrace where you can have breakfast and take aways in the evenings. The internet and email service with wi-fi (a wireless connection for personal laptops) is very popular and can be accessed with a normal French telephone card at local-call prices. A disco is held once a week, and twice a month you can enjoy a theme meal with entertainment.

Provence-Alpes-Côte d'Azur

Ceyreste

Rating	7.3
Tariff range	€€€
Town	Ceyreste
Department	Bouches-du-Rhône
Postal Code	13600
Map	6 B2
Tel	04-42830768
Fax	04-42831992
e-mail	campingceyreste@yahoo.fr
Open	01 Apr – 10 Nov

From A50 turn off at La Ciotat, then D3 towards Ceyreste. In village turn left before Cooperative Oléicole de Ceyreste, then follow signs for approx 500mtrs. (Last 100mtrs has 15% gradient)

Size (hectares) 3
Touring pitches 50   **Static pitches** 30
Sanitary facilities rating 7.6
close to the coast • quiet and plenty of shade • interesting village nearby • beautiful coastline • beautiful countryside • Ceyreste (0.5 km)
Electric hook-ups/amps 50/2-6

Being able to enjoy the Mediterranean without the hustle and bustle of the Côte d'Azur is Ceyreste's biggest selling point. The campsite is situated about 3 km from the sandy beaches of La Ciotat. It has plenty of aromatic pine trees to provide enough shade, almost creating the impression that you are in the middle of a wood. The pitches (all with their own tap and worktop) are spacious enough and are neatly laid out in terraces. The steep slopes and small retaining walls can sometimes make it difficult to manoeuvre with a caravan. The sanitary facilities are plentiful and well maintained.

The owner has been planning to install a swimming pool for a number of years, but has unfortunately not yet been granted permission. Instead there is a mini golf course on the site. Guests can hire a refrigerator, there is an ice cream shop with outdoor seating, and some organised activities for children. The Mediterranean is only ten minutes away and the village of Ceyreste is within easy walking distance where the locals regularly hold parties and other events.

Monplaisir

Rating	8.1
Tariff range	€€€
Town	St-Rémy-de-Provence
Department	Bouches-du-Rhône
Postal Code	13210
Map	5 H3
Tel	04-90922270
Fax	04-90921857
e-mail	reception@camping-monplaisir.fr
Open	01 Mar – 10 Nov

D99 to St-Rémy-de-Provence, take D5 NW towards Maillane. After 100mtrs turn left. Site on left approx 400mtrs.

Size (hectares) 2.8
Touring pitches 122
Sanitary facilities rating 8.1
a warm welcome • peaceful and well-maintained • they serve their own wine • authentic villages • Les Alpilles • St-Rémy-de-Provence (1 km)
Electric hook-ups/amps 122/6

Monplaisir has matured from a farmhouse campsite 27 years ago with only six pitches to a fully-fledged one with all modern conveniences and a friendly character. The site is tastefully designed and offers a peaceful environment with carefully-planted cypress trees and oleanders. The pitches are a good size and are bounded by hedges. It can sometimes prove difficult to find a pitch with sufficient shade on the newer part of the site.

The sanitary facilities are well-maintained, and you can buy fruit and vegetables from the farmhouse kitchen garden. It has its own swimming pool and a beautiful sunny meadow. Those looking for fun on the campsite will be content with the boules area and the small playground for the children – a disco would just not fit in here. However, there are all sorts of interesting sights in the surrounding area. The Camargue is a veritable paradise for birdwatchers, while historians will be interested in the Roman excavations and ramblers will just love the Alpilles.

Mas de Nicolas

Rating	7.7
Tariff range	€€€
Town	St-Rémy-de-Provence
Department	Bouches-du-Rhône
Postal Code	13210
Map	5 H3
Tel	04-90922705
Fax	04-90923683
e-mail	camping-masdenicolas@nerim.fr
Open	15 Mar – 15 Oct

Site NE of town. Take D99 NE from stadium. Turn left 300mtrs, and site in 200mtrs.

Size (hectares) 3.5
Touring pitches 117
Sanitary facilities rating 8
beautiful landscaped campsite • quiet and very tidy • beautiful views • Roman villa • walking routes • St-Rémy-de-Provence (1 km)
Electric hook-ups/amps 117/6

Mas de Nicolas is a delightful spacious campsite with neatly kept lawns and grassy areas, majestic cypress trees, oleanders in full bloom and some beautiful old trees. From the cosy park benches on the lawns you can enjoy the breathtaking views of St-Rémy and, in the distance, the Alpilles or the 'Little Alps'. There are many sights to be seen in the surrounding area, and plenty of walks to be had. The tall hedges between the pitches give a feeling of seclusion, and the sanitary facilities are fairly new and very well maintained.

As you gaze across the sunny meadows surrounding the circular swimming pool, you can almost taste the opulent lifestyle of the Romans who once lived nearby in Glanum near St-Rémy. There is a small playground for the kids and a farmyard, but otherwise it is a quiet campsite. The facilities are fairly minimal, and shopping is limited to fresh bread orders. However, the village has plenty of shops and restaurants and is within walking distance. The campsite bar is open throughout the day, but no alcohol is served.

La Vieille Ferme

Rating	9.1
Tariff range	€€€€
Town	Embrun
Department	Hautes-Alpes
Postal code	05200
Map	6 B4
Tel	04-92430408
e-mail	info@campingembrun.com
Open	01 May – 01 Oct

Take N94 from Embrun towards Gap. Straight on at rdbt and turn left after 500mtrs. Then follow site signs.

Size (hectares) 2.6
Touring pitches 95
Sanitary facilities rating 9.3
enthusiastic management • countless activities • magnificent landscape • nature reserve • adventure sports • Embrun (1 km)
Electric hook-ups/amps 95/6-10

La Vieille Ferme is set by a stream on the outskirts of Embrun, and offers many sporting opportunities in a delightful, well-maintained and comfortable holiday spot. The pitches are attractive and open too, the sanitary facilities clean, and simple meals are available. The owner supervises the rafting, canyoning and mountain biking himself, and other instructors run rock climbing and abseiling. The Hautes Alpes are a mountain-sports paradise: the Durance Gorge is a highpoint for wild water rafters, and there are several steep inclines in the vicinity that even top cyclists need to warm up for!

If you prefer the quieter side of things, you can go hiking – with or without a guide – and enjoy the splendour of the Parc National des Écrins; end the day with a refreshing dip in the Lac de Serre-Ponçon. There is also a playground, swimming pool, tennis courts and mini golf. Budding young cowboys and jugglers can be left in the capable hands of the recreation team while you relax and enjoy the view of Mont Guillaume. This mountain is the preferred take-off point for para-gliders who have their landing zone directly alongside the campsite.

Provence-Alpes-Côte d'Azur

Le Petit Liou

Rating   7.2
Tariff range   €€€
Town   Embrun
Department   Hautes-Alpes
Postal code   05200
Map   6 B4
Tel   04-92431910
Fax   04-92436928
e-mail   info@camping-lepetitliou.com
Open   20 Apr – 30 Sep
Leave N94 at rdbt to S of Durance, take D40 towards Les Orres. Turn left after 700mtrs, site in 500mtrs.
Size (hectares) 4
Touring pitches 200
Sanitary facilities rating 7.5
densely wooded terrain • comfortable family campsite • good management • mountain walks • nature reserve • Embrun (1 km)
Electric hook-ups/amps 200/3-10

Le Petit Liou is a simple campsite situated in the French Alps. A lovely recreational lake lies 3 km away, offering almost endless sports and leisure activities. The campsite is run by Mark Audier, who takes great pleasure in his job and is eager to please his guests. The pitches vary from spacious and open, to shady and screened off by bushes and trees. Although there are no special activities for younger campers, they will be happy with the simple swimming pool and paddling pool and a set of fantastic climbing frames. The old trees, bushes and play areas have been transformed into a magical and fascinating playground where children up to the age of 15 can play.

As well as the Embrun lake, another lake, the Lac de Serre-Ponçon, is within easy reach. The towering Alps remain the main attraction for hiking and cycling enthusiasts, though if heights are not your thing, don't worry: close to the campsite the landscape is densely wooded and flat. Fresh bread twice a day, delightful pavement cafés and many shops are all just 1km from the campsite.

St-James Les Pins

Rating   7.2
Tariff range   €€
Town   Guillestre
Department   Hautes-Alpes
Postal code   05600
Map   6 C4
Tel   04-92450824
Fax   04-92451865
e-mail   camping@lesaintjames.com
Open   All year
Site 1.5km SW of Guillestre. From N94 (Gap- Briançon), take D902a to Guillestre. Turn right after 1 km. Site 600mtrs further on left.
Size (hectares) 3.5
Touring pitches 80
Sanitary facilities rating 7.6
sheltered location • friendly atmosphere • helpful management • Parc des Écrins • Parc du Queyras • Guillestre (1 km)
Electric hook-ups/amps 80/3-5

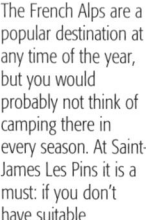 

The French Alps are a popular destination at any time of the year, but you would probably not think of camping there in every season. At Saint-James Les Pins it is a must: if you don't have suitable equipment for winter camping you can stay in a log cabin; the ski slopes of Vars and Risoul are a mere 13 km away, though the access road is quite narrow. St-James Les Pins does have the most to offer in the summer months however. It is a simple, well-maintained site with roomy but not separate pitches.

The atmosphere is friendly, and there is entertainment, though younger ones in particular are quite happy on bikes and amusing themselves in the little play area. The stream that flows beside the site is also a great attraction for them, as is the swimming pool 600m away. The area lends itself to various levels of excursion on foot or on mountain bike. The campsite stands with one foot in the Écrins glacier nature reserve and the other in the Queyras, where the beautiful landscape is dotted with atmospheric artists villages. Rafting, and canoe and kayak excursions are available on the fast-flowing rivers.

Provence-Alpes-Côte d'Azur

Au Blanc Manteau

Rating 8.1
Tariff range €€€
Town Manteyer
Department Hautes-Alpes
Postal code 05400
Map 6 B4
Tel 04-92578256
Open All year
Leave D994 (Veynes-Gap) at La Roche-des-Arnauds, take D18 towards Manteyer. Site 800mtrs on right.
Size (hectares) 4
Touring pitches 41
Sanitary facilities rating 8.2
peace and quiet • lovely grounds • take-away meals • walking • horse riding (for beginners) • Gap (14 km)
Electric hook-ups/amps 41/2-10

Au Blanc Manteau is open all year round, but you will only find snow here in the winter months. Winter guests come here in search of skiing, and there are plenty of suitable places in the alpine ski area of Gap-Ceuse, or cross-country skiing across the wider surrounding area. Pierre and Judith Wampach run the campsite in an extremely friendly and helpful way, but there is a set of strict house rules. For example, overnight campers are not welcome, and the gates do not open before 9am.

There are no organised activities and children aged over twelve may find little to do. For younger children there is a lovely swimming pool (open from June through August) with a small slide, and parents can keep an eye on them from the outdoor café, or use the tennis courts. There are separate heated toilet facilities for the disabled. The surrounding area is ideal for hiking, and both early and late in the season the flowers are either in bloom or the autumn colours are spectacular. Three kilometres from the campsite, you will find riding stables. Au Blanc Manteau is particularly attractive for older campers.

Les Princes d'Orange

Rating 7.5
Tariff range €€€
Town Orpierre
Department Hautes-Alpes
Postal Code 05700
Map 6 B3
Tel 04-92662253
Fax 04-92663108
e-mail campingorpierre@wanadoo.fr
Open 01 Apr – 28 Oct
Follow N75 (Serres-Sisteron-Eyguians). Right onto D30 to Orpierre. In town centre S up hill for 300mtrs to site.
Size (hectares) 20
Touring pitches 60
Sanitary facilities rating 7.6
activities • friendly owners • situated in the foothills • hiking • alpine sports • Larange (8 km)
Electric hook-ups/amps 60/4-10

This terraced campsite lies in the foothills of the Hautes Alpes, not far from the Drôme. Although the sloping grounds may present you with some practical problems, this is par for the course when you're in the Alps! Orpierre acts as a magnet for athletic youngsters who come here for all kinds of alpine sports. Les Princes d'Orange is an excellent campsite for active families. Mum and Dad may not, however, succeed in convincing the kids to go on a mountain hike – after all the swimming pool, trampoline, table tennis and youth clubhouse are stiff competition. And adjacent to the campsite you will find a football pitch.

Most teenagers will be exhausted when they return the next morning from the organised overnight camp-out held on Tuesday and Friday nights. Also on Tuesdays and Fridays, there is an activities programme for smaller children. Parents can hit the dance floor of the pavement café at the weekend. However, the majority of guests are more than satisfied to sit and enjoy the magnificent view in all directions.

Provence-Alpes-Côte d'Azur

Domaine des 2 Soleils

Rating	7.1
Tariff range	€€€
Town	Serres
Department	Hautes-Alpes
Postal Code	05700
Map	6 B3
Tel	04-92670133
Fax	04-92670802
e-mail	dom.2.soleils@wanadoo.fr
Open	01 May – 30 Sep

From Serres follow N75 towards Sisteron. On outskirts of Serres turn left up mountain. Follow site signs up steep road, 800mtrs to site entrance.

Size (hectares) 26
Touring pitches 98
Sanitary facilities rating 7.3
beautiful location • ample privacy • activities • hiking • adventure trips • Serres (2 km)
Electric hook-ups/amps 98/6

Domaine des 2 Soleils is beautifully situated in the mountains of Provence at an altitude of 800m. It is 2 km outside the hillside town of Serres, but apart from the town, the inhabited world is quite some distance away. The campsite is ideally suited to relaxing with your children. There is plenty of shade, with its demarcated terraced pitches, and these come in a variety of size and price. The sanitary facilities are spread across three units, and although not luxurious, they are more than adequate. The swimming pool with a separate children's pool and water slide provides plenty of aquatic fun.

You can sign up for beginners' riding lessons on both ponies and horses, or you may prefer to go out hiking. The entertainment team organises various activities, but the languages spoken are always French and English. In the evenings, under the stars, you can enjoy regular outdoor film screenings (with Dutch subtitles), dance nights and karaoke. If this is all too tame for you, you can go paragliding, abseiling or caving in the immediate vicinity.

Le Diamant

Rating	8
Tariff range	€€€
Town	St-Jean-Saint-Nicolas
Department	Hautes-Alpes
Postal code	05260
Map	6 B4
Tel	04-92559125
Fax	04-92559597
e-mail	camping.diamant@libertysurf.fr
Open	01 May – 30 Sep

Follow N85 until Brutinel, 10 km to N of Gap. Then W on D14 (becomes D944) towards Chabottes/Orcières to Pont-du-Fossé.

Size (hectares) 3.8
Touring pitches 70   **Static pitches** 10
Sanitary facilities rating 8.2
situated alongside a stream • no frills but good • youth activities organiser • lake for water sports • marked hiking routes • Gap (26 km)
Electric hook-ups/amps 70/1-10

Many campers return to Le Diamant year after year, lured by its simplicity and peaceful location in the valley of Champsaur. The atmosphere is unmistakeably French, comfortable and friendly towards foreign visitors. What you will find at this little jewel of a site is a no frills attitude that can be summed up as 'no fuss, no bother and no complaints'. This applies to the size of the pitches, as well as the sanitary facilities, the range of goods in the shop, and the meals available. The entertainment includes boules, table tennis, mini golf, a camp fire and a good entertainment programme for children.

The trees provide ample shade and there are two open fields as well, from which you can enjoy a magnificent view of the Écrins Massif. The Écrins are the main attraction for many visitors, and the whole area is ideally suited to active holidaymakers who like alpine sports: hiking and abseiling in the towering Alps, or caving and mountain biking. Seven kilometres from the campsite you will find plenty to do at the lake – and you can go wild-water rafting in the vicinity. It is a good home base for sporty campers, but it also offers its less active guests something to do, like fishing for trout.

Provence-Alpes-Côte d'Azur

Esterel Caravaning

Rating 7.8
Tariff range €€€€
Town Agay
Department Var
Postal Code 83530
Map 6 C2
Tel 04-94820328
Fax 04-94828737
e-mail contact@esterel-caravaning.fr
Open 15 Mar – 27 Sep

Take exit 38 on A8 towards St-Raphaël to Agay via N98. Follow Valescure signs at bay. After fly-over into valley on N100. Site on right in approx 5 km.
Size (hectares) 12.5
Touring pitches 200
Sanitary facilities rating 8.1
all-in club campsite • non-stop recreation team • five swimming pools • Esterel Massif • from Saint-Tropez to Cannes • Agay (4 km)
Electric hook-ups/amps 200/6

Tents are not allowed in the grounds of Esterel Caravaning. It is a beautifully situated, luxurious campsite with a Mediterranean ambience and an extensive recreational programme. It is a true club where all activities – with the exception of horse riding – are included in the price. Even the tennis lessons are free of charge. There are no fewer than five swimming pools – two of which are heated – competing with the beach 4 km away at Agay. The non-stop recreation team takes all age groups into account, and there is the disco in the evenings – situated underground so that almost no noise escapes into the caravan park grounds.

As its name suggests, the park is located in the Esterel Massif with its imposing pink rock formations. Various pedestrian-only tracks and paths crossing the hills are ideal for horse riding, hiking and mountain biking. You can admire the magnificent calanques along the coast – rocky outcrops and breathtaking bays that are best viewed from the sea. A boat trip along the coast is an unforgettable experience, as is scuba diving in the crystal-clear, warm waters. All the pitches are shady, and equipped with electricity, water and drainage. Eighteen caravans have private sanitary facilities.

Camp du Domaine

Rating 8.7
Tariff range €€€€
Town Bormes-les-Mimosas
Department Var
Postal Code 83230
Tel 04-94710312
Fax 04-94151867
e-mail mail@campdudomaine.com

From Hyères take D559 through Bormes-les-Mimosas towards La Favière. Site on left after 3 km.
Size (hectares) 45
Touring pitches 1200
Sanitary facilities rating 8.3
camping on the beach • many facilities • sport and entertainment • Îles d'Hyères • Port-Cros national park • Bormes (4 km)
Electric hook-ups/amps 830/10

This campsite's unique feature is that you can camp right on the beach! Even if all the beach pitches are taken (and they do go fast), there are always pitches with a sea view on the hillside. The great-grandfather of the current owners was not very pleased when the first campers put up their tents on his beach and chased them off his land, until a grape picker let slip that camping was the future.

Now this is one of the largest campsites on the Côte d'Azur, providing home to around 7,000 people in the high season, although because of the hills, the shape of the campsite and the trees, you would hardly notice them. However, in July and August you will have to queue to use the sanitary facilities.

Six tennis courts, two basket ball pitches, plenty of other sports, a kiddies club, three bars, a pizzeria, a supérette and a butcher's shop can be found here.

Provence-Alpes-Côte d'Azur

Flower Camping Beau Vezé

Rating	7.5
Tariff range	€€€€
Town	Carqueiranne
Department	Var
Postal Code	83320
Map	6 B2
Tel	04-94576530
Fax	04-94576530
Web	www.camping-beauveze.com
Open	15 May – 15 Sep

From Toulon, take A570, leave at exit 7. At rdbt take N98 towards Toulon/La Moutonne. After 1.5 km, turn left onto D76 (La Moutonne). Turn right in La Moutonne. Site in 1 km.

Size (hectares) 7
Touring pitches 150
Sanitary facilities rating 7.6
parkland campsite • swimming pool and fun pools for the kids • restaurant with outdoor seating • Îles d'Hyères • Massif des Maures • Carqueiranne (3 km)
Electric hook-ups/amps 128/6-10

A well-designed, wooded parkland, where in some places you feel completely secluded, though there are also busier areas. You will find small and larger pitches offering enough space for a large bungalow tent: state your preference when you book. The site is spread across the hillside in several terraces and is surrounded by woodland and the owner's vineyard. Plenty of shade is provided by the mature foliage.

The swimming pool includes two fun pools for the children, one with a mini slide. Near the pool is the restaurant's outside dining area, where you can get a variety of meals at reasonable prices. The entertainer divides his time equally between the age groups. The site also has table tennis facilities, boules, a volleyball pitch and a tennis court. For the adults, there is organised entertainment in the restaurant every other night. It is a lively campsite, but also one that offers some peace and quiet. The climate is great, the sandy beach offers excellent windsurfing and the islands just off the coast are great for diving. The only downside is that some of the sanitary facilities need modernising, although they are well maintained.

Cros de Mouton

Rating	8.1
Tariff range	€€€€
Town	Cavalaire-sur-Mer
Department	Var
Postal Code	83240
Map	6 C2
Tel	04-94641087
Fax	04-94646312
e-mail	info@crosdemouton.com
Open	15 Mar – 31 Oct

From Cavalaire follow site signs. Site N of village.

Size (hectares) 5
Touring pitches 133
Sanitary facilities rating 8.1
family atmosphere • swimming pool with sea views • Camping Cheques are accepted • St-Tropez and the coast • Îles d'Hyères • Cavalaire-sur-Mer (2 km)
Electric hook-ups/amps 133/10

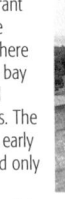 

From the swimming pool, the restaurant and some of the higher pitches, there are views of the bay of Cavalaire and wooded hillsides. The campsite opens early in the spring and only closes in late October, because it is so popular even in the low season. The solar-heated swimming pool stays open as long as there are enough people, and fresh bread is always available to order.

If you do not want to risk taking the caravan up to the terraced pitches yourself, the owner will tow it for you with his jeep. This is the sort of campsite where you know you are in good hands. You soon make friends with your neighbours and discover that they have been coming here for years. The big attractions are the climate, the shops and nearby Saint-Tropez. And then there's the countryside further inland with its Provençal towns, weekly markets, lavender fields, reservoirs and gorges.

In July and August, the campsite belongs to families with young children. The kids love the 4km-long beach (only 1.5 km away) and the shady pitches. The old guard return in September, hoping that there is still plenty of fresh fish on the menu. And at a price that puts the rest of the Côte to shame!

Provence-Alpes-Côte d'Azur

Les Pins Parasols

Rating	7.9
Tariff range	€€€€
Town	Fréjus
Department	Var
Postal Code	83600
Map	6 C2
Tel	04-94408843
Fax	04-94408199
e-mail	lespinsparasols@wanadoo.fr
Open	05 Apr – 27 Sep

On A8 towards Nice, take exit 38 towards Fréjus centre. Turn right at rdbt towards Caïs then 1.5 km. Turn right onto D4 at end of road. After 1.5 km site on right.

Size (hectares) 5
Touring pitches 167
Sanitary facilities rating 7.9

48 private sanitary facilities • quiet haven near the coast • swimming pool with three pools • Côte d'Azur • Esterel Massif • Fréjus (3 km)
Electric hook-ups/amps 167/6-10

This site offers 48 pitches with private sanitary facilities but almost no organised recreation. Although the beautiful, yellow mimosa blossoms can only be seen in winter, the trees provide welcome shade in the summer. The oleander hedgerows ensure the necessary privacy and are in bloom all year round. The restaurant food is typically French, with two menus, a daily special and the option of take-away meals. The swimming pool (with three separate pools) has an extra-long slide that is a favourite with children.

Although guests on the lower grounds will hear passing traffic, the noise level is not annoying. The same road will take you to the motorway in a few minutes, and on to Toulon, Hyères islands, Cannes, Nice and Monaco to Ventimiglia in Italy. But there are enough attractions in the close vicinity: the hiker's paradise of the Esterel Massif is nearby. Or, you can pack a rucksack and stroll down to the adjacent coast, famous for its rock formations and hidden sandy beaches – only accessible on foot or by boat.

Le Moulin de Verdagne

Rating	6.9
Tariff range	€€€
Town	Gassin
Department	Var
Postal Code	83580
Map	6 C2
Tel	04-94797821
e-mail	info@moulindeveragne.com
Open	01 Apr – 31 Oct

From main rdbt near Port-Grimaud take D559 towards La Croix-Valmer. Turn left before La Croix-Valmer, then towards Le Brost & Gassin, past football stadium. After 2 km turn left. Site approx 200mtrs.

Size (hectares) 5
Touring pitches 80
Sanitary facilities rating 6.8

quiet, rustic location • inexpensive • open all year • Saint-Tropez • outcrops of rock in the sea • La Croix-Valmer (2 km)
Electric hook-ups/amps 80/6

Le Moulin de Verdagne is located between the Gulf of Saint-Tropez to the north and the 4 km of sandy beach at Cavalaire-sur-Mer in the south. To the east is the even longer beach at Pampelonne. The campsite must be unique on the Côte d'Azur, enjoying a countryside location surrounded by vineyards and with no major roads nearby. The price is much lower than the beach campsites and the pitches are greener. The only thing missing is entertainment. But pleasure-seekers will find all the fun they need in St-Tropez, Ste-Maxime and Cavalaire which are renowned for their nightlife.

In the past the owner has accepted young holidaymakers in the high season when all the beach campsites were full, not wanting them to miss out on their beach holiday. But he quickly regretted it as there was nothing there for them. When they got bored they became a nuisance to the other guests, mainly families with small children. He now sticks to families, and with them in mind has upgraded the sanitary facilities. Le Moulin de Verdagne is ideal if you are thinking of taking the kids on a beach holiday to a quiet though inexpensive campsite.

Provence-Alpes-Côte d'Azur

Le Presqu'île de Giens

Rating 8
Tariff range €€€€
Town Hyères
Department Var
Postal Code 83400
Map 6 B2
Tel 04-94582286
Fax 04-94581163
e-mail info@camping-giens.com
Open 22 Mar – 05 Oct
From Hyères take D97 towards Giens. Just before Giens turn right towards Madrague, then turn left immediately.
Size (hectares) 7
Touring pitches 170
Sanitary facilities rating 8.4
campsite with no frills • also suitable for small tents • many facilities • Îles d'Hyères • Port-Cros national park • Giens (1 km)
Electric hook-ups/amps 170/6-16

This is the place to come for a real beach and surf holiday, with its two long sandy beaches close to the campsite. The one at Almanarre is a particular favourite amongst windsurfers, and the site can arrange windsurfing lessons. On the other side of the double peninsula that links Giens to the coast, past the salt pans and the thousands of flamingos, there is a slightly narrower beach sheltered from the wind. Diving lessons can be taken at the La Tour Fondue campsite (see below), which has the same owner as La Presqu'île de Giens.

Le Presqu'île de Giens offers many facilities and has a reasonably extensive activities programme. There is a disco, shop, shows and sports facilities. The pitches are slightly too small for a caravan with an awning and a car, unless you take a pitch near the static caravans. There are plenty of those, all quite close together in neat rows. Many of the guests hire their pitch for the entire year, so you could almost call it a village. A lot of the wooded hillside provides a home to the younger guests with small tents, and these are not accessible by car.

La Tour Fondue

Rating 7.7
Tariff range €€€€
Town Hyères
Department Var
Postal Code 83400
Map 6 B2
Tel 04-94582286
Fax 04-94581163
e-mail info@camping-giens.com
Open 22 Mar – 02 Nov
From Hyères follow D97 towards Giens to La Tour Fondue. Site near point where boats depart for Porquerolles.
Size (hectares) 2
Touring pitches 119
Sanitary facilities rating 8
simple and quiet • has its own diving club • directly located on rocky coast • Îles d'Hyères • Port-Cros national park • Giens (2 km)
Electric hook-ups/amps 119/6-10

The campsite is on a rocky coast with a row of pitches right above the waves, where the subtropical islands are renowned as a diving paradise; La Tour Fondue also has its own diving club where you can take lessons, and hire all the equipment. Because there is no activities programme, swimming pool or beach, the price is modest and relaxation guaranteed. Entertainment can be found on La Presqu'île (see previous entry), a campsite about 1.5 km away belonging to the same owner. You can also scramble over the rocks to a couple of mini beaches below the site. Two piers for the diving boats serve as diving boards for the kids. There are larger beaches within walking distance.

The pitches are a little small for a caravan with an awning and a car, and there is little privacy and limited shade. The sea breeze is cooling, but in the early and late season you will be thankful for every ray of sun. A pizzeria with an outdoor dining area serves snacks and gives a friendly welcome. This is a rare site where, even in high season, the majority are people of all ages without children who love diving, surfing and the natural coast.

Provence-Alpes-Côte d'Azur

SA Sélection Camping

Rating 8.4
Tariff range €€€€
Town La Croix-Valmer
Department Var
Postal Code 83420
Map 6 C2
Tel 04-94551030
Fax 04-94551039
e-mail camping-selection@wanadoo.fr
Open 15 Mar – 15 Oct
From Cavalaire-sur-Mer take D559 towards La Croix-Valmer, then follow Barbigoua from rdbt. Site approx 200mtrs N.
Size (hectares) 4
Touring pitches 136
Sanitary facilities rating 8.6
400 m from the sandy beach • new heated swimming pool • sufficient shade • St-Tropez • rocky outcrops and small bays • Cavalaire-sur-Mer (3 km)
Electric hook-ups/amps 136/10

A shady campsite about 400m from the beach with a heated swimming pool that is open right through the season. The beach is sandy (not pebbles) and about 4 km long. Where the road from the campsite meets the beach, you will also find some restaurants, boutiques and kiosks. There is even a small pier, the departure point for boats that regularly cross between the islands of Porquerolles and Port-Cros.

Port-Cros is a maritime national park with walks clearly marked though some of them are under water! You can take your first diving lesson in the campsite pool and then join the diving class on the beach. Connoisseurs claim that it is the most beautiful in the whole of France. Even with only a snorkel, there is plenty of colourful sea life to be seen amongst the rocks that mark the end of the beach. The 400m that separate Sélection from the beach are enough to dissipate the sounds of the coastal road, making it a quiet campsite. There is plenty to do, including a disco, live music, a conjuror and other entertainers, sports events, and a kiddies' club.

Les Moulières

Rating 8.2
Tariff range €€€€
Town La Londe-les-Maures
Department Var
Postal Code 83250
Map 6 B2
Tel 04-94015321
Fax 04-94015322
e-mail camping.les.moulieres@wanadoo.fr
Open 01 Jun – 02 Sep
From Hyères take N98 towards La Londe. Just before La Londe follow signs for Les Plages. Site just S of La Londe.
Size (hectares) 3.5
Touring pitches 250
Sanitary facilities rating 8.4
surprisingly quiet • spacious and clean • restaurant and bar • ideal cycling country • charming harbour • La Londe (1 km)
Electric hook-ups/amps 250/6

Les Moulières is about 1 km from the beach in a landscape of flat vineyards and wooded hillsides. You will appreciate its beauty and it has the advantage over other campsites along the coast: they are often crowded where guests and tents can get overwhelmed with sand every time the wind blows! The pitches at Les Moulières are extremely well-proportioned and the campsite is clean and tidy. There are no barriers between the pitches which means that there can be a lack of privacy and quiet during the high season. When booking, make sure you ask for one at the edge of the site, where you will also find more shade.

There isn't a swimming pool, but the beach is just a short cycle ride away. The harbour at La Londe has charming shops and restaurants that are easily accessible from the beach. The site also has its own restaurant and bar where prices are reasonable and portions are generous. An added bonus is the campsite's own bakery oven, which means that the baguettes and croissants are always fresh.

Provence-Alpes-Côte d'Azur

Les Cigales

Rating	8.3
Tariff range	€€€€
Town	Le Muy
Department	Var
Postal code	83490
Map	6 C2
Tel	04-94451208
Fax	04-94459280
e-mail	contact@les-cigales.com
Open	01 Apr – 28 Sep

Take A8, and from exit 36 onto N555 towards Le Muy. Approx 300mtrs, just before junct with N7, turn left. Site in 1 km.

Size (hectares) 13
Touring pitches 198
Sanitary facilities rating 8.4
rope-ladder course • 9 playgrounds • donkey trekking in the countryside • Côte d'Azur • Massif Esterel • Le Muy (3 km)
Electric hook-ups/amps 198/6-10

The enthusiastic family that runs this campsite is mad about nature, animals, games, gardens and, above all, children. Mix these interests together and you have Les Cigales, a campsite full of surprises. The grounds are partly in woodland and partly on the slopes under old umbrella pines, with a view of the hills of Les Maures. Hidden away here is the exciting Lost Valley, an adventure course of rope ladders, chain bridges and nets strung high up in the trees. It is not a short, boring course, but one with a high Indiana Jones factor that goes down a storm with children. There are different versions for toddlers, small children and older ones. Another activity is a donkey trek.

Love of games and horticulture are combined in César and Léonie's Garden, where you can play all kinds of exotic games, and it's all free. Les Cigales is otherwise a comfortable site with everything you would expect. The motorway is so close, but luckily the design of the campsite takes that into account, so that on the pitches you are hardly bothered by it.

Au Paradis des Campeurs

Rating	8.5
Tariff range	€€€€
Town	Les Issambres
Department	Var
Postal Code	83380
Map	6 C2
Tel	04-94969355
Fax	04-94496299
Web	www.paradis-des-campeurs.com
Open	20 Mar – 16 Oct

On A8 take exit 36 towards Le Muy. Follow N7 to Roquebrune-sur-Argens then take D7 towards St-Aygulf. Then N98 towards St-Tropez. After 2 km site on right in Les Issambres.

Size (hectares) 3.7
Touring pitches 180
Sanitary facilities rating 8.4
tranquil campsite • sandy beach • well-designed sanitary facilities • Saint-Tropez • rock formations and bays • Saint-Aygulf (2 km)
Electric hook-ups/amps 180/6

For beach-lovers, this campsite is a true paradise. The sea lies directly on the other side of the coastal road, and the site has its own underground passage to the beach; children can therefore make their way safely on their own. The beach is sandy, lying in a bay of less than a kilometre across, between rocks where the fishing and snorkelling is excellent. The campsite's restaurant – with shop and snack bar – cuts off most of the noise from the coastal road. This road can be a driver's nightmare on summer weekends – not because people drive fast, but because the traffic simply does not move!

You can enjoy the sun on the restaurant terrace, or take away a pizza. There is another restaurant on the beach with a veranda overlooking the sea. The former sanitary facilities were good, but the new unit is actually beautiful: columns, arches, a courtyard with a Moorish fountain – a picture straight out of an architecture magazine! The water supply to each pitch is a nice touch. For party animals, this paradise may be a trifle tame given that there are organised activities only three times a week, and these may not appeal to young adults. However, most of the guests are families with young children and they feel completely at home.

Provence-Alpes-Côte d'Azur

Les Pins

Rating	8.5
Tariff range	€€€
Town	Les Salles-sur-Verdon
Department	Var
Postal Code	83630
Map	6 B3
Tel	04-98102380
Fax	04-94842327
e-mail	camping.les.pins@wanadoo.fr
Open	01 Apr – 18 Oct

Site W of Les Salles-sur-Verdon. On D957 take Les Salles-sur-Verdon exit and follow Le Lac south.

Size (hectares) 2
Touring pitches 104
Sanitary facilities rating 8.7

neat and tidy family campsite • nearby village accessible on foot • close to a pebble beach • Gorges du Verdon • Plateau de Valensole • Les Salles-sur-Verdon (0.5 km)

Electric hook-ups/amps 73/6

Les Pins and La Source (see below) are situated opposite one another and offer the same facilities. The sanitary facilities at La Source are slightly better, but at Les Pins the pitches are larger. La Source is a true terraced campsite, while Les Pins has a level area with some terraces higher up. Both campsites are neat and tidy, clean and well maintained.

The two sites share a common, long, pebble beach as well as the crystal clear waters of the Lac de Ste-Croix reservoir in Verdon with a water temperature of 26°C in the summer. Verdon is also home to a breathtaking canyon – reminiscent of Arizona's Grand Canyon. Both campsites back onto a low hillside crowned by the village of Les Salles, easily accessible on foot at a distance of 200 metres. The village of Les Salles has shops, cafés and restaurants, and for this reason neither of the campsites offers such facilities – nor do either of them have a swimming pool. Both sites are on the same no-through road that is only used by cars going to and from the campsites. La Source or Les Pins, heads or tails – it's a choice between equals.

La Source

Rating	7.9
Tariff range	€€€
Town	Les Salles-sur-Verdon
Department	Var
Postal Code	83630
Map	6 B3
Tel	04-94702040
Fax	04-94702074
Web	www.provence-campings.com/verdon/lasource
Open	23 Mar – 10 Oct

Site W of Les Salles-sur-Verdon. On D957 take Les Salles-sur-Verdon exit. Follow site signs through village.

Size (hectares) 2
Touring pitches 89
Sanitary facilities rating 8.2

neat, tidy and clean family campsite • village in walking distance • close to pebble beach • Gorges du Verdon • Plateau de Valensole • Les Salles-sur-Verdon (0.5 km)

Electric hook-ups/amps 89/6-10

La Source and Les Pins (see above) are situated opposite one another and offer the same facilities. The sanitary facilities at La Source are slightly better, but at Les Pins the pitches are larger. La Source is a true terraced campsite, while Les Pins has a level area with some terraces higher up. Both campsites are neat and tidy, clean and well maintained.

The two sites share a common, long, pebble beach as well as the crystal clear waters of the Lac de Ste-Croix reservoir in Verdon with a water temperature of 26°C in the summer. Verdon is also home to a breathtaking canyon – reminiscent of Arizona's Grand Canyon. Both campsites back onto a low hillside crowned by the village of Les Salles, easily accessible on foot at a distance of 200 metres. The village of Les Salles has shops, cafés and restaurants, and for this reason neither of the campsites offers such facilities – nor do either of them have a swimming pool. Both sites are on the same no-through road that is only used by cars going to and from the campsites. La Source or Les Pins, heads or tails – it's a choice between equals.

Provence-Alpes-Côte d'Azur

La Bastiane

Rating	8.5
Tariff range	€€€€
Town	Puget-sur-Argens
Department	Var
Postal Code	83480
Map	6 C2
Tel	04-94555594
Fax	04-94555593
e-mail	info@labastiane.com
Open	21 Mar – 18 Oct

Take exit 37 on A8. Follow N7 towards Le Muy. At Puget, turn right at traffic lights. After 500mtrs left, follow country lane for 1 km. Site 2 km N of Puget-sur-Argens.

Size (hectares) 3
Touring pitches 80
Sanitary facilities rating 8.8

club-like atmosphere • varied activities • theme evenings • Côte d'Azur • Esterel Massif • Puget-sur-Argens (3 km)

Electric hook-ups/amps 80/6

La Bastiane calls itself a campsite with the atmosphere of a club, though many activities are charged extra. Pony rides and the disco afternoons for children are free, and there is a great deal to do besides. A music club is held every evening at the disco (situated off the campsite grounds), and there are organised games and sports competitions held at the swimming pool which is heated in the off-season. Three times a week you can enjoy a themed meal with accompanying music, and you can take part in organised walks through the surrounding area. Children's washrooms in a separate area are new.

The umbrella-pine forest that borders the campsite is ideal for jogging and walking. These beautiful pine trees create welcome shade and are typical of the area around Saint-Tropez. The sea is 8km away, near Fréjus, but you have the choice of many other beaches. The campsite is not located on the coast so you do not have the daily problem of traffic jams. The motorway is close by, allowing you to travel easily to the urban areas of the Côte d'Azur, Cannes, Nice and Monaco.

Les Tournels

Rating	7.9
Tariff range	€€€€
Town	Ramatuelle
Department	Var
Postal Code	83350
Map	6 C2
Tel	04-94559090
Fax	04-94559099
e-mail	info@tournels.com
Open	01 Jan – 07 Jan, 13 Mar – 31 Dec

From St-Tropez take D93 towards Ramatuelle. After 7.5 km turn left before Ramatuelle towards Phare de Camarat. Site approx 1 km.

Size (hectares) 20
Touring pitches 698
Sanitary facilities rating 7.7

beach reachable by bike or bus • lots of sports and entertainment • has its own vineyard and wine • the port at St-Tropez • Plage de Pampelonne • Ramatuelle (3 km)

Electric hook-ups/amps 698/6-10

This campsite produces its own wine and it is quite a good one too – a red Côtes-de-Provence cuvée spéciale that you can easily leave to mature for a few years. From the hill, there are fabulous views of the sea, though most pitches don't have sea views. They do provide plenty of shade, though. The sea is only a short distance away, about fifteen minutes by bike or less with the campsite bus. The famous Plage de Pampelonne is about 5 km long and only a stone's throw from Saint-Tropez. There are some smaller beaches between the rocks to the south of Ramatuelle.

Les Tournels is a large campsite with lots of facilities and an extensive entertainment programme that lasts until one o'clock in the morning. In some ways, however, it could be improved. For many of the electrical outlets, you still need a French plug and the walk to the tap from some of the pitches without their own water is considerable. Although clean, the sanitary facilities are dated; having said that, there are plenty of facilities on the site and there is plenty to do.

Provence-Alpes-Côte d'Azur

Domaine de la Bergerie

Rating	8.9
Tariff range	€€€€
Town	Roquebrune-sur-Argens
Department	Var
Postal Code	83520
Map	6 C2
Tel	04-98114545
Fax	04-98114546
e-mail	info@domainelabergerie.com
Open	15 Feb – 15 Nov

A8 exit 36, N7 towards Roquebrune-sur-Argens. D8 towards St-Aygulf. At rdbt after Roquebrune take D8 towards San-Peire-sur-Mer. Site in 2 km.

Size (hectares) 60
Touring pitches 160   **Static pitches** 40
Sanitary facilities rating 9.2

static caravans on large pitches • lots to do • plenty of shade • from St-Tropez to Cannes • the Esterel massif • St-Aygulf (7 km)
Electric hook-ups/amps 160/5-10

This campsite is spread out across the hillsides with lovely views over the Mediterranean landscape. Caravans can be hired throughout the season, as can the privately-owned holiday homes, many of which have been lovingly decorated with flowers and have charming patios and pergolas. The campsite provides a subtropical and friendly atmosphere. The hillsides are peaceful, in stark contrast to the tent and caravan section of the campsite lower down, where you will be camping amidst the hustle and bustle of the campsite's many facilities and the entertainment that La Bergerie provides throughout the day and evening.

The site boasts a large partially-covered swimming pool complex with a whole host of sporting facilities, including five tennis courts, a fitness centre, a busy entertainment crew and a disco that holds more than 300 people. For those staying in the static caravans or holiday homes especially, the site offers rest and relaxation, great views and an action-packed holiday for the kids. The campsite is only 7 km from the beach at Les Issambres.

Leï Suves

Rating	8.4
Tariff range	€€€€
Town	Roquebrune-sur-Argens
Department	Var
Postal code	83520
Map	6 C2
Tel	04-94454395
Fax	04-94816313
e-mail	camping.lei.suves@wanadoo.fr
Open	01 Apr – 15 Oct

Take exit 37 (Fréjus/Le Muy) on A8 and follow N7 towards Fréjus/Le Muy. At rdbt by Roquebrune-sur-Argens take tunnel. Site N of Roquebrune-sur-Argens.

Size (hectares) 7
Touring pitches 160
Sanitary facilities rating 8.4

suitable for families • many facilities • flowers in bloom year round • Côte d' Azur • Massif Esterel • Roquebrune-sur-Argens (4 km)
Electric hook-ups/amps 160/6

Even in October the flowers are still blooming at Leï Suves, the work of the campsite founder who could never bear to be idle. There are old olive trees among the flowers in large containers on the restaurant terrace, and everywhere you walk he has planted scented lavender and rosemary. The area for tents looks like an open cork-oak woodland: in fact 'Leï Suves' means 'the cork oaks' in the Provençal dialect. Nowadays the old man's son runs the campsite and his granddaughter works in reception.

Although the view of the hills gives you the feeling of being deep in the heart of the countryside, the Mediterranean is not far away. After a day on the beach it is pleasant to return to the peace of the country, characterised by chirping of cicadas. You can walk, or take a mountain bike, to Rocher de Roquebrune or the Gorges du Blavet, while the pink Massif Esterel is criss-crossed by footpaths. Thanks to the motorway, trips to Nice and Monaco are very easy. A 25-m swimming pool with a large paddling pool for the children, a tennis court and courts for volleyball, handball and basketball are some of the on-site amenities.

Provence-Alpes-Côte d'Azur

Campasun Mas de Pierredon

Rating	7.8
Tariff range	€€€€
Town	Sanary-sur-Mer
Department	Var
Postal Code	83110
Map	6 B2
Tel	04-94742502
Fax	04-94746142
e-mail	pierredon@campasun.com
Open	05 Apr – 15 Sep

From Aix-en-Provence take A50 and turn off at Ollioules. Then take D11 towards Sanary-sur-Mer. Turn right before autoroute viaduct. Site on right in 1 km.

Size (hectares) 3
Touring pitches 70
Sanitary facilities rating 8
pitches with individual sanitary facilities • lots to do for the children • various sports activities on offer • Îles d'Hyères • the port at Sanary • Sanary-sur-Mer (3 km)
Electric hook-ups/amps 70/10

The owner of this campsite usually mans the reception desk to get to know the guests and to be on hand to deal with any problems that may arise. She also makes sure that there is plenty to do in the high season. Every morning there is painting and other activities for the younger children and a special morning programme entertains the 12 to 14-year olds; there is fun geared towards the older kids in the afternoon. Tennis, mini golf, volleyball and football are available on site. Dogs are welcome, but must be kept on a lead. The swimming pool and kiddies fun pool are ideally located at the foot of the restaurant terrace.

Eighteen pitches have their own private sanitary facilities, which is a great bonus. However, this means these pitches are smaller and not particularly suitable for larger tents. Static caravans and tents are also available for hire. The owner's straightforward approach – "Don't hide the fact that we're close to the motorway" – explains why people return year after year. There is some traffic noise, but people seem to stop noticing very quickly. What might start out as a stop-over site rapidly becomes a favoured holiday spot for children and parents alike.

Le Brégoux

Rating	7.3
Tariff range	€€
Town	Aubignan
Department	Vaucluse
Postal code	84810
Map	6 A3
Tel	04-90626250
Fax	04-90626521
e-mail	camping-lebregoux@wanadoo.fr
Open	01 Mar – 31 Oct

From Aubignan take D55 towards Caromb. From D55, while still in built-up area, follow sign to right.

Size (hectares) 4
Touring pitches 170
Sanitary facilities rating 7.4
central location • cheap • simple and clean • cycling and walking trips • beautiful natural surroundings • Aubignan (0.5 km)
Electric hook-ups/amps 170/6

Located at the heart of the region, Le Brégoux is simple, clean and inexpensive. It makes an attractive base for anyone wishing to stay in a beautiful area with lots to see, without having to pay for all kinds of frills at the campsite itself. Its position in the heart of Provence, between Mont Ventoux and the Dentelles de Montmirail, makes Le Brégoux a first-class point of departure for exploring the area. You can visit some pretty villages here; some of them, such as Gigondas and Vacqueyras, are renowned centres of wine production.

The pitches are separated by hedges but there is little shade, and the simple sanitary facilities are well maintained. Numerous paths criss-cross the grounds, with floral names such as Allée des Acacias and Allée des Forsythias. There is no shop, but you can buy food and other things in the pleasant village of Aubignan, which is within walking distance of the site. There is no swimming pool, either, though there is a nice play area for children. If you want to swim, there is the lake at Mormoiron 15 km away. Entertainment is provided in the evening, and now and then a local band puts on a performance.

Provence-Alpes-Côte d'Azur

Domaine Naturiste de Bélézy

Rating 7.5
Tariff range €€€€
Town Bédoin
Department Vaucluse
Postal code 84410
Map 6 A3
Tel 04-90656018
Fax 04-90659445
e-mail info@belezy.com
Open 15 Mar – 06 Oct
From Bédoin take D974 towards Mont Ventoux. After 300mtrs turn left. 600mtrs follow sign to site reception.
Size (hectares) 25
Touring pitches 160 **Static pitches** 60
Sanitary facilities rating 7.3
luxurious camping • cultural programme • many facilities • Mont Ventoux • Avignon, city of the Popes • Bédoin (1 km)
Electric hook-ups/amps 160/16

As one of the oldest naturist campsites in France, Domaine de Bélézy, at the foot of Mont Ventoux, offers a wealth of luxury for the camper with high expectations. You will find three beautiful swimming pools, filtered using special techniques, one of which is specially for small children. In the restaurant many dishes are prepared with truffles, a very expensive delicacy that grows unseen under the earth of the campsite itself.

The founder of Bélézy was a music teacher, and even now there are many cultural events on offer, among them concerts, and literary and poetry evenings. For book lovers there is even a library. Those who prefer to play sports can make use of extensive pitches for football or volleyball courts.

Programmes for the children include building a Native American village, morning exercises, and a treasure hunt. A children's farm and recreation areas complete the delights available for them. The older ones have plenty of activities from adventure games to weekends camping out on Mont Ventoux. Adults can spoil themselves with a sauna or hydrotherapy.

Lou Comtadou

Rating 7.5
Tariff range €€€
Town Carpentras
Department Vaucluse
Postal code 84200
Map 6 A3
Tel 04-90670316
Fax 04-90460181
e-mail info@campingloucomtadou.com
Open 01 Mar – 31 Oct
In Carpentras follow signs for 'Lou Comtadou' sports complex. From Carpentras take D4 towards St-Didier.
Size (hectares) 2
Touring pitches 92
Sanitary facilities rating 7.4
central location • fairly new • quiet, even in the high season • Mont Ventoux • Le Lubéron • Carpentras (0.5 km)
Electric hook-ups/amps 92/6

CCI

Some of the advantages of a fairly new campsite such as Lou Comtadou is that it is clean and tidy, with good sanitary facilities. Another good point is the size of the attractive pitches, which are all bordered by colourful oleanders to create adequate privacy. The managers (who speak English) keep the site in excellent condition, and the grass is mown every day. Lou Comtadou is fairly central for all the sights of Provence – Mont Ventoux, Le Lubéron, Avignon and pretty villages, and few of them are more than 30 kilometres away. Another convenient aspect is that the local bus stops outside – handy for a visit to the lively centre of Carpentras.

The campsite itself is very peaceful, with not much in the way of entertainment for children and teenagers. There are a couple of play areas for younger children, with soft surfaces in case they fall. Everyone enjoys a discount at the swimming pool (which has a slide) in the Lou Comtadou sports complex next door, where the tennis court and other facilities are free. The restaurant serves a limited range of simple dishes at good prices.

Provence-Alpes-Côte d'Azur

Airotel La Sorguette

Rating	8.1
Tariff range	€€€€
Town	l'Isle-sur-la-Sorgue
Department	Vaucluse
Postal Code	84800
Map	6 A3
Tel	04-90380571
Fax	04-90208461
e-mail	sorguette@wanadoo.fr
Open	15 Mar – 15 Oct

Take A7 and turn off at Avignon-Nord, towards Carpentras. Take D6 towards Vedène, through St-Saturnin towards Châteauneuf-de-Cadagne. Take N100 towards l'Isle-sur-la-Sorgue. Site 1.5 km E of l'Isle-sur-la-Sorgue.

Size (hectares) 5
Touring pitches 127
Sanitary facilities rating 7.8
simple, but clean • plenty of planting • inexpensive • bric-a-brac market on Sundays • villages in the Luberon mountains • l'Isle-sur-la-Sorgue (1 km)
Electric hook-ups/amps 127/4-10

La Sorguette is a great place to experience a relaxed lifestyle. There is no unnecessary bustle, and it is a safe environment for the kids. The sanitary facilities are good, the showers are hot and the wash basins are cubicled. The site has its own shop and snack bar, and takeaway meals are available in the high season. Each pitch is surrounded by a hedge and there are always at least two trees to provide the necessary shade.

Various activities are organised for the children. It does not have a fun pool for them, so to cool off, you will have to take a dip in the waters of the Sorgue. The water is fairly shallow and therefore not really suitable for swimming. However, campsite guests can visit the local municipal swimming baths (2 km away) at a reduced rate. For the keen oarsman, canoes are available for hire at the site for trips along the Sorgue. It also makes an excellent base for visits to the Sunday bric-a-brac market in l'Isle-sur-la-Sorgue.

Font Neuve

Rating	8
Tariff range	€€€
Town	Malemort-du-Comtat
Department	Vaucluse
Postal code	84570
Map	6 A3
Tel	04-90699000
Fax	04-90699177
e-mail	camping.font-neuve@libertysurf.fr
Open	01 May – 30 Sep

In village, follow Méthamis signs (approx 1.5 km). Turn left, and site on left in 50mtrs. Site SE of Malemort-du-Comtat.

Size (hectares) 1.5
Touring pitches 50
Sanitary facilities rating 8.3
authentic Provençal surroundings • pleasant campsite • friendly staff • Mont Ventoux • the Nesque gorges • Malemort-du-Comtat (2 km)
Electric hook-ups/amps 50/6-20

The Font Neuve campsite is set amidst a typical Provençal landscape and offers a terrific view of the Dentelles de Montmirail and the red roofs of Malemort-du-Comtat. The owners of the site, the Gleize family from the village, offer their guests a very warm, sincere welcome.

It is a genuinely pleasant no-frills family campsite, although it does have a very good swimming pool. The sunshine is very strong here in the foothills of Mont Ventoux. Those seeking the shade will have to find themselves a reasonably-sized olive tree to hide under.

The sanitary facilities are not spectacular, but are kept clean. The restaurant offers good local fare and has a different menu every day. In short, Font Neuve is an excellent base for anyone looking to discover all aspects of Provence. The only drawback is the lack of organised entertainment for children, apart from a tennis tournament. The advantage of this lack of time-tabled activities is that you never have to clock-watch while you are out and about, to make sure you are back in time for the kiddies karaoke show!

Provence-Alpes-Côte d'Azur

La Coucourelle

Tariff range €€
Town Pernes-les-Fontaines
Department Vaucluse
Postal code 84210
Map 6 A3
Tel 04-90664555
Fax 04-90613246
e-mail camping@ville-pernes-les-fontaines.fr
Open 01 Apr – 30 Sep
From Pernes-les-Fontaines take D28 towards St-Didier. Approx 300mtrs turn left, follow signs for 'Camping Municipal'.
Size (hectares) 1
Touring pitches 39
Sanitary facilities rating
small • cheap • central location • municipal sports complex • Mont Ventoux • Pernes-les-Fontaines (1 km)
Electric hook-ups/amps 39/10

La Coucourelle is a small, inexpensive, centrally located place with clean facilities for an overnight stay. The municipal sports complex next door contains a large swimming pool, football and rugby pitches, tennis courts and a gym. If you are staying at the campsite, you can use these for little or no charge. For cyclists, the real challenge is a bit further away at Mont Ventoux. Walkers can look forward to a variety of marked routes, such as a trip around the fourteen fountains in the surrounding area. The campsite is also an excellent base for visiting famous towns of Provence, such as Avignon, Carpentras, Gordes, Orange and pretty Pernes-les-Fontaines itself.

Those seeking a big, lively campsite with all kinds of facilities and entertainment will not find it here. There is no shop (it is a ten-minute walk to the village), no restaurant, no bar (or snack bar) and no terrace. On the other hand, the sanitary facilities are clean and the pitches are separated by high hedges to provide peace and privacy, though on a new section, they have not yet fully grown. The only facility for children is the play area.

Le Soleil de Provence

Rating 7.6
Tariff range €€€
Town St-Romain-en-Viennois
Department Vaucluse
Postal code 84110
Map 6 A3
Tel 04-90464600
Fax 04-90464037
e-mail info@camping-soleil-de-provence.fr
Open 15 Mar – 31 Oct
From D938 Vaison-la-Romaine/Nyons take C2 to St-Romain-en-Viennois. Then turn left and site 300mtrs.
Size (hectares) 4
Touring pitches 141
Sanitary facilities rating 7.6
fantastic panoramic view • beautiful swimming pool • gleaming sanitary facilities • Mont Ventoux • Dentelles de Montmirail • Vaison-la-Romaine (4 km)
Electric hook-ups/amps 137/10

Set on a hill in the middle of the Provençal landscape, Le Soleil de Provence does full justice to its name. Here sun worshippers have every opportunity to pamper themselves, but it is not a place for those who would rather be in the shade, although the young trees do offer a certain amount of protection from the burning sun. Luckily there is a splendid swimming pool, with palm trees to provide much needed cool areas. There is no toddlers' or children's pool although there is a play area for little ones.

From the spacious pitches you are treated to a wonderful panorama, with Mont Ventoux as the literal high point. It is irresistible for anyone who cannot get enough of the typical Provençal landscape with its vineyards and hills. The campsite is fairly new, as you can see from the facilities which are clean and well maintained. There is a small shop at the site where you can order bread. The nearest village is the quiet Saint-Romain-en-Viennois. There is sometimes a karaoke, but Le Soleil de Provence is a quiet place in the evenings.

Provence-Alpes-Côte d'Azur

Le Théâtre Romain

Rating 8
Tariff range €€€€
Town Vaison-la-Romaine
Department Vaucluse
Postal code 84110
Map 6 A3
Tel 04-90287866
Fax 04-90287876
e-mail info@camping-theatre.com
Open 15 Mar – 05 Nov
Site N of town. Signed from D95 approx 500mtrs W of D975/D938 rdbt towards Orange.
Size (hectares) 1.5
Touring pitches 69
Sanitary facilities rating 8.2
beautiful location • good privacy • clean • Roman ruins • hiking routes • Vaison-la-Romaine (0.5 km)
Electric hook-ups/amps 69/5-10

Peace, cleanliness and every convenience right outside your door are some of the advantages of Le Théâtre Romain campsite, close to the famous Roman theatre in Vaison-la-Romaine. The neatly arranged pitches are separated by high hedges, and the site is encircled by a salmon-pink wall which provides plenty of privacy. The sparkling toilet and shower blocks are just as neat and clean. If you want to cool off, there is the swimming pool. You will not come across many children on this site, as the play area is the only thing it has to offer them.

Because Le Théâtre Romain lies on the outskirts of Vaison, there are plenty of facilities close at hand (excellent restaurants, nice shops and opportunities for days out in Provence). Excavations of Roman ruins, the Mont Ventoux and the Dentelles de Montmirail are all just a stone's throw away. It is an excellent place if you want to spend the night in a pleasant little town but prefer not to use a hotel. The owner believes that a good atmosphere and cleanliness are very important, though he does not provide much by way of entertainment.

Les Verguettes

Rating 7.6
Tariff range €€€€
Town Villes-sur-Auzon
Department Vaucluse
Postal code 84570
Map 6 A3
Tel 04-90618818
Fax 04-90619787
e-mail info@provence-camping.com
Open 01 Apr – 15 Oct
From Carpentras take D942 via Mazan to Villes-sur-Auzon. Site on right, W of village.
Size (hectares) 2
Touring pitches 81
Sanitary facilities rating 7.6
in central Provence • close to an attractive village • simple and peaceful • Provencal villages • magnificent steep gorges • Villes-sur-Auzon (0.5 km)
Electric hook-ups/amps 81/6-10

Everywhere in Provence you come across attractive villages, and whether lively or sleepy, they all allow you to sample the atmosphere of the region. At Les Verguettes in Villes-sur-Auzon, where a small, friendly campsite lies not far from the village square, you can experience one at close quarters. The site does not have many facilities, but you can walk over to the village bakery to buy fresh bread. Mont Ventoux forms a magnificent backdrop to your morning stroll. In the afternoon you can sit and enjoy a pastis on the cosy terrace near the little restaurant, and you can even take some chips back to your tent.

The swimming pool is not very big, but it has a toddlers' pool. The sanitary facilities are simple but clean. A long avenue of cypress and pine trees crosses the campsite, and along it there are small areas, each with slightly compact pitches in groups of six. Les Verguettes is especially aimed at those seeking peace and quiet, so there is not much in the way of playground equipment for the children. A beer at an outdoor café in the village can be very pleasant.

Le Colombier

Rating 8.2
Tariff range €€€
Town Culoz
Department Ain
Postal Code 01350
Map 6 B5
Tel 04-79871900
Fax 04-79871900
e-mail camping.colombier@free.fr
Open 18 Apr – 21 Sep
Culoz NW of Lac du Bourget on D904. Site approx 800mtrs E of village near rdbt.
Size (hectares) 1.4
Touring pitches 64   **Static pitches** 14
Sanitary facilities rating 8.2
sports and games • excellent sanitary facilities • beautiful setting • National Park • Lac du Bourget • Seyssel (5 km)
Electric hook-ups/amps 58/10

A few years ago the municipal campsite in Culoz was privatised, and since then Jean-Claude Le Guillou has given it its own identity. Although quite a few facilities are to be found away from the site, they are all under his management: the swimming area with sandy beach that gets fresh water from a brook, the tennis court, the mini golf course, the volleyball area and football pitch, the table tennis tables and the boules ground. The pitches, separated by hedges, are on level park-like terrain surrounded by green slopes. On some there is sunshine all day, while others are almost permanently in the shade. The very clean sanitary facilities come as a pleasant surprise, and shopping is only 500m from the campsite.

There are some interesting museums and workshops in hospitable Bugey, between the Rhône Valley and the Grand Colombier (1534m). The landscape offers enough variety, from unusual rock formations to waterfalls and wetlands. The long distance walking route Grande Randonnée no. 9 crosses the area. On your way to Aix-les-Bains (26 km), a sophisticated spa and shopping town, you pass the vast Lac du Bourget, where all kinds of watersports are practised.

Municipal Les Genêts

Rating 8.4
Tariff range €€
Town Gex
Department Ain
Postal Code 01170
Map 6 B6
Tel 04-50416146
Fax 04-50416877
e-mail camp-gex@cc-pays-de-gex.fr
Open 27 May – 17 Sep
Site E of Gex. Follow D984c to Divonne-les-Bains. Turn right after 12 km and follow signs.
Size (hectares) 3.2
Touring pitches 140
Sanitary facilities rating 8.4
quiet • much privacy • friendly owners • Geneva • Mont-Blanc range • Divonne (2 km)
Electric hook-ups/amps 99/16

Geneva and its lake are only a stone's throw away from this campsite, which lies within walking distance of Gex. Most visitors are either on their way to or from Switzerland, and have planned a short stay to explore the sights of the city.

On the way to the site you pass Voltaire's mansion, and the splendid panoramas of the Haut-Jura National Park will leave an unforgettable impression on you. The latter is a perfect walking area, and thanks to the cable cars on Mont-Rond tourists with limited walking ability can share the experience. Jean-Pierre Laplace and Veronique Duhollard speak several languages, including English, and they offer a very friendly welcome to Les Genêts.

Because of the high hedges the view is limited to the mountain peaks, but the grounds and all facilities are neat and clean. You can enjoy a drink or a snack or just sit on the terrace. There are a few small playgrounds and opposite the site is a swimming pool (reduced entrance fee for campers). At a short distance away you can rent mountain bikes or book a tour on horseback.

Rhône-Alpes

L' Ile Chambod

Rating 7.8
Tariff range €€€
Town Hautecourt-Romanèche
Department Ain
Postal Code 01250
Map 6 A6
Tel 04-74372541
Fax 04-74372828
e-mail camping.chambod@free.fr
Open 26 Apr – 27 Sep
From Bourg-en-Bresse towards Geneva, then follow D979 to Nantua. Turn right after 20 km in Hautecourt (towards Chambod). Site on right (3 km).
Size (hectares) 2.4
Touring pitches 94   **Static pitches** 6
Sanitary facilities rating 8.1
spacious lay-out • pleasant atmosphere, quiet • a real family camp site • bread and wine route • Cerdon • Poncin (5 km)
Electric hook-ups/amps 94/5-10

This campsite is set in the wooded valley of the River Ain in an almost forgotten part of France, far from the motorway. The most striking aspect is the spacious lay-out, with lots of trees yet still a wide view of the wooded hills. There you will find a network of footpaths over 150 km in total length. The valley itself is suitable for cycling trips.

A totally different view can be seen from the river; you can rent a canoe at the campsite to explore the Ain, which is only a short distance away. In Merpuis you can board a flat-bottomed boat, and enjoy the water and the natural environment of Gorges de l'Ain. Explore under ground on a visit to the caves of Cerdon. In and around Cerdon you can spend some time in one of the museums – also interesting for children – or on a visit to the wine cellars. On your way you will see the bread ovens that are so characteristic of the Bugey region.

In many picturesque villages artists and craft workers display their products. On a hot day you might prefer to stay on the sandy beach of Chambod, a recreation island, or in the swimming pool on the site.

Le Point Vert

Rating 7.7
Tariff range €€€
Town Serrières-de-Briord
Department Ain
Postal Code 01470
Map 6 A5
Tel 04-74361345
Fax 04-74367166
e-mail nelly@camping-ain-bugey.com
Open 02 Apr – 30 Sep
1.5 W of Serrieres-de-Briord. Follow 'Base de Loisirs du Point Vert' signs.
Size (hectares) 2.5
Touring pitches 77   **Static pitches** 53
Sanitary facilities rating 7.7
riverside location • many recreational facilities • good atmosphere • wine route • cycling along the Rhône • Montalieu (12 km)
Electric hook-ups/amps 69/6

On the bank of the River Rhône lies the recreation park of Serrières-de-Briord, part of which serves as a campsite. To enjoy the water and the sandy beaches you don't need to go as far south as the mouth of the river. Here you can spend your time on a pedalo, a surf board or a boat. Large lawns are a wonderful spot for children to play, and you can have a picnic without getting sand on your baguettes. Sports enthusiasts can enjoy a game of tennis or a tour on a mountain bike (hired at the campsite).

High plane trees give plenty of shade, and you can always cool off in the swimming pool. The low mountains of the Bugey region make a pleasant setting together with the picturesque villages on the wooded hills, where vineyards form perfect geometric patterns. A characteristic feature is the open-air bread ovens you find here and there; in the summertime these are often the centre of folk festivals during weekends. Try the delicious farm bread, but don't miss the traditional walnut cake and a glass of chardonnay or gamay. The high peaks of the Alps are not very far away.

Merle Roux

Rating	8
Tariff range	€€€€
Town	Baix
Department	Ardèche
Postal code	07210
Map	5 H4
Tel	04-75858414
Fax	04-75858307
e-mail	info@lemerleroux.com
Open	01 Apr – 31 Oct

6km NW from Baix. A7, exit 16 (Loriol). Follow N86 to Teil. After 4km, before railway station, turn right onto D22A. Approx 900mtrs to left; site in 1.5km

Size (hectares) 16
Touring pitches 124
Sanitary facilities rating 7.9
Dutch camp site • magnificent panoramic view • all ages welcomed • Eyrieux Valley • Valence and Montélimar
Electric hook-ups/amps 124/6

A Dutch-run camp site that has a convenient travellers' area as it is only 10km from the Autoroute du Soleil; this site proves popular for a one night stay on the way through France. However many people return for a longer stay partly because of the magnificent panoramic views of the Ardèche and the Rhône Valley, the spacious pitches (particularly on the upper terraces) and for the relaxed atmosphere created by the owners, Wim and Annet.

Young people also like staying here - they often meet up with the friends they made the previous year and have their own clubhouse. Sometimes they arrive on their own and pitch their tents next to that of their parents. There are lovely swimming pools, which the owners are very proud of, and a restaurant, open all season, run by a Dutch cook who offers a French menu. The campsite is right in the heart of the Ardeche and the Drôme so there are many interesting trips you can take. These are all detailed in the book that every guest receives on arrival.

Le Chamadou

Rating	7.8
Tariff range	€€€€
Town	Balazuc
Department	Ardèche
Postal code	07120
Map	5 H4
Tel	08-20366197
Fax	04-75890969
e-mail	reservations@camping-le-chamadou.com
Open	22 Mar – 31 Oct

S from Aubenas on D579 to Ruoms. Turn left 1.5 km beyond St-Maurice-d'Ardèche, follow narrow road for 1.5 km uphill to site.

Size (hectares) 1
Touring pitches 69
Sanitary facilities rating 7.5
beautiful lay-out • well tended • very quiet • medieval village • gorge of the River Ardèche • Balazuc (3 km)
Electric Hook-ups/amp 69/6

Balazuc is known to be one of the most attractive villages in France, and Le Chamadou matches it as one of the most attractive campsites in France. When it comes to location and landscaping it is hard to beat. Many fragrant flower boxes, dividing walls, beautiful terraces, pretty ponds with water lilies, and grand cypresses along the main road enhance the site's beauty. Even the clean and well kept toilet buildings are decorated with flowering oleanders.

Old vines and conifers provide guests with the necessary privacy and shade, although tents and caravans are often in full sun on the new part of the site. On the other hand the view over the valley and the vineyards is magnificent. Lake Le Chamadou, to which the site owes its name, is a short distance away and a trout fisherman's paradise (free of charge); however it is not suited to any other activities. Le Chamadou is mostly a campsite for people who just want to relax in a quiet atmosphere. There is not much entertainment for children, with just some games to play in and around the swimming pool next to the water garden, or a game of mini golf. From time to time a magician entertains campers while they are having dinner in the restaurant.

La Digue

Rating	8
Tariff range	€€€€
Town	(Chauzon)/Ruoms
Department	Ardèche
Postal code	07120
Map	5 H4
Tel	04-75396357
Fax	04-75397517
e-mail	info@camping-la-digue.fr
Open	15 Mar – 25 Oct

800mtrs from Chauzon. Take D 308 and C1 to Balazuc. Follow signs. 1km partly through Chauzon

Size (hectares) 3
Touring pitches 75
Sanitary facilities rating 8.3
simple and typically French • beautiful playgrounds • large store • beautiful rual scenery • pleasant villages • Ruoms (1km)
Electric Hook-ups/amp 75/6-10

The opportunity to swim and the many local places of interest prove important factors for visitors to this camp site. The site is situated just outside Ruoms, between the vineyards and groves near Chauzon. Motorists with caravans have to drive with care because the street that leads through the picturesque village is rather narrow.

The pitches are laid out in a typical French way: somewhat chaotic! This certainly has its charm, but unfortunately there is little privacy because the pitches lie close to one another. The land, with the several shady trees, is well maintained by the manager. The sanitary buildings are kept clean and in good condition. The swimming pool is rather small, but fortunately the little river nearby proves an additional attraction at the height of the season. This site is popular with families, and the manager has created playgrounds and some activity programs. A word of warning however: La Digue adjoins a neighbouring camp site where the manager isn't very fond of 'intruders'!

L'Oasis

Rating	8.2
Tariff range	€€€
Town	Eclassan
Department	Ardèche
Postal code	07370
Map	5 H4
Tel	04-75345623
Fax	04-75344794
e-mail	oasis.camp@wanadoo.fr
Open	19 Apr – 28 Sep

Exit N86 near Sarras and take D6 to St-Jeure d'Ay/Fourany. Follow signs.

Size (hectares) 6.5
Touring pitches 41
Sanitary facilities rating 8.8
swimming pool and paddling river • very luxurious sanitary facilities • well tended • steam train Tournon-Lamastre • Peaugres safari park • Sarras (7 km)
Electric Hook-ups/amp 36/3-6

The attractive side of this small-scale campsite in the northern part of the Ardèche region is the attention paid to detail. Take for instance the solar panels that heat the swimming pool, and the fact that you can sit on the restaurant terrace without having to order a drink.

In spite of the limited number of pitches the sanitary facilities are heated; they even include two large rooms with baths so that parents can wash their children. The owner prepares take-away meals as well as the plat du jour in the restaurant. It can take five hours to prepare a traditional dish, so orders should be placed by 12 noon. The price of the meals is attractive, and families staying here often use the restaurant.

Children can hug and feed old bread to the little goats that walk around. There is no kids' club, but funny and creative games. At the bottom of the terraced hill there is a paddling river with playgrounds and a sunbathing area, a barbecue site for common use and picnic tables.

La Nouzarède

Rating 7.4
Tariff range €€€€
Town Joyeuse
Department Ardèche
Postal code 07260
Map 5 G3
Tel 04-75399201
Fax 04-75394327
e-mail campingnouzarede@wanadoo.fr
Open 29 Mar – 27 Sep

Site on N side of village, close to centre. Turn right at Le Champion supermarket.

Size (hectares) 2
Touring pitches 43
Sanitary facilities rating 6.8

close to a nice village • swimming in the river • flat terrain • Gorges de l'Ardèche • Gorges de la Baume • Joyeuse (1 km)

Electric Hook-ups/amp 43/10

Joyeuse is a lovely French village with old limestone houses and the largest weekly market of the region, held under the plane trees. Within walking distance of the centre lies La Nouzarède, surrounded by vineyards and a park-like forest that stretches as far as the banks of the River Baume. This river is famous for its narrow gorge downstream which can be explored by canoe. A short footpath leads from the campsite to the river beach. Buoys mark the limit of the swimming area, which is generally under supervision during the summer. The site has its own swimming pool with two paddling pools, and a terrace with a snack bar. The ground is flat, and you will find some shade under the poplars. The sanitary facilities are in good order.

An old limestone building houses the bar and the shop, as well as a number of gîtes that stay open throughout the year. Twice a week an old vaulted building behind the bar serves as a discotheque. La Nouzarède is especially suitable for children in July and August; off season it attracts older visitors who are drawn to the mild climate and the beautiful surroundings.

Les Ranchisses

Rating 8.7
Tariff range €€€€
Town Largentière
Department Ardèche
Postal code 07110
Map 5 G4
Tel 04-75883197
Fax 04-75883273
e-mail reception@lesranchisses.fr
Open 12 Apr – 02 Nov

Site 3 km N of Largentière on D5.

Size (hectares) 4
Touring pitches 100
Sanitary facilities rating 8.5

many facilities • excellent swimming pool • spacious lay-out • Gorges de l'Ardèche • rivers and caves • Largentière (2 km)

Electric Hook-ups/amp 100/10

There is no need to leave Les Ranchisses: it is a village in itself, complete with an old farmhouse, a French gourmet restaurant, three swimming pools, a cellar with a small museum where you can taste regional wines, sleepy terraces and a river to walk along.

The first impression you get when entering the campsite is the spacious and pleasant lay-out. You can pitch your tent or park your caravan in the verdant grounds, with trees and hedges and a view of the wooded hillsides. The renovated sanitary facilities are close to all pitches. The luxurious swimming facilities come as a pleasant surprise: three pools, including a paddling pool, where you can keep an eye on the children from the shady terrace.

The youngest guests are invited to take part in karaoke and other games. Older children can rent a kayak or a mountain bike, and go to the weekly disco in a practically sound-proof recreation room above the restaurant. A small bridge leads to the pride of Les Ranchisses, the vaulted restaurant where you can eat a fresh 'salade ardèchoise', which can also be served on the terrace if you wish. The owner will gladly show you every part of the site in his golf cart, which is the only means of public transport in this holiday 'village'.

Rhône-Alpes

Domaine des Plantas

Rating 8.6
Tariff range €€€€
Town Les Ollières-sur-Eyrieux
Department Ardèche
Postal code 07360
Map 5 H4
Tel 04-75662153
Fax 04-75662365
e-mail plantas.ardeche@wanadoo.fr
Open 05 Apr – 20 Sep
From A7, junct Loriol, take N86 to La Voulte and D120 to Le Cheylard. In Les Ollières follow signs.
Size (hectares) 9
Touring pitches 112
Sanitary facilities rating 8.8
swimming in the river • restaurant in manor house • French-Dutch owners • Eyrieux Valley • volcanoes and waterfalls • Les Ollières-sur-Eyrieux (2 km)
Electric Hook-ups/amp 112/10

For many campers a river next to the campsite is more important than a swimming pool. The Franco-Dutch management of Domaine des Plantas understand this, and the River Eyrieux is the place where everything happens. The sandy beach is located in a bend of the river where the water is shallow and safe for children. On an outside bend you can go swimming and diving. Sun lovers can relax in their deck chairs by the river or in the shade on the sunbathing area behind the beach. The playground and the beach volleyball pitch are also near the river.

Pitches are located on a higher part of the campsite, and although the trees make it impossible to enjoy a view of the river, the site faces north which guarantees some coolness. The main building is a manor house; the restaurant inside has a stylish atmosphere and offers both gastronomic meals and ordinary dishes, including pizzas and snacks. The vaulted cellar serves as a discotheque with limited noise seeping out. After closing time the dancers often don't go back to their tents, but head for the beach for a final get-together before returning later to their parents' tents and caravans. Domaine des Plantas is a quiet camp site, situated at the end of a lane and relatively safe for little children.

La Plaine

Rating 8.5
Tariff range €€€€
Town Ruoms
Department Ardèche
Postal Code 07120
Map 5 G3
Tel 04-75396583
Fax 04-75397438
e-mail info@yellohvillage-la-plaine.com
Open 01 Apr – 20 Sep
From Ruoms take D579 SE towards Vallon-Pont-d'Arc. After 2 km turn right onto D111 towards St-Ambroix/Alès. Site approx 300mtrs on left before bridge over the Ardèche.
Size (hectares) 4
Touring pitches 160
Sanitary facilities rating 8.7
spacious and peaceful • clean sanitary facilities • friendly • nature walks nearby • swimming in the river • Ruoms (3 km)
Electric hook-ups/amps 160/6

La Plaine started life as a vineyard that also had a field for tent pitches – you can still catch the flavours of the vine in the air sometimes. The campsite is still surrounded by acres of vineyards, and retains its original character. It is a friendly site offering all the essentials, and an excellent spot for anyone who dreams of finding a quiet spot along the Ardèche for their tent or caravan. La Plaine offers its guests the space to relax. Its pitches are generous and offer more than enough shade. The washing facilities are extremely well equipped and very clean.

The site has its own beautiful pool, and swimming is easily available in the river. There is a beautiful sandy beach along the riverbanks, offering excellent views of the awe-inspiring rock faces on the other side of the river. Between 10am and 12, there are supervised sessions for children to play or do some drawing and painting. For older children there is a cabaret and karaoke every evening. And while they are away having fun, it is an ideal moment for mum and dad to sit back, relax and enjoy a bottle of wine.

La Garenne

Rating 8.5
Tariff range €€€€
Town St-Laurent-du-Pape
Department Ardèche
Postal code 07800
Map 5 H4
Tel 04-75622462
e-mail info@lagarenne.org
Open 01 Mar – 31 Oct
On A7 take junct 16 (Loriol) to Le Pouzin; then follow N86 to La Voulte. Left and follow D120 to St-Laurent. Right after 300mtrs, before post office.
Size (hectares) 4
Touring pitches 120
Sanitary facilities rating 8.9
pleasant and lots of activities • suitable for thematic holidays • facilities within walking distance • Eyrieux Valley • volcanoes and waterfalls • La Voulte-sur-Rhône (3 km)
Electric Hook-ups/amp 120/4-6

A pleasant atmosphere, an impressive amount of tourist information, and many off-season activities are some of the advantages of this campsite under Dutch ownership. The site specialises in early and late season bridge competitions; participation is optional and for a small fee. Three times a week during this period you can join an excursion organised by enthusiastic walkers. In May, June and September, Dutch artist Lucy Beckers runs drawing and painting courses five mornings a week.

During the high season most activities are geared towards children and sports enthusiasts. Bedtime stories are in Dutch, but the survival training is international. Teenagers are invited to a special gathering when they all sleep without their parents in small tents and have fun together. There are canoeing trips, canyonning adventures and abseiling courses. The campsite is located just outside the village, and shops and restaurants are within walking distance. Cross the bridge over the Eyrieux and you will find some small riverside beaches.

La Revire

Rating 7.8
Tariff range €€
Town St-Martin-d'Ardèche
Department Ardèche
Postal Code 07700
Map 5 H3
Tel 04-75987114
Fax 04-75987755
e-mail campinglarevire@wanadoo.fr
Open 26 Mar – 31 Oct
From N86, turn right at St-Just, follow D290. Site on left, approx 200mtrs NE of village.
Size (hectares) 1
Touring pitches 55
Sanitary facilities rating 8
good stop-over campsite • adjacent river and beach • spacious and clean • the gorges of the Ardèche • crocodile farm in Pierrelatte • St-Martin-d'Ardèche (1 km)
Electric hook-ups/amps 55/16

This small campsite close to the Ardèche River looks like an orchard, and offers very generous caravan pitches, with a separate tenting area to keep children together. The sanitary facilities are extremely hygienic, though no other facilities are available. Neighbouring St-Martin has all the facilities you need. The river at this point is wide and calm, and a path takes you down to the beach only 100m away, where you can enjoy views to the other side of the water, including the village of Aiguèze with its fortress ruins.

The water is suitable for paddling and swimming, and canoes can be hired from the campsite. From the beach, you can go boating in either direction because the flow of the river is minimal and you can also start out further upstream and then spend the day heading back to base. This journey takes you past the awe-inspiring gorges de l'Ardèche. La Revire opens earlier and closes later than most other sites in the Ardèche when most visitors come looking for the quiet life on the water, or are just stopping off on the way to Spain. The autoroute is only 19 km away.

Rhône-Alpes

La Résidence

Rating 7.1
Tariff range €€€
Town St-Remèze
Department Ardèche
Postal Code 07700
Map 5 H3
Tel 04-75042687
Fax 04-75043952
e-mail mail@campinglaresidence.net
Open 30 Mar – 30 Sep
From Bourg-St-Andéol 16 km on D4 to St-Remèze. Left at rdbt, site in village centre.
Size (hectares) 1.7
Touring pitches 40
Sanitary facilities rating 7.1
personal touch • quiet spot near the busy gorges • grape picking • the gorges of the Ardèche • the natural rock arch at Pont d'Arc • Saint-Remèze (0.5 km)
Electric hook-ups/amps 40/5

One day in September, the campers at La Résidence all muck in together to harvest the wine grapes. The grape picking is followed by a delicious meal as a thank you for the help. The 7,000 bottles of wine made here every year often win prizes; they have even won a gold medal. The campsite owners Zahia, who is originally from Paris, and Allan from Denmark, got their first campsite customers by accidentally having an article printed in Denmark's largest camping magazine.

Zahia and Allan like to have a mix of nationalities at the site, and English seems to have become the unofficial language. So if you are in the Ardèche and you are looking for a small and fairly quiet campsite with a personal touch, look no further. The wine harvest usually attracts the over-55s, but in the high season it's mainly families with small children. This friendly site is situated in the village, and has a good number of semi-shady pitches and clean sanitary facilities. Also worth mentioning is that if two people hire a four-berth caravan, they only pay for two.

Soleil Vivarais

Rating 8.1
Tariff range €€€€
Town Sampzon
Department Ardèche
Postal Code 07120
Map 5 G3
Tel 04-75396756
Fax 04-75396469
e-mail info@soleil-vivarais.com
Open 05 Apr – 14 Sep
From Ruoms take D579 SE towards Vallon-Pont-d'Arc. After about 3 km turn right onto D761, over bridge towards Sampzon. Site on right.
Size (hectares) 12
Touring pitches 103
Sanitary facilities rating 8.2
offers all modern amenities • quiet location along the river • many activities available • the natural rock arch at Pont d'Arc • rustic setting • Vallon-Pont-d'Arc (4 km)
Electric hook-ups/amps 103/10

The Club Soleil Vivarais campsite has got something for everyone. For the swimmer, there is a choice of clear blue swimming pools to choose from, while nature lovers will find pleasure on one of the private beaches alongside the beautiful river. A fun pool at Les Jardins is a new addition that will keep the smaller kids amused. The newer section of the campsite offers peace and quiet, while the section around the recreation area is ideal for those who like to be at the heart of things.

The day starts early with aqua gym or jazz gym followed by kayaking, mountain climbing, cave trips, jeep safari and lots, lots more.

The smaller children will not miss out, and can learn to canoe, go pony riding or join in the fun with the kids' club. The restaurant offers good food and there is a spectacular stage show. The pitches are spacious enough, but some are fairly close together. All amenities are available on site, including a bar, shop, pizzeria, launderette and modern sanitary facilities. There is also plenty to do in the surrounding area, although there are probably some guests who never leave the excitement of the campsite.

Domaine de Gil

Rating	8.5
Tariff range	€€€€
Town	Ucel
Department	Ardèche
Postal code	07200
Map	5 G/H4
Tel	04-75946363
Fax	04-75940195
e-mail	info@domaine-de-gil.com
Open	12 Apr – 21 Sep

In Aubenas take road to Privas. Left after crossing bridge over Ardèche, follow D578b to Ucel. Site on left, 500mtrs beyond Ucel.

Size (hectares) 4.5
Touring pitches 40
Sanitary facilities rating 8.5

many families with children • riverside location • various activities • Gorges de l'Ardèche • volcanoes and waterfalls • Vals-les-Bains (2 km)

Electric Hook-ups/amp 40/3-10

The swimming pool with its rocks and waterfall is ample proof that this is a luxurious campsite, and it is matched by the high quality tented playground, the sanitary facilities and the pitch-and-putt field for golfers. The restaurant, however, is the kind of average eating-house that you will find on any other campsite.

The riverside, with pebble beaches and plenty of room for playing and sun-bathing, is another bonus. This is the Ardèche River, long before it reaches the famous gorges; a dam creates a broad waterfall, and on the opposite bank is the ruin of an old water mill. At the foot of the dam the river is deep enough for swimmers, but elsewhere you can only go paddling in shallow water. It is also very suitable for canoeing. Small children go to the 'miniclub' in the morning, and in the afternoon there are sports competitions, guided tours and walks in the area. Playing golf and tennis is free, while children can do go-karting and play paintball for half price. Three times a week there is an evening disco party next to the bar, with the dancing terrace ending at the floodlit swimming pool. After 11pm all outdoor activities are continued indoors, allowing a good night's sleep for those who want it.

La Rouvière les Pins

Rating	7.4
Tariff range	€€€
Town	Vagnas
Department	Ardèche
Postal code	07150
Map	5 G3
Tel	04-75386141
e-mail	rouviere07@aol.com
Open	27 Mar – 15 Sep

from N follow D579 to bridge at Vallon-Pont-d'Arc. Cross bridge, turn right towards Barjac; turn right beyond Vagnas, follow road signs.

Size (hectares) 3
Touring pitches 95
Sanitary facilities rating 7.6

wonderful landscape • many sights • quiet family campsite • typical French villages • Cèze Valley • Barjac (6 km)

Electric Hook-ups/amp 95/6-10

You don't have to stand with your feet in the water to enjoy a river. That is the philosophy of some visitors to La Rouvière les Pins, a campsite that is only a stone's throw away from the tourist flood yet is an oasis of tranquillity. As you approach the site you soon realise how true this is: vast vineyards and bushes separate La Rouvière from the accessible outside world, including the village of Vagnas.

It is easy to find a spot with a magnificent view over the vineyards and enough room for your tent or caravan. Some pitches are really idyllic, but all offer the comfort of your own kitchen sink and hot running water. The swimming pool was built on the opposite side of the road to the campsite, so you will not be disturbed by the noise from the bathers. The luxurious sanitary facilities are well kept and clean.

Children can use the small playground or play games under supervision, though there is not much entertainment for older children. You might decide to go to Barjac where there is always something to do, especially on a cultural level.

Rhône-Alpes

Aire Naturelle la Goule

Tariff range €€€
Town Vallon-Pont-d'Arc
Department Ardèche
Postal Code 07150
Map 5 H3
Tel 04-75386124
Fax 04-75386322
e-mail campinglagoule-peschaire@aliceadsl.fr
Open 16 Mar – 01 Oct
From Vallon-Pont-d'Arc take D579 across bridge towards Barjac. After 4 km turn left, follow to Labastide-de-Virac. Site on left after approx 2 km.
Size (hectares) 1.5
Touring pitches 25
spacious, quiet and secluded • owners are always on site • surrounded by vineyards • the gorges of the Ardèche • caves at Orgnac • Vallon-Pont-d'Arc (8 km)
Electric hook-ups/amps 15/6

Guests at La Goule come here for rest and relaxation. Anyone wondering whether the site also provides a disco for the kids will leave disappointed. La Goule does not go in for this type of entertainment, although it does have its own swimming pool. Camping here means good old-fashioned peace and quiet in the midst of the beautiful vineyards and hills. The pitches are very generous, so no need to worry about having your neighbour's washing blowing in your face.

When you have come for peace and quiet, extensive facilities become irrelevant. However, the gentle aroma of freshly-baked bread will greet you every morning when you wake up, and the local butcher visits once a week to sell you his best cuts. The small shop stocks all the basics, such as butter and drinks. Now and again, the owner's wife will treat the guests to some spit-roasted chicken. The owners do all they can to keep their guests happy, but every evening from 10pm they like to enjoy their own peace and quiet.

Le Chauvieux

Rating 8
Tariff range €€€
Town Vallon-Pont-d'Arc
Department Ardèche
Postal code 07150
Map 5 H3
Tel 04-75880537
Fax 04-75880537
e-mail camping.chauvieux@wanadoo.fr
Open 28 Apr – 10 Sep
From Vallon-Pont-d'Arc take D579 to Barjac (southward). Cross bridge over Ardèche, turn left at rdbt.
Size (hectares) 1.8
Touring pitches 87
Sanitary facilities rating 8.3
classic campsite • favourable location • not expensive • beautiful nature • ruins of Salavas Castle • Vallon-Pont-d'Arc (1 km)
Electric Hook-ups/amp 87/6

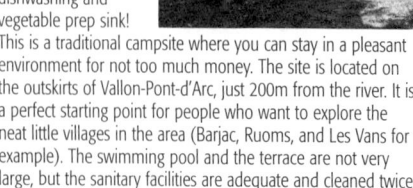

They don't like that much fuss at Le Chauvieux, so you'll find no modern background music in the toilets, for example. But every pitch here has its own dishwashing and vegetable prep sink! This is a traditional campsite where you can stay in a pleasant environment for not too much money. The site is located on the outskirts of Vallon-Pont-d'Arc, just 200m from the river. It is a perfect starting point for people who want to explore the neat little villages in the area (Barjac, Ruoms, and Les Vans for example). The swimming pool and the terrace are not very large, but the sanitary facilities are adequate and cleaned twice a day.

Pitches tend to be spacious and generally offer enough shade. Some activities are put on for children, such as face painting, making decorations and doing karaoke. What they offer seems to be popular, and many campers return year after year. Some are real veterans, who knew the present owners when they were still babies. Of course this doesn't include the French teenagers who come to the campsite at weekends for a kayak trip. But even for them the general rule applies: no noise after midnight.

Beau Rivage

Rating 8.1
Tariff range €€€€
Town Vallon-Pont-d'Arc
Department Ardèche
Postal code 07150
Map 5 H3
Tel 04-75880354
Fax 04-75880354
e-mail campingbeaurivage@wanadoo.fr
Open 01 May – 13 Sep
From Vallon-Pont-d'Arc take D579 to Ruoms/Aubenas (NW). Turn left after 2 km (towards Les Mazes). Site just before Les Mazes.
Size (hectares) 2
Touring pitches 86
Sanitary facilities rating 8.2
beautiful setting • close to attractions • many activities • gorges of the Ardèche • neat little villages • Vallon-Pont-d'Arc (2 km)
Electric Hook-ups/amp 86/6

Owner M Massot is very proud of the swimming pool he built, which even includes a jacuzzi. His enthusiasm is one of the reasons why many campers have come to this site for several years running. But that is not the only reason: Beau Rivage is set in the vineyards where his parents planted the first trees in 1972. It has now become one of the most attractive campsites in and around Vallon-Pont-d'Arc.

The beautiful spacious pitches offer magnificent views over the river, with plenty of shade and privacy for all. Sanitary facilities are good and kept clean and tidy. As there are no roads, children can run around as much as they like. There are daily activities, including song contests and a puppet theatre; rock climbing and kayak trips are also offered. There is a paddling pool, a play room, a room with pinball machines and even a small children's farm.

You can swim to the floating raft in the river that also serves as a diving board. M Massot knows how to create a pleasant atmosphere and the only rule here is absolute silence after 11pm, so that everyone can sleep in peace.

Mondial

Rating 8
Tariff range €€€€
Town Vallon-Pont-d'Arc
Department Ardèche
Postal Code 07150
Map 5 H3
Tel 04-75880044
Fax 04-75371373
e-mail reserve-info@mondial-camping.com
Open 15 Mar – 30 Sep
From Vallon-Pont-d'Arc follow 'Routes des Gorges' (D290) for approx 1.5 km. Site on right.
Size (hectares) 4.2
Touring pitches 206
Sanitary facilities rating 7.9
ideal for small children • attention to detail • clean facilities • walking and canoeing nearby • picture-postcard villages • Vallon-Pont-d'Arc (1 km)
Electric hook-ups/amps 206/6-10

At Mondial, the whole family chips in to keep the campsite looking spic and span from Grandpere to the children. The campsite is particularly popular with families with small children.
Despite being so close to the busy banks of the Ardèche and the bustling tourist hub of Vallon-Pont-d'Arc, Mondial offers plenty of peace and quiet. From 11pm onwards is the strictly-enforced quiet time, so the campsite is not ideal for boisterous teenagers. However, there is plenty to do for the younger kids, who can paint and draw or play games under supervision.

While they are busy playing, their parents can leave their shady pitches and take a canoe down the river or relax by the pool. The owner of Mondial adds new improvements every year. Some of the showers are so spacious that you can almost take the whole family with you! However, the one thing that does not change is that Mondial is the closest campsite along the Ardèche to the natural rock arch at Pont d'Arc.

Rhône-Alpes

Le Provençal

Rating 8.1
Tariff range €€€€
Town Vallon-Pont-d'Arc
Department Ardèche
Postal Code 07150
Map 5 H3
Tel 04-75880048
Fax 04-75880200
e-mail camping.le.provencal@wanadoo.fr
Open 09 Apr – 18 Sep
From Vallon-Pont-d'Arc follow D290 ('Route des Gorges') SE for approx 2 km.
Size (hectares) 3.5
Touring pitches 178
Sanitary facilities rating 7.9
canoeing on the Ardèche • shady pitches • activities for children • authentic villages • beautiful countryside • Vallon-Pont-d'Arc (1 km)
Electric hook-ups/amps 178/8

The only noise that is allowed to disturb the peace and quiet on the campsite is the sound of canoes being stacked, and all the guests of Le Provençal know it! You can take a canoe directly from the campsite for a trip along the Ardèche, and even when it is busy there is no shortage of canoes – just as well as it's a very popular activity. The generous and shady pitches are bounded by hedges that provide the right amount of shelter.

For anyone who prefers to have a view of the action, there are a number of spots along the riverbank with seating. The children will be kept busy as Le Provençal organises all sorts of fun and games for them. The campsite also offers its own tennis, volleyball, table tennis and boules. The sanitary facilities are very good and ideal for cleaning up after the day's activities.

The swimming pool is reasonably luxurious and is bordered by beautiful lavender bushes. The neoclassical fencing around the pool exudes opulence, and the staff have an excellent command of English.

Domaine Le Pommier

Rating 8.6
Tariff range €€€€
Town Villeneuve-de-Berg
Department Ardèche
Postal Code 07170
Map 5 H5
Tel 04-75948281
Fax 04-75948390
e-mail info@campinglepommier.com
Open 26 Apr – 30 Sep
From Montelimar W towards Aubenas on N102. Site E of Villeneuve-de-Berg.
Size (hectares) 7.7
Touring pitches 330
Sanitary facilities rating 8.8
entertainment for young and old • spacious pitches • multipurpose swimming complex • the gorges of the Ardèche • waterfall at Ray-Pic • Villeneuve-de-Berg (1 km)
Electric hook-ups/amps 330/6

In the low season Domaine Le Pommier attracts guests of a certain age, who come for the free watercolour painting workshops and lessons in boules. There are also organised walks, folk dancing classes and card tournaments, all free of charge. For the more adventurous, there are canoe trips along the Ardèche with the expert supervision of an instructor and the canoe rental included in the price. There is an air of calm during the off-season, and the terraced pitches are more popular than the lower ones. The higher terraces afford campers plenty of sun and views all the way to the Cévennes.

What a difference from the height of the summer, when the focus is undoubtedly the 25-m swimming pool and its winding 37-m long waterslide. Entertainment at night is provided by Le Garage, the fully soundproof disco. For the outdoor sports types, there is mountain biking and canyoning, as well as night-time orienteering missions. Free activities for the kids include pony riding, kite making and a game of 'smuggler' in the woods. All this, and Le Pommier is still a campsite with spacious pitches and highly modern sanitary facilities.

Le Gallo Romain

Rating 8.2
Tariff range €€€€
Town Barbières
Department Drôme
Postal code 26300
Map 6 A4
Tel 04-75474407
Fax 04-75474407
e-mail info@legalloromain.net
Open 26 Apr – 14 Sep

Take D101 from Barbières towards Léoncel/Col de Tourniol. Site in 1.5 km (signed).

Size (hectares) 3
Touring pitches 61
Sanitary facilities rating 8.1

quiet family campsite • Roman styling • natural surroundings • gorges and caves • fairyland (Hostun) • Romans-sur-Isère (12 km)

Electric hook-ups/amps 61/6

A Roman villa houses the sanitary facilities, columns surround the swimming pool and aromatic lavender bushes grow around the outbuildings. The owners initially intended to base the design of the campsite on local architecture – many of the farms in the Barbières region use traditional farmhouse architecture – but in the end they opted for a Roman design, which is both different and fun. The Mediterranean colours and the terracotta pots filled with flowers help to make this a great place.

The pitches are very green and spread across several level terraces, which descend towards a brook like a staircase – a favourite haunt of children. They are separated by natural planting which is not quite as dense as a hedgerow would be. With the exception of the odd pétanque competition, there is no organised entertainment or dancing, but instead guests entertain themselves, either in and around the swimming pool or near the brook. The stunning Vercors nature reserve, situated just around the corner, is a paradise for nature-lovers (birds of prey, orchids, etc). It can be explored by bike or on foot.

Le Couspeau

Rating 7.4
Tariff range €€€€
Town le Poët-Célard
Department Drôme
Postal code 26460
Map 6 A4
Tel 04-75533014
Fax 04-75533723
e-mail info@couspeau.com
Open 15 Apr – 17 Sep

Take D538 Crest/Bourdeaux. Turn right onto D538b to Poët-Célard approx 3 km before Bourdeaux. After 2.6 km, turn left onto D538a towards Dieulefit. Site on left after 800mtrs.

Size (hectares) 8
Touring pitches 100
Sanitary facilities rating 7.4

view across valley and mountains • safe for children • electric rental bicycles • Forêt de Saou • gorges and caves • Bourdeaux (5 km)

Electric hook-ups/amps 100/6

Camping Le Couspeau is set opposite the Forêt de Saou, an enormous hollow rock formation that has been eroded on all sides. Viewed from above, it looks as though someone has dropped an enormous letter 'U' in the middle of the countryside. Seen from the campsite, all you see is the large outer rock face. The valley inside the 'U' is covered in old trees and makes for a great place to walk. Whether you're sitting in your tent, dining in the restaurant or sunbathing beside the swimming pool, the view is equally good.

The site is mainly used by guests, often with small children, who value tranquillity and great walks, as well as the mountains which are not quite as daunting as the Alps. Anyone who'd rather cycle can rent one of the electric bikes on offer, and cheat on the steepest parts. The restaurant is frequented by people who live or stay elsewhere, which is usually a sign of quality. A plat du jour, a small carafe of wine and a cup of coffee cost a mere €8. The pitches vary in size, which you may want to bear in mind when booking, particularly if you have a large caravan.

Rhône-Alpes

Gervanne Camping

Rating 7.9
Tariff range €€€
Town Mirabel-et-Blacons
Department Drôme
Postal Code 26400
Map 6 A4
Tel 04-75400020
Fax 04-75400397
e-mail info@gervanne-camping.com
Open 01 Apr – 31 Oct
Take D164 (Crest-Aouste-Die). Site W of River Drôme bridge in Mirabel-et-Blacons.
Size (hectares) 3.5
Touring pitches 164
Sanitary facilities rating 8.4
located alongside a river • luxurious swimming pool • excellent transient campsite • gorges and caves • Forêt de Saou • Crest (5 km)
Electric hook-ups/amps 164/4-6

Gervanne allows you to take a beach vacation without needing to travel to the sea. The pebble beach along the clear green water of the River Drôme is long, and sections of it are dammed off during the summer months to create a swimming pool. The water in the pool is calm – ideal for swimming or splashing about. The campsite gets its name from a river that discharges into the Drôme. Although the Gervanne is quite cold (some would argue that it is too cold for swimming), it offers good fishing.

The campsite also has a swimming pool with a heated part including a jacuzzi and a baby pool, located beside the snack bar terrace. The pitches are on both sides of the road, and connected by a car-free bridge across the Gervanne. The camping field to the north is more recent; the trees have not yet matured, and allow more sun through. The southern field, which includes several pitches along the River Drôme, is covered in older trees. Gervanne is frequently used by campers heading towards – or returning from – the south, especially during the summer months.

Les Clos

Rating 8
Tariff range €€€
Town Nyons
Department Drôme
Postal code 26110
Map 6 A3
Tel 04-75262990
Fax 04-75264944
e-mail info@campinglesclos.com
Open 15 Mar – 12 Oct
From Nyons take D94 towards Serres. Site on right approx 2 km.
Size (hectares) 2
Touring pitches 74
Sanitary facilities rating 8.6
good pitches • sunny climate • friendly owners • Côtes du Rhône vineyards • Mont Ventoux • Nyons (1 km)
Electric hook-ups/amps 74/6-10

The owners of the Les Clos campsite are very friendly, and since they took over in 2002 they have made a number of improvements. The most notable of these are more shade, improved electric hook-ups and more space for sports and games. Try and get one of the pitches by the river, as few campsites offer views as good as these.

Les Clos has put special safety measures in place because of the risk of flooding, and was the first in France to install an automated warning system. May, June and October are risky months, and if the alarm goes off, the lower section of the campsite (the best bit) is evacuated. However, the place has been incident-free since 1992. Most people are unperturbed and come back year after year, not least because of the sunny micro-climate, and chalets can be rented all year round.

The nearby historic town of Nyons offers plenty of facilities and activities within walking distance, as well as a large Provençal market on Thursdays. One slight drawback for those with tents is the gravelly pitches.

La Vallée Bleue

Rating	7.6
Tariff range	€€€
Town	Sahune
Department	Drôme
Postal code	26510
Map	6 A5
Tel	04-75274442
Fax	04-75274442
e-mail	info@lavalleebleue.com
Open	01 Apr – 30 Sep

From Nyons take D94 to Serres. Just before Sahune follow signs for site.

Size (hectares) 3
Touring pitches 51
Sanitary facilities rating 8.5

lovely view • river with pebble beach • located under fruit trees • old towns and villages • Côtes-du-Rhône wines • Nyons (14 km)
Electric Hook-ups/amp 51/6

Lovely views over the mountains and a sunny microclimate are the trump cards of La Vallée Bleue. Added to this is the adjacent bright green River Eygues, with its pebble beach and sunbathing area, and you can understand why the campsite is such a sought after holiday spot. There are several reminders that the site used to be an orchard, and the old fruit trees with their spreading branches provide the necessary shade. La Vallée Bleue (The Blue Valley) attracts guests of all nationalities, but especially Dutch, Flemish and French; British campers are few in number but very welcome.

Not many campers have children under the age of 12, so the entertainment is largely based around the countryside. For example, about 10 km from the campsite is a colony of over a hundred wild vultures that you can watch during guided walking tours. Once a week there is an excursion to see the natural habitats of either beavers or chamois. A particularly great experience is the two-day tour on horseback, which is equally suitable for children with their parents, or people without any riding experience. Food and equipment are transported separately, and you spend the night in the open air.

La Mer de Glace

Rating	8.2
Tariff range	€€€€
Town	Chamonix-Mont-Blanc
Department	Haute-Savoie
Postal code	74400
Map	6 C5
Tel	04-50534403
Fax	04-50536083
e-mail	info@chamonix-camping.com
Open	25 Apr – 05 Oct

From Chamonix towards Swiss border. Turn right in Les Praz, immediately after rdbt; then cross railway and follow signs.

Size (hectares) 2.2
Touring pitches 150
Sanitary facilities rating 8.5

quiet and well tended • outdoor sports • nice chalets • glacier and ice caves • Aiguille du Midi • Chamonix-Mont-Blanc (2 km)
Electric Hook-ups/amp 75/3-10

La Mer de Glace is a campsite geared towards mountaineers. You will find your tent surrounded by lightweight expedition tents, and can watch the climbers practising their rope techniques before they leave for the highest peaks. As the name suggests the site is located close to the Mer de Glace. The view is dominated by the granite triangle of the Aiguille de Dru, a rock slab 1,000m high and a real challenge for the experienced climber.

The owner is a former ski instructor who offers useful tips if you want to go hiking. He started the campsite on a piece of land that had belonged to his grandfather, which gave him the opportunity to make some money in summer as well. La Mer de Glace is above all a place for guests who practise outdoor sports, so you will find a good range of leaflets and hiking maps at reception. The entrance looks attractive, with authentic wooden chalets housing the main services like shop and toilets. These chalets are also a good place to sit and read a book while waiting for good weather. There are some pitches in the woods, and others in the central part of the site where there is enough shade.

Rhône-Alpes

L'Oustalet

Rating 8.5
Tariff range €€€
Town Châtel
Department Haute-Savoie
Postal code 74390
Map 6 C6
Tel 04-50732197
Fax 04-50733746
e-mail oustalet@valdabondance.com
Open 24 Jun – 02 Sep , 23 Dec – 29 Apr
D902 (Thonon-Châtel), junct D22, then right before
La Ville-du-Nant, follow signs.
Size (hectares) 3.8
Touring pitches 86
Sanitary facilities rating 8.9
excellent sanitary facilities • fine swimming pool •
entertainment programme • walking and mountain biking •
close to Switzerland • Chatêl (0.5 km)
Electric Hook-ups/amp 86/2-10

This pleasant campsite can be found in the skiing and hiking resort of Châtel, in the Franco-Swiss border region. A public road separates the two sections of the site, but each has its own, very clean sanitary facilities and a TV room. The local baker has his shop right next to the site. The first attraction is the heated swimming pool, with a roof that opens in fine weather. It has a paddling pool with a fountain in the shape of a clown. Other delights include a toy cable car in the garden next to reception, moving between two boulders, and a life-size draughts set.

The Thoule family organise all sorts of activities for their guests, the majority of whom are mountain hikers; Marie-Jo, for example, leads experienced hikers over the mountain footpaths around Châtel. You can also rent a mountain bike (in French: vélo tout terrain or VTT) and follow the same route. The Thoules also offer instruction in other outdoor sports, like rafting and archery. Children under the age of 11 can go on a mountain picnic tour. Older children can take the hiking trip of their dreams: climb the mountains, spend the night in a tent and walk back next morning. They may even spot an ibex or a mountain goat.

International du Lac Bleu

Rating 8.3
Tariff range €€€€
Town Doussard
Department Haute-Savoie
Postal code 74210
Map 6 B5
Tel 04-50443018
Fax 04-50448435
e-mail lac-bleu@nwc.fr
Open 01 Apr – 30 Sep
Site 1.5 km N of Doussard, between N508 (Annecy- Albertville)
and Lake Annecy (south side).
Size (hectares) 3.3
Touring pitches 220
Sanitary facilities rating 8.6
swimming and paddling pool • entertainment for children •
day nursery • Lake Annecy • walking and cycling • Doussard
(1.5 km)
Electric Hook-ups/amp 220/8

Holidaymakers who choose Camping International du Lac Bleu (on the southern shore of Lake Annecy) are advised not to stay near reception, where a sharp bend in the main road causes a lot of traffic noise. It is better to pick your spot by the lake, where geese walk on the pebble beach, or near the jetty, where you can dive into the lukewarm water.

The campsite is located on a bay where you have a good view of the windsurfers, sailing boats, catamarans, motor boats and even watch paragliders practising emergency landings on the water. Boating fans will also feel at home, and families with children will be pleased that a lot of activities are organised by the management. There is a nice swimming pool (with paddling pool), although the lake probably attracts more swimmers. Children can have fun in the kids' club or on the beach. The campsite covers a large area and is neatly arranged, with simple but adequate sanitary facilities. The planting of trees between the pitches, however, is too sparse to guarantee shade and privacy. But when the sun is shining brightly there is always the cool lake.

La Serraz

Rating 7.6
Tariff range €€€€
Town Doussard
Department Haute-Savoie
Postal code 74210
Map 6 B5
Tel 04-50443068
e-mail info@campinglaserraz.com
Open 01 May – 13 Sep
Site in centre of Doussard, opposite post office. Doussard on N508, on south shore of Lake Annecy.
Size (hectares) 4
Touring pitches 126
Sanitary facilities rating 7.5
farmyard atmosphere • two swimming pools • entertainment programme • water sports • French Alps • Doussard
Electric Hook-ups/amp 126/6-16

La Serraz has a farmyard atmosphere, and it's not surprising since this flat terrain between the mountains and the lake was once used for agricultural purposes. The bricks are overgrown with ivy, and blossoms hang from wooden balconies and shutters. In the playground next to the farmhouse stands an old well; in the old days water was drawn by the cast iron equipment that is now decorated with geranium boxes.

The owners turned the farm into a campsite in 1962 and built a swimming pool and a children's pool behind the house. The toilets, the washbasins and even the TV room are housed in the former granaries. The best places to erect your tent are those along the straight lanes that run through the orchard, where trees offer sufficient shade but still let plenty of sunlight through. Elsewhere the layout is more like the average campsite, with pitches separated by high hedges. The view over the mountain ranges of the Savoy Alps that surround the lake is wonderful. The slopes are a deep green, but here and there you can see a glimpse of the limestone rocks. The whole area is a perfect place for long walks and mountaineering. For boating fans the beautiful lake with the clearest water in France is only 1 km away.

Le Plan du Fernuy

Rating 8.3
Tariff range €€€€
Town La Clusaz
Department Haute-Savoie
Postal code 74220
Map 6 B5
Tel 04-50024475
Fax 04-50326702
e-mail fernuy@franceloc.fr
Open 01 Jan – 29 Apr, 16 Jun – 22 Sep
Site 2 km E of Vallée des Confins. From La Clusaz follow signs for ski resort to site (2 km).
Size (hectares) 1.4
Touring pitches 61
Sanitary facilities rating 8.2
quiet • fine indoor swimming pool • open in winter • walking routes • Chamonix • La Clusaz (1 km)
Electric Hook-ups/amp 61/4-13

Le Plan du Fernuy is located on the slopes of the Des Aravis mountain range, 1,200m above sea level. Higher up you can see the ski lifts which are active in winter but resting in summer. Jean-Luc Laborde has been running this campsite since the '70s, and ten years ago he had the land levelled and laid out in terraces. The pitches are simple but spacious; and if there is hardly any shade it doesn't matter, because sunshine is most welcome at this altitude, especially in the evenings and in spring and autumn.

Winter campers with caravans can use this site in the darkest months of the year. If you prefer some luxury, you can rent a mobile home or an apartment. The clean sanitary facilities are somewhat outdated. The luxurious heated pool is housed in a wooden chalet. Guests are welcomed in the bar, where a blackboard gives information on local markets and badminton competitions in the neighbourhood. You can retire to the living room, where you will find a sofa and a bookcase. Beyond the entrance there is a steep road, and motorists driving uphill can be a bit noisy.

Rhône-Alpes

Les Fontaines

Rating 8
Tariff range €€€€
Town Lathuile
Department Haute-Savoie
Postal code 74210
Map 6 B5
Tel 04-50443122
Fax 04-50448780
e-mail info@campinglesfontaines.com
Open 01 May – 30 Sep
Site 200mtrs S of Chaparon on road to Lathuile (caravans should use road through Lathuile), 3 km W of the southern part of Lake Annecy.
Size (hectares) 3
Touring pitches 170
Sanitary facilities rating 8.5
fine swimming pools • good restaurant • entertainment • Lake Annecy • French Alps • Doussard (2 km)
Electric Hook-ups/amp 170/6

Everything at Les Fontaines was built by André Rulland himself, from the swimming pools to the bar stools. He has designed a real family campsite, where there is a lot of fun during the day, and silence and safety are promised in the evening and during the night.

All the required facilities are here: a shop for your newspapers or baguettes, a laundrette, a bar and a restaurant. From early in the morning until late in the afternoon there are plenty of activities and performances, including jugglers, fire-eaters, sack races, and table tennis for the kids. After dinner (try the tartiflettes or some other Savoy dish) there is either a dance party or a karaoke show.

The first swimming pool, next to reception, is eye-catching with its spectacular water slides. The second pool, a heated one, is located in the central part of the grounds. To fulfill his ambitions André has built a third pool specially for little children. But a day trip is still well worth while. Along the clearest lake in France is a cycling route that has been laid out on the flat track of the former railway line from Annecy to Doussard.

Les Dômes de Miage

Rating 8.1
Tariff range €€€
Town St-Gervais-les-Bains
Department Haute-Savoie
Postal code 74170
Map 6 C5
Tel 04-50934596
Fax 04-50781075
e-mail info@camping-mont-blanc.com
Open 01 May – 21 Sep
Genève-Chamonix, junct Le Fayet, towards St-Gervais. Then take D902 to Les Contamines; follow signs. Site on left, beyond St-Gervais.
Size (hectares) 2.5
Touring pitches 150
Sanitary facilities rating 8.2
quiet and well tended • shiny sanitary facilities • helpful caretaker • beautiful walking area • Chamonix-Mont-Blanc • Saint-Gervais-les-Bains (1 km)
Electric Hook-ups/amp 120/3-10

Camping Les Dômes de Miage is located at the foot of the icy north side of the Dômes de Miage, a promontory of Mont Blanc. The campsite lies close to a forest where herds of deer roam, and sometimes show themselves on the site in the early evening. You can choose either a pitch in the quiet part or one in the central section. The very clean shower building has a heated floor, and large windows offer a good view of the snow-capped mountains. Even on busy days there is never a shortage of hot water.

Owner Stéfan hates entertainment programmes, and refuses to see his park as a leisure centre. Most of his guests make their own plans, and there is nobody around during the day. Exploring the mountains is what people come to do, and they are given all the information they need. Stéfan will gladly draw a cycling route on your map, and he speaks English fluently. There are more services available here, like the detailed météo (weather forecast). You can book tickets for the mountain trains in Chamonix, and the cable car to the Aiguille du Midi is free. The reception is a library full of maps and leaflets.

Les Nations

Rating	8.1
Tariff range	€€€
Town	Auberives-sur-Varèze
Department	Isère
Postal code	38550
Map	5 H5
Tel	04-74849513
Fax	04-74849513
e-mail	jacquet.g@wanadoo.fr

From Lyon, exit A7 at junct Vienne, from Valence junct Chanas. Site S of Auberives.

Size (hectares) 1.5
Touring pitches 56
Sanitary facilities rating 7.9
typical transit campsite • excellent sanitary facilities • swimming pool • Rhône Valley and Vienne • Mont Pilat (Parc Régional) • Auberives-sur-Varèze (2 km)
Electric Hook-ups/amp 56/6-10

Les Nations is a typical transit campsite with simple, no-nonsense pitches and functional facilities. Travellers on their way to the Mediterranean, Italy or Spain will find clean toilets and washrooms, a swimming pool in which to relax after the long journey, and a snack bar with a terrace so they don't have to do any cooking unless they want to. This is what this campsite was made for. There is some noise from the N7.

Yet this is actually a fascinating region. Vienne, with its Roman ruins, is only a few kilometres away. Lyon, a gourmet's paradise not often visited, waits to be discovered. The old centre, situated at the confluence of two major rivers, the Rhône and the Saône, is much more interesting than most travellers could imagine.

A pleasant day trip might be a ride on the little steam train that runs from Tournon through the northern Ardèche. Or head east to the limestone mountains of the Chartreuse region or the caves, gorges, crevasses and steep rock faces of Vercors.

Les 4 Saisons

Rating	7.8
Tariff range	€€€
Town	Gresse-en-Vercors
Department	Isère
Postal Code	38650
Map	6 B4
Tel	04-76343027
Fax	04-76343952
e-mail	pieter.aalmoes@wanadoo.fr
Open	01 Jan – 15 Mar, 01 May – 30 Sep

Take N75 (Grenoble-Serres) to Monestier, W on D8a towards Gresse-en-Vercors. Left onto D8D at church. Country lane 1.3km (on left) to site.

Size (hectares) 2.2
Touring pitches 90
Sanitary facilities rating 7.7
superb view • quiet, easy-going atmosphere • winter sports facilities • Mont Aiguille • Lac du Monteynard • Monestiers-de-Clermont (13 km)
Electric hook-ups/amps 60/2-10

The mighty limestone wall of Vercors rises up behind the campsite, and offers a magnificent backdrop which draws many people to stay at Les 4 Saisons. The sanitary facilities are a model of cleanliness and practicality. Most people are families with small children, who come here for its tranquillity and high altitude. At 1200m, the nights are cool, even in the middle of summer, and there's usually a fresh breeze during the day, which makes up for the absence of shady spots.

The surrounding area is magnificent, and turns any walk or car trip into an expedition. The landscape varies between 'rugged' mountain scenery with gorges and limestone peaks, and lovely rolling hills in a hotchpotch of meadows and forests. The swimming pool is the campsite's only form of entertainment – there are no organised activities, children's clubs or disco evenings. Gresse (a mere 500m away) offers just about everything you can imagine. Although the site is closed in September, it reopens for the winter season, when it primarily attracts cross-country skiers. Hence the name.

Rhône-Alpes

Neige et Nature

Rating 8.5
Tariff range €€€
Town La Ferrière
Department Isère
Postal Code 38580
Map 6 B5
Tel 04-76451984
e-mail contact@neige-nature.fr
Open 10 May – 15 Sep
Situated 200mtrs W of La Ferrière. From Allevard follow D525 towards Les-Sept-Laux-Le-Pleney.
Size (hectares) 1.4
Touring pitches 42
Sanitary facilities rating 8.9
small, simple, clean • sports facilities • suited to nature lovers • Les Sept Laux • Crêt du Poulet • Allevard (12 km)
Electric hook-ups/amps 42/10

'Neige' does not refer to the snow that falls in winter, but to the snow-capped tops of the nearly 3,000m-high mountains in the Belledonne range. The River Bréda valley looks as if it has been ignored by both tourism and agriculture, but this is a perfect destination for hikers. There are walking routes of various levels of difficulty, though most of them are relatively easy. The finest day trip is the route to Les Sept Laux, seven lakes at an altitude of 2,000m. You need to be in good physical condition to tackle this stretch, but after a few days of training even the oldest walkers are able to rise to the challenge, returning with excited stories.

The campsite is small and simple, but the sanitary facilities are clean and heated. Th snack bar/reception area has a cosy fireplace. The trees are still immature, so there is not much shade. Children can play table tennis, volleyball and badminton, and sometimes there are competitions. A small swimming pool has now been completed, adding an important amenity to the site's beautiful natural setting.

Le Château

Rating 8.2
Tariff range €€€€
Town Le Bourg-d'Oisans
Department Isère
Postal Code 38520
Map 6 B4
Tel 04-76110440
Fax 04-76802123
e-mail jcp@camping-le-chateau.com
Open 24 May – 13 Sep
Take D526 E from Rochetaillée (7 km NW of Le Bourg-d'Oisans). Site on left, approx 150mtrs.
Size (hectares) 3
Touring pitches 83
Sanitary facilities rating 8
located in château grounds • entertainment • fitness area and sauna • Écrins national park • l'Alpe-d'Huez • Le Bourg-d'Oisans (7 km)
Electric hook-ups/amps 83/6-10

The drive is lined by stately chestnut trees, and you pitch your tent in the château grounds, play mini golf through the gates of a fortress, and dine underneath the château vaults. The owner has a clear grasp of his guests' desires which are plenty of clean sanitary facilities, a comparatively inexpensive restaurant, private, shaded or sunny pitches to choose from, a heated swimming pool and internet facilities.

Entertainment programmes are available during the morning for toddlers and the afternoon for slightly older children, and include badminton tournaments and treasure hunts. In the evenings, there's either a magician, a mime concert, a fashion show starring your own children or a slide presentation of the region (or combinations thereof). The campsite's sports facilities include a climbing wall and a fitness centre with a view across the mountains. And if you've played an outdoor sport in one of the neighbouring villages or cycled to Alpe d'Huez, you'll certainly appreciate the sauna.

Le Colporteur

Rating 7.9
Tariff range €€€€
Town Le Bourg-d'Oisans
Department Isère
Postal Code 38520
Map 6 B4
Tel 04-76791144
Fax 04-76791149
e-mail info@camping-colporteur.com
Open 10 May – 21 Sep
From city centre take N91 towards Briançon. Right at Total garage (300mtrs). Site in 300mtrs.
Size (hectares) 3.7
Touring pitches 130
Sanitary facilities rating 7.6
ideal for col fanatics • superb views • surrounded by high mountains • Écrins national park (20 km) • l'Alpe-d'Huez • Le Bourg-d'Oisans (400 m)
Electric hook-ups/amps 130/15

Passionate cyclists can just see Alpe d'Huez while sitting underneath their awning, and most cannot resist the challenge to sweat their way to the top. This site attracts hikers and nature-lovers.

The high mountains (Écrins Massif) are truly magnificent.

Although the site is located a mere 400m from the lively town of Le Bourg d'Oisans, it is very peaceful with plenty of things to do. The inter-campsite competitions are exceptionally tough contests between six sites in the Le Bourg region. At night, you'll probably hear the sound of music (jazz, chanson or country), or come across a magician. The organised entertainment focuses on toddlers. The swimming pool is located just outside the entrance, and anyone staying at Le Colporteur for at least five days can pick up free entry tickets. It also has a restaurant (local dishes), a pizzeria and a snack bar. Children tend to congregate in the recreation area, which has a billiards table, a pinball machine and video games. You'll additionally find a computer with internet access.

Le Coin Tranquille

Rating 8.4
Tariff range €€€€
Town Les Abrets
Department Isère
Postal Code 38490
Map 6 B5
Tel 04-76321348
Fax 04-76374067
e-mail contact@coin-tranquille.com
Open 22 Mar – 01 Nov
From Les Abrets follow N6 to Chambéry. Approx 2 km E of Les Abrets, site on left
Size (hectares) 8
Touring pitches 178   **Static pitches** 14
Sanitary facilities rating 8.5
perfect service • cooking lessons • good entertainment • lake district • walking area • Les Abrets (2 km)
Electric hook-ups/amps 160/2-10

Is it the friendly welcome that makes you want to stay here? Is it the privacy of the spacious pitches located between hedges and flowering shrubs? Is it the marvellous view of the mountains from the slopes where the campsite is set? Or is it the superb cooking with which owner and chef Gilles Vallon attracts customers from outside the camp? He also gives cookery lessons, and creates dishes anyone can prepare in their own caravan. The lessons are so popular that you need to book well in advance. No wonder that in 2000 Le Coin Tranquille was proclaimed Campsite of the Year.

But despite this the site remains a quiet corner ('coin tranquille' in French) off the beaten track. Martine Vallon says they don't accept more guests than they can accommodate, and the pitches are still spacious with great views. Above all this is a family site during the high season, and families with small children like the organised entertainment. Off season they concentrate on elderly people without children – both groups guarantee a good night's rest! One of the appealing services provided here is to take the guests out on a walking trip in the area where they can enjoy the splendid Alpine scenery.

Caravaneige Les Buissonnets

Rating	8.5
Tariff range	€€€
Town	Méaudre
Department	Isère
Postal Code	38112
Map	6 B4
Tel	04-76952104
Fax	04-76952614
e-mail	camping-les-buissonnets@wanadoo.fr
Open	01 Jan – 01 Nov

On A48 (Lyon-Grenoble), take Villard-de-Lans exit (D531). Then take D106 to Méaudre. Site on right just after village.

Size (hectares) 2.7
Touring pitches 69
Sanitary facilities rating 9
charming view • pétanque facilities • tranquillity • Gorges de la Bourne • Les Grands Goulets • Méaudre (1 km)
Electric hook-ups/amps 69/2-10

Don't be put off by the site entrance, a gravel area with slightly too many caravans. The camping facilities for touring caravans and tents are located to the right, behind a thick hedge, on a green field with modern sanitary facilities and a wonderful view across the rolling hills. There are meadows at the bottom (you'll hear the sound of cowbells) and woods at the top. It has several shops and restaurants as well as a discotheque. The swimming pool is located about 300m down the road, with reduced rates for guests of Les Buissonnets. The site is a very peaceful place in the heart of Vercors. You won't notice its rough character – ravines, vertical cliff faces, caves and treeless plains featuring rare plants – from the site. The Gorges de Méaudre, a prelude to the famous Gorges de la Bourne, start a mere 2 km down the road. Make sure you drive through the Grands Goulets, which are so deep and narrow that it feels like night time. During the winter months, Méaudre is a family winter sports resort and ideally suited to cross-country skiing.

La Base de Loisirs du Moulin

Rating	7.8
Tariff range	€€
Town	Meyrieu-les-Étangs
Department	Isère
Postal code	38440
Map	6 A5
Tel	04-74593034
Fax	04-74583612
e-mail	contact@camping-meyrieu.com
Open	15 Apr – 30 Sep

From Lyon junct Bourgoin-Jallieu. Then take D522 to St-Jean-de-Bournay. Right after 12 km in Meyrieu-les-Étangs, follow signs to Base de Loisirs. Site SW of village.

Size (hectares) 1.5
Touring pitches 72
Sanitary facilities rating 7.6
in a recreation park • lakeside location • safe for children • plenty of fish in the lakes • Vienne and La Côte-St-André • St-Jean-de-Bournay (5 km)
Electric Hook-ups/amp 66/6-10

It doesn't look much like a natural lake, and it is actually used more as a swimming pool. But 'le basse' is better than any normal campsite pool, with its sandy beach, sunbathing lawn and no chlorinated water. There is room enough for both campers and local holidaymakers on its shores, and while the latter will have to pay an entrance fee, campers don't. A 'baywatch' character keeps an eye on swimmers from his lookout, though quite a few non-swimmers spend hours on and around the lake canoeing, on a pedalo, and fishing.

The recreation park and the campsite that is part of it are both looked after by security guards. During the night the gates around the park and the site are locked while a guard stays on duty leaving campers feeling safe. There are hedges to protect the pitches and provide privacy; some pitches are spacious while others are not, so it is best to mention the size of your tent or caravan when booking. On the beach you will find a café/snack bar with take-away meals. The site has a multi-purpose room housing the kids' club, tables to play cards and a dance floor. During the summer season there is always something going on, either here or by the snack bar, except on Sundays.

Le Daxia

Rating	8.5
Tariff range	€€€
Town	St-Clair-du-Rhône
Department	Isère
Postal code	38370
Map	5 H4
Tel	04-74563920
Fax	04-74564557
e-mail	info@campingledaxia.com
Open	01 Apr – 30 Sep

A7, junct Vienne, then take D4 to Clair-du-Rhône. Site on CD4, (country road on left) leading to St-Clair.

Size (hectares) 7.5
Touring pitches 75
Sanitary facilities rating 8.5

along the road to the South • tidy, clean, colourful • pool and river beach • Rhône Valley and Vienne • Mont Pilat (Parc régional) • St-Clair-du-Rhône (3 km)

Electric Hook-ups/amp 75/6

Off season, Le Daxia is a perfect stop on the way to or from the Mediterranean, Italy or Spain. Even without a booking you will find a pitch. Most of the 'real' transit campsites along the N7 through the Rhône Valley are rather boring and noisy because of the traffic on the highway. Transit guests often stay on Le Daxia longer than planned, as this is a pleasant, quiet site in an interesting region. There is Vienne with its Roman ruins, the city of Lyon, often ignored, and Mont Pilat in the nature reserve of the same name.

In summer most guests are families with children, which means that transit guests must make a booking as early as possible. Le Daxia is tidy, clean and attractive because of its colourful design. The swimming pool, for example, has a great variety of tiles and ceramics, and an ultramodern fountain; the large paddling pool reminds you of rolling waves. Paddling is also possible in a small river. The pitches by the riverside are very popular, in spite of the lack of shade. Here there is a small pebble beach with a shower, and a sheltered barbecue stand that is highly appreciated. Put some wood on the fire when you return after a wet low-season day trip, and you will quickly warm up.

Saumont

Rating	8.2
Tariff range	€€€
Town	Ruffieux
Department	Savoie
Postal Code	73310
Map	6 B5
Tel	04-79542626
e-mail	camping.saumont@wanadoo.fr
Open	01 May – 30 Sep

From Aix-les-Bains follow D991 (E side of lake) northbound via Brison to Ruffieux. Site on left of D991, W of Ruffieux.

Size (hectares) 4
Touring pitches 45
Sanitary facilities rating 8.7

typical French atmosphere • entertainment for children • fine tennis courts • wine tasting • Lac du Bourget • Aix-les-Bains (20 km)

Electric hook-ups/amps 40/6-10

This campsite is as French as can be, and particularly suitable for people who want to brush up their knowledge of the language. This may be difficult for children who want to join the entertainment programme (generally in the morning for young children, sometimes from 12 noon), but they can learn while playing. The site, surrounded by forests, has a heated swimming pool with paddling section, a table tennis table, two tennis courts, a volleyball and football pitch, and a boules field.

You can rent kayaks or canoes for a trip down the river that runs past the campsite. Between 5 and 10 km from here you can practise all kinds of watersports on Lac du Bourget. This part of Savoy, La Chautagne (on the north side of the lake), produces AC-wines; visit one of the wine-tasting cellars, where you can also buy your preferred bottles. The whole region gains from the opportunities offered by the lake area and the mountains. There are many footpaths and steep rocks to climb or to experience a free fall. The landscape offers a great variety, including caves and waterfalls.

Rhône-Alpes

Les 7 Laux

Rating	8.5
Tariff range	€€€
Town	Theys
Department	Isère
Postal Code	38570
Map	6 B5
Tel	04-76710269
Fax	04-76710885
e-mail	camping.les7laux@wanadoo.fr
Open	01 Jun – 15 Sep

A41 (Grenoble-Chambéry), junct Goncelin, D29, D30 to Theys, D280 to Le Col-des-Ayes. Site on right, 4 km S of Theys.
Size (hectares) 2.7
Touring pitches 59
Sanitary facilities rating 8.7
for walking fans • neat but playful • no site caravans • cable train • beautiful mountain landscape • Theys (4 km)
Electric hook-ups/amps 59/4-10

This whole region looks distinctly Austrian, with its bare mountains, forests, farmhouses, meadows and cattle. But it is France, and a lovely part of it. Here you can still find the wooden country architecture that has disappeared elsewhere in the French Alps, and mountain agriculture is far more important than tourism. The first row of pitches on the site offers a great view of this idyllic landscape. The owners, themselves farmers by origin, have an almost Austrian sense of tidiness and order. To prevent their site looking too austere, they brought some gigantic boulders to give it a more pleasant appearance by dividing it into separate sections.

The site is bordered by old trees, though those surrounding the pitches are still rather young. Most guests are walking enthusiasts, and they can use the swimming pool, as well as a simple café with a bar where you can have breakfast, and a shop selling bread and other necessities. There is a recreation room for children with pinball machines and table football. Outdoors they will find a table tennis table and a playground. But most children prefer to walk into the forest next to the campsite, where they can play adventure games in and around a hut.

Alp'aix

Rating	7.9
Tariff range	€€
Town	Aix-les-Bains
Department	Savoie
Postal Code	73100
Map	6 B5
Tel	04-79889765
Open	01 May – 30 Sep

From A43 junct Chambéry take N201 to Aix-les-Bains. In Aix follow 'Lac' and 'Camping' signs to boulevard; site on right, behind aquarium.
Size (hectares) 1.2
Touring pitches 62
Sanitary facilities rating 8.2
casual atmosphere • good management • lakeside boulevard • Lac du Bourget • Bauges • Aix-les-Bains (1 km)
Electric hook-ups/amps 52/6-10

This small campsite, now under new ownership, is on the outskirts of Aix-les-Bains; as the name suggests, the view is dominated by the French Alps. Actually there is hardly any view at all; the broad-leaved trees on the site do not allow you to enjoy the panorama, but they let enough sunshine through and guarantee a lot of privacy. There is not much to do here – a small playground, a table-tennis table and of course a boules field. But Alp'aix is a quiet starting point to explore the surrounding area.

In spring and autumn the majority of the guests are elderly people for whom Aix is primarily a spa offering various kinds of health treatments. During the high season the campers are much younger, here to enjoy the facilities around the lake. On the other side of the boulevard you can find everything you need, whether it is fishing, windsurfing, sailing, canoeing, pedalos or swimming that you are seeking. Petit-Port is a good bathing area for those who don't like deep water. The nature reserves nearby offer opportunities for parasailing, mountaineering and mountain biking.

Les Trois Lacs

Rating 7.8
Tariff range €€€€
Town Belmont-Tramonet
Department Savoie
Postal Code 73330
Map 6 B5
Tel 04-76370403
Fax 04-76373760
e-mail info@les3lacs.com
Open 01 May – 21 Sep

A43, junct Chimilin/Pont-de-Beauvoisin, follow D592. Turn right in Aoste, take N516 to St-Genix. Right again and follow D916a to Le Pont-de-Beauvoisin (3 km).

Size (hectares) 5
Touring pitches 66
Sanitary facilities rating 8.1

pleasant atmosphere • entertainment • river • mountain walking • Lac d'Aiguebelette • Le Pont-de-Beauvoisin (3 km)

Electric hook-ups/amps 66/6-10

Whatever the reason for choosing this campsite, you will certainly receive a friendly reception and have an enjoyable time. This is undoubtedly true for young children especially, who will enjoy the entertainment. Owner Pascal Froger and his Dutch wife Lidewij Tetrode know exactly how to infect the entire staff in the snack bar and the recreation team with their own enthusiasm.

The site is located in a beautiful setting in the woodlands by the River Guiers, where you can go fishing, paddling or sailing. Mountain bikes can be rented, and there is also a nice swimming pool. Teenagers gather around the undercover table tennis tables or play a game of volleyball or tennis. The nearby Chartreuse Mountains challenge experienced hikers and cyclists, while picturesque villages like Le Pont-de-Beauvoisin are unmistakably French.

Don't forget to plunge into Lake Aiguebelette, which has the highest water temperature in Europe. As many families nowadays want to enjoy the pleasure of camping without having to bring a lot of equipment, the owners offer luxurious site caravans, tent-shaped huts and fully-equipped tents.

Le Versoyen

Rating 7.6
Tariff range €€€
Town Bourg-Saint-Maurice
Department Savoie
Postal code 73700
Map 6 C5
Tel 04-79070345
Fax 04-79072541
e-mail leversoyen@wanadoo.fr
Open 01 Jan – 24 Apr, 27 May – 01 Nov

From Bourg-Saint-Maurice, follow D119 towards Les Arcs. After supermarket follow site signs. Site 2 km E of Bourg-Saint-Maurice.

Size (hectares) 3.5
Touring pitches 185
Sanitary facilities rating 7.4

well situated • rafting available from the campsite • open in the summer and winter • mountain climbing • skiing • Bourg-Saint-Maurice (2 km)

Electric hook-ups/amps 170/4-10

The campsite offers an unlimited supply of walks in the Vanoise national park, ranging through valleys and alpine meadows in the rugged mountain landscape. Wild water rafting and a visit to museums and other cultural events will offer a complete contrast for the adventurous, and there are plenty of opportunities to relax as well. There are also a number of specialities on offer, such as cycle rides ranging from 15 km along the riverside path to various Tour de France mountain passes. Mountain bikers are well catered for here. Paragliders can often be seen swooping through the air against the green backdrop.

As it is a municipal campsite, some of the facilities are actually off-site, such as the swimming pool, the tennis courts and the mini golf. Groceries can be bought nearby in one of the two supermarkets. The concrete patch in the middle of the site is reserved for the winter season skiers who come to visit Les Arcs and Les Trois Vallées, as well as some smaller slopes. Le Versoyen offers good facilities all year round.

Rhône-Alpes

Le Vieux Moulin

Rating 7.4
Tariff range €€€
Town Flumet
Department Savoie
Postal code 73590
Map 6 B5
Tel 04-79317006
Fax 04-79317006
Open All year

From Flumet take N212 to Megève; turn right 1 km beyond Flumet, just before bridge (follow signs). Keep to right on rdbt. Site 1.5 km beyond Flumet.

Size (hectares) 1.5
Touring pitches 60
Sanitary facilities rating 7.6

quiet • simple • open in winter • walking • skiing • Megève (9 km)

Electric Hook-ups/amp 50/3-10

A holiday in the heart of Savoie is not to be missed, and an ideal place to stay is the Old Mill campsite that gets it electricity from a nearby river. It is located close to Mont-Blanc, and the majority of guests are mountain hikers. You don't have to start with ropes and pickaxes to enjoy this activity though: set off along the river, and a gradual climb of two or three hours will take you to the Signal du Sac (1682m). Once there you can decide whether to continue your walk to the Hameau du Tandieu or not. The greatest challenge in these parts is the Mont-Charvin.

The tourist office has useful illustrated documentation on walking routes and gives good advice. Every day experienced guides lead parties into the mountains. Interestingly, the finest view of Mont-Blanc is the one you get when driving on the motorway to Switzerland and Italy. Winter is high season in this part of France, when Alpine meadows and footpaths turn into ski runs. The huge, open flat meadows are within easy reach of the site, and the excellent sanitary facilities here are heated. Apart from table tennis there are no playing facilities.

Caravaneige du Col

Rating 8
Tariff range €€€
Town Fontcouverte-la-Toussuire
Department Savoie
Postal code 73300
Map 6 B5
Tel 04-79830080
Fax 04-79830367
e-mail campingducol@free.fr
Open 15 Dec – 18 Apr, 27 Jun – 31 Aug

From St-Jean-de-Maurienne take D926 towards Vallée de l'Arvan. After 4 km take D78 towards La Toussuire (NB: not St-Pancrace). Site in approx 10 km (3 km NW of Fontcouvert).

Size (hectares) 0.8
Touring pitches 32
Sanitary facilities rating 8.6

beautiful views • winter facilities • simple • Vanoise national park • tourist trails • St-Jean-de-Maurienne (16 km)

Electric hook-ups/amps 32/2-10

Caravaneige du Col is a level campsite high up in the Savoie, looking out to the Maurienne Valley. Once the realm of the Dukes of Savoy, you will feel like royalty in this countryside. All seasons have their attraction here: you will notice that some of the caravans are equipped for the colder months (some pitches are seasonal), and the sanitary facilities are centrally heated too. The breathtaking views from your tent, and the sun rising slowly over the hills are everyday delights.

Throughout the winter the access road remains clear, and there is a free shuttle service to the nearby ski slopes. In the summer, the site is a good starting point for mountain bike trips or walks. In the village of La Toussuire about 1 km away, children's activities are divided into four age groups. The lake, the climbing wall, mini golf, tennis courts and various other facilities in the village can all be used on an individual basis. In the evenings, the restaurant serves local fare (daily menu), and on colder evenings you are more than welcome to stay on in the restaurant for a game, or just to watch TV, or quietly read a book.

L'Eden

Rating	8.6
Tariff range	€€€
Town	Landry
Department	Savoie
Postal code	73210
Map	6 C5
Tel	04-79076181
Fax	04-79076217
e-mail	info@camping-eden.net
Open	17 Dec – 01 May, 25 May – 30 Sep

Site approx 500mtrs N of Landry, accessed via N90, (Moûtiers-Bourg-St-Maurice): turn off at Landry, over bridge, turn left before railway. (Landry 7 km SW of Bourg-St-Maurice).

Size (hectares) 2.7
Touring pitches 132
Sanitary facilities rating 8.6

beautiful views • quiet and secluded • spacious pitches • mountain climbing • Savoy culture • Bourg-St-Maurice (6 km)

Electric hook-ups/amps 132/10

Established in 1995, this wooded campsite is beautiful and well kept, just the way the guests like it. The owners, Georges and Nicole, like sharing their piece of paradise with others, especially if they in turn share their love of peace and quiet. Anyone who creates a disturbance can expect the wrath of Georges. You won't find entertainment seekers here, as the walks and trips in the surrounding area are too tiring to leave you with any energy for other activities.

You can choose between mountain climbing, mountain biking, paragliding, white water rafting and horse riding. The heated swimming pool is a delight in itself, although Plan d'Eau 3 km away offers even more water fun. The campsite remains open and accessible throughout the winter. The 13-km cycle path between Aime and Bourg-Saint-Maurice is used for cross-country skiing in the winter, although most winter visitors come for the slopes at Les Arcs and La Plagne. Ski passes are available at the campsite with a 30% discount. The modern sanitary facilities are heated and skis are available to hire.

Le Curtelet

Rating	7.9
Tariff range	€€
Town	Lépin-le-Lac
Department	Savoie
Postal Code	73610
Map	6 B5
Tel	04-79441122
Fax	04-79441122
e-mail	lecurtelet@wanadoo.fr
Open	15 May – 30 Sep

Site E of Lépin-le-Lac, parallel to rail line and on D921b.

Size (hectares) 1.3
Touring pitches 89   **Static pitches** 2
Sanitary facilities rating 8

clean • great fun for the kids • private lakeside beach • lake recreation • walking • Le Pont-de-Beauvoisin (10 km)

Electric hook-ups/amps 89/2-6

Gilles Guicherd knows his campsite inside and out; he is a jack-of-all-trades: cleaner, attendant, and entertainer at Camping Le Curtelet, and his wife is the receptionist. They both work hard to create a great atmosphere on their small, clean site. It is like a micro-community where people treat each other with respect within the framework of a basic set of rules. The trains that pass the site at high speed, however, show no respect at all, and they may disturb your early morning peace, though you get used to it.

Le Curtelet is located on the bank of Lac d'Aiguebelette, a fine example of a clear and clean lake with the highest water temperature in Europe. A section of the beach is reserved for campers, and it is advisable to bring your own rubber boat or canoe. There are woodlands around the lake, but the site itself is open. Many families come here every year, mostly at the request of their children, who have a lot of space in which to play games or practise sports. From time to time football and volleyball competitions are held, and close to the campsite you can play tennis or mini golf. The mountains offer an invitation to go hiking, but it might not be easy to convince your children to come with you.

Rhône-Alpes

Les Combes

Rating 7.9
Tariff range €€€
Town Modane
Department Savoie
Postal code 73500
Map 6 C4
Tel 04-79050023
Fax 04-79050023
e-mail camping-modane@wanadoo.fr
Open 01 May – 30 Sep, 15 Dec – 30 Mar
In Modane follow signs for 'Tunnel de Fréjus' (D215), then from W through Modane-Gare. Site is signed and approx 800mtrs SW of Modane.
Size (hectares) 3.5
Touring pitches 66
Sanitary facilities rating 7.8
lively campsite • caravans and tents are separate • friendly staff • Vanoise national park • the 'baroque route' • Modane (1 km)
Electric hook-ups/amps 66/10

This campsite offers the shelter of a pine forest and is the ideal base for walks in the high ridges of the Savoie. It is a simple site, where Silvia De Rosa and Gilles Gagnière offer their guests a warm reception and wave you off when you leave. There are two distinct sections for caravans and tents, and the latter do not have electric hook-up facilities or clearly marked pitches. The campsite is situated on the edge of Modane, offering beautiful views of the surrounding mountains.

You can discover the relatively new climbing sport of 'via ferrata', or climbing and scrambling along the steep paths and deep crevices of Thabor. Modane is the nearest place for shopping, and also offers a swimming pool. It is one of the villages and towns along the Baroque route, with their churches and chapels filled with 17th-century altar pieces and expressive statues that provide a vivid contrast to their surroundings. A road runs past the campsite, and the railway line can sometimes disturb the quiet at night, but there are many compensations.

Les Lanchettes

Rating 7.3
Tariff range €€€
Town Peisey-Nancroix
Department Savoie
Postal code 73210
Map 6 C5
Tel 04-79079307
Fax 04-79078833
e-mail lanchettes@free.fr
Open 01 Jan – 30 Apr, 01 Jun – 30 Sep
Take D90 towards Moutiers/Bourg-St-Maurice, turn off at Peisey-Nancroix onto D87, through Nancroix.
Site 3 km SE of Peisey-Nancroix on D87.
Size (hectares) 2.2
Touring pitches 80
Sanitary facilities rating 7.1
well situated • rest and relaxation • good river fishing • mountain sports in the summer • winter sports • Bourg-Saint-Maurice (12 km)
Electric hook-ups/amps 50/3-10

This terraced campsite is situated high in the Vanoise national park and is the ideal spot for lovers of sport. Nature is seen at her best here, and you can enjoy the mountain flora and fauna, including the chamois, the ibex and the marmots. Guides are available for tours through the Vanoise, and you can even arrange to take a mule along to lighten the load. Walks spanning several days are very impressive and offer overnight stays in mountain huts. The steep rock faces make excellent scrambling terrain.

If water is your thing, there is something for everyone, including fishing in the river by the campsite and the challenging sport of white water rafting. One holiday is probably not long enough to discover all the sports available in the Savoie. Skiing is offered throughout the summer on the glacier slopes of Les Arcs, but it is probably best left to the winter season when the campsite becomes a veritable ski resort and there is a shuttle service to the ski lifts. Whichever season you choose, simplicity and the quiet life are the key to a stay at Les Lanchettes.

Index

CARAVAN & CAMPING IN FRANCE

Index

Index

CARAVAN & CAMPING IN FRANCE

Index

CARAVAN & CAMPING IN FRANCE